The Thinker's Guide to College Success

The Thinker's Guide to College Success

John Chaffee, Ph.D.

LaGuardia College,

City University of New York

Houghton Mifflin Company   Boston   Toronto

Geneva, Illinois   Palo Alto   Princeton, New Jersey

This book is dedicated to Charlotte and Hubert Chaffee, with love.

Sponsoring editor: Bill Webber

Senior project editor: Rosemary Winfield

Senior production/design coordinator: Jill Haber

Senior manufacturing coordinator: Marie Barnes

Marketing manager: Charles Cavaliere

Cover design by Karen Lehman. Cover image © 1995 M. C. Escher/Cordon Art, Baarn, Holland. All rights reserved.

Text and art credits begin on page 431.

Printed in the U.S.A.

Library of Congress Catalog Card Number: 95-76932

ISBN: 0-395-72730-8

123456789-QM-98 97 96 95

Brief Contents

Contents

6   Reading Critically   199

Preface

Freshmen arrive at college excited and full of hope, somewhat anxious about the challenges of college life, and often with limited understanding of what the college experience is about. Recognizing that this condition creates special freshman needs, colleges and universities have created courses designed to help entering students make the transition from high school or the world of work back to college life. *The Thinker's Guide to College Success* is a text designed for academically oriented courses that are intended not only to introduce students to the culture of college life but also to help students develop the abilities needed to succeed in their academic and personal lives.

The "culture" of higher education that students are entering is both challenging and typically very different from their previous experiences. In order to be successful, they need to possess important skills, knowledge, and insight, which this text is designed to help them develop:

- A foundation of thinking and language abilities so that they can negotiate rigorous college courses,
- An array of "studenting" skills in the areas of studying, note taking, and test taking,
- Key "life skills" that will enable them to organize their time, manage money, stay healthy, and deal with stress, and
- A mature understanding of important aspects of their new community involving issues like relationships, sexuality, diversity, communication, and social responsibility.

The Thinker's Guide to College Success grows out of a nationally recognized program in critical and creative thinking I established in 1979 at LaGuardia College (The City University of New York) that involves 1,200 students annually. This program is based on the assumption, supported by research, that learning to think more effectively is a synthesizing process, knitting critical thinking abilities together with academic content and the fabric of students' experiences. The evaluation results of this approach over the past sixteen years have been consistent and compelling: students develop sophisticated reasoning and problem-solving abilities; they exhibit accelerated development of language skills; and they demonstrate increased self-awareness, maturity, and responsibility. The curriculum for the program's keystone course, "Critical Thinking Skills," is my textbook *Thinking Critically,* which is entering its fifth edition and has been adopted at over 350 colleges and universities. Building on this solid foundation, *The Thinker's Guide to College Success* will help students become more knowledgeable and mature thinkers, equipped with the abilities to succeed in every aspect of their experience at college, and beyond.

The Thinker's Guide to College Success goes far beyond traditional student success coverage (goal setting, time management, note taking, and test taking) to include other topics essential to academic, career, and life success, such as

- Thinking Critically and Creatively
- Solving Problems and Making Decisions
- Reading Critically and Writing Effectively
- Discussing and Debating
- Discovering and Establishing Learning Styles
- Recognizing and Evaluating Arguments
- Creating a Life Philosophy

Student-relevant readings provide substantive contexts to help students deal effectively with the personal and social issues confronting them, such as career exploration, friendships, alcohol use and abuse, depression, eating disorders, gender miscommunication, sexuality and date rape, living in a diverse community, and creating a life philosophy. Critical thinking and writing activities follow each selection and throughout the text reinforce students' development into mature and thoughtful critical thinkers.

The Thinker's Guide to College Success addresses the values and purposes of college education by focusing on the very foundation of higher education, reflective thinking. The readings and activities in the textbook reveal to students that the educated person is someone who takes a disciplined and thoughtful approach to creating meaning from human experience and who, when faced with important issues and problems, chooses to practice careful reasoning to reach decisions about these matters.

Teaching a course from a critical thinking perspective is one of the most inspiring and rewarding experiences that a teacher can have. Because the thinking process is such an integral part of who we are as people, the prospect of expanding students' thinking implies expanding who they are as human beings—the perspective from which they view the world, the concepts and values they use to guide their choices, and the impact they have on the world as a result of those choices. Teaching people to become critical thinkers does not mean simply equipping them with certain academic skills and intellectual tools; it involves their personal transformation and its commensurate impact on the quality of their lives and those around them. This is truly education at its most inspiring! It is a teaching experience that involves embarking on high adventure, a journey that is full of unanticipated challenges and unexpected triumphs. I have written *The Thinker's Guide to College Success* to serve as an effective guide for this journey. In the final analysis, however, you must embark on the journey by joining it with your expertise and critical thinking abilities to provide productive educational experiences for your students.

Features of *The Thinker's Guide to College Success*

- **Helps students develop the patterns of thinking, habits of behavior, and language abilities needed for academic, career, and life success.** Students will develop the abilities to learn effectively, reason logically, solve challenging problems, achieve their goals, and think critically about themselves and the complex world in which they live.

- **Takes a critical thinking approach to study and life skills.** This process-oriented and developmentally sequenced approach is much more effective than simply presenting students with advice and lists of tips.

- **Relates academic skills and thinking abilities to students daily lives.** By asking students to think critically about themselves and their experience, the text fosters their personal development as mature and responsible critical thinkers.

- **Incorporates student-relevant thematic units** ("Thinking Passages") into each chapter. These readings provide substantive contexts for students to develop their skills in a meaningful and lasting fashion. At the same time, students are thinking, reading, and writing (through "Questions for Analysis") about important personal and social issues that they confront. The text stimulates and guides students to think clearly about these complex issues and make informed decisions in their lives about them.

- **Provides students with opportunities to actively engage in the learning process** through sequenced exercises ("Thinking Activities") that ask students to respond to the text, express their own ideas, and critically examine their own and others' thinking in order to improve their abilities.

- **Includes chapter-opening cognitive maps** that lay out each chapter's framework and help students break down the ideas behind the main concept of the chapter. In a student success/note taking context, these maps also illustrate the concept of mind mapping.

- **Includes original illustrations and photographs** that communicate key ideas in visually creative and intellectually stimulating ways.

- **Is accompanied by an informative Instructor's Resource Guide** to assist in using *The Thinker's Guide to College Success* most effectively and a Test Bank of Questions to stimulate students to think critically about the ideas in the text.

- **Is accompanied by a provocative critical thinking videotape.** "Thinking Toward Decisions" (1989) is a one-hour critical thinking videotape developed by the author that is designed to work in conjunction with Chapter 2, "Thinking Critically." The tape creatively interweaves drama, expert testimony, and a student seminar group in order to engage students' critical thinking abilities (free with adoption).

- **Is accompanied by Roundtable Discussion videotapes** that cover "Study Strategies" (note taking, reading, memory, testing) and "Life Skills" (goal setting, time management, stress management). These two videos feature five college students who discuss and seek solutions to the problems they face in college and in life (contact your local Houghton Mifflin representative for further information).

- **Includes a Critical Thinking Test** developed by the author that provides for a comprehensive evaluation of student thinking and language abilities. Using a court case format arising from a fatal student drinking incident, students are challenged to gather and weigh evidence, ask relevant questions, evaluate expert testimony and summation arguments, and reach a verdict. The test is included in the Instructor's Resource Manual in a form that can be reproduced.

Acknowledgments

A book is a living thing, nurtured in its development by the contributions of many people. I have been fortunate to work with a dedicated and talented "family" at Houghton Mifflin who helped bring *The Thinker's Guide to College Success* into vibrant existence. Alison Husting Zetterquist provided the spark that created the soul of this book, and she served as guide and inspiration during its formative stages; Bill Webber brought inexhaustible energy and an expansive vision for the book's possibilities; Melissa Plumb gave new meaning to the word "professionalism" with her conscientious and timely handling of numerous responsibilities. The art program was coordinated in outstanding fashion by Connie Gardner, who brought exceptional dedication, insight, and a contagious optimism. The artist for the book, Warren Gebert, had the extraordinary ability to capture key concepts in illustrations that are visually creative and intellectually provocative. As the senior project editor, Rosemary Winfield integrated all of the disparate elements of the book into a coherent whole. June Smith, executive vice president of the College Division, provided strong institutional support for the book, and Mike Goulding, district sales manager, convinced me to write the book in the first place.

A number of educators graciously provided invaluable assistance, including Judith Gazzola, director of the Career Resource Center at LaGuardia College; Catherine Charlton, director of Health Education at New York University; and Dr. Paul Grayson, director of Counseling Services at New York University. I would also like to give special acknowledgment to Fred Janzow of Southeast Missouri State University. In adapting my textbook *Thinking Critically* to the exemplary Freshman Year Experience program at his university, Dr. Janzow and his colleagues developed ideas and curriculum materials that served as valuable resources for *The Thinker's Guide to College Success* and the accompanying Instructor's Resource Manual. Additionally, the following educators provided insight and expertise in reviewing the evolving manuscript: Deb Carlson, Wayne State College (NE); Carolyn Hopper, Middle Tennessee State University; Fred Janzow, Southeast Missouri State University; Margaret D. Long, Lewis University (IL); Susan L. Neste, University of North Dakota; Jacqueline Richardson, Metropolitan State University (MN); Adam Palmer, Southampton Institute (UK); Toby Rose, Northern Michigan University; Gwendolyn Roundtree, Westchester Community College (NY); Gwendolyn Stevens, United States Coast Guard Academy (CT).

I wrote *The Thinker's Guide to College Success* as a professional educator and as a parent. As an educator, I wanted to write the kind of book that I would have enjoyed using during my first bewildering year at college. The students I have been privileged to encounter during my twenty years of teaching have enriched my thinking and changed my life. These students, their dreams for the future, and their commitment to improving their lives through the liberating power of education are woven into every page of this book.

As a parent of two remarkable children, writing this book had a special meaning for me. Jessie and Joshua have taught me all of my important lessons about the incredibly complex processes of teaching and learning. They have consistently challenged my thinking, expanded my understanding, and reminded me how to view the world in fresh, creative ways. In writing this book, I wanted to bring my love for education and the best of my experience to them, creating a vehicle that will help them enjoy a college experience that is life altering, mind expanding, and personally memorable. As enthusiastic participants in the project, they were a demanding yet sensitive audience, providing field testing that was both up close and personal.

Finally, I want to thank my wife Heide for consistently challenging me to achieve my best, both in my writing and in my life. Her expert guidance, unwavering support, and enduring love have stimulated my growth as a person and enriched my life with special meaning.

J.C.

The Thinker's Guide to College Success

Reaching Your Goals

Working Toward Goals

IDENTIFY THE GOALS
Identify the appropriate goal(s).
Rank them in order of importance.
Select the most important goals.
DEVISE EFFECTIVE PLANS
List all steps in order.
Estimate the time each will take.
Plan the steps in your schedule.

Why College?

Making Decisions

1. *Define* the decision clearly
2. *Consider* all possible choices.
3. *Gather* all relevant information and evaluate the pros and cons of each choice
4. *Select* the choice(s) that best meet the needs of the situation
5. *Implement* a plan of action and monitor the results

Deciding on a Career

CREATING YOUR DREAM JOB
DISCOVERING "WHO" YOU ARE:
• Your interests?
• Your abilities?
FINDING THE RIGHT MATCH

Becoming an Educated Thinker

Welcome to college! Your decision to enter college says a great deal about you as a person. It suggests that you are someone who dreams of great accomplishments, who seeks a challenging career that will make use of your unique talents, who yearns to develop your mind to the fullest extent possible, who desires to become an informed, educated thinker. However, although enrolling in college is an important step in your life, it is only the first step on what can be a fascinating journey.

In many ways college is a new world, different from any you may have experienced. You will likely find that your courses are more challenging than those you took in high school. Not only will you be expected to do *more* work in your courses, but you will also be expected to do this work at a higher level: to *read critically*, to *write more analytically*, to *think more conceptually*. You will likely encounter a greater diversity of people in your classes than you are used to, people from many walks of life, locations, and ethnic backgrounds. If you are living away from home for the first time, you will encounter challenges in managing your time, your money, and your life. If you are balancing the demands of work and family obligations and now have added college as a new dimension, you will find that your college experiences will influence other areas of your life as well. In any case, you will find yourself thinking about and discussing important issues that affect not only you but also the college community of which you are a member and the society and world in which you live.

The purpose of this book is to help you develop the knowledge and abilities you will need to be successful at college:

- adapting to the college culture
- identifying a major

Attending college means becoming a member of a diverse community composed of people from many walks of life and ethnic backgrounds, who are interested in learning and improving the quality of their lives.

- studying effectively and taking useful class notes
- mastering tests
- reading and writing effectively
- discussing and debating ideas

In addition to learning these essential skills, you also will explore important issues that you will encounter as a member of the college community:

- fostering productive relationships
- nurturing your physical and psychological health
- communicating effectively with diverse people

Finally, as you learn these college skills and explore these important issues, you will also be developing essential thinking abilities that will help you in every area of your life:

- becoming a critical thinker
- learning to solve problems
- reasoning logically
- reaching your goals
- creating a life philosophy

After successfully completing this course, you will have established a foundation on which you can build a rewarding college career. Of course, like most valuable accomplishments in life, completing this course will involve your dedication and hard work. There's no time to lose, so let's get started!

Why College?

Although you may not think of yourself as an artist, you are in fact the artist of your own life, painting your individual portrait. Each of us creates our life every day, and decisions are the tools that we use to define ourselves and shape a positive future. Your decision to enter college is an important part of that portrait, and in order to plan your future, you should think carefully about the history of this decision. In the space provided below, describe the reasons that you decided to attend college:

1. _____
2. _____
3. _____

When you compare your responses to those of other students in the class, you'll probably discover that people come to college for a variety of reasons. Near the

New Possibilities:
College opens up a new world full of possibilities for developing yourself and discovering your life work.

top of most people's lists is the desire to choose and prepare for a career, their life's work. However, every list ought to contain the reason "to become an educated thinker." Why is this goal so important? College provides you with a unique opportunity to develop your mind in the fullest sense. Entering college initiates you into a community of people dedicated to learning, and each discipline, or subject area, represents an organized effort to understand some significant dimension of human experience. As you are introduced to various disciplines, you learn new ways to understand the world, and you elevate your consciousness as a result. You may never have the same opportunity in your life to expand your mind and develop your sensibilities, so you should make the most out of college.

Becoming an "educated thinker" will help you achieve your career goals as well. In this rapidly evolving world, it is impossible to predict with precision your exact career (or *careers*) or the knowledge and skills that this career will require. But as an educated thinker you will possess the essential knowledge and abilities that will enable you to adapt to whatever your career situation demands. In addition, becoming an educated thinker will elevate your understanding of the world in which you live and help you develop insight into your "self" and that of others, qualities that are essential to high achievement in most careers. Let's examine how your previous learning experiences have contributed to your emerging portrait as an educated thinker by embarking on your first Thinking Activity.

Thinking Activities are designed to stimulate your thinking process and provide the opportunity to express your ideas about important topics. Thinking is an active process, and we learn to do it better by becoming aware of and actually using the thought process, not simply by reading about it. By participating in the Thinking Activities contained in this text and applying these ideas to your own experiences, you will find that your thinking—and language— abilities are becoming sharper and more powerful. By sharing these ideas with other members of the class, you are not only expanding your own thinking; you are also expanding theirs. Each student in the class has a wealth of experiences and insights to offer to the class *community.*

Thinking Activity 1.1

Think back on the most memorable learning experience you have had (in school or outside of school). Describe that experience in detail, and explain why it had such a significant and lasting impact on you. Discuss how this experience contributed to your development as an educated thinker.

"Preconceptions" are ideas that you have about what an experience is going to be like before you actually have the experience. Often, your preconceptions are not accurate. They may be based on what others have told you, things you have read, or even your own fantasies. For example, you may believe any or all of the following statements:

- Most college students are more intelligent than you are.
- College students are extremely competitive and not particularly friendly.
- In order to be popular at college, you have to drink and party.

The problem with inaccurate preconceptions is that they may influence you to act inappropriately. For instance, you may threaten your success at college by drinking and partying excessively, not realizing there are more constructive ways to have an active social life and enjoy yourself. In these cases, it is important to correct your misconceptions as soon as possible. In the space below, identify some of the preconceptions you had about college, and evaluate the accuracy of these ideas based on what you have discovered since beginning your college career. For example,

Preconception: College students are extremely competitive and not particularly friendly.

Evaluation of accuracy: Although there are a few students who are very competitive, most of the students aren't like that at all and are friendly.

1. *Preconception:* _____

    _____

    Evaluation of accuracy: _____

    _____

2. *Preconception:* _____

    _____

    Evaluation of accuracy: _____

The final step in thinking about your decision to enroll in college is to consider the results you hope to achieve as a result of your college experience. One helpful way to do this is to project yourself into the future, imagining as specifically as possible the kind of person you would like to be after completing your college education.

Thinking Activity 1.2

1. Describe, as specifically as possible, how you believe that *your life* will be different after completing your college education.
2. Describe, as specifically as possible, how you believe that *you* will be different after completing your college education.

Working Toward Goals

Ah, but a man's reach should exceed his grasp, Or what's a heaven for?

—Robert Browning

My future career goal is to become a professional photographer, working for *National Geographic Magazine* and traveling around the world. I originally had different dreams, but gradually drifted away from them and lost interest. Then I enrolled in a photography course and loved it. I couldn't wait until the weekend was over to attend class on Monday or to begin my next class project—reactions that were really quite unusual for me! Not everyone is certain about what they would like to become, and I think it is important to discover a career you will enjoy because you are going to spend the rest of your life doing it. I have many doubts, as I think everyone does. Am I good enough? The main thing I fear is rejection, people not liking my work, a possibility that is unavoidable in life. There is so much competition in this world that sometimes when you see someone better at what you do, you can feel inadequate. These problems and obstacles that interfere with my goals will have to be overcome. Rejection will have to be accepted and looked at as a learning experience, and competition will have to be used as an incentive for me to work at my highest level. But through it all, if you don't have any fears, then what do you have? Lacking competition and the possibility of rejection, there is no challenge to life.

As revealed in this student passage, goals play extremely important functions in your life by organizing your thinking and giving your life order and direction. Whether you are preparing food, preparing for an exam, or preparing for a career, goals suggest courses of action, influence your decisions, and provide a sense of accomplishment when you achieve them. Goals contribute meaning to your life.

Most of your behavior is based on a purpose or purposes, a goal or goals, that you are trying to reach. We can begin to discover the goals of our actions by asking the question *why* of what we are doing or thinking. For example, answer the following question as specifically as you can:

Why did you come to this class today? _____

_____

This question may have stimulated any number of responses:

■ because I want to pass this class

■ because I was curious about the topics to be discussed

■ because I woke up early and couldn't get back to sleep

Whatever your response, it reveals at least some of your goals in attending class. You attempt to make sense of what people, including yourself, are doing by figuring out the goal or purpose of the behavior, by asking for the reason *why*. Asking *why* about your goal usually leads to additional *why* questions because a specific goal in your life is part of larger goal patterns. As a result, one approach you can use to try to discover your goal pattern is to ask *why* you did something and then to ask *why* about the answer and so on. Although this approach is reminiscent of the maddening *why* game played by children at grownups' expense, it can lead to some interesting results, as revealed in the following activity.

Using your response to the question "Why did you come to class today?" as a starting point, try to discover part of your goal patterns by asking a series of *why* questions. After each response, ask *why* again. (For example: Why did you come to class today? Because I want to pass this course. Why do you want to pass this course? Because. . . .) Try to give thoughtful and specific answers.

Why did you come to class today? (See your response above.)

Why do you want to _____

_____?

Because _____

_____

Why do you want to _____

_____?

Because _____

_____

Why do you want to _____

_____?

Because _____

_____

As you may have found in completing the activity, this "child's game" begins to reveal the network of goals that structure your experience and leads you to progressively more profound questions regarding your basic goals in life, such as "Why do I want to be successful?" or "Why do I want a happy and fulfilling life?" These are complex issues that require thorough and ongoing exploration. A first step in this direction is to examine the way your mind works to achieve your goals (which is the goal of this section). If you can understand the way your mind functions when you think effectively, then you can use this knowledge to improve your thinking abilities. To begin this process, think about an important goal you have achieved in your life, and then complete Thinking Activity 1.3.

1. Describe an important goal that you recently achieved.
2. Identify the steps you had to take to achieve this goal in the order in which they were taken, and estimate the amount of time each step took.
3. Describe how you felt when you achieved your goal.

Achieving Short-term Goals

By examining your response to Thinking Activity 1.3, you can see that thinking effectively helps you achieve your goals by performing two distinct, interrelated activities:

1. identifying goals
2. devising effective plans to achieve your goals

You are involved in this goal-seeking process in every aspect of your daily life. Some of your goals are more immediate (short-term) than others—for example, planning your activities for the day or preparing for an upcoming exam. While achieving these short-term goals should be a manageable process, our efforts meet with varying degrees of success. We don't always achieve our goals for the day, and we may *occasionally* find ourselves inadequately prepared for a test. By improving your mastery of the goal-seeking process, you should be able to improve the quality of every area of your life. Let's explore how you can do this. *Identify* five short-term goals that you would like to achieve in the next week:

Short-term Goals for Next Week

_____

_____

_____

_____

_____

Now *rank* these goals in order of importance, ranging from the goals that are most essential for you to achieve to those that are less significant.

Once this process of identifying and ranking your goals is complete, you

Goals:

Reaching your goals involves identifying the right goals, developing a realistic plan, and following through with committment.

can then focus on devising effective plans and strategies to achieve your goals. In order to complete this stage of the goal-seeking process, select the goal that you ranked first or second and then *list* all the steps in the order in which they need to be taken to achieve this goal. Next, *estimate* how much time each step will take and plan the step in your daily or weekly schedule. For example, if your goal is to prepare for a quiz in biology, your steps might look like the following:

Goal: Prepare for biology quiz in 2 days

Steps to be taken	Time involved	Schedule
1. Photocopy the notes for the class I missed last week	20 minutes	after next class
2. Review reading assignments and class notes	2 hours	tonight

3. Make a summary review sheet	1 hour	tomorrow night
4. Study the review sheet	30 minutes	right before quiz

Goal: _____

Steps to be taken	*Time involved*	*Schedule*
1. _____	_____	_____
2. _____	_____	_____
3. _____	_____	_____
4. _____	_____	_____

Methods for Achieving Short-term Goals

Step 1: Identify the goals.

■ *Identify* the short-term goals.

■ *Rank* the goals in order of importance.

■ *Select* the most important goals to focus on.

Step 2: Devise effective plans to achieve your goals.

■ *List* all the steps in the order in which they should be taken.

■ *Estimate* how much time each step will take.

■ *Plan* the steps in your daily or weekly schedule.

Although this method may seem a little mechanical the first few times you use it, it will soon become integrated into your thinking processes and become a natural and automatic approach to achieving the goals in your daily life. We often fail to achieve our short-term goals because we skip one or more of the steps in this process. For example, some common thinking errors include the following:

■ We neglect to explicitly identify important goals.

■ We concentrate on less important goals first, leaving insufficient time to work on more important goals.

■ We don't identify all of the steps required to achieve our goal, or we approach them in the wrong order.

■ We underestimate the time each step will take or fail to plan the steps in our schedule.

A worksheet that will guide you in your initial goal analysis is located on page 12.

Goal Worksheet

Step 1: Identify the goals.

Priority rank

1. _____   _____
2. _____   _____
3. _____   _____
4. _____   _____
5. _____   _____

Step 2: Devise an effective plan.

Steps to take   *Estimated time*

1. _____   _____
2. _____   _____
3. _____   _____
4. _____   _____
5. _____   _____
6. _____   _____
7. _____   _____

Integrate these steps into your daily or weekly schedule.

Achieving Long-term Goals

Identifying short-term goals tends to be a fairly simple procedure, but identifying the appropriate long-term goals is a much more complex and challenging process: career goals, plans for marriage, paying for children's college, goals for personal development. For example, think about the people you know who have full-time jobs. How many of these people get up in the morning excited and looking forward to going to work that day? The unfortunate fact is that many people have not been successful in identifying the most appropriate career goals for themselves, goals that reflect their true interests and talents.

In many areas of life, people are often unaware of the most appropriate goals for themselves. For example, people often have goals that are not really their own but have been inherited from someone else. Have you ever been in this position? Consider the following student's experience:

The goal I inherited was to be a nurse. Since my mother was a nurse, she wanted me to be one. In fact, she wanted all of her daughters to be nurses. They had all tried it and didn't like it at all. She said I would be very happy, but I tried and hated it. It's not that I don't like helping others, it's just that it's not for me. I was very confused and didn't know what to do. I finally spoke to her and explained that being a nurse holds no future for me—I'm not happy in that field of work. She was hurt, but better her than me for the rest of my life.

How do you identify the most appropriate long-term goals for yourself? To begin with, you need to develop an in-depth understanding of yourself: your talents, your interests, the things that stimulate you and bring you satisfaction. You also need to discover what your possibilities are, either through research or actual experience. Of course, your goals do not necessarily remain the same throughout your life. It is unlikely that the goals you had at the age of eight are the ones you have now. As you grow, change, and mature, it is natural for your goals to change and evolve as well. The key point is that you should keep examining your goals to make sure that they reflect your own thinking and current interests.

Research studies have shown that high-achieving people are able to envision a detailed, three-dimensional picture of their future in which their goals and aspirations are clearly specified. In addition, these people are able to construct a mental plan that includes the sequence of steps they will have to take, the amount of time each step will involve, and strategies for overcoming the obstacles they are likely to encounter. Such realistic and compelling concepts of the future enable these people to make sacrifices in the present to achieve their long-term goals. Of course, they may modify these goals as circumstances change and they acquire more information, but they retain a well-defined, flexible plan that charts their life course.

On the other hand, research also reveals that people who are low achievers tend to live in the present and the past. Their concept of the future is vague and ill defined: "I want to be happy" or "I want a high-paying job." This unclear concept of the future makes it difficult for them to identify the most appropriate goals for them, to devise effective strategies for achieving these goals, and to make the necessary sacrifices in the present that will ensure that the future becomes a reality. For example, imagine that you are faced with the choice of studying for an exam or going out with your friends. What would you do? If you are focusing mainly on the present rather than the future, then the temptation to go out with your friends may be too strong. On the other hand, if you see this exam as connected to a future that is extremely important to you, then you are better equipped to sacrifice a few hours of pleasure for your future happiness.

Apply to a situation in your life some of the insights we have been examining about working toward goals.

1. Describe as specifically as possible an important long-term goal that you want to achieve. Your goal can be academic, professional, or personal.

2. Explain the reasons that led you to select the goal that you did and why you believe that your goal makes sense.

3. Identify both the major and minor steps you will have to take to achieve your goal. List your steps in the order they need to be taken, and indicate how much time you think each step will take. Make your responses as specific and precise as possible.

4. Identify some of the sacrifices that you may have to make in the present in order to achieve your future goal.

Making Decisions

In order to reach your goals, you have to learn to make effective decisions your-self. Although we all make decisions, we don't always make the most *informed* or *intelligent* decisions possible. In fact, most of us regularly have the experience of mentally kicking ourselves because we realize that we made a poor decision. Describe in the space below a decision you made that you would make differently if you had an opportunity to do it over again.

_____

_____

_____

_____

_____

Many of our poor decisions involve relatively minor issues—for example, selecting an unappealing dish in a restaurant, agreeing to go out on a blind date, or taking a course that does not live up to expectations. Although these decisions may result in unpleasant consequences, the discomfort is neither life threatening nor long lasting, although a disappointing course may *seem* to last forever! However, there are many more significant decisions in our lives in which poor decisions can result in considerably more damaging and far-reaching consequences. For example, one reason for the current divorce rate in the United States of 50 percent is the poor decisions that people make before or after the vows "till death do us part." Similarly, the fact that many employed adults wake up in the morning unhappy about going to their jobs, anxiously waiting for the end of the day and the conclusion of the week (TGIF!) so they are free to do what they *really* want to do, suggests that somewhere along the line they made poor career decisions or felt trapped by circumstances they couldn't control. Jobs should be much more than just a way to earn a paycheck: they should be vehicles for using professional skills, opportunities for expressing creative talents, stimulants to personal growth and intellectual development, and experiences that offer feelings of fulfillment and success. In the final analysis, careers are central elements of people's lives and important dimensions of life portraits. A career decision is one that we better try to get right!

An important part of becoming an educated thinker is learning to make effective decisions. Let's explore the process of making effective decisions, and then apply your knowledge to the challenge of deciding on the most appropriate career for you.

1. Think back on an important decision you made that turned out well, and describe the experience as specifically as possible.

2. Reconstruct the reasoning process that you used to make your decision. Did you
   - clearly define the decision to be made and the related issues?
   - consider various choices and anticipate the consequences of these various choices?
   - gather additional information to help in your analysis?
   - evaluate the various pros and cons of different courses of action?
   - use a chart or diagram to aid in your deliberations?
   - create a specific plan of action to implement your ideas?
   - periodically review your decision to make necessary adjustments?

An Organized Approach to Making Decisions

As you reflected on the successful decision you wrote about in Thinking Activity 1.5, you probably noticed your mind worked in a more or less systematic way as you thought your way through the decision situation. Of course, we often make important decisions with less thoughtful analysis by acting impulsively or relying on our "intuition." Sometimes these decisions work out well, but often they don't, and we are forced to live with the consequences of these mistaken choices. People who approach decision situations thoughtfully and analytically tend to be more successful decision makers than people who don't. Naturally, there are no guarantees that a careful analysis will lead to a successful result: there are often too many unknown elements and uncontrollable factors. But we can certainly improve our success rate as well as our speed by becoming more knowledgeable in the decision-making process. Expert decision makers can typically make quick, accurate decisions based on intuitions that are informed, not merely impulsive. However, as with most complex abilities in life, we need to learn to "walk" before we can "run," so let's explore a versatile and effective approach to making decisions.

The decision-making approach we will be using consists of five steps. As you gradually master these steps, they will become integrated into your way of thinking, and you will be able to apply them in a natural and flexible way.

Step 1: Define the decision clearly.
This seems like an obvious step, but a lot of decision making goes wrong at the starting point. For example, imagine that you decide that you want to have a "more active social life." The problem with this characterization is that it defines the situation too generally and therefore doesn't give any clear direction for your analysis. Do you want to develop an intimate, romantic relationship? Do you want to cultivate more close friendships? Do you want to engage in more social activities? Do you want to meet new people? In short, there are many ways to more clearly define the decision to have a "more active social life." The more specific your definition of the decision to be made, the clearer your analysis and the greater the likelihood of success.

> **Strategy:** *Write a one-page analysis that articulates your decision-making situation as clearly and specifically as possible.*

Step 2: Consider all the possible choices.
Successful decision makers explore all of the possible choices in their situation, not simply the obvious ones. In fact, the less obvious choices often turn out to be the most effective. For example, a student in a recent class of mine was undecided on whether he should major in accounting or business management. In discussing his situation with other members of the class, he revealed that his true interest was in the area of graphic design and illustration. Although he was very talented, he considered this area to be only a hobby, not a possible career choice. Class members pointed out to him graphic design might turn out to be his best career choice, but he needed to first *see* it as a possibility.

> **Strategy:** *List as many possible choices for your situation as you can, both obvious and not obvious. Ask other people for additional suggestions, and don't censor or prejudge any ideas.*

Step 3: Gather all relevant information, and evaluate the pros and cons of each possible choice.
In many cases we lack sufficient information to make an informed choice. Unfortunately, this situation doesn't

prevent people from plunging ahead anyway, making a decision that is often more a gamble than an informed choice. Instead of this questionable approach, it makes a lot more sense to seek out the information we need in order to determine which of the choices we identified has the best chance for success. For example, in the case of the student mentioned above, there is important information he would need to secure in order to determine whether he should consider a career in graphic design and illustration: What are the specific careers within this general field? What sort of academic preparation and experience are required for the various careers? What are the prospects for employment in this area, and how well do these jobs pay?

Strategy: *For each possible choice that you identified, create questions regarding information that you need, and then locate that information.*

In addition to locating all relevant information, each of the possible choices you identified has certain advantages and disadvantages, and it is essential that you analyze these pros and cons in an organized fashion. For example, in the case of the student described above, the choice of pursuing a career in accounting may have *advantages* such as ready employment opportunities, the flexibility of working in many different situations and geographical locations, moderate-to-high income expectations, and job security. On the other hand, *disadvantages* might include the fact that accounting may not reflect a deep and abiding interest of the student, he might lose interest over time, and the career might not result in the personal challenge and fulfillment that he seeks.

Strategy: *Using a format similar to the decision-making worksheet below, analyze the pros and cons of each of your possible choices.*

Decision-Making Worksheet

Define the decision: _____

	Possible choices	*Information needed*	*Pros*	*Cons*
1.	_____	_____	_____	_____
2.	_____	_____	_____	_____
3.	_____	_____	_____	_____
4.	_____	_____	_____	_____
5.	_____	_____	_____	_____

Select the best choice: _____
Create a plan of action and monitor the results.

Step 4: Select the choice that seems to meet the needs of the situation. The first four steps of this approach are designed to help you *analyze* your decision situation: to clearly define the decision, generate possible choices, gather relevant information, and evaluate the pros and cons of the choices you identified. In the final step, you must attempt to *synthesize* all that you have learned into a conclusion, weaving together all of the various threads into a choice that you believe to be your "best" one. How do you do this? There is no one simple way to identify your "best" choice, but there are some useful strategies for guiding your deliberations.

Strategy: *Identify and prioritize the goals of your decision situation, and determine which of your choices best meets these goals.*

This process will probably involve reviewing and perhaps refining your perception of the decision situation. For example, in the case of the student who we have been considering, some goals might include choosing a career that will

1. provide financial security
2. provide personal fulfillment
3. make use of his special talents
4. offer plentiful opportunities and job security

Once identified, goals can be ranked in order of their priority, which will then suggest what the "best" choice will be. For example, if the student ranks goals 1 and 4 at the top of the list, then a choice of accounting or business administration might make sense. On the other hand, if the student ranks goals 2 and 3 at the top, then pursuing a career in graphic design and illustration might be the best selection.

Strategy: *Anticipate the consequences of each choice by "preliving" the choices.*

Another helpful strategy for deciding on the best choice is to project yourself into the future, imagining as realistically as you can the consequences of each possible choice. As with previous strategies, this process is aided by writing your thoughts down and discussing them with others.

Step 5: Implement a plan of action and then monitor the results, making necessary adjustments.

Once you have selected what you consider to be your best choice, you need to develop and implement a specific, concrete plan of action. As we discovered in the last section, the more specific and concrete your plan of action, the greater its likelihood of success. For example, if the student in the case we have been considering decides to pursue a career in graphic design and illustration, his plan should include reviewing the major that best meets his needs, discussing his situation with students and faculty in that department, planning the courses he will be taking, and perhaps speaking to people in the field.

Strategy: *Create a schedule that details the steps you will be taking to implement your decision and a time line for taking these steps.*

Naturally, your plan is merely a starting point for implementing your decision. As you actually begin taking the steps in your plan, you will likely discover that changes and adjustments need to be made. In some cases, you may find that, based on new information, the choice you selected appears to be the wrong one. For example, as the student we have been discussing takes courses in the graphic design and illustration major, he may find that his interest in the field is not as serious as he thought and that although he likes this area as a hobby, he does not want it to be his life's work. In this case, he should return to considering his other choices and perhaps add choices that he did not consider before. The fact is that we often learn as much about what we want from choices that don't work out as from those that do.

Strategy: *After implementing your choice, evaluate its success by identifying what's working, noting what isn't, and making the necessary adjustments to improve the situation.*

Method for Making Decisions

Step 1: Define the decision clearly.

Strategy: Write a one-page analysis that articulates your decision-making situation as clearly and specifically as possible.

Step 2: Consider all the possible choices.

Strategy: List as many possible choices for your situation as you can, both obvious and not obvious. Ask other people for additional suggestions, and don't censor or prejudge any ideas.

Step 3: Gather all relevant information, and evaluate the pros and cons of each possible choice.

Strategy: For each possible choice that you identified, create questions regarding information that you need, and then locate that information.

Strategy: Using a format similar to the decision-making worksheet on page 17, analyze the pros and cons of each of your possible choices.

Step 4: Select the choice that seems to meet the needs of the situation.

Strategy: Identify and prioritize the goals of your decision situation, and determine which of your choices best meets these goals.

Strategy: Anticipate the consequences of each choice by "preliving" the choices.

Step 5: Implement a plan of action and then monitor the results, making necessary adjustments.

Strategy: Create a schedule that details the steps you will be taking to implement your decision and a time line for taking these steps.

Strategy: After implementing your choice, evaluate its success by identifying what's working, noting what isn't, and making the necessary adjustments to improve the situation.

Thinking Activity 1.6

1. Describe an important decision that you will have to make in the near future.

2. Using the five-step decision-making approach we just explored, analyze the situation and conclude with your "best" choice.

3. Share your analysis with other members of the class, and listen carefully to the feedback they give you.

Deciding on a Career

> Work is a search for daily meaning as well as daily bread, for recognition as well as cash . . . in short, for a life rather than a Monday through Friday sort of dying.
>
> —Studs Terkel, *Working*

"What are you going to be when you grow up?" You have doubtless been asked this pivotal question many times throughout your life by well-intentioned people. As children, this question is fun to contemplate, because life is an adventure and the future is unlimited. However, now that you are grown, this question may elicit more anxiety than enjoyment. "What *am* I going to be?" "*Who* am I going to be?" Enrolling in college is certainly an intelligent beginning. The majority of professional careers require college education. And the investment is certainly worthwhile in monetary terms: the average college graduate can expect lifetime earnings of $830,000 more than peers who didn't go beyond high school and $600,000 more than those who started college but didn't graduate (*The Occupational Outlook Quarterly*, Winter 1995).

Perhaps you are entering college right out of high school, or perhaps you are returning to college after raising a family, working in a variety of jobs, or serving in the armed forces. The question is the same: "What is the right decision to make about a career?" Some people have no idea how to answer this question; some have a general idea about a possible career (or careers) but aren't sure exactly which career they want or precisely how to achieve their goals. Even if you feel sure about your choice, it makes sense to engage in some serious career exploration to ensure that you fully understand your interests and abilities, as well as the full range of career choices that match up with your talents.

Most students entering college will change their majors a number of times

The Career Ladder: Your career choice is an important element of your life portrait, enabling you to use your professional abilities and express your creative talents and offering feelings of fulfillment and success.

before graduating. (I changed my major two weeks after beginning college!) Although many students are concerned that these changes reveal instability and confusion, in most cases these changes are, in reality, a healthy sign. The changes suggest that students are actively engaged in the process of career exploration: considering possible choices, trying them out, revising their thinking to exploring other possibilities. Often we learn as much from discovering what we *don't* want as from what we *do* want. The student who plans to become a veterinarian may end up concluding that "I never want to see a sick animal the rest of my life," as one of my students confided after completing a work internship in a veterinary clinic.

The best place to begin an intelligent analysis of your career future is by completing a review of what you already know about your career orientation. Your personal history contains clues about which career directions are most appropriate for you. By examining the careers you have considered in your life and by analyzing the reasons that have motivated your career choices, you can start creating a picture of yourself that will help you define a fulfilling future for yourself. With these considerations in mind, complete the following activity as a way to begin creating your individual "career portrait."

Describe two careers that you have considered for yourself in the past few years along with the reason(s) for your choices.

1. *Career:* _____

   Reason(s) selected: _____

   _____

2. *Career:* _____

   Reason(s) selected: _____

   _____

Thinking Activity 1.7

Describe in a two-page paper your *current* thoughts and feelings about your career plans. Be very honest, and include the following:

1. A specific description of the career(s) you think you might enjoy

2. A description of the history of this choice(s) and the reasons why you think you would enjoy it (them)

3. The doubts, fears, and uncertainties you have about your choice(s)

4. The problems you will have to solve and the challenges you will have to overcome in order to achieve your career goal

Too often, people choose careers for the wrong reasons, including the following:

- They consider only those job opportunities with which they are familiar, and fail to discover countless other career possibilities.

- They focus on certain elements—such as salary or job security—while ignoring others—such as job satisfaction or opportunities for advancement.

- They choose careers because of pressure from family or peers, rather than selecting careers that they really want.

- They drift into a job by accident or circumstance and never re-evaluate their options.

- They fail to fully understand their abilities and long-term interests, and what careers will match these.

- They don't pursue their "dream jobs" because they are afraid they will not succeed.

- They are reluctant to give up their current unsatisfactory job for more promising possibilities because of the risk and sacrifice involved.

Whatever the reasons, the sad fact is that many people wind up with dead-end, unsatisfying jobs that seem more like lifetime prison sentences than their "field of dreams." However, such depressing outcomes are not inevitable. This text is designed to help you develop the thinking abilities, knowledge, and insight you will need to find the right career.

Where Are You?

Your third grade	Mother was a nurse.
teacher said	Now you are.
you had a problem with math.	Why are you
You gave up on	where you are?
math, and you forever	Because you want
eliminated two-thirds	to be there?
of the jobs available in	Think about it.
this world.	Maybe you ought to be
Somebody	somewhere else. Maybe it's
decided the	not too late
Navy needed	to figure out
a cook.	where, and how
After your	to get there.
hitch, you opened	
a restaurant.	

Source: © United Technologies Corporation, Hartford, Ct., 1984. Used by permission.

Creating Your Dream Job

One of the powerful abilities you possess is the capacity to think imaginatively. In order to discover the career that is right for you, it makes sense to use your imagination to create an image of the job that you believe would make you feel most fulfilled. Too often, people settle for less than they have to because they don't believe they have any realistic chance to achieve their dreams. Using this self-defeating way of thinking virtually guarantees failure in a career quest. Another thinking error occurs when people decide to pursue a career simply because it pays well, even though they have little interest in the work itself. This approach overlooks the fact that in order to be successful over a long period of time, you must be highly motivated; otherwise, you may "run out of gas" when you most need it. Interestingly enough, when people pursue careers that reflect their true interests, their success often results in financial reward because of their talent and accomplishments, even though money wasn't their main goal!

So the place to begin your career quest is with your dreams, not your fears. In order to get started, it's best to imagine an ideal job in as much detail as possible. Of course, any particular job is only one possibility within the field of your career choice. It is likely that you will have a number of different jobs as you pursue your career. However, your imagination works more effectively when conjuring up *specific* images. In the space below, provide a brief but detailed description of your ideal job, including the following elements:

Discovering the right career for you is an important part of achieving personal fulfillment and happiness in your life.

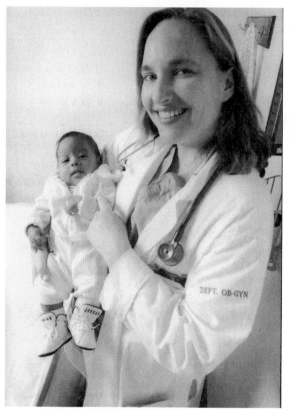

- *physical setting or environment* in which you would like to spend your working hours
- *types of activities* you would like to spend your time doing
- *kinds of people* you would like to be working with
- *personal goals and accomplishments* you would like to achieve as part of your work

Physical setting or environment: _____

_____

_____

Activities: _____

_____

_____

People: _____

_____

_____

Personal goals/accomplishments: _____

_____

_____

Of course, these initial responses are merely the first step toward giving your career exploration a genuine and appropriate direction. There is a great deal of thinking, research, and action required in order to transform your dreams into reality. An ancient Chinese proverb advises that "the journey of a thousand miles begins with just one step." We might add that in order to reach your desired destination, you must make sure that your first step is in the right direction!

Thinking Activity 1.8

Using your responses above as a guide, write a two-page description of your ideal job. Spend time letting your imagination conjure up a specific picture of your job, and don't let negative impulses ("I could never get a job like that!) interfere with your creative vision. Be sure to address each of the four features of your ideal job: (1) physical setting and environment, (2) activities, (3) people, and (4) personal goals and accomplishments.

Discovering "Who" You Are

Each of us possesses an original combination of interests, abilities, and values that characterizes our personalities. Discovering the appropriate career for yourself involves becoming familiar with your unique qualities: the activities that interest you, the special abilities and potentials you have, and the values that define the things you consider to be most important. Once you have a reasonably clear sense of "who" you are and what you are capable of, you can then begin exploring those careers that are a good match for you. Many people are still in the early stages of self-understanding, which makes identifying the appropriate career particularly difficult.

What Are Your Interests?

In order to find a career that will be stimulating and rewarding to you over the course of many years, you must choose a field involving activities in which you have a deep and lasting interest. If you want to be a teacher, you should find helping people learn to be an inspiring and fulfilling activity. If you want to be an architect, you should find the process of creating designs, working with

Your career choice should involve activities for which you have a lasting interest and natural ability.

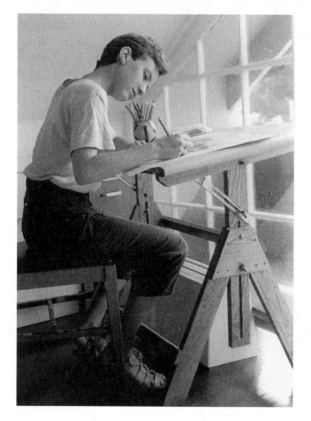

clients, and solving construction problems to be personally challenging activities. When people achieve a close match between their natural interests and the activities that constitute a career, they are assured of working in a profession that will bring them joy and satisfaction.

Achieving a positive match between your natural interests and potential careers means first identifying what your natural interests actually are. Each of us has many interests in our lives, and many of these do not appear directly relevant to our career decisions. However, if we examine the situation more closely, we can see that the many interests that we pursue form *patterns* of interests that are very relevant to our career decisions. For example, identify possible careers that might be appropriate matches for people who list the following interests, and explain your reasons why:

■ I enjoy listening to my friends' problems and trying to help them figure out the best thing for them to do.

■ I have volunteered to help out with an organization devoted to helping young people with substance abuse problems.

■ I am particularly interested in the psychology courses I have taken because I find the human personality to be incredibly fascinating.

Possible careers: _____

Explanation: _____

_____

- When I read the newspaper, I always begin with the business section.
- I have always enjoyed selling products to others—Christmas cards, Girl Scout cookies—and I have always been very successful!
- I have always dreamed of owning my own business and have even drawn up plans for exactly how it's going to work.
- I find that the more business courses I take, the more I want to take.

Possible careers: _____

Explanation: _____

_____

- I worked on the school newspaper and was responsible for all of the layout and design.
- Art has always been a major interest for me, and I have drawn and painted for as long as I remember. I feel that art enables me to express my creative ideas.
- I am fascinated by the designs of products and the advertising created for them. I have a large collection of particularly unusual and effective examples.
- I have always excelled in my art courses, particularly design classes. They just seem to come naturally to me.

Possible careers: _____

Explanation: _____

_____

While there might not be a direct connection between your interests and your eventual career, carefully examining your interests should nevertheless provide you with valuable clues toward discovering a career that will bring you lifelong satisfaction.

Thinking Activity 1.9

1. Create a list of the interests in your life, describing each one as specifically as possible. Begin with the present and work backward as far as you can remember, covering the areas of *employment, education,* and *general activities.* Make the list as comprehensive as you can, including as many interests as you can think of. Ask people who know you how they would describe your interests.

2. Once you have created your list, classify the items into groups based on similarity. Don't worry if the same interest fits in more than one group.

3. For each group you have created, identify possible careers that might be

→

related to the interests described in the group. A student example is included below.

Interest Group 1

- I enjoy helping people solve their problems.
- I am interested in subjects like hypnotism and mental therapy.
- I have always been interested in the behavior of people.
- I enjoy reading books on psychology.

Possible careers: clinical psychologist, occupational therapist, social worker, gerontologist, behavioral scientist, community mental health worker, industrial psychologist

Interest Group 2

- I am interested in sciences, especially chemistry and anatomy.
- I like going to hospitals and observing doctors and nurses at work.
- When I was in high school, I always enjoyed biology and anatomy labs.
- I am interested in hearing about people's illnesses and injuries.

Possible careers: doctor, nurse, physical therapist, paramedic, biomedical worker, chemical technician, mortician, medical laboratory technician

Interest Group 3

- I enjoy going to museums and theaters.
- I enjoy painting and drawing in my free time.
- I enjoy listening to music: classical, jazz, and romantic.
- I enjoy reading magazines like *Vogue, Vanity Fair, Vanidades.*

Possible careers: actor, publicist, advertising executive, interior design, fashion design

What Are Your Abilities?

In general, the activities that you have a sustained interest in over a period of time are activities that you will be good at. This is another key question for you to address as you pursue your career explorations: "What are my special abilities and talents?" Each of us has a unique combination of special talents, and it is to our advantage to select careers that exploit these natural abilities. Otherwise, we will find ourselves competing against people who *do* have natural abilities in that particular area. For example, think of courses you have taken that seemed extremely difficult despite your strenuous efforts, while other students were successful with apparently much less effort (or vice versa: courses that seemed easy to you but very difficult for other students). There is a great deal of competition for *desirable* careers, and if you are to be successful, you need to be able to use your natural strengths.

I once gave a simulated job interview to a woman who was majoring in business. She possessed wonderful social skills—she was personable, articulate, engaging—but when I reviewed her transcript, it was clear that she had done poorly in most of her business courses while performing very well in a variety of liberal arts courses. When I asked her about her academic record, she said, "I guess I just don't have a head for numbers." Unfortunately, for people to excel in business, it is important for them to have a "head for numbers," or they will likely be seriously handicapped in their career aspirations. On the other hand, the student clearly had exceptional abilities in areas that her career direction might not make full use of.

How do you go about identifying your natural abilities? One productive approach to begin identifying your abilities is to examine important accomplishments in your life, a strategy described in Thinking Activity 1.10. In addition, there are career counselors and computer software programs that can help you zero in on your interests and strengths. However, we sometimes possess unknown abilities because we simply haven't had the opportunity to discover and use them. With this in mind, it makes sense for you to explore unfamiliar areas of experience to become aware of your full range of potentials.

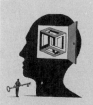

Thinking Activity 1.10

1. Identify the ten most important accomplishments in your life. From this list of ten, select the three accomplishments of which you are most proud. Typically, these will be experiences in which you faced a difficult challenge or complex problem that you were able to overcome with commitment and talent.

2. Compose a specific and detailed description (1–2 pages) of each of these three accomplishments, paying particular attention to the skills and strategies you used to meet the challenge or solve the problem.

3. After completing the descriptions, identify the abilities that you displayed in achieving each accomplishment. Then place them into groups, based on their similarity to one another. A student example is included below.

Accomplishments

1. Graduating from high school
2. Moving into my own apartment
3. Getting my real estate license
4. Finding a job
5. Succeeding at college
6. Getting my driver's license
7. Owning a dog
8. Buying a car
9. Winning a swimming championship
10. Learning to speak another language

→

Accomplishment 1: Graduating from high school

The first accomplishment I would like to describe is graduating from high school. I never thought I would do it. In the eleventh grade I became a truant. I only attended classes in my major, after which I would go home or hang out with friends. I was having a lot of problems with my parents and the guy I was dating, and I fell into a deep depression in the middle of the term. I decided to commit suicide by taking pills. I confided this to a friend, who went and told the principal. I was called out of class to the principal's office. He said he wanted to talk to me, and it seemed like we talked for hours. Suddenly my parents walked in with my guidance counselor, and they joined the discussion. We came to the conclusion that I would live with my aunt for two weeks, and I would also speak with the counselor once a day. If I didn't follow these rules, they would place me in a group home. During those two weeks I did a lot of thinking. I didn't talk to anyone from my neighborhood. Through counseling I learned that no problems are worth taking your life. I joined a peer group in my school, which helped me a lot as well. I learned to express my feelings. It was very difficult to get back into my schedule in school, but my teachers' help made it easier. I committed myself to school, and did very well, graduating the following year.

Abilities and Skills from Accomplishment 1

1. I learned how to analyze and solve difficult problems in my life.

2. I learned how to understand and express my feelings.

3. I learned how to work with other people in order to help solve each other's problems.

4. I learned how to focus my attention and work with determination toward a goal.

5. I learned how to deal with feelings of depression and think positively about myself and my future.

Finding the Right Match

The purpose of these past few sections has been to help you use your thinking abilities to begin identifying your interests, abilities, and values. Discovering "who" you are is one part of identifying the appropriate career for you. The second part involves researching the careers that are available in order to determine which ones match up with your interests, abilities, and values. There are literally thousands of different careers, most of which you are unfamiliar

The Right Match:
Career exploration involves discovering the right match between your interests and abilities and the various career possibilities.

with. How do you find out about them? There are a number of tools at your disposal. To begin with, your college probably has a career resource center containing reference books, periodical publications, videotapes, and software programs that describe various occupations. Career counselors are also available, either at your school or in your community. Speaking to people working in various careers is another valuable way to learn about what is really involved in a particular career. Work internships, summer jobs, and volunteer work are other avenues for learning about career possibilities and whether they might be right for you. At the end of this chapter (pages 34–44) is an article titled "Solving the Job Puzzle" that might also help you in your explorations.

As you begin your career explorations, don't lose sight of the fact that your career decisions will likely evolve over time, reflecting your growth as a person and the changing job market. Many people alter their career paths often, so you should avoid focusing too narrowly. Instead, concentrate on preparing for broad career areas and developing your general knowledge and abilities. For example, by learning to think critically, solve problems, make intelligent decisions, and communicate effectively, you are developing the basic abilities needed in virtually any career. As an "educated thinker" you will be able to respond quickly and successfully to the unplanned changes and unexpected opportunities that you encounter as you follow—and create—the unfolding path of your life.

Discovering the right career is an adventure that involves careful analysis, comprehensive research, and patience. For people who are willing to embark on this adventure, the result will be a career that will bring them a lifetime of challenges, accomplishments, and rewards. Instead of TGIF, we may actually say TGIM ("Thank God it's Monday!").

Becoming an Educated Thinker

This chapter has focused on the role of college in preparing people for a career. However, as we noted early on, another main goal of a college education is to help you become an educated thinker. As an educated thinker you will possess the thinking abilities and the knowledge needed not only to excel in your college studies, but to be successful in your chosen career as well.

What exactly is *thinking*? Thinking is the extraordinary cognitive process we use every waking moment to make sense of our world and our lives. Throughout this chapter we have been exploring the different ways our thinking enables us to make sense of the world by working toward our goals and making decisions. Of course, our thinking helps us make sense of the world in other ways as well. When we attend a concert, listen to a lecture, discuss a complicated issue, or try to understand someone's behavior, it is our thinking that enables us to figure out what is happening. In fact, these attempts to make sense of what is happening are going on all the time in our lives, and they represent the heart of the thinking process.

If we review the different ways of thinking we have been exploring in this chapter, we can reach several conclusions about thinking:

1. *Thinking is an active process.* Whether we are trying to reach a goal or make a decision, we are actively using our minds to figure out the situation.

2. *Thinking is directed toward a purpose.* When we think, it is usually for a purpose—to reach a goal, make a decision, or solve a problem.

3. *Thinking is an organized process.* When we think effectively, there is usually an order or organization to our thinking. For each of the thinking activities we explored, we saw that there are certain steps or approaches to take that help us reach goals and make decisions.

We can put together these conclusions about thinking to form a working definition of the term:

Thinking

An active, purposeful, organized cognitive process that we use to make sense of our world.

Thinking is a process that develops with use over a lifetime, whether we are trying to decide what courses to take in school, which career to pursue, or simply how much to bet on a poker hand. By continuing to develop our thinking abilities, we become even better prepared to make sense of our world, to explore the choices available to us, and to make appropriate decisions.

We can improve our thinking in an organized and systematic way by following these three steps:

1. *Becoming aware of our thinking process.* We usually take thinking for granted and do not pay much attention to it. Developing our thinking means that we have to "think about the way we think."

2. *Carefully examining our thinking process and the thinking process of others.* In this chapter we have explored various ways in which our thinking works. By focusing our attention on these (and other) thinking approaches and strategies, we can learn to think more effectively.

3. *Practicing our thinking abilities.* To improve our thinking, we actually have to think for ourselves, to explore and make sense of thinking situations by using our thinking abilities. Although it is important to read about thinking and learn how other people think, there is no substitute for actually doing it ourselves.

The ability to think for ourselves by carefully examining the way that we make sense of the world is one of the most satisfying aspects of being a mature, educated human being. We will refer to this ability to think carefully about our thinking as the ability to *think critically*. Using our definition of *thinking* as a starting point, we can define *thinking critically* as follows:

Thinking critically

The cognitive process we use to carefully examine our thinking and the thinking of others in order to clarify and improve our understanding.

We are able to think critically because of our natural human ability to *reflect*—to think back on what we had been thinking, doing, or feeling. By carefully thinking back on our thinking, we are able to figure out the way our thinking operates and therefore learn to do it more effectively. In the following chapters we will systematically explore many dimensions of the way that our minds work, providing us the opportunity to deepen our understanding of the thinking process and stimulating us to become more effective thinkers. As you become a more sophisticated thinker, you will also be developing the knowledge and abilities you will need to be successful at college, and exploring important issues that you will encounter as a member of the college community.

Of course, carefully examining the ideas produced by the thinking process assumes that there are ideas worth examining. Producing such ideas is made possible by our ability to *think creatively*, that dimension of our thinking process by which we create ideas that are original, useful, and worthy of further elaboration. From this perspective, we can define *thinking creatively* as follows:

Thinking creatively

The cognitive process we use to develop ideas that are unique, useful, and worthy of further elaboration.

Examining creative thinking is a rich and complex enterprise that is integrally tied to critical thinking. In fact, these two dimensions of the thinking process are so tightly interwoven that both must be addressed in order to understand either one. For example, when you imagined your "dream job" on page 25, you were using your creative thinking abilities to visualize an ideal career situation. With this idea as a starting point, you could use your critical thinking abilities to refine your idea and then research existing career opportunities. Once a clear career goal is established, you can use your creative thinking abilities to generate possible ideas for achieving this goal, while your critical thinking abilities will help you evaluate your various options and devise a practical, organized plan.

It is apparent that creative and critical thinking work as partners to produce effective thinking, enabling us to make informed decisions and lead successful lives. As this text unfolds, you will be given the opportunity to become familiar with and develop both of these powerful forms of thought. With these essential abilities as a foundation, you will possess the intellectual tools to excel in your college studies, to succeed in your career, and to become an educated thinker.

"Solving the Job Puzzle"

The following article, written by the economists Anne W. Clymer and Elizabeth McGregor, provides additional guidance in your career explorations. The first section describes additional strategies for identifying your interests and abilities, and it also suggests various resources for researching information about potential careers. The second section helps you match your personal interests and abilities with the characteristics of potential careers. After carefully reviewing the article, answer the questions that follow.

Solving the Job Puzzle

by Anne W. Clymer and Elizabeth McGregor

"I am myself reminded that we are not alike; there are diversities of natures among us which are adapted to different occupations." These words, which Plato attributed to Socrates, are still true today.

Anne W. Clymer and Elizabeth McGregor are economists in the Office of Employment Projections, BLS. ⟶

Choosing a career is one of the hardest jobs you will ever have. You should devote extensive time, energy, and thought to make a decision with which you will be happy. Even though undertaking this task means hard work, view a career as an opportunity to do something you enjoy, not simply as a necessity or as a means of earning a living. Taking the time to thoroughly explore career options can mean the difference between finding a stimulating and fulfilling career or hopping from one job to the next in search of the right job. Finding the best occupation for you also is important because work influences many aspects of your life—from your choice of friends and recreational activities to where you live.

Choosing a career is work that should be done carefully. As you gain experience and mature, however, you may develop new interests and skills which open doors to new opportunities. Work is an educational experience and can further focus your interests or perhaps change your career preferences. The choice you make today may not be your last. In fact, most people change occupations several times during their careers. With careful consideration of the wide range of occupations available, you should be able to find the right career.

There are many factors to consider when exploring career options and many ways to begin solving your job puzzle. Everyone has certain expectations of his or her job—these may include career advancement, self-expression or creativity, a sense of accomplishment, or a high salary. Deciding what you want most from your job will make choosing a career easier.

This article can assist you in your search for a suitable career. It discusses things to consider—personal interests, educational and skill requirements, and job outlook—and lists sources of additional information. The accompanying chart (which begins on page 41) is an exploratory tool to help you pair personal interests, skills, and educational qualifications with those usually associated with a particular occupation. This will help you identify some potential occupational choices.

Interests

Identifying your interests will help in your search for a stimulating career. You might start by assessing your likes and dislikes, strengths and weaknesses. If you have trouble identifying them, consider the school subjects, activities, and surroundings that appeal to you. Would you prefer a job that involves travel? Do you want to work with children? Do you like science and mathematics? Do you need flexible working hours? Does a particular industry, such as health services, appeal to you? These are just a few questions to ask yourself. There are no right or wrong answers, and only you know what's important. Decide what job characteristics you require, which ones you prefer, and which ones you would not accept. Then rank these characteristics in order of importance to you.

Perhaps job setting ranks high on your list of important job characteristics. You may not want to work behind a desk all day. The chart indicates many diverse occupations—from building inspectors, to surveyors, to real estate agents—that require work away from an office. Or maybe you always dreamed of a job that involves instructing and helping others; in this case, child care workers, teachers, and physicians are among the occupations that might interest you.

Geographic location may also concern you. If so, it could influence your career decision because employment in some occupations and industries is concentrated in certain regions or localities. For example, aerospace jobs are concentrated in three States—California, Texas, and

Washington—while advertising jobs are concentrated in large cities. If you choose to work in one of these fields, you probably will have to live in one of these States or in a large city. Or, if you live in Denver or the Southeast, for instance, you should learn which industries and occupations are found in those locations. On the other hand, many industries such as hotels and motels, legal services, and retail trade, as well as occupations such as teachers, secretaries, and computer analysts, are found in all areas of the country.

Earnings potential varies from occupation to occupation, and each person must determine his or her needs and goals. If high earnings are important to you, look beyond the starting wages. Some occupations offer relatively low starting salaries, but earnings substantially increase with experience, additional training, and promotions. In the end, your earnings may be higher in one of these occupations. For example, insurance sales workers may have relatively low earnings at first; after years of building a clientele, however, their earnings may increase substantially.

Job setting, working with a specific group of people, geographic location, and earnings are just a few occupational characteristics that you may consider. Be open minded. Consider occupations related to your initial interests. For example, you may be interested in health care, and certain qualities of nursing may appeal to you, such as patient care and frequent public contact. Exploring other health occupations that share these characteristics—including doctors, respiratory therapists, and emergency medical technicians—may stimulate your interest in a health field other than nursing.

Don't eliminate any occupation or industry before you learn more about it. Some occupations and industries invoke certain positive or negative images. For some people, fashion designers produce a glamorous image, while production occupations in manufacturing industries bring to mind a less attractive image. However, jobs often are not what they first appear to be, and misconceptions are common. Exciting jobs may have dull aspects, while less glamorous occupations may interest you once you learn about them. For example, the opportunity to travel makes a flight attendant's job seem exciting, but the work is strenuous and tiring; flight attendants stand for long periods and must remain friendly when they are tired and passengers are unpleasant. On the other hand, many people consider automotive assembly work dirty and dull; however, production workers in the motor vehicle manufacturing industry are among the highest paid in the Nation.

Skills

One way to choose an occupation is to examine the skills required to perform the job well. Consider the skills you already have, or your ability and interest in obtaining the skills or training required for specific occupations. Some occupations that require mechanical ability, for instance, include elevator installers and repairers and automotive mechanics. If you do not plan to attend college, consider occupations that require less formal education. If you are interested in engineering, for example, but do not want to pursue a college degree, drafters and engineering technicians are two occupations you can enter with 1 or 2 years of postsecondary training.

Some skills—analysis, persuading, and mechanical ability, for example—are specific to certain occupations and are included in the accompanying chart. However, certain skills are needed, in varying degrees, in virtually all occupations, from factory workers to top executives.

→

Because these skills apply to so many occupations, they are not found in the chart, but are discussed here.

Skills Common to All Jobs

As the marketplace becomes increasingly competitive, a company's ability to succeed depends upon its workers' skills—in particular, basic skills in reading, writing, and mathematics. These skills allow workers to learn and adapt to rapid technological advances and changing business practices in their jobs. This adaptability is crucial to one's survival in the job market.

Reading skills are essential to perform most jobs. Workers must often read and understand text, graphs, charts, manuals, and instructional materials. Writing skills are necessary to communicate thoughts, ideas, and information in written forms such as memorandums, invoices, schedules, letters, or information requests. Many jobs require basic mathematical skills to take measurements and perform simple calculations. Lack of these skills can lead to many problems, including poor quality products and missed deadlines. These problems can then result in a decline in sales and increased customer complaints.

Reading, writing, and mathematical skills are as important for a research scientist as they are for occupations that require little formal education, such as a stockroom clerk at a manufacturing plant. Although a computer system may be designed to track inventory by electronically recording all transactions, the clerk is responsible for verifying the information. The clerk must be able to read and do simple calculations to confirm that stockroom inventory matches what the computer registers. Any inaccuracies in counting, computing, or recording of this inventory could result in a slowdown in production.

Workers also need good listening and speaking skills to interact with others. Greater interaction among workers is evident in factories, offices, and laboratories. Problems often are solved through communication, cooperation, and discussion, and workers must be able to listen, speak, and think on their feet. When dealing with customers, workers must listen and understand customers' needs and communicate solutions and ideas. It is not good enough to merely take a customer's order; workers must provide customers with useful information.

The banking industry illustrates the importance of listening and speaking skills. Banks face competition from other industries—including insurance companies, credit unions, and investment houses—that offer a growing array of financial products. Tellers, customer service representatives, and bank managers need strong communication skills to explain, promote, and sell the bank's services to potential customers. Customer satisfaction can only be achieved by understanding what the customer wants and by providing that service as quickly as possible.

Good interpersonal skills are critical as the workplace becomes more team-oriented. Apparel plants, for instance, are replacing the traditional assembly line with modular manufacturing. On the traditional assembly line, workers performed a specific task independent of other workers and were compensated accordingly. Today, groups of workers, called modules, work as a team to produce garments, solve problems as they occur, and make suggestions to improve production or working conditions. Group interaction is important because an individual's earnings are based upon the group's performance.

Workers at all levels must be willing to learn new techniques. Computers, for instance, were once found primarily in office settings; today, computers are found in every work setting

→

from factories to classrooms. The introduction of computers into the manufacturing process is transforming many craft and factory occupations; many of these jobs now require the use of computer-controlled equipment. For example, most elevators are computerized and electronically controlled. In order to install, repair, and maintain modern elevators, elevator repairers need a thorough knowledge of electronics, electricity, and computer applications. Even though a high school education generally is the minimum requirement for entering this field, workers with postsecondary training in electronics usually have better advancement opportunities than those with less training. As technological changes continue, retraining will be essential for workers in many fields.

Matching Personal and Job Characteristics

Having looked at the job puzzle, you can now focus your career search. The accompanying table matches 18 job characteristics to over 200 occupations studied in the occupational outlook program. You can use it to match yourself with the characteristics associated with various occupations. Be realistic when matching your interests, skills, and goals to a career. For example, you can't become a neurosurgeon without completing college and many years of advanced study, and elementary school teachers do not make $100,000 per year. Being realistic will help you eliminate some possible career choices and identify others that may interest you.

The table can be used in various ways. If you are interested in a specific occupation, you can find out some general characteristics of that occupation. If you are considering psychology, for example, the table indicates that psychologists need a college degree, treat and advise others, and do analysis and evaluation. If the field of education appeals to you, the table provides information about various jobs in that field. If you have no idea about an occupation or field but do know what skills you possess, the table can help you identify careers that might interest you.

Although this table presents information on occupations and skills, it is intended only as a general guide. Don't rule out an occupation because one or two characteristics don't appeal to you. The table addresses primary characteristics of a typical job in that occupation. Not all jobs in an occupation are alike. There may be some differences by specialty, employment setting, or level of experience. For example, jewelers in retail stores deal with the public daily, while those in manufacturing rarely have contact with the public. Counseling psychologists work with people in offices, while experimental psychologists may work with animals in laboratories. Furthermore, you could find two dissimilar occupations that share some characteristics. For example, public relations specialists and dietitians are unrelated occupations, but both require analyzing and troubleshooting ability.

Most occupations cannot be easily categorized by job characteristics. The process of selecting and defining occupational characteristics relies upon the best judgment of analysts who study trends of the selected occupations. Because final decisions rely upon judgment, there may be some questions as to which characteristics apply to a particular occupation. For instance, teachers spend much of their day on their feet, which is physically tiring. However, the table does not indicate physical stamina as a key characteristic of teachers because they can teach while sitting at a desk. Construction laborers, in comparison, must lift heavy objects and endure physical stress and strain to perform their work. Take the time to learn more about

→

occupations that interest you; this may include following the suggestions mentioned in the section on additional information.

The characteristics matched in the table with occupations studied in the occupational outlook program are defined below. The characteristics are grouped under five headings: Education, data/information, people, things, and working conditions. Specific occupations are mentioned with the definitions to illustrate how the characteristics apply to the job.

Education

High school diploma (HS)—requires a high school diploma or the equivalent.

Postsecondary training (PS)—requires training beyond high school but less than a bachelor's degree, including formal on-the-job training, technical or vocational school, or junior or community college.

College and above (C)—requires at least a bachelor's degree.

No educational level indicated—occupation may be entered with less than a high school education.

In some cases, more than one level of educational attainment is indicated for an occupation, reflecting a range of formal educational requirements. For example, some high school graduates become administrative services managers by advancing through the ranks of an organization. Even though a higher degree is not always required for administrative services managers, postsecondary or college education usually enhances their chance of advancing to top-level management positions. Educational requirements may also vary within an occupation. For instance, registered nursing can be entered by earning a diploma, associate degree, or bachelor's degree.

Data/Information

Researching and compiling: Gathering and organizing information or data by reading, conducting tests or experiments, or interviewing experts. Through research, scientists gather information to develop new theories, products, and processes, such as a new medicine to cure a disease. Paralegals conduct research and compile information to identify appropriate laws, legal articles, and judicial decisions that might be used in a client's case. Credit clerks and authorizers compile and update information for credit reports.

Analyzing and evaluating: Examining data or information to develop conclusions or interpretations. After conducting research and compiling data, paralegals may analyze the information and write reports that are used by attorneys to decide how a case should be handled. Retail buyers study sales data to determine purchasing trends, and budget analysts examine financial data to determine the most efficient distribution of funds and resources for their company.

Troubleshooting: Identifying, diagnosing, and solving problems. A degree of analysis may be required to form opinions and make decisions. Involves a reaction to a situation or problem that arises. Elevator repairers diagnose and repair electrical defects quickly to ensure that elevators continue running smoothly. Automotive mechanics diagnose problems with cars and make adjustments or repairs. Managers must deal with various problems, such as a decline in an employee's performance or budget reductions requiring layoffs.

→

Artistic expression: Designing, composing, drawing, writing, or creating original works or concepts. Interior designers need creativity to develop designs to use in preparing working drawings and specifications for interior construction of buildings. They need an artistic sense to coordinate colors, select furniture and floor coverings, and design lighting and architectural details. Newspaper columnists convey their views on political, social, and economic issues.

People

Instructing: Teaching people by explaining or showing. Often requires ability to develop new methods and approaches. Adult education teachers demonstrate various techniques to students, including the use of tools or equipment. Manufacturers' and wholesale sales representatives show their customers how to operate and maintain new equipment.

Treating and advising: Counseling or caring for others. Dietitians advise people on proper nutrition. Psychologists and counselors help people deal with vocational and marital problems. Securities and financial services sales representatives advise people on financial investments and planning.

Supervising: Directing, organizing, and motivating people and groups. Blue-collar worker supervisors coordinate and supervise the activities of subordinates. Education administrators provide direction, leadership, and day-to-day management of educational activities in schools and instructional organizations in private businesses.

Persuading: Influencing the feelings of others. Preaching, selling, promoting, speechmaking, negotiating, and mediating are among the skills included in this occupational characteristic. Lawyers attempt to persuade a jury to believe a client's case. Advertising executives try to influence consumers to buy the products they are promoting.

Public contact: Meeting, assisting, and dealing directly with the public frequently on a daily basis. Reference librarians work directly with people, helping them locate information. Bank tellers cash checks and process deposits and withdrawals for customers. Real estate agents help customers find homes that meet their needs.

Things

Mechanical ability: Extensively using and understanding machines or tools. Setting up, operating, adjusting, and repairing machines may also be required. Textile machinery operators make minor repairs and restart looms when malfunctions occur. Musical instrument repairers tune and adjust pianos and other instruments. Marine engineers maintain and repair engines, boilers, generators, and other machinery on boats and ships.

Operating a vehicle: Driving and controlling vehicles or equipment. Busdrivers, industrial truck operators, and aircraft pilots are several examples.

Working Conditions

Repetitious: Work in which the same duties are performed continuously in a short period of time. Sometimes a machine sets the pace of work. Examples include workers on automotive assembly lines, as well as cashiers and bank tellers.

$\longrightarrow$

Geographically concentrated: Occupations concentrated in a particular region or locality. Most textile workers are concentrated in a few States. Advertising workers are found mainly in large cities.

Mobile: Requires frequent movement between various work locations, such as office buildings and construction sites. Can involve a combination of different work settings. Workers do not stay in a single office, factory, or laboratory. For example, in addition to working in an office, property and real estate managers frequently visit properties they oversee, while manufacturing sales representatives travel to different cities to visit customers. Messengers deliver packages to various locations.

Physical stamina: Physically demanding. Workers must endure significant physical stress and strain, including lifting heavy objects. Construction work is often strenuous, and workers spend most of the day on their feet—bending, kneeling, lifting, and maneuvering heavy objects.

Part time: Opportunities for part-time work are favorable. Most waiters and waitresses work part time, as do retail salesworkers.

Irregular hours: Working a schedule other than the standard 8-hour day, including night or weekend shifts, rotating schedules, or working for several days and then having several days off. Many nurses and security guards work nights or weekends. Other occupations that work on shifts include firefighters, pilots, and roustabouts.

	Education	Researching and compiling	Analyzing and evaluating	Troubleshooting	Artistic expression	Instructing	Treating and advising	Supervising	Persuading	Public contact	Mechanical ability	Operating a vehicle	Repetitious	Geographically concentrated	Mobile	Physical stamina	Part time	Irregular hours
Management and financial occupations																		
Accountants and auditors	C	●	●	●														
Administrative services managers	HS, PS, C		●	●				●										
Financial managers	C	●	●	●				●										
General managers and top executives	C		●	●				●	●									
Hotel managers and assistants	C		●	●				●		●								●
Personnel, training, and labor relations specialists and managers	C		●	●				●		●								

→

Column groups: **Data/Information** (Researching and compiling, Analyzing and evaluating, Troubleshooting, Artistic expression) · **People** (Instructing, Treating and advising, Supervising, Persuading, Public contact) · **Things** (Mechanical ability, Operating a vehicle, Repetitious) · **Working Conditions** (Geographically concentrated, Mobile, Physical stamina, Part time, Irregular hours)

Occupation	Education	Researching and compiling	Analyzing and evaluating	Troubleshooting	Artistic expression	Instructing	Treating and advising	Supervising	Persuading	Public contact	Mechanical ability	Operating a vehicle	Repetitious	Geographically concentrated	Mobile	Physical stamina	Part time	Irregular hours
Mathematical, scientific, and related occupations																		
Agricultural scientists	C	●	●															
Architects	C	●	●		●													
Biological scientists	C	●	●															
Computer programmers	C		●	●														
Computer systems analysts	C	●	●	●														
Engineers (aerospace, chemical, civil, electrical and electronic, industrial, mechanical, metallurgical, mining, nuclear, petroleum)	C	●	●	●														
Landscape architects	C	●	●		●										●			
Physical scientists (chemists, geologists and geophysicists, meteorologists, physicists, astronomers)	C	●	●															
Legal, social science, and human service occupations																		
Anthropologists and archaeologists	C	●	●												●	●		
Archivists, curators, and historians	C	●	●															
Human services workers	PS, C	●	●				●			●					●			●
Lawyers and judges	C	●	●	●			●		●	●								
Paralegals	PS	●	●							●								
Psychologists	C	●	●	●			●		●	●								
Religious workers (ministers, rabbis, priests)	PS, C					●	●	●	●	●					●			●
Social workers	C	●	●	●			●		●	●					●			
Urban and regional planners	C	●	●	●					●	●								
Education and related occupations																		
Adult education teachers and college faculty	C	●	●	●		●	●										●	●
Counselors	C		●	●		●	●		●	●								
Kindergarten, elementary, and secondary school teachers	C		●	●		●	●											
Librarians	C	●		●						●							●	●
Preschool workers	HS, PS, C			●		●	●			●							●	

→

	Education	Data/Information								People	Things					Working Conditions		
		Researching and compiling	Analyzing and evaluating	Troubleshooting	Artistic expression	Instructing	Treating and advising	Supervising	Persuading	Public contact	Mechanical ability	Operating a vehicle	Repetitious	Geographically concentrated	Mobile	Physical stamina	Part time	Irregular hours
Health care occupations (chiropractors, dentists, optometrists, physicians, podiatrists, veterinarians)																		
Clinical laboratory technologists and technicians	PS, C	•												•				
Dietitians and nutritionists	C		•	•		•	•			•							•	
Emergency medical technicians	PS		•	•			•			•					•	•		•
Health diagnosing practitioners	C	•	•	•		•	•			•								•
Licensed practical nurses	PS						•			•						•	•	•
Occupational therapists	C		•	•		•	•			•								
Physical therapists	C		•	•		•	•			•						•	•	
Physician assistants	C		•	•			•			•								•
Registered nurses	PS, C		•	•		•	•			•						•	•	•
Speech-language pathologists and audiologists	C		•	•			•			•								
Surgical technicians	PS						•			•								
Communication, visual arts, and performing arts occupations																		
Actors, dancers, musicians					•					•					•	•	•	•
Designers	HS, PS, C				•					•								
Directors, choreographers, and conductors		•	•	•	•	•		•	•	•					•			•
Marketing, advertising, and public relations managers	C		•	•	•			•	•	•				•				
Photographers and camera operators	PS				•					•	•			•				
Radio and television announcers and newscasters	HS, PS, C	•	•		•				•	•								•
Visual artists	HS, PS, C				•													
Writers and editors	PS, C	•	•		•				•	•								
Sales and related occupations																		
Insurance agents and brokers	PS, C	•	•				•		•	•								
Manufacturers' and wholesale sales representatives	C	•	•	•		•			•	•				•				
Real estate agents, brokers, and appraisers	HS, PS	•	•	•			•		•	•				•		•	•	

→

Occupation	Education	Data/Information			People						Things			Working Conditions				
		Researching and compiling	Analyzing and evaluating	Troubleshooting	Artistic expression	Instructing	Treating and advising	Supervising	Persuading	Public contact	Mechanical ability	Operating a vehicle	Repetitious	Geographically concentrated	Mobile	Physical stamina	Part time	Irregular hours
Sales and related occupations (cont'd)																		
Securities and financial services sales representatives	C	●	●					●	●	●								
Wholesale and retail buyers and merchandise managers	PS, C	●	●	●				●	●									
Administrative support occupations																		
Adjusters, investigators, and collectors	HS, PS, C	●	●							●								
Clerical supervisors and managers	HS, PS, C		●	●				●										
Service occupations																		
Firefighting occupations	HS			●			●			●		●			●	●		●
Police, detectives, and special agents	HS	●	●	●			●			●		●			●	●		●
Transportation occupations																		
Aircraft pilots	C			●								●			●			●
Air traffic controllers	HS, PS, C			●														●
Marine engineers and captains	C			●				●			●	●			●			●

Questions for Analysis

1. With your work in the career exploration section of this chapter as a foundation, identify at least two careers that you think you might be interested in pursuing.

2. Research the careers you have identified by using some of the resources identified in this article. Make notes to record the important information that you discover.

3. Using the chart in this article as a guide, identify the central characteristics of the careers that you have identified.

4. Compare what you have discovered about these potential careers with your interests and abilities. Are they a good match? Explain why or why not.

Thinking Critically

**Thinking for
Ourselves**

**Viewing
Situations
from Different
Perspectives**

THINKING CRITICALLY:
Carefully examining our thinking
(and the thinking of others),
in order to clarify and improve
our understanding.

**Carefully
Exploring
Situations with
Questions**

Fact   Interpretation
Analysis   Synthesis
Evaluation Application

**Supporting
Perspectives
with Evidence
and Reasons**

Thinking Actively

Reading Actively
Annotate text
Identify questions
Elaborate ideas

Listening Actively
Take clear and comprehensive notes

Participating Actively
Make thoughtful contributions

A college education is the road that can lead you to your life's work, a career that will enable you to use your unique talents to bring you professional fulfillment. However, there are many other benefits to a college education, among them the opportunity to become what we have called an "educated thinker." Becoming an educated thinker is essential for achieving the greatest possible success in your chosen career, and it enriches your life in many other ways as well. In the space below, describe some of the qualities that you believe are part of being an "educated thinker."

An educated thinker is someone who

1. _____

2. _____

3. _____

Traditionally, when people refer to an "educated thinker," they mean someone who has developed a knowledgeable understanding of our complex world; a thoughtful perspective on important ideas and timely issues; the capacity for penetrating insight and intelligent judgment; and sophisticated thinking and language abilities. These goals of advanced education have remained remarkably similar for several thousand years. In ancient Greece, most advanced students studied Philosophy in order to achieve "wisdom." (The term *philosophy* in Greek means "lover of wisdom.") In today's world, many college students are hoping through their studies to become the modern-day equivalent: informed, critical thinkers.

The word *critical* comes from the Greek word for *critic (kritikos),* which means to question, to make sense of, to be able to analyze. It is by questioning, making sense of things and people, and analyzing that we examine our thinking and the thinking of others. These activities aid us in reaching the best possible conclusions and decisions. The word *critical* is also related to the word *criticize,* which means to question and evaluate. Unfortunately, the ability to criticize is often used destructively, to tear down someone else's thinking. However, criticism can also be *constructive*—analyzing for the purpose of developing a better understanding of what is going on. We engage in constructive criticism as we develop our ability to think critically.

Thinking is the way you make sense of the world; thinking critically is thinking *about* your thinking so that you can clarify and improve it. If you can understand the way your mind works when you work toward your goals, make informed decisions, and solve complex problems, then you can learn to think more effectively in these situations. In this chapter you will explore ways to examine your thinking so that you can develop it to the fullest extent possible. That is, you will discover how to *think critically*.

Thinking critically

The cognitive process we use to carefully examine our thinking and the thinking of others in order to clarify and improve our understanding.

Thinking Independently:
Becoming a critical thinker transforms you in positive ways by enabling you to become an expert learner, think independently, and make informed choices.

Becoming a critical thinker transforms you in positive ways by enabling you to become an expert learner, view the world clearly, and make productive choices as you shape your life. Thinking critically is not simply one way of thinking; it is a total approach to understanding how you make sense of a world that includes many different features. This chapter explores the various activities that make up thinking critically, including the following:

- Thinking actively
- Carefully exploring situations with questions
- Thinking for ourselves
- Viewing situations from different perspectives
- Supporting diverse perspectives with reasons and evidence

Thinking Actively

When you think critically, you are *actively* using your intelligence, knowledge, and abilities to deal effectively with life's situations. When you think actively, you are

- *Getting involved* in potentially useful projects and activities instead of remaining disengaged
- *Taking initiative* by making decisions on your own instead of waiting passively to be told what to think or do
- *Following through* on your commitments instead of giving up when you encounter difficulties
- *Taking responsibility* for the consequences of your decisions rather than unjustifiably blaming others or events "beyond your control"

When you think actively, you are not just waiting for something to happen. You are engaged in the process of achieving goals, making decisions, and solving problems. When you react passively, you let events control you or permit others to do your thinking for you. To make an intelligent decision about your future career, for example, you have to work actively to secure more information, try out various possibilities, speak with people who are experienced in your area of interest, and then critically reflect on all these factors. Thinking critically requires that you think actively—not react passively—to deal with life's situations.

Influences on Your Thinking

As our minds grow and develop, we are exposed to influences that encourage us to think actively. However, we also have many experiences that encourage us to think passively. For example, some analysts believe that when people, especially children, spend much of their time watching television, they are being influenced to think passively, thus inhibiting their intellectual growth. Listed here are some of the influences people generally experience along with space for you to add your own influences. As you read through the list, place an *A* next to those items that you believe influence you to think *actively* and a *P* next to those you consider to be generally *passive* influences.

Activities	*People*
Reading books	Family members
Writing	Friends
Taking drugs	Employers
Dancing	Advertisers
Drawing/painting	School/college teachers
Playing video games	Police officers
Playing sports	Religious leaders
Listening to music	Politicians
_____	_____
_____	_____
_____	_____

 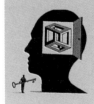

Thinking Activity 2.1

All of us are subject to powerful influences on our thinking that we are often unaware of. For example, advertisers spend billions of dollars to manipulate our thinking in ways that are complex and subtle.

Select one of your favorite commercials and perform an in-depth analysis of it. If you have a VCR, replay the commercial a number of times, with and without the sound. Explain how each of the commercial's elements—images, language, music—work to influence your thinking. Pay particular attention to the symbolic associations of various images and words, and identify the powerful emotions that these associations elicit.

Of course, in many cases people and activities can act as both active and passive influences, depending on the specifics of situations and our individual responses. For example, consider employers. If we are performing a routine, repetitive job, like the summer I spent in a peanut-butter-cracker factory hand-scooping 2,000 pounds of peanut butter a day, the very nature of the work tends to encourage passive, uncreative thinking (although it might also lead to creative daydreaming!). We are also influenced to think passively if our employer gives us detailed instructions for performing every task, instructions that permit no exception or deviation. On the other hand, when our employer gives us general areas of responsibility within which we are expected to make thoughtful and creative decisions, then we are being stimulated to think actively and independently.

These contrasting styles of supervision are mirrored in different approaches to raising children. Some parents encourage children to be active thinkers by teaching them to express themselves clearly, make independent decisions, look at different points of view, and choose what they think is right for themselves. Other parents influence their children to be passive thinkers by not letting them do things on their own. These parents give the children detailed instructions they are expected to follow without question, and they make the important decisions for their children. They are reluctant to give their children significant responsibilities, creating (unintentionally) dependent thinkers who are not well adapted to making independent decisions and assuming responsibility for their lives.

Becoming an Active Learner

Critical thinkers actively use their intelligence, knowledge, and abilities to deal with life's situations. Similarly, active thinking is one of the keys to effective learning. Each of us has our own knowledge framework that we use to make sense of the world, a framework that incorporates all that we have learned in our lives. When we learn something new, we have to find ways to integrate this new information or skill into our existing knowledge framework. For example, if one of our professors is presenting material on Sigmund Freud's concept of the Unconscious or the role of Werner Heisenberg's Uncertainty Principle in the theory of quantum mechanics, you need to find ways to relate these new ideas to things you already know in order to make this new information "your own." How do you do this? By actively using your mind to integrate new information into your existing knowledge framework, thereby expanding the framework to include this new information.

For example, when your professor provides a detailed analysis of Freud's concept of the Unconscious, you use your mind to call up what you know about Freud's theory of personality and what you know of the concept of the Unconscious. You then try to connect up this new information to what you already know, integrating it into your expanding knowledge framework. In a way, learning is analogous to the activity of eating: you ingest food (information) in one form, actively transform it through digestion (mental processing), and then integrate the result into the ongoing functioning of your body (minds). Let's examine the strategies you can use to promote active learning.

Reading Actively. Your success at college largely depends upon your becoming an effective reader, yet most students read very inefficiently because they are not actively involved with the material. Instead, they read passively, using only a small portion of their minds to engage the material as they mechanically turn the pages. Effective reading demands mental action—asking and trying to answer questions, elaborating points, reorganizing material, relating ideas to knowledge you already have. There are a variety of strategies you can use to promote this mental action:

- Underline and number important points, and circle key words.
- Write notes in the margins that exemplify or extend the ideas, and use question marks to indicate what you don't understand.
- Use notebook paper to write more extended responses, and use more elaborate diagrams to illustrate important ideas and their relationships.

By taking an active posture in your reading, you are relating and reshaping the material to conform to your own mind, "digesting" it so that it can be integrated into your own knowledge framework. If you don't make an effort to transform the material in this way, what you are reading tends to remain outside of your thinking, not being incorporated into your mind in an essential and meaningful way. When this happens, your understanding of what you are reading is superficial: you don't understand it deeply, connect it to what you already know, or retain it very long. You will be examining the entire process of "critical reading" in more detail in Chapter 6, but for the present you should begin practicing the strategies of active reading immediately. For example, in using this book, be sure to complete all the write-on lines because they are designed to stimulate your thinking and provide an opportunity for you to express your ideas. *Make this book your own* by customizing it with your own personal notes and responses, and treat your other college books the same way.

Thinking Passage

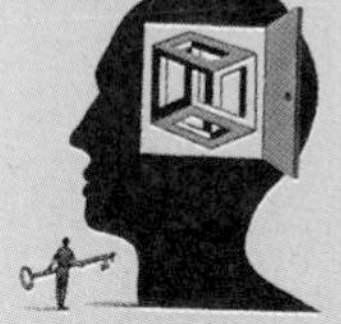

Read and annotate the following passage, using active reading strategies to help you transform and integrate the ideas. After annotating the article, detach it from the book, and compare your notes to those completed by other members of the class. This will give you an opportunity to learn active reading strategies from each other.

From *Creative Thinking and Critical Thinking*

Gardner Lindzey, Calvin S. Hall, and Richard F. Thompson

CREATIVE THINKING
Partnership and Conflict
CRITICAL THINKING

Creative thinking is thinking that results in the discovery of a new or improved solution to a problem. *Critical thinking* is the examination and testing of suggested solutions to see whether they will work. Creative thinking leads to the birth of new ideas, while critical thinking tests ideas for flaws and defects. Both are necessary for effective problem-solving, yet they are sometimes incompatible—creative thinking can interfere with critical thinking, and vice versa. To think creatively we must let our thoughts run free. The more spontaneous the process, the more ideas will be born and the greater the probability that an effective solution will be found. A steady stream of ideas furnishes the raw material. Then critical judgment selects and refines the best ideas, picking the most effective solution out of the available possibilities. Although we

→

must engage in the two types of thinking separately, we need both for efficient problem-solving. . . .

Inhibitions to Creative Thinking

Conformity—the desire to be like everyone else—is the foremost barrier to creative thinking. People are afraid to express new ideas because they think they will make fools of themselves and be ridiculed. This feeling may date back to childhood, when their spontaneous and imaginative ideas may have been laughed at by parents or older people. During adolescence, conformity is reinforced because young people are afraid to be different from their peers. Then, too, history teaches us that innovators often are laughed at and even persecuted.

Censorship—especially self-imposed censorship—is a second significant barrier to creativity. External censorship of ideas, the thought control of modern dictatorships, is dramatic and newsworthy, but internal censorship is more effective and dependable. External censorship merely prevents public distribution of proscribed thoughts; the thoughts may still be expressed privately. But people who are frightened by their thoughts tend to react passively rather than think of creative solutions to their problems. Sometimes they even repress those thoughts, so they are not aware they exist. Freud called this internalized censor the *superego.* . . .

A third barrier to creative thinking is the *rigid education* still commonly imposed upon children. Regimentation, memorization, and drill may help instill the accepted knowledge of the day, but these classroom methods cannot teach students how to solve new problems or how to improve upon conventional solutions to old problems.

A fourth barrier to creative thinking is the great *desire to find an answer quickly.* Such a strong motivation often narrows one's consciousness and encourages the acceptance of early, inadequate solutions. People tend to do their best creative thinking when they are released from the demands and responsibilities of everyday living. Inventors, scientists, artists, writers, and executives often do their most creative thinking when they are not distracted by routine work. The value of a vacation is not that it enables people to work better on their return but rather that it permits new ideas to be born during the vacation.

Daydreamers often are criticized for wasting time. Yet without daydreams, society's progress would be considerably slower, since daydreaming often leads to the discovery of original ideas. This is not to suggest that all daydreaming or leisurely contemplation results in valid and workable ideas—far from it. But somewhere, among the thousands of ideas conceived, one useful idea will appear. Finding this one idea without having to produce a thousand poor ones would achieve a vast saving in creative thinking. But such a saving seems unlikely, especially since creative thinking is generally enjoyable whether its results are useful or not.

Listening Actively. As a college student, you will spend more time than you care to imagine listening to professors speak to you during lectures. Some of these lectures will be articulate and entertaining, filled with engaging examples, lively anecdotes, and thought-provoking questions. Others will be less so. Regardless, you must find ways to learn the ideas and information being presented. In the same way that you need to develop active reading strategies to comprehend and integrate ideas into your knowledge framework, you have to develop active listening strategies to achieve the same learning goals. Too often during lectures you can find yourself slipping into a passive mode, similar to the zonked-out state we sometimes achieve watching television, in which we just let the words wash over us. Eventually your mind starts to wander, you drift away, and by the end of the class, you have very little new understanding to show for the time you just spent.

To counteract this tendency, you need to reach out and actively engage the material being presented: relate it to what you already know, reshape it into a form that is intelligible to you, and integrate it into your knowledge framework.

How do you accomplish these goals? Note taking is the primary tool we have for training our minds and attention. In Chapter 6, we will explore several effective note-taking models. For the present time, however, the most immediate objective is to actually *take* notes, as clear and detailed as possible. Too often we believe that we will recall the material being presented and discussed but actually end up failing to do so. As you practice your note taking and learn the note-taking models, you will gradually develop expertise with this essential learning tool. After the class, when you have a chance, go over your notes and add ideas and information. Also, it is very helpful to have a "partner" in the class with whom you compare notes, discussing the class and enhancing your notes. Some students like to tape-record classes (with the permission of the instructor), and for students with sight and hearing challenges, this strategy is essential.

Participating Actively.　　The British philosopher Bertrand Russell once said, "Most people would rather die than think—and most do!" The best way for you to develop and sharpen your capacity to think is for you to be actively involved in your classes. This means not only *listening actively* but also *participating* in the class discussions and responding to the instructor's questions. In addition to demonstrating your eagerness to learn and contribute to the class, participating gives you the opportunity to express your thinking and have others respond to your ideas. These are invaluable experiences for developing your skills and confidence as an educated thinker.

For some people, participating in group discussions comes easily; for others, it is a fate worse than a painful, torturous death. If the prospect of speaking in groups paralyzes you with anxiety, you are not alone. Many people face a similar challenge. However, this is a difficulty that can be overcome, and it is worth doing so. First, it is important to separate irrational fantasy from reality. The fantasy of many is that they will say something foolish and that everyone in the class will ridicule them. The truth is that quiet students almost never make an uninformed comment. And on those rare occasions when a student does make an inappropriate or mistaken comment, other classmates rarely laugh. They empathize with that student's predicament and know they may find themselves in the same place one day! Second, set modest goals for yourself. Answer questions you are sure you know the answer to. As your confidence increases, take more chances. Every student has important ideas and experiences to contribute to the class, and you should not deprive the other students of what you have to offer.

Of course, some teachers (unfortunately) do not encourage student participation, or the classes are too large to give all students enough chances to participate. However, when opportunities to participate do present themselves, seize them! You will enrich your learning.

Thinking Activity 2.2

Keep a record of your class participation during the next several weeks, using the following format:

Date	Course	Kind of participation	Response	The way I felt
10/24	Biology	I answered a question about metabolism.	The teacher said I was 95% right.	I was nervous, but afterward I felt proud and more confident.

Carefully Exploring Situations with Questions

As we have just seen, thinking critically involves actively using your thinking abilities to attack problems, meet challenges, and analyze issues. An important dimension of thinking actively is carefully exploring the situations you are involved in with relevant questions. In fact, the ability to ask appropriate and penetrating questions is one of the most powerful thinking tools you possess, although many people do not make full use of it. Active learners explore the learning situations they are involved in with questions that enable them to understand the material or task at hand and then integrate this new understanding into their knowledge framework. In contrast, passive learners rarely ask questions. Instead, they try to absorb information like sponges, memorizing what is expected and then regurgitating what they memorized on tests and quizzes.

Questions come in many different forms and are used for many different purposes. For instance, questions can be classified in terms of the ways people organize and interpret information, and we can identify six such categories of questions:

1. Fact
2. Interpretation
3. Analysis
4. Synthesis

5. Evaluation
6. Application

Active learners are able to ask appropriate questions from all of these categories in a very natural and flexible way. These various types of questions are closely interrelated, and an effective thinker is able to use them together productively. Listed below is a summary of the six categories of questions along with sample forms of questions from each category.

1. ***Questions of fact:*** Questions of fact seek to determine the basic information of a situation: who, what, when, where, how. These questions seek information that is relatively straightforward and objective.

    Who, what, when, where, how _____?

    Describe _____.

2. ***Questions of interpretation:*** Questions of interpretation seek to select and organize facts and ideas, discovering the relationships between them. Examples of such relationships include the following:

    Chronological relationships: relating things in time sequence

    Process relationships: relating aspects of growth, development, or change

    Comparison/contrast relationships: relating things in terms of their similar/different features

    Causal relationships: relating events in terms of the way some events are responsible for bringing about other events

    Retell _____ in your own words.

    What is the *main* idea of _____ ?

    What is the *time sequence* relating the following events: _____?

    What are the steps in the *process of growth* or *development* in _____?

    How would you *compare and contrast* the features of _____ and _____?

    What was the *cause* of _____? What was the *effect* of _____ ?

3. ***Questions of analysis:*** Questions of analysis seek to separate an entire process or situation into its component parts and understand the relation of these parts to the whole. These questions attempt to classify various elements, outline component structures, articulate various possibilities, and clarify the reasoning being presented.

    What are the *parts* or *features* of _____?

    Classify _____ according to _____.

    Outline/diagram/web _____.

    What *evidence* can you present to support _____?

    What are the *possible alternatives* for _____?

    Explain the *reasons* that you think _____.

4. **Questions of synthesis:** Questions of synthesis have as their goal combining ideas to form a new whole or come to a conclusion, making inferences about future events, creating solutions, and designing plans of action.

What would you *predict/infer* from _____?

What ideas can you *add* to _____?

How would you *create/design* a new _____?

What might happen if you *combined* _____ with _____?

What *solutions/decisions* would you suggest for _____?

5. **Questions of evaluation:** The aim of evaluation questions is to help us make informed judgments and decisions by determining the relative value, truth, or reliability of things. The process of evaluation involves identifying the criteria or standards we are using and then determining to what extent the things in common meet those standards.

How would you *evaluate* _____, and what *standards* would you use?

Do you agree with _____? Why or why not?

How would you *decide* about _____?

What *criteria* would you use to *assess* _____?

6. **Questions of application:** The aim of application questions is to help us take the knowledge or concepts we have gained in one situation and apply them to other situations.

How is _____ an *example* of _____?

How would you *apply* this rule/principle to _____?

Mastering these types of questions and using them appropriately will serve you as powerful tools in the learning process. Let's explore further by completing Thinking Activity 2.3.

Thinking Activity 2.3

Review the reading on page 51 and develop at least two questions regarding the reading from each of the six question categories. For example,

1. *Questions of fact:* How would you *describe* the creative process?

2. *Questions of interpretation:* How would you *compare* and *contrast* the features of creative thinking and critical thinking?

3. *Questions of analysis:* Explain the *reasons* that you think that being creative is important.

4. *Questions of synthesis:* How would you *design* a more creative approach to living your life?

→

5. *Questions of evaluation:* How would you *evaluate* how creative a piece of music is, and what *standards* would you use?

6. *Questions of application:* How is inventing a recipe for a new dish an *example* of being creative?

Becoming an expert questioner is an ongoing project, and you can practice it throughout the day. Even when you are talking to people about everyday topics, get in the habit of asking questions from all of the different categories. Similarly, when you are attending class, taking notes, or reading assignments, make a practice of asking—and trying to answer—appropriate questions. You will find that by actively exploring the world in this way you are discovering a great deal and retaining what you have discovered in a meaningful and lasting fashion.

As children we were natural questioners, but this questioning attitude was often discouraged when we entered the school system. Often we were given the message, in subtle and not so subtle ways, that "Schools have the questions, and your job is to learn the answers." The educator Neil Postman has said this: "Children enter schools as question marks and they leave as periods." In order for us to become critical thinkers and effective learners, we have to become question marks again.

Review the following decision-making situation (based on an incident that happened in Springfield, Missouri, in 1989), and then critically examine it by posing questions from each of the six categories we have considered in this section:

1. Fact
2. Interpretation
3. Analysis
4. Synthesis
5. Evaluation
6. Application

Imagine that you are a member of a student group at your college that has decided to stage the controversial play *The Normal Heart* by Larry Karma. The play is based on the lives of real people and dramatizes their experiences in the early stages of the AIDS epidemic. It focuses on their efforts to publicize the devastating nature of this disease and to secure funding from a reluctant federal government to find a cure. The play is

→

considered controversial because of its exclusive focus on the AIDS subject, its explicit homosexual themes, and the large amount of profanity contained in the script. After lengthy discussion, however, your student group has decided that the educational and moral benefits of the play render it a valuable contribution to the life of the college.

While the play is in rehearsal, a local politician seizes it as an issue and mounts a political and public relations campaign against it. She distributes selected excerpts of the play to the newspapers, religious groups, and civic organizations. She also introduces a bill in the state legislature to withdraw state funding for the college if the play is performed. The play creates a firestorm of controversy, replete with local and national news reports, editorials, and impassioned speeches for and against it. Everyone associated with the play is subjected to verbal harassment, threats, crank phone calls, and hate mail. The firestorm explodes when the house of one of the key spokespersons for the play is burned to the ground. The director and actors go into hiding for their safety, rehearsing in secret and moving from hotel to hotel.

Your student group has just convened to decide what course of action to take. Analyze the situation by using the six types of questions listed above, and then conclude with your decision and the reasons that support your decision.

Thinking for Ourselves

Answer the following questions, based on what you believe to be true:

Yes   *No*   *Not Sure*

1. Is the earth flat?
2. Is there a God?
3. Is abortion wrong?
4. Is democracy the best form of government?
5. Should men be the breadwinners and women the homemakers?

Your responses to these questions reveal aspects of the way your mind works. How did you arrive at these conclusions? Your views on these and many other issues probably had their beginnings with your families, especially your parents. When we are young, we are very dependent on our parents, and we are influenced by the way they see the world. As we grow up, we learn how to think, feel, and behave in various situations. In addition to our parents, our

Critical thinkers carefully consider all possible perspectives, develop thoughtful conclusions based on reasons and evidence, and discuss issues in a productive way.

"teachers" include brothers and sisters, friends, religious leaders, schoolteachers, books, television, and so on. Most of what we learn we absorb without even being aware of it. Many of your ideas about the issues raised in the questions above were most likely shaped by the experiences you had growing up.

As a result of our ongoing experiences, however, our minds—and our thinking—continue to mature. Instead of simply accepting the opinion of others, we gradually develop the ability to examine this opinion and to decide whether it makes sense to us and whether we should accept it. As we think through such ideas, we use this standard to make our decision: Are there good reasons or evidence that support this thinking? If there are good reasons, we can actively decide to adopt these ideas. If they do not make sense, we can modify or reject them.

Of course, we do not *always* examine our own thinking or the thinking of others so carefully. In fact, we very often continue to believe the same ideas with which we were brought up without ever examining and deciding for ourselves what to think. Or we often blindly reject the beliefs with which we have been brought up without ever really examining them.

How do you know when you have examined and adopted ideas instead of simply borrowing them from others? One indication of having thought through your ideas is being able to explain *why* you believe them, explaining the reasons that led you to these conclusions.

For each of the views you expressed at the beginning of this section, explain how you arrived at it and give the reasons and evidence that you believe support it.

1. *Example:* Is the earth flat?

   Explanation: I was taught by my parents and in school that the earth was round.

   Reasons/evidence:

   a. *Authorities:* My parents and teachers taught me this.

   b. *References:* I read about this in science textbooks.

   c. *Factual evidence:* I have seen a sequence of photographs taken from outer space that show the earth as a globe.

   d. *Personal experience:* When I flew across the country, I could see the horizon line changing.

2. Is there a God?

   Explanation: _____

   _____

   Reasons/Evidence:

   a. *Authorities:* _____

   b. *References:* _____

   c. *Factual evidence:* _____

   d. *Personal experience:* _____

3. Is abortion wrong?

4. Is democracy the best form of government?

5. Should men be the breadwinners and women the homemakers?

Of course, not all reasons and evidence are equally strong or accurate. For example, before the fifteenth century the common belief that the earth was flat was supported by the following reasons and evidence:

■ *Authorities:* Educational and religious authorities taught people that the earth was flat.

■ *References:* The written opinions of scientific experts supported belief in a flat earth.

■ *Factual evidence:* No person had ever circumnavigated the earth.

■ *Personal experience:* From a normal vantage point, the earth *looks* flat.

Many considerations go into evaluating the strengths and accuracy of reasons and evidence, and we will be exploring these areas in this chapter and future ones. Let's examine some basic questions that critical thinkers automatically consider when evaluating reasons and evidence.

Thinking Activity 2.5

Evaluate the strengths and accuracy of the reasons and evidence you identified to support your beliefs on the five issues listed above by addressing questions such as the following:

■ *Authorities:* Are the authorities knowledgeable in this area? Are they reliable? Have they ever given inaccurate information? Do other authorities disagree with them?

■ *References:* What are the credentials of the authors? Are there other authors that disagree with their opinions? On what reasons and evidence do the authors base their opinions?

■ *Factual evidence:* What is the source and foundation of the evidence? Can the evidence be interpreted differently? Does the evidence support the conclusion?

■ *Personal experience:* What were the circumstances under which the experiences took place? Were distortions or mistakes in perception possible? Have other people had either similar or conflicting experiences? Are there other explanations for the experience?

The opposite of thinking for yourself is when you simply accept the thinking of others without examining or questioning it. Imagine that a friend tells you that a course you are planning to take is very difficult and suggests that you register for a less demanding course. Although the thinking of your friend may have merit, it still makes sense for you to investigate the evidence for that particular view yourself. For example, consider the following situation. Explain how you would respond to the ideas that are being suggested to you, and then give the reasons that support your views.

> One of your professors always wears blue jeans and sneakers to class. He says that the clothes you wear have nothing to do with how intelligent or how capable you are or the quality of your work. Other people should judge you on *who* you are, not on the clothes you wear. However, your supervisor at work has just informed you that you have been dressing too casually. How do you respond?

Response: _____

_____

Reasons that support your response: _____

_____

Thinking for yourself doesn't always mean doing exactly what you want to; it may mean becoming aware of the social guidelines and expectations of a given situation and then making an informed decision about what is in your best interests. In this situation, even though you may have a legal right to choose whatever clothes you want at the workplace, if your choice doesn't conform to the employer's guidelines or "norms," then you may suffer unpleasant consequences as a result. In other words, thinking for yourself often involves balancing your views against those of others—integrating yourself into social structures without sacrificing your independence or personal autonomy.

Learning to become an independent, critical thinker is a complex, ongoing process that involves all the abilities we have been examining in this chapter to this point:

■ Thinking actively

■ Carefully exploring situations with questions

■ Thinking for yourself

As you confront the many decisions you have to make in your life, try to gather all the relevant information, review your priorities, and then carefully weigh all the factors before arriving at a final decision. One helpful strategy for exploring thinking situations is the one we have been practicing: *identify* the important questions that need to be answered, and then try to *answer* these questions.

Viewing Situations from Different Perspectives

While it is important to think for yourself, others also may have good ideas from which you can learn and benefit. A critical thinker is a person who is willing to listen to and examine carefully other views and new ideas. In addition to your viewpoint, other viewpoints may be equally important and will need to be considered if you are to develop a more complete understanding of a situation.

As children, we understand the world from only our own point of view. As we grow, we come into contact with people with different viewpoints and begin to realize that our viewpoint is often inadequate, that we are frequently mistaken, and that our perspective is only one of many. If we are going to learn and develop, we must try to understand and appreciate the viewpoints of others. For example, consider the following situation:

Imagine that you have been employed at a new job for six months. Although you enjoy the challenge of your responsibilities and you are doing well, you simply cannot complete all your work during office hours. To keep up, you have to work late, take work home, and even work occasionally on weekends. When you explain the situation to your employer, she says that although she is sorry that the job interferes with your personal life, it has to be done. She suggests that you view this time spent as an investment in your future and that you try to work more efficiently. She reminds you that there are many people who would be happy to have your position.

1. Describe this situation from your employer's standpoint, identifying reasons that might support her views: _____

_____

_____

Being Open-Minded:
Critical thinkers are open to new ideas and different viewpoints, with the flexibility to view situations from many perspectives instead of being dogmatic and singleminded.

2. Describe some different approaches that you and your employer might take to help resolve this situation: _____

_____

_____

   For most of the important issues and problems in our lives, one viewpoint is simply not adequate to provide a full and satisfactory understanding. To increase and deepen your knowledge, you must seek *other perspectives* on the situations you are trying to understand. You can sometimes accomplish this task by using your imagination to visualize other viewpoints. Usually, however, you need to seek actively (and *listen* to) the viewpoints of others. It is often very difficult for people to see things from points of view other than their own, and if we are not careful we can make the very serious mistake of thinking that the way we see things is the way things really are. As well as identifying with perspectives other than your own, you also have to work to understand the *rea-*

sons that support these alternate viewpoints. This approach deepens our understanding of the issues and also stimulates us to evaluate our beliefs.

Describe a belief of yours that you feel very strongly about. Then explain the reasons or experiences that led you to this belief.

Next, describe a point of view that is *different* from your belief. Identify some of the reasons that someone might hold this belief. See the following student example:

A Belief That I Feel Strongly About

I used to think that we should always try everything in our power to keep a person alive. But now I strongly believe that a person has a right to die in peace and with dignity. The reason why I believe this now is because of my father's illness and death.

It all started on Christmas Day, December 25, 1987, when my father was admitted to the hospital. The doctors diagnosed his condition as a heart attack. Following this episode, he was readmitted and discharged from several different hospitals. On June 18, 1988, he was hospitalized for what was initially thought to be pneumonia but which turned out to be lung cancer. He began chemotherapy treatments. When complications occurred, he had to be placed on a respirator. At first he couldn't speak or eat. But then they operated on him and placed the tube from the machine in his throat instead of his mouth. He was then able to eat and move his mouth. He underwent radiation therapy when they discovered he had three tumors in his head and that the cancer had spread all over his body. We had to sign a paper which asked us to indicate, if he should stop breathing, whether we would want the hospital to try to revive him or just let him go. We decided to let him go because the doctors couldn't guarantee that he wouldn't become brain-dead. At first they said that there was a forty percent chance that he would get off the machine. But instead of that happening, the percentage went down.

It was hard seeing him like that since I was so close to him. But it was even harder when he didn't want to see me. He said that by seeing me suffer, his suffering was greater. So I had to cut down on seeing him. Everybody that visited him said that he had changed dramatically. They couldn't even recognize him.

The last two days of his life were the worst. I prayed that God would relieve him of his misery. I had come very close to taking him off the machine in order for him not to suffer, but I didn't. Finally, he passed away on November 22, 1988, with not the least bit of peace or dignity. The loss was great then and still is, but at least he's not suffering. That's why I believe that when people have terminal

→

diseases with no hope of recovery, they shouldn't place them on machines to prolong their lives of suffering, but instead they should be permitted to die with as much peace and dignity possible.

Somebody else might believe very strongly that we should try everything in our power to keep people alive. It doesn't matter what kind of illness or disease the people have; what's important is that they are kept alive, especially if they are loved ones. Some people want to keep their loved ones alive with them as long as they can, even if it's by a machine. They also believe it is up to God and medical science to determine whether people should live or die. Sometimes doctors give them hope that their loved ones will recover, and many people wish for a miracle to happen. With these hopes and wishes in mind, they wait and try everything in order to prolong a life, even if the doctors tell them that there is nothing that can be done.

Being open to new ideas and different viewpoints means being *flexible* enough to change or modify your ideas in the light of new information or better insight. Each of us has a tendency to cling to the beliefs we have been brought up with and the conclusions we have arrived at. If we are going to continue to grow and develop as thinkers, however, we have to be willing to change or modify our beliefs when evidence suggests that we should. For example, imagine that you have been brought up with certain views concerning an ethnic group—black, white, Hispanic, Asian, Native American, or any other. As you mature, you may find that your experience conflicts with the views you have been raised with. As critical thinkers, we have to be *open* to receiving this new evidence and *flexible* enough to change and modify our ideas on the basis of it.

In contrast to open and flexible thinking, *un*critical thinking tends to be one-sided and narrow. People who think this way are convinced that they alone see things as they really are and that everyone who disagrees with them is wrong. The words we use to describe this type of person include *dogmatic, subjective,* and *egocentric.* It is very difficult for such people to step outside their own viewpoint in order to see things from other people's perspectives. Part of being an educated person is being able to think in an open-minded and flexible way.

Supporting Diverse Perspectives with Reasons and Evidence

When you are thinking critically, what you think makes sense and you can give good reasons to back up your ideas. As we have seen and will continue to see throughout this book, it is not enough simply to take a position on an issue or make a claim; we have to *back up our views* with other information that

For most of the important issues and problems in our lives, one viewpoint is simply not adequate to provide a full and satisfactory understanding. What is your interpretation of this photograph?

supports our position. In other words, there is an important distinction and relationship between *what* you believe and *why* you believe it.

If someone questions *why* you see an issue the way you do, you probably respond by giving reasons or arguments that support your belief. For example, take the question of what sort of college to attend: two-year or four-year, residential or commuter. What are some of the reasons you might offer to support your decision to attend the kind of college in which you enrolled?

1. _____
2. _____
3. _____

Although all the reasons you just gave for attending your sort of college support your decision, some are obviously more important to you than others. In any case, although going to your college may be the right thing for you to do, this decision won't be the right one for everybody. In order for you to fully appreciate this fact, to see both sides of the issue, you have to put yourself in the position of others and try to see things from their points of view. What are some of the reasons or arguments someone might give for attending a different kind of college?

1. _____
2. _____
3. _____

The Educated Thinker:

"Educated thinkers" are better equipped to deal with the difficult challenges that life poses; to solve problems, to establish and achieve goals and to make sense of complex issues.

The responses you just gave demonstrate that if you are interested in seeing all sides of an issue, you have to be able to give supporting reasons and evidence not just for *your* views but for the views of *others* as well. Seeing all sides of an issue thus combines these two critical-thinking abilities:

- Viewing issues from different perspectives
- Supporting diverse viewpoints with reasons and evidence

Combining these two abilities enables you not only to understand other views about an issue, but also to understand *why* these views are held. Consider the issue of whether seat-belt use should be mandatory. As you try to make sense of this issue, you should attempt to identify reasons that support your view and reasons that support other views. The following are reasons that support each view of this issue.

Issue

Seat-belt use should be mandatory.   Seat-belt use should not be mandatory.

Supporting Reasons

1. Studies show that seat belts save lives and reduce injury in accidents.

Supporting Reasons

1. Many people feel that seat belts may trap them in a burning vehicle.

Now see if you can identify additional supporting reasons for each of these views on making use of seat belts mandatory.

Supporting Reasons

2. _____

   _____

3. _____

   _____

4. _____

   _____

Supporting Reasons

2. _____

   _____

3. _____

   _____

4. _____

   _____

Thinking Activity 2.6

For each of the following issues, identify reasons that support each side of the issue.

Issue

1. Multiple-choice and true/false exams should be given in college-level courses.

Multiple-choice and true/false exams should not be given in college-level courses.

Issue

2. It is better to live in a society that minimizes the role of government in the lives of its citizens.

It is better to live in a society in which the government plays a major role in the lives of its citizens.

Issue

3. The best way to deal with crime is to give long prison sentences.

Long prison sentences will not reduce crime.

Issue

4. When a couple divorces, the children should choose the parent with whom they wish to live.

When a couple divorces, the court should decide all custody issues regarding the children.

Thinking Activity 2.7

Working to see different perspectives is crucial in getting a thorough understanding of the ideas being expressed in material that you read. Read each of the following passages and then do these tasks:

1. Identify the main idea of the passage.
2. List the reasons that support the main idea.
3. Develop another view of the main issue.
4. List the reasons that support the other view.

Most wicked deeds are done because the doer proposes some good to himself. The liar lies to gain some end; the swindler and thief want things that, if honestly got, might be good in themselves. Even the murderer may be removing an impediment to normal desires or gaining possession of something that his victim keeps from him. None of these people usually does evil for evil's sake. They are selfish or unscrupulous, but their deeds are not gratuitously evil. The killer for sport has no such comprehensible motive. He prefers death to life, darkness to light. He gets nothing except the satisfaction of saying "Something that wanted to live is dead. There is that much less vitality, consciousness, and, perhaps, joy in the universe. I am the Spirit that Denies." When a human wantonly destroys one of humankind's own works, we call him Vandal. When he wantonly destroys one of the works of God, we call him Sportsman.

More than at any other time in history, America is plagued by the influence of cults, exclusive groups that present themselves as religions devoted to the worship of a single individual. Initially, most Americans were not terribly concerned with the growth of cults, but then in 1979 more than nine hundred cult members were senselessly slaughtered in the steamy jungles of a small South American country called Guyana. The reason for the slaughter was little more than the wild, paranoid fear of the leader, the Reverend Jim Jones, who called himself father and savior. Since that time, evidence has increased that another cult leader, the Reverend Sun Myung Moon, has amassed a large personal fortune from the purses of his followers, male and female "Moonies," who talk of bliss while peddling pins and emblems preaching the gospel of Moon. Cults, with their hypnotic rituals and their promises of ecstasy, are a threat to American youth, and it is time to implement laws that would allow for a thorough restriction of their movements.

If we want auto safety but continue to believe in auto profits, sales, styling, and annual obsolescence, there will be no serious accomplishments. The moment we put safety ahead of these other values,

→

something will happen. If we want better municipal hospitals but are unwilling to disturb the level of spending for defense, for highways, and for household appliances, hospital service will not improve. If we want peace but still believe that countries with differing ideologies are threats to one another, we will not get peace. What is confusing is that up to now, while we have wanted such things as conservation, auto safety, hospital care, and peace, we have tried wanting them without changing consciousness, that is, while continuing to accept those underlying values that stand in the way of what we want. The machine can be controlled at the "consumer" level only by people who change their whole value system, their whole world view, their whole way of life. One cannot favor saving our wildlife and wear a fur coat.

Becoming a Critical Thinker

In this chapter we have discovered that critical thinking is not just one way of thinking—it is a total approach to the way we make sense of the world, and it involves an integrated set of thinking abilities and attitudes that includes the following:

- *Thinking actively* by using our intelligence, knowledge, and skills to question, explore, and deal effectively with ourselves, others, and life's situations
- *Carefully exploring situations* by asking—and trying to answer—relevant questions
- *Thinking for ourselves* by carefully examining various ideas and arriving at our own thoughtful conclusions
- *Viewing situations from different perspectives* to develop an in-depth, comprehensive understanding
- *Supporting diverse perspectives with reasons and evidence* to arrive at thoughtful, well-substantiated conclusions

These critical thinking qualities are a combination of cognitive abilities, basic attitudes, and thinking strategies that enable you to clarify and improve your understanding of the world. By carefully examining the process and products of your thinking—and the thinking of others—you develop insight into the thinking process and learn to do it better. However, becoming a critical thinker does not simply involve mastering certain thinking abilities; it affects the entire way that you view the world and live your life. For example, the process of striving to understand other points of view in a situation changes the way you

Many factors come together to make a fine student, including curiosity, discipline, risk-taking, initiative, and enthusiasm.

think, feel, and behave. It catapults you out of your own limited way of viewing things, helps you understand others' viewpoints, and broadens your understanding. All these factors contribute to your becoming a sophisticated thinker and a mature human being.

Critical thinkers are better equipped to deal with the difficult challenges that life poses: to solve problems, to establish and achieve goals, and to make sense of complex issues. The foundation of thinking abilities and critical attitudes introduced in these first two chapters will be reinforced and elaborated in the chapters ahead, helping to provide you with the resources to be successful at college, in your chosen career, and throughout the other areas of your life as well.

"On Becoming a Better Student"

In this article, certified yoga teacher Donna Farhi Schuster discusses life skills that are important for success in all of your endeavors: curiosity, discipline, risk taking, initiative, and enthusiasm. She also includes a number of practical suggestions for performing well in your courses, strategies that are particularly helpful in viewing things from your teachers' perspectives. After carefully reviewing the reading, answer the questions that follow.

→

On Becoming a Better Student

Donna Farhi Schuster

A Zen master invited one of his students over to his house for afternoon tea. After a brief discussion the teacher poured tea into the student's cup and continued to pour until the cup was overflowing.

Finally the student said, "Master, you must stop pouring; the tea is overflowing—it's not going into the cup."

"That's very observant of you," the teacher replied. "And the same is true with you. If you are to receive any of my teachings, you must first empty out what you have in your mental cup."

As students we expect a great deal from our teachers. We expect them to be enthusiastic. We expect them to be reliable. We may even have expectations that they be endless repositories of skill and knowledge from which we may partake at will.

As a teacher I have come to feel weighted by these expectations and have begun to see that it is really not possible to teach. All the words and theories and techniques are of no use to students who have yet to open themselves with receptivity and to take it upon themselves to practice. So in a sense I have given up trying to "teach," for I've come to believe that the greatest thing I can offer my students is to help them learn how to find themselves through their own investigation.

Many factors come together to make a fine student. Find someone you think is extraordinary, and you will find many, if not all, of the following qualities. People who learn a great deal in what seems like a very short time embody these qualities.

Curiosity

Such people are tremendously curious. The whole world is of interest to them, and they observe what others do not. Nobel Prize-winning physician Albert Szent-Gyorgyi put it well when he said, "Discovery consists of looking at the same thing as everyone else and thinking something different."[1] With this curiosity comes an "investigative spirit"; the learning is not so much the acquisition of information as it is an investigation—a questioning, a turning over of the object of study to see all sides and facets. It is not knowing in the sense of having a rigid opinion, but the ability to look again at another time, in a different light, as Gyorgyi suggests, and to form a new understanding based on that observation.

One way to develop curiosity is to cultivate "disbelief." By disbelieving what we often take for granted, we begin to investigate and explore on our own. In the process, we stop mindlessly parroting our teachers and begin to find how their understanding works in our own experience. Disbelief can be a major step toward creative exploration. In my own classes I encourage students to investigate, to question my instructions in their own practice. "How does this movement affect my body? What happens if I do it another way? How am I reacting to this posture?" The mere act of saying "What if . . . ?" opens a completely new dimension of thought. This kind of questioning has led to some of the most exciting inventions of our time.

Discipline

Any discipline—but especially those with great subtlety and complexity, like yoga or t'ai chi—can be a lifelong pursuit. Persistence, consistency, and discipline are required. Without these, our learning is but froth without substance. There are no shortcuts. The fruit of these seemingly dry qualities (which we prefer to admire in others) is the satisfaction of having tasted the fullness of completion, or the thrill of meeting a difficult challenge with success. Perhaps, though, our culture is in need of redefining what it means to study. If we can look at our chosen discipline or craft as an ongoing process rather than as a discrete accomplishment, the potential for learning can be infinite. With this attitude we may find ourselves treating even the most mundane discovery with wide-eyed wonder and joy.

Almost anyone can recognize when another's understanding has true substance. The admiration we bestow on great dancers, musicians, and artists comes from our sense that these people have stepped into the unknown. When we see something extraordinary, we sense the unexpressed third dimension of our own two-dimensional, limited selves. When we take it upon ourselves to step into the unknown, we stop asking our teachers to give our lives meaning and start asking how we ourselves can bring meaning to all aspects of our lives.

Risk-Taking

Why is it, then, that so few people live up to their true potential? Beyond the well-paved roads and secure structures we usually build for ourselves lie demons, unsure footing—and unfelt pleasures. To be a student is to take risks. Yet most education discourages people from venturing far enough to take risks to make mistakes. "Children enter school as question marks and leave as periods," observes educator Neil Postman. What kind of punctuation mark do you represent? Do you find yourself looking for tidy answers that give you a feeling of security? By learning to find the one right answer, we may have relinquished our ability to find other answers and solutions. We learn, then, not to put ourselves into situations where we might fail, because failure has tremendous social stigma. When we try different approaches and do things that have no precedence in our experience, we will surely make mistakes. A creative person uses these "failures" as stepping stones.

Initiative

Can we begin, then, to see that our teachers are guides on our journey, but that the journey itself is our own responsibility? There is nothing quite so satisfying as undergoing a difficult process and after long hard work discovering the true nature of that process. It could be as simple as throwing a perfect pot, or as complex as formulating a new theory of physics. The satisfaction we feel will be directly proportional to the amount of work we do by ourselves to achieve our goal. Successful students do not expect to be spoon-fed, but take their own initiative. Wanting answers from my teacher has often been a way for me to avoid taking the initiative to discover my own answers through my own practice.

Speaking from the other side of the fence, yoga teacher Dona Holleman helps clarify the teacher's role in this relationship when she says: "Helping the pupil must come as a reward for

→

long and persistent work on the part of the pupil. It should be spare and rare. The pupil should do all the work himself, and then the occasional slight help comes as a 'bonus.'"[2]

Looking at our own unexplored terrain helps to strengthen weak areas and to nurture latent talent to fruition. One teacher who profoundly influenced how I learn was the famous Russian ballet teacher Mia Slavenska. After a quick, steely glance at my dance technique, she announced that I could forget everything I had ever learned because it would be of no use to me. Then for one year she demanded that I lift my leg no higher than twelve inches off the floor so that I would learn how to "move from the right place," instead of merely showing off with displays of outward form. When we give up trying to impress the teacher with what we already know and instead humble ourselves to what we do not know, we enter into a learning mode. Mia was rarely impressed by anyone and rarely offered praise, but, when she did, you knew you deserved it! She claimed that it took a good eight to ten years to train an excellent dancer, and her prodigies, many of whom entered renowned companies, showed the exceptional brilliance and truth of the combined dedication of teacher and student.

Enthusiasm

To learn, then, is to open oneself. Jim Spira, director of the Institute for Educational Therapy in Berkeley, California, asks his students to prepare themselves to learn in this way: "Drop your prior knowledge . . . [and] attempt to grasp the new framework in its own context. The student complains, 'But I know what is important.' If what you know is important, then it should be there when you finish the course. If you continually 'hold onto it,' then you'll only see what is presented in terms of the old knowledge/framework and never really grow in new ways."

"Drop your self-image . . . [and] become what you are involved with to the fullest. The student says, 'But what I am is important.' I reply, 'Don't get trapped by what you like and dislike.' Being willing to go through each activity as fully as possible will expand your potential well beyond your present limitations."

When I am lucky enough to meet people like Jim Spira, who live life as explorers, I find myself uplifted by their presence. These people, who inspire all of us, seem to have tapped into a limitless supply of enthusiasm. They excite us, they enlighten us, and we want some of whatever it is they have. The Greek word *enthousiasmos* means "infused with the divine."

We often go to classes because we need the enthusiasm of the teacher to bolster us or push us forward, and then we carry that enthusiasm home with us like a fragile package and often watch it diminish until the next class. But eventually we must find a way to stop resisting our own "infusion of the divine." Advanced students of any discipline are constantly finding new ways to connect with the enthusiastic part of themselves that "wants to do." These are the people who will go beyond replication of their teachers or systems to bring fresh new ideas and an iconoclastic vision to fields that have otherwise become jaded and ingrown.

I do not mean to advocate disrespect or casual regard for teachers. They are great gifts to us, but eventually we must become our own person—and the best teachers will help us move in that direction. By devoting yourself to one teacher, you help that teacher learn how best to help you. At the same time, you can develop trust in your teacher and can begin to understand his or her particular vocabulary. Contrary to the belief that more is better, studying

→

simultaneously with many different teachers and packing in one workshop after another may not be the best way to learn. Don't be a teacher or workshop junkie. If you find that you practice little on your own but take many classes and workshops, it may be time to assess how much you are really learning. Only through practice (by yourself) and time can you assimilate new information. Integrate new concepts and ideas into your practice in a meaningful way before stuffing yourself with more information and techniques.

Finally, as we each advance on our own unique journey, let us live each day as beginners. Being "advanced" has its own pitfalls—among them complacency and pushing or forcing. To go deeper may mean to be still, to progress more patiently, or to devote more time to other areas of our lives as yet green and immature. As F. M. Alexander, of the Alexander technique, once said to his students as they strained and labored, "Give up trying too hard, but never give up."[3]

Tips for the Aspiring Student

The information that follows is designed as a guide. The author welcomes correspondence from those who can add to it.

- Be attentive. Teachers will usually go out of their way to help a self-motivated and interested student.

- Be seen. If you want the teacher to know that you are serious, sit or stand in the front of the class. Make eye contact and introduce yourself, either before or after class.

- Be on time. Consistent lateness is a sign of disrespect. If you take your teacher's skills so lightly, why should he or she take you seriously? Missing the beginning of class can also be physically dangerous if you have missed explanations and work meant to prepare you for more difficult movements.

- Be consistent. The quality of any class improves when there is a collective commitment to regular attendance. In this way you can gain a cumulative knowledge and progress at a more rapid pace. On a more practical level, your attendance may be your teacher's livelihood.

- Listen with your whole body. We have come to treat words like the background noise of a radio. Plant words in the pertinent area of your body so that information can be "embodied."

- Appreciate constructive criticism. Remember why you're there—to break through restrictive habit patterns and to change. Teachers usually reserve the most scathing criticism for their most promising students!

- Questions can help clarify and enrich both teacher and student if the student's questions are pertinent. If, on the contrary, the student is asking questions because he or she is late or inattentive, the student is being disrespectful to the teacher and fellow classmates and is consequently lowering the quality of the class. Highly personal questions with little relevance to the subject at hand are best asked after class.

- You have the right to disagree—but you do not always have the right to express it.

→

Sometimes it is appropriate to challenge a teacher. It is unethical, however, to argue with a teacher or to badger a teacher in public. If you thoroughly object to what is being taught, you are free to leave and learn elsewhere.

■ Let your teacher know how much you appreciate him or her. Teachers need encouragement like everyone else. Giving them feedback when something has proved particularly beneficial or injurious to you can help them improve the quality of their teaching.

Notes

1. Roger Vaon Oech, *A Whack on the Side of the Head* (New York: Warner, 1983).
2. Dona Holleman, *Centering Down* (Firenze, Italy: Tipografia Giuntina, 1981).
3. Michael Gelb, *Body Learning* (New York: Delilah Books, 1981).

Questions for Analysis

1. Explain what you think Szent-Gyorgyi meant when he said, "Discovery consists of looking at the same thing as everyone else and thinking something different"? Describe an example from your own life when you had a similar experience.

2. Think of an achievement in your life that required a lot of discipline. Do you find that same kind of discipline in your academic accomplishments? If not, why not? Describe strategies for cultivating such discipline in the rest of your college career.

3. Explain whether you agree with what Schuster says about your right to disagree with a teacher and the limits she suggests. Where would you draw the line?

4. To borrow the analogy of Neil Postman, do you feel more like a question mark or a period at this stage of your academic career? Why?

5. Abraham Maslow, the founder of humanistic psychology, used to ask his students at Brandeis University who among them aspired to become great. Very few students ever raised their hands. Would you have raised your hand? Why or why not?

These questions are based on those developed by John Lawry in his book *College 101*.

3

Solving Problems

AN ORGANIZED APPROACH TO SOLVING PROBLEMS

Accepting the Problem

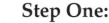

Step One:
What Is the Problem?

What do I know about the situation?
What results am I aiming for?
How can I define the problem?

Step Five:
How Well Is the Solution Working?

What is my evaluation?
What adjustments are necessary?

Step Two:
What Are the Alternatives?

What are the boundaries?
What are possible alternatives?

Step Four:
What Is the Solution?

Which alternative(s) will I pursue?
What steps can I take?

Step Three:
What Are the Advantages and/or Disadvantages of Each Alternative?

What are the advantages?
What are the disadvantages?
What additional information do I need?

Solving the Problem of Not Enough Money

Solving the Problem of Not Enough Time

Throughout your life, you continually solve problems. As a student, for example, you are faced with a steady stream of academic assignments: quizzes, exams, papers, homework projects, oral presentations. In order to solve these problems effectively—to do well on an exam, for instance—you need to *define* the problem (what areas will the exam cover, and what will be the format?), identify and evaluate various *alternatives* (what are possible study approaches?), and then put all these factors together to reach a *solution* (what will be my study plan and schedule?). Let's explore the problem-solving process by completing the following activity:

1. Describe an important *problem* you have solved recently.

   _____

   _____

   _____

   _____

2. Identify the *alternatives* that you considered in working through your problem.

   Alternative A: _____

   Alternative B: _____

   Alternative C: _____

3. Describe the *advantages* that you identified for each alternative.

   A. _____

   B. _____

   C. _____

   Describe the *disadvantages* that you identified for each alternative.

   A. _____

   B. _____

   C. _____

4. Describe which alternative you selected as a *solution* and then describe your *plan of action.*

   Alternative: _____

   Plan of action: _____

   _____

5. Describe how well your *solution* worked, including any modifications that you needed to make.

   _____

   _____

   _____

   _____

In the situation you just described, the analysis of your problem led to a series of decisions. This is what the thinking process is all about—trying to make sense of what is going on in our world and acting appropriately in response. When we solve problems effectively, our thinking process has a coherent organization similar to the general approach we have just explored. If we can understand the way our mind operates when we are thinking effectively, then we can apply this understanding to new, challenging situations. We can summarize this problem-solving approach as follows:

Problem-Solving Method

1. What is the *problem*?
2. What are the *alternatives*?
3. What are the *advantages* and/or *disadvantages* of each alternative?
4. What is the *solution*?
5. How well is the solution *working*?

We will be applying this method to solving problems that many college students face: "not enough money" and "not enough time." For example, imagine yourself in the following situation. What would your next move be, and what are your reasons for it?

You are about to begin your second year of college, following a very successful first year. To this point, you have financed your education through a combination of savings, financial aid, and a part-time job (16 hours/week) at a local store. However, you just received a letter from your college reducing your financial aid package by half due to budgetary problems. The letter concludes, "We hope this aid reduction will not prove to be too great an inconvenience." From your perspective, the loss of financial aid isn't an inconvenience—it's a disaster! Your budget last year was already tight, and with your job, you had barely enough time to study, participate in a few college activities, and have a modest (but essential) social life. To make matters worse, your mother has been ill, reducing her income and creating financial problems at home. You're feeling panicked and more than a little stressed. What in the world are you going to do?

When we first approach a difficult problem such as this, it often seems a confused tangle of information, feelings, alternatives, opinions, considerations, and risks. These kinds of problems are complicated situations that may not seem to offer a single simple solution. Very often when we are faced with such a difficult problem, we simply do not know where to begin, and we may

Analyzing Problems:

Effective problem solvers are able to analyze complex problems—like "time" and "money"—in an organized way and then develop creative solutions.

1. *Act impulsively,* without thought or consideration. (For example, "I'll just quit school.")

2. *Do what someone else suggests* without seriously evaluating the suggestion. (For example, "Tell me what I should do—I'm tired of thinking about this.")

3. *Do nothing* as we wait for events to make the decision for us. (For example, "I'll just wait and see what happens before doing anything.")

None of these approaches is likely to succeed in the long run, and they can gradually reduce our confidence in our ability to deal with complex problems. An alternative to these reactions is to *think critically* about the problem, analyzing it with an organized approach similar to the five-step method we identified above. Before applying a method like this to your problem, however, you need to first ready yourself by *accepting* the problem.

Accepting the Problem

To solve a problem, you must first be willing to *accept* the problem by *acknowledging* that it exists and *committing* yourself to trying to solve it. Sometimes you may have difficulty in recognizing there *is* a problem, unless it is pointed out to you. Other times you may actively *resist* acknowledging a problem, even when it is pointed out to you. The person who confidently states "I don't really have any problems" sometimes has very serious problems but is simply unwilling to acknowledge them.

On the other hand, mere acknowledgment is not enough to solve a problem. Once you have identified a problem, you must commit yourself to trying to solve it. Successful problem solvers are highly motivated and willing to persevere through the many challenges and frustrations of the problem-solving process. How do you find the motivation and commitment that prepare you to begin the problem-solving process? There are no simple answers, but a number of strategies may be useful to you:

1. ***List the benefits.*** Making a detailed list of the benefits you will derive from successfully dealing with a problem is a good place to begin. Such a

College students are confronted with many complicated and challenging problems which can threaten their academic success if the problems are not solved.

process helps you clarify why you might want to tackle the problem, motivates you to get started, and serves as a source of encouragement when you encounter difficulties or lose momentum.

2. ***Formalize your acceptance.*** When you formalize your acceptance of a problem, you are "going on record," either by preparing a signed declaration or by signing a "contract" with someone else. This formal commitment serves as an explicit statement of your original intentions that you can refer to if your resolve weakens.

3. ***Create a worst case scenario.*** Some problems may persist because you are able to ignore their possible implications. When you create a "worst case" scenario, you need to remind yourself, as graphically as possible, of the potentially disastrous consequences of your actions for yourself and for others in your life. For example, using vivid color photographs and the conclusions of scientific research, you can remind yourself that excessive smoking, drinking, or eating can lead to myriad health problems and social and psychological difficulties as well as an early death.

4. ***Identify the constraints.*** If you are having difficulty accepting a problem, it may be because something is holding you back. For example, you might be worried about making changes in your life or reluctant to expend the time and effort required to solve the problem. Whatever the constraints, using this strategy involves identifying and describing all the factors that are preventing you from attacking the problem and then addressing these factors one at a time.

Solving the Problem of Not Enough Money

Money difficulties are the number-one reason that students drop out of college. Too often, however, students leave college before exploring all their options for increasing their income or decreasing their expenses.

Step One: What Is the Problem?

A problem like this is actually much more complicated than the simple characterization of "I don't have enough money." If you are like many people, you will live much of your life feeling that you don't have "enough" money. Although you will likely be earning more money in the future, you will also probably have more expenses as well. Somehow the amount of money we spend (or want to spend) always seems greater than the money we earn. So the problem isn't merely "not having enough money"; the problem is not *managing* your money in a way that enables you to have the things that are most important to you. Managing your money involves both regulating your expenses *and* maximizing your income.

What Do I Know About the Situation? Solving a problem begins with determining what information you *know* to be the case and what information you *think* might be the case. Sometimes a situation may appear to be a problem when it really isn't, simply because your information isn't accurate. For example, you might be worried about staying in college because you believe you are not eligible for additional financial assistance. If this belief is inaccurate, however, then your "problem" may not really exist.

The best place to begin the analysis of your money situation is to complete an inventory of where you currently stand. With this information as a foundation, you can construct an intelligent budget that reflects your priorities and then engage in some longer range financial planning.

Analyze your current financial situation by first outlining your sources of *income* by category—for example, paycheck, financial aid, savings, contributions from family. Specify these figures on a weekly and monthly basis. Next, analyze your *expenses* by first making a list of all the relevant categories: rent, utilities, food, tuition, books, transportation, clothes, CD's and tapes, entertainment, and so on. Then organize these expenses on a weekly and monthly basis. Use the worksheet on page 84 to guide your analysis of both income and expenses.

Having completed your inventories, think about your income and expense patterns. How would you describe your financial situation? Did you find any surprises? How does your total annual income compare to your total annual expenses?

What Results Am I Aiming for in This Situation? The first part of the question "What is the problem?" consists of identifying the specific *results* or objectives you are trying to achieve. The results are those aims that will eliminate the problem if you are able to attain them. To identify your results, you need to ask yourself this question: "What are the objectives that, once achieved, will have the effect of solving my problem?" Let's see how this applies to your financial situation.

After compiling your income and expense inventory, you need to evaluate your financial situation and plan changes, if needed. Begin by prioritizing your expenses.

- Identify the expenses that are *essential,* and indicate when they are due. Many of these expenses are fairly constant and recurring, such as rent, utilities, food, and haircuts. Other expenses are intermittent and variable, such as medical fees and car repair.
- Identify expenses that are *important*, such as new clothes.
- Identify the expenses that are *attractive* but not really important, such as entertainment and vacations.

Financial Inventory

	INCOME					EXPENSES						
Day	Paycheck	Financial Aid	Family	Savings	Other	Rent	Utilities	Tuition	Food	Books	Transportation	Entertainment
M												
T												
W												
TH												
F												
M												
T												
W												
TH												
F												
M												
T												
W												
TH												
F												
M												
T												
W												
TH												
F												
Totals												

After completing your work, evaluate whether the amounts you are spending in the various categories are appropriate. If you think that you are spending too much, put a reduced amount in the appropriate column. If you think that you are spending too little, record an increased amount in the appropriate column. These targets represent the expense goals that you will try to achieve.

Next, critically evaluate your income, using the same worksheet. Break down your income into fixed sources—paychecks or financial aid—and intermittent sources—such as money that comes from working on special projects or occasional contributions by your family. Identify the areas where you would like to increase your income, and estimate the increased amounts you would *realistically* like to achieve. These amounts represent the income goals that you will try to reach.

As a final step, add up all your proposed expenses for a year and compare this amount to your total projected income. The income figure should be significantly larger than the expense figure—there are always unexpected emergencies, and we tend to underestimate our expenses and overestimate our income. If your income total is not substantially larger than your expense total, you should probably review your anticipated expenses to try to reduce them.

How Can I Define the Problem? You complete the first step by defining the problem as clearly and specifically as possible. Sometimes defining the problem is relatively straightforward, such as "I need to find enough time to exercise." Often, however, identifying the central issue of a problem is a much more complex process. For example, the statement "My problem is not being able to succeed to the extent I am capable" suggests a complicated situation that resists simple definition. In fact, you may begin to develop a clear idea of the problem only as you engage in the process of trying to solve it. You might begin by believing that your problem is, say, not having the *ability* to succeed and end by concluding that the problem is really a *fear* of success. Although there are no simple formulas for defining challenging problems, you can pursue several strategies to identify the central issue most effectively:

1. ***View the problem from different perspectives.*** Perspective taking is a key ingredient of thinking critically, and it can help you zero in on many problems as well. For example, when you describe how various individuals might view a given problem—such as your financial difficulties—the essential ingredients of the problem begin to emerge.

2. ***Identify component problems.*** Larger problems are often composed of component problems. To define the larger problem, it is often necessary to identify and describe its subproblems. For example, poor performance at school might be the result of a number of factors—ineffective study habits, inefficient time management, and preoccupation with a personal problem. Defining and dealing effectively with the larger problem means dealing with the subproblems first.

3. ***State the problem clearly and specifically.*** A third defining strategy is to state the problem as clearly and specifically as possible, based on your examination of the problem's objectives. If you do so, then your description will begin to suggest actions you can take to solve the problem. Examine the differences between the statements of the following problem:

General: "My problem is money."

More specific: "My problem is budgeting my money so that I won't always run out near the end of the month."

Most specific: "My problem is developing the habit and the discipline to budget my money so that I won't always run out near the end of the month."

Using the analyses that you have completed and the strategies described above, summarize your financial situation in the space below, including the goals you established in the areas of income and expenses.

_____

_____

_____

_____

_____

Step Two: What Are the Alternatives?

Once you have identified your problem clearly and specifically, your next move is to examine each of the possible actions that might help solve the problem. Of course, identifying all the possible alternatives is not easy; in fact, it may be part of the problem. You may not see a way out of a problem because your thinking is set in certain ruts, fixed in certain perspectives. You may be blind to other approaches, either because you reject them before seriously considering them ("That will never work!") or because they simply do not occur to you. You can use several strategies to overcome these obstacles:

1. ***Discuss the problem with other people.*** Thinking critically involves being open to seeing situations from different viewpoints and discussing ideas with others in an organized way. As critical thinkers we live—and solve problems—in a community, not simply by ourselves. Other people can suggest possible alternatives that you haven't thought of, in part because they are outside the situation and thus have a more objective perspective, and in part because they naturally view the world differently than you do, based on their past experience. In addition, discussions are often creative experiences that generate ideas the participants would not have come up with on their own.

2. ***Brainstorm ideas.*** Brainstorming, a method introduced by Alex Osborn, builds on the strengths of working with other people to generate ideas and solve problems. In a typical brainstorming session, a group of people work

Successful problem solvers often work with other people to view problems from different perspectives and develop the productive solutions.

together to generate as many ideas as possible in a specific period of time. As ideas are produced, they are not judged or evaluated, for this tends to inhibit the free flow of ideas and discourages people from making suggestions. Evaluation is deferred until a later stage. People are encouraged to build on the ideas of others, since the most creative ideas are often generated through the constructive interplay of various minds.

Alternatives for managing your money fall into the two categories of reducing your expenses and increasing your income. After reviewing the approaches described below, write down additional alternatives that are appropriate to your own situation. Use one or more of the strategies described above to help you break out of your typical ways of thinking.

Alternative 1: Create a weekly and monthly budget.
Using the expense and income inventories that you completed in Step One as a guide, create a weekly and monthly budget for yourself. Do your best to stick to it, and note any unexpected expenses that occur. At the end of each week, revise your monthly budget based on what you have actually earned and spent. A worksheet to guide you is located on page 89.

Alternative 2: Avoid credit-card purchases whenever possible, and pay your total balance each month.
Institutions that administer

Generating Alternatives:

The best approach to solving problems involves viewing the problem from diverse perspectives, generating many possibile alternatives instead of just a few.

credit cards are counting on you to feel that using a credit card is not the same thing as spending money. That's why it's so easy to roll up large amounts on a credit card, amounts you would never spend if you were using cash. Once you charge more than you can pay back at the end of the month, you get drawn into a system of outrageously high interest, typically 18% or more. This creates an on-going balance that never seems to shrink significantly, no matter how hard you try, in part because 20% of your spending money is being used for interest.

Alternative 3: Comparison shop for your purchases. There are
remarkable discrepancies between what different stores charge for the same items. With a little effort, you can significantly cut your expenses by finding the lowest prices. For example, buy a month's supply of toiletries and cosmetics at a discount drugstore. Purchase your computer equipment and software through college-sponsored consortiums. Buy your plane tickets far enough in advance to qualify for discount fares.

Alternative 4: Limit the spending money in your wallet. People tend
to find ways to spend the cash that is available to them. Decide in advance how

Monthly Budget

| | INCOME | | | | | | EXPENSES | | | | | |
Day	Paycheck	Financial Aid	Family	Savings	Other	Rent	Utilities	Tuition	Food	Books	Transpor-tation	Entertain-ment
M												
T												
W												
TH												
F												
M												
T												
W												
TH												
F												
M												
T												
W												
TH												
F												
M												
T												
W												
TH												
F												
Totals												

much you want to spend that day or evening, and take along just that amount, with an extra $20 tucked away for emergencies *only.*

Alternative 5: Avoid impulse buying.   On the spur of the moment, we often buy things that we wouldn't if we had time to think. To combat this tendency, wait a day or two to decide on a purchase, asking the question "Do I really *need* this?"

Alternative 6: If you are not employed, consider getting a part-time job.   Having a part-time job not only increases your income; it also helps you structure your time and become more efficient. If you can secure employment in a field related to your career interests, you are gaining valuable experience as well. Many colleges have work/study and internship programs, and many employers offer career opportunities that will sponsor your college study.

Alternative 7: Create your own job.   If you can't find a job that suits your needs, consider creating a service that uses your skills. For example, to increase my income in college, I advertised myself as a custom woodworker and began building custom furniture. Since I had no formal experience, I began with simple designs like bookshelves (which everybody needs!) and then branched out to wall units, beds, tables, and drawer units. Eventually I even published a book titled *Designing and Making Fine Furniture.* Similarly, you may have skills that you can market such as hair cutting or braiding, tutoring in specific areas like languages or math, word-processing, pet- or baby-sitting.

Alternative 8: Explore all possibilities for financial assistance.
Although it takes time to research all the grants and scholarships that you might qualify for and to complete the required applications, your effort represents a sound investment. If necessary, student loans are also available through the college and local lending institutions. However, don't lose sight of the fact that these loans must be repaid, usually with interest.

Alternative 9:   _____

_____

Alternative 10:   _____

_____

Step Three: What Are the Advantages and Disadvantages of Each Alternative?

Once you have identified the various alternatives, the next step is to *evaluate* them. Each possible course of action has certain *advantages* (potential positive results) and certain *disadvantages* (potential risks or negative consequences). Additionally, for each alternative there may be information you need in order to determine whether the alternative makes sense. Carefully review the alternatives described above, as well as those that you identified, and then for each alternative describe the advantages, disadvantages, and further information needed. For example:

Alternative 1: Create a weekly and monthly budget.

Advantages: Creating a weekly and monthly schedule will help you organize and control your finances, and become aware of your spending habits. Since it will bring some predictability to your financial situation, a budget will help you feel more relaxed and confident about money while teaching you important money management skills that you will use throughout your life.

Disadvantages: Trying to stick to a budget can be time-consuming and annoying. In addition, it is difficult to estimate every expense, and there are often unexpected expenses that throw a budget out of whack.

Information needed: Can I learn to use a budget in a natural and flexible way? Can I learn to adapt to unexpected expenses? Do I have the determination to stick to my budget?

Alternative 2: Avoid credit-card purchases whenever possible, and pay your total balance each month.

Advantages: _____

Disadvantages: _____

Information needed: _____

Alternative 3: Comparison shop for your purchases.

Alternative 4: Limit the spending money in your wallet.

Alternative 5: Avoid impulse buying.

Alternative 6: If you are not employed, consider getting a part-time job.

Alternative 7: Create your own job.

Alternative 8: Explore all possibilities for financial assistance.

Alternative 9: _____

Alternative 10: _____

Step Four: What Is the Solution?

The purpose of the first three steps is to analyze our problem in a systematic and detailed fashion—to work through the problem in order to become thoroughly familiar with it and with the possible solutions. After breaking down the problem in this way, you should try to put the pieces back together—that is, decide on a thoughtful course of action based on your increased understanding. Even though this sort of problem analysis does not guarantee finding a specific solution to the problem, it should give you some very good ideas about your general direction and the immediate steps you should take.

What Alternative(s) Will I Pursue?   There is no simple formula or recipe to tell you which alternatives to select. As you work through the different courses of action that are possible, you may find that you can immediately rule some out. However, it may not be so simple to select which of the other alternatives you wish to pursue. How do you decide?

The decisions you make usually depend on what you believe to be most important to you—your *values.* Your values strongly influence your decisions and help you set *priorities* in life—that is, decide what aspects of your life are most important to you. For example, you might decide that for right now, going to school is a higher priority than having an active social life. Let's examine some strategies for selecting alternatives that can help you solve problems.

1. ***Evaluate and compare alternatives.*** Although each alternative may have certain advantages and disadvantages, not all advantages are equally desirable or potentially effective. Thus, it makes sense to try to evaluate and rank the various alternatives, based on how effective they are likely to be and how they match up with our value system. A good place to begin is the "Results" stage in Step One. Examine each of the alternatives and evaluate how well it will contribute to achieving the results you are aiming for. You may want to rank the alternatives or develop your own rating system to assess their relative effectiveness and desirability, based on your needs, interests, and value system. After completing these two evaluations, you can then select the alternative(s) that seems most appropriate.

2. ***Synthesize a new alternative.*** After reviewing and evaluating the alternatives you generated, develop a new alternative that combines the best qualities of several options while avoiding their disadvantages. For example, you can productively combine "Avoid credit-card purchases," "Limit the money in your wallet," and "Avoid impulse buying" to create an effective spending strategy.

3. ***Try out each alternative in your imagination.*** Focus on each alternative and try to imagine, as concretely as possible, what it would be like if you actually selected it. Visualize what impact your choice would have on your problem and what the implications would be for your life as a whole. By visualizing the alternative, you can sometimes avoid unpleasant results or unexpected consequences. As a variation of this strategy, you can sometimes test alternatives on a very limited basis in a practice situation. For example, if you were trying to overcome your fear of speaking in groups, you could practice various speaking techniques with your friends or family until you found an approach you were comfortable with.

Your analysis of the various alternatives for managing money should have provided you with some productive ideas. Using one or more of the strategies

for selecting alternatives explained above, identify below one or more
alternatives that you plan to implement.

Alternative 1: _____

_____

Alternative 2: _____

_____

Alternative 3: _____

_____

What Steps Can I Take to Act on the Alternative(s) Chosen? Once
you have decided on the correct alternative(s) to pursue, your next move is to
plan the steps you will have to take. For each of the alternatives that you identified, design a plan of action that specifies the steps that you need to take to
implement it. Don't forget to include a schedule. And remember that plans do
not implement themselves. Once you know what actions you have to take, you
need to commit yourself to taking the necessary steps. This is where many
people stumble in the problem-solving process, paralyzed by inertia or fear.
Sometimes, to overcome these blocks and inhibitions, you need to reexamine
your original acceptance of the problem, perhaps making use of some of the
strategies we explored on pages 81–92. Once you get started, the rewards of
actively attacking your problem are often enough incentive to keep you focused
and motivated.

Step Five: How Well Is the Solution Working?

As you work toward reaching an informed conclusion, don't fall into the trap of
thinking that there is only one "right" decision and that all is lost if you do not
figure out what this decision is and carry it out. You should remind yourself that
any analysis of problem situations, no matter how careful and systematic, is ultimately limited. You simply cannot anticipate or predict everything that is going
to happen. As a result, many decisions you make are provisional, in the sense
that your ongoing experience will inform you if your choices are working out
or if they need to be modified. This is precisely the attitude of the critical
thinker—someone who is *receptive* to new ideas and experiences and *flexible*
enough to change or modify beliefs based on new information. Critical thinking
is not a compulsion to find the "right" answer or make the "correct" decision; it
is an ongoing process of exploration and discovery. In many cases the relative
effectiveness of your efforts will be apparent. In other cases it will be helpful to
pursue a more systematic evaluation along the lines suggested in the following
strategies.

1. ***Compare the results with the goals.*** The essence of evaluation is
   comparing the results of your efforts with the initial goals you were trying
   to achieve. Compare the anticipated results of the alternative(s) you

Evaluating Possible Solutions:
Selecting the most promising solution results from carefully evaluating all of the alternatives and trying to anticipate which alternative(s) will best meet the problem-solving goals we established. How well is the solution working?

selected. To what extent will your choice meet these goals? Are there goals that are not likely to be met by your alternative(s)? Which ones? Could they be addressed by other alternatives? Asking these and other questions will help you clarify the success of your efforts and provide a foundation for future decisions.

2. ***Get other perspectives.*** As we have seen throughout the problem-solving process, getting the opinions of others is a productive strategy at virtually every stage, and this is certainly true for evaluation. Naturally, the evaluations of others are not always better or more accurate than our own, but even when they are not, reflecting on these different, possibly more objective views usually deepens our understanding of the situation. To receive specific, practical feedback from others, you need to ask specific, practical questions that will elicit this information. General questions ("What do you think of this?") typically result in overly general, unhelpful responses ("It sounds OK to me"). Be focused in soliciting feedback, and remember: you *do* have the right to ask people to be *constructive* in their comments, providing suggestions for improvement rather than flatly expressing what they think is wrong.

As a result of your review, you may discover that the alternative you selected is not feasible or is not leading to satisfactory results. When this occurs, don't get discouraged or give up! Instead, go back and review the other alternatives to identify another possible course of action. Or you may find that the alternative you selected is working out fairly well but still requires some adjustments as you continue to work toward your desired outcomes. In fact, this is a typical situation you should expect to occur. Even when things initially appear to be working reasonably well, an active thinker continues to ask such questions as "What might I have overlooked?" and "How could I have done this differently?" Of course, asking—and trying to answer—questions of this sort is even more important if solutions are hard to come by (as they usually are in real-world problems) and if you are to retain the flexibility and optimism you need to tackle a new option.

Thinking Activity 3.2

Select an important *unsolved* problem from your own life, one that you are currently grappling with and have not yet been able to solve. After selecting the problem you want to work on, strengthen your *acceptance* of the problem by using one or more of the strategies described on pages 81–82 and describing your efforts. Then analyze your problem using the problem-solving method we have explored in the chapter, which is outlined below.

As you work through your analysis, discuss the problem with other class members, individually and in small groups, to generate fresh perspectives and unusual alternatives that might not have occurred to you. Write your analysis in outline style, giving specific responses to the questions in each step of the problem-solving method. Although you might not reach a "guaranteed" solution to your problem, you should deepen your understanding of the problem and develop a concrete plan of action that will help you move in the right direction. Implement your plan of action, and then monitor the results.

⟶

Acceptance: Have I acknowledged the problem and committed myself to solving it?

1. *Step One: What is the problem?*
   a. What do I know about the situation?
   b. What are the results I am aiming for in this situation?
   c. How can I define the problem?
2. *Step Two: What are the alternatives?*
   a. What alternatives are possible?
3. *Step Three: What are the advantages and disadvantages of each alternative?*
   a. What are the advantages of each alternative?
   b. What are the disadvantages of each alternative?
   c. What additional information do I need to evaluate each alternative?
4. *Step Four: What is the solution?*
   a. Which alternative(s) will I pursue?
   b. What steps can I take to act on the alternative(s) chosen?
5. *Step Five: How well is the solution working?*
   What is my evaluation, and what adjustments are necessary?

Solving the Problem of Not Enough Time

Another problem commonly faced by students is that of "not having enough time." In addition to the demands of school, students must often integrate employment, family responsibilities, athletics, and extracurricular and volunteer activities. Let's apply the method we have been using to analyze the problem of *not enough time.*

Accepting the Problem

While many people complain about not having enough time, not all of them are ready to acknowledge their responsibility in creating their predicament and to commit themselves to improving it through thoughtful analysis and determined action. If you find that you have these sorts of difficulties, perhaps you could use one or more of the strategies described on pages 81–82.

Step One: What Is the Problem?

What Do I Know About the Situation? Since we cannot actually *create* time (we're all stuck with 24 hours per day, or 168 hours per week), we need to think of ways that we can *use* the time we have more efficiently and productively. In order to begin this process, it is helpful to analyze how you are currently using the time allocated to you. Complete the time inventory in Thinking Activity 3.3.

Thinking Activity 3.3

Describe a typical week in your life, using the following categories:

morning preparations	evening preparations	meals	sleep
classes	study	work	travel
socializing	exercise/sports	activities (specify)	
television/music	reading	other (specify)	

Use the worksheet format on page 98 as a guide in this task. After completing the worksheet, add up the total hours that you spend in each of the different categories. How would you analyze the result? Did you find any surprises?

What Are the Results I Am Aiming for in This Situation? Review the time inventory that you just created, and think about your own situation with respect to time. In which areas of your life do you feel particularly squeezed? On the other hand, in which areas do you feel you are spending too much time? With these ideas in mind, identify the major "time" results that you would like to achieve.

Result 1: _____

_____

Result 2: _____

_____

Result 3: _____

_____

How Can I Define the Problem? Based on what you have discovered, describe in the space below your essential problem with respect to time. Use one or more of the strategies described on pages 85–86 to assist you in defining your problem.

_____

_____

_____

_____

_____

Time Inventory

	7:00 am	8:00 am	9:00 am	10:00 am	11:00 am	12:00 pm	1:00 pm	2:00 pm	3:00 pm	4:00 pm	5:00 pm	6:00 pm
Monday												
Tuesday												
Wednesday												
Thursday												
Friday												
Saturday												
Sunday												

	7:00 pm	8:00 pm	9:00 pm	10:00 pm	11:00 pm	12:00 am	1:00 am	2:00 am	3:00 am	4:00 am	5:00 am	6:00 am
Monday												
Tuesday												
Wednesday												
Thursday												
Friday												
Saturday												
Sunday												

Step Two: What Are the Alternatives?

Beyond chanting the refrain "I need more time" or cutting down on their sleep, many people have few strategies for better managing their time. Yet there are many successful approaches we can use to create time by living our lives more efficiently. Some of these strategies are described below. After reviewing them, write down additional alternatives that are appropriate to your situation. Use one or more of the strategies described on page 86 to help you break out of your typical ways of thinking.

Alternative 1: Create a weekly plan to organize your time. Using the time inventory that you created in Thinking Activity 3.3 and taking into consideration the changes you proposed after reviewing your inventory, create a weekly schedule for yourself. You can use the blank schedule located on page 99, following or you can create your own.

Alternative 2: Prioritize your activities so that you can concentrate on the most important things. Make a list on an index card of the things you would like to get done that day. Then prioritize them by using the following key:

Weekly Schedule

	7:00 am	8:00 am	9:00 am	10:00 am	11:00 am	12:00 pm	1:00 pm	2:00 pm	3:00 pm	4:00 pm	5:00 pm	6:00 pm
Monday												
Tuesday												
Wednesday												
Thursday												
Friday												
Saturday												
Sunday												

	7:00 pm	8:00 pm	9:00 pm	10:00 pm	11:00 pm	12:00 am	1:00 am	2:00 am	3:00 am	4:00 am	5:00 am	6:00 am
Monday												
Tuesday												
Wednesday												
Thursday												
Friday												
Saturday												
Sunday												

+++ absolutely essential

++   important

+   desirable

At the end of the day, create a new prioritized list for the following day, placing on the list the things that you didn't get to that day.

Alternative 3: Synthesize your schedule to make it more efficient.
Carefully examine your schedule to see how you can organize it more efficiently. For example, try to schedule your classes close together to cut down on extra travel and waiting time between classes (although the extra time between classes can be used to study and process the material you just learned, or prepare for your upcoming class). Try to make your key locations—home, school, work, child care—as close to one another as possible, in order to save travel time. Combine your shopping trips and errands in order to complete them more efficiently. See if there are other strategies you can use to better synthesize your schedule and so "create" more time.

Alternative 4: Make use of the small blocks of time in your schedule.
Although it's best to study in time blocks of one hour or greater, much of our daily schedule has smaller periods of time sandwiched in. Often we don't even attempt to make productive use of these smaller intervals, but they can be valuable resources for us if we approach them creatively. As we will discover in the next chapter, studying for short, intense intervals can be extremely effective. And if you're prepared to get right to work, you can get things accomplished in as little as 15 or 20 minutes. After all, three 20-minute periods do add up to one hour. Similarly, time spent traveling can be used productively, whether riding on public transportation or even driving in your car, when you can listen to tape-recorded versions of class notes.

Alternative 5: Create a diversely integrated schedule.
Although it may seem logical to create large time blocks for various activities—for example, allowing four hours to study history—the fact is that this is not the most effective approach. Instead, you work more effectively when you alternate activities in order to stay "fresh." For example, it may make more sense to schedule your four-hour time block along the following lines:

study History	60 minutes
snack break	15 minutes
Philosophy paper	60 minutes
physical exercise	15 minutes
review notes for Biology	45 minutes
English reading	45 minutes

This type of diverse scheduling helps you avoid the loss of concentration that often occurs when you are doing one activity for too long. It also encourages you to avoid Parkinson's Law, the observation by C. Northcote Parkinson that work expands to fit the time allotted. By scheduling shorter time periods to complete activities, you are challenged to work in a more focused and efficient mode.

Alternative 6: Target the time wasters in your life, and try to reduce or eliminate them.
Each of us has our own time temptations, activities that we slip into doing and end up wasting precious hours. It may be hanging out with friends, watching the soaps on TV, talking on the phone, or simply daydreaming. Identify your time wasters, and then make a concerted effort to reduce or even eliminate them from your schedule.

Alternative 7: Avoid perfectionism and procrastination.
These are distinct though often related time maladies that infect many people. Perfectionism is the need to complete all your work to the highest possible standards. Although this approach is admirable in intent, you often don't have the time to meet these high standards in all your activities. Some important projects may demand your highest quality work, but you can often use more reasonable standards in other activities.

Procrastination is a more common problem, one in which you postpone responsibilities until you run out of time. Many of the strategies we have been discussing in this chapter will help you overcome procrastination, but you need to use your determination to break these deeply ingrained habits. In fact, procrastination is sometimes so deeply rooted in your personality and way of relating to the world that you need to give it its own individual problem analysis!

Alternative 8: _____
_____

Alternative 9: _____
_____

Step Three: What Are the Advantages and/or Disadvantages of Each Alternative?

Carefully review the alternatives described as well as those that you identified, and then for each alternative describe the advantages, disadvantages, and further information needed. For example,

Alternative 1: Create a weekly plan to organize your time.

Advantages: A weekly schedule will help you create a total design that includes all the activities you need to accomplish. It will encourage you to plan ahead and also prevent you from spending excessive time on any one activity. It will also discourage time-wasting activities, give your life more stability, and help you feel "in control."

Disadvantages: Weekly schedules can be applied in an overly rigid way. There are also unknown factors and unforeseen circumstances that might interfere with your plans, and if you try to follow the schedule above all else, you may end up doing more harm than good.

Information Needed: Will I be able to stick to the schedule once I have created it? Will I be able to use it flexibly, making the necessary adjustments when the unexpected occurs?

Alternative 2: Prioritize your activities so that you can concentrate on the most important things.

Advantages: _____

Disadvantages: _____

Information needed: _____

Alternative 3: Synthesize your schedule to make it more efficient.

Alternative 4: Make use of small blocks of time in your schedule.

Alternative 5: Create a diversely integrated schedule.

Alternative 6: Target the time wasters in your life, and try to reduce or eliminate them.

Alternative 7: Avoid perfectionism and procrastination.

Alternative 8: _____

Alternative 9: _____

Step Four: What Is the Solution?

Which Alternative(s) Will I Pursue? Your analysis of the various alternatives for managing time should have provided you with some useful ideas that you can use. Review the strategies for selecting alternatives explained on page 92, and then identify one or more alternatives that you plan to implement.

Alternative 1: _____

_____

Alternative 2: _____

_____

Alternative 3: _____

_____

What Steps Can I Take to Act on the Alternative(s) Chosen? For each of the alternatives that you identified, design a plan of action that specifies the steps that you need to take to implement it. Don't forget to include a schedule!

Step Five: How Well Is the Solution Working?

As you implement your plans of action, monitor how successfully they are helping you. If you find that you need to make adjustments to improve their effectiveness, then make them. If you find that a plan is not working, go back, review your list of alternatives, and try another one. If you discover your motivation to manage time is diminishing and you find yourself slipping back into some of your old time-wasting habits, review the strategies that you used during the acceptance stage of your analysis (pages 81–82) in an effort to recommit yourself to solving this problem. Additional evaluation strategies are located on pages 93–95.

Thinking Activity 3.4

Analyze one of the following problems using the problem-solving approach presented in this chapter.

Problem 1

The most important unsolved problem that exists for me is the inability to make that crucial decision of what to major in. I want to be secure with respect to both money and happiness when I make a career for myself, and I don't want to make a mistake in choosing a field of study. I want to make this decision before beginning the next semester so that I can start immediately in my career. I've been thinking about managerial studies. However, I often wonder if I have the capacity to make executive decisions when I can't even decide on what I want to do with my life.

Problem 2

One of my problems is my difficulty in taking tests. It's not that I don't study. What happens is that when I get the test I become nervous and my mind goes blank. For example, in my social science class, the teacher told us on Tuesday that there would be a test on Thursday. That afternoon I went home and began studying for the test. By Thursday I knew most of the work, but when the test was handed out, I got nervous and my mind went blank. For a long time I just stared at the test, and I ended up failing it.

Problem 3

My problem is "the weed." I have been smoking cigarettes for over five years. At first I did it because I liked the image, and most of my friends were smoking as well. Gradually, I got hooked. It's such a part of my life now that I don't know if I can quit. Having a cup of coffee, studying, talking to people—it just seems natural to have a cigarette in my hand. I know there are a lot of good reasons for me to stop. I've even tried a few times, but I always ended up bumming cigarettes from friends and then giving up entirely. I don't want my health to go up in smoke, but I don't know what to do.

⟶

Problem 4

One of the serious problems in my life is learning English as a second language. It is not so easy to learn a second language, especially when you live in an environment where only your native language is spoken. When I came to this country three years ago, I could speak almost no English. I have learned a lot, but my lack of fluency is getting in the way of my studies and my social relationships.

Problem 5

This is my first year of college, and in general I'm enjoying it a great deal. The one disturbing thing I have encountered is the amount of drinking that students engage in when they socialize. Although I enjoy drinking in moderation, most students drink much more than "in moderation" at parties. They want to "get drunk," "lose control," "get wasted." And the parties aren't just on weekends—they're every night of the week! The problem is that there is a lot of pressure for me to join in the drinking and partying. Most of the people I enjoy being with are joining in, and I don't want to be left out of the social life of the college. But it's impossible to party so much and still keep up-to-date with my course work. And all that drinking certainly isn't good for me physically. But on the other hand, I don't want to be excluded from the social life, and when I try to explain that I don't enjoy heavy drinking, my friends make me feel immature and a little silly. What should I do?

Solving Nonpersonal Problems

The problems we have analyzed up until this point are "personal" problems in the sense that they represent individual challenges encountered by us as we live our lives. However, problems are not only of a personal nature. We also face problems as members of a community, a society, and the world. As with personal problems, we need to approach these kinds of problems in an organized and thoughtful way in order to explore the issues, develop a clear understanding, and decide on an informed plan of action. For example, the abuse of alcohol (and other drugs) is a serious problem on many college campuses, interfering with academic study and causing antisocial behavior. Experts from different fields have offered a variety of explanations to account for this behavior. In the space provided, describe why you believe alcohol abuse is such a serious problem among college students and what should be done to address the problem.

Making sense of a complex, challenging situation like this is not a simple process. Although the problem-solving method we have been using in this chapter is a powerful approach, its successful application depends on having sufficient information about the situation we are trying to solve. As a result, it is often necessary for us to research articles and other sources of information to develop informed opinions about the problem we are investigating. The articles at the conclusion of this chapter provide important information and analysis regarding the abuse of alcohol at college.

The famous journalist H. L. Mencken once said, "To every complex question there is a simple answer—and it's wrong!" Although complex problems do not admit simple solutions, by working through these problems thoughtfully and systematically, we can achieve a deeper understanding and develop strategies for solving them.

Becoming an effective problem solver does not merely involve applying a problem-solving method in a mechanical fashion, anymore than becoming a mature critical thinker involves mastering a set of thinking skills. Rather, solving problems, like thinking critically, reflects a total approach to making sense of experience. When we think like problem solvers, we approach the world in a distinctive way. Instead of avoiding difficult problems, we have the courage to meet them head-on and the determination to work through them. Instead of acting impulsively or relying exclusively on the advice of others, we are able to make sense of complex problems in an organized way and develop practical solutions and initiatives.

A sophisticated problem solver employs all of the critical thinking abilities that we have examined so far and those that we will explore in the chapters ahead. And while we might agree with H. L. Mencken's evaluation of simple answers to complex questions, we might endorse a rephrased version: "To many complex questions there are complex answers—and these are worth pursuing!"

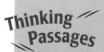

Thinking Passages

"Bad Times at Hangover U." and "College Women and Alcohol"

The following articles deal with the problem of excessive alcohol use on college campuses. The first, "Bad Times at Hangover U.," discusses the widespread use of alcohol at many colleges. The second article, "College Women and Alcohol," analyzes the social and psychological factors that encourage alcohol abuse, particularly among women. After carefully reviewing these articles, think critically about this problem by answering the questions that follow.

Bad Times at Hangover U.

Debra Rosenberg

College parties lead to the ER or the drunk tank

Marty woke up at 5 A.M. when the nurse slapped him in the face. It had been a long night: the party started with beer and graduated to Russian vodka. Marty downed shot after shot until he vomited on someone's leg. He thinks he spent an hour face down in the middle of the street.

→

The ambulance ride to the hospital was a blur, too. In fact, Marty's only vivid memory of his 18th birthday is the morning after. "Hangovers are not fun," says the Harvard freshman.

Like Marty, more and more college students are ending the party in the emergency room. At Boston College, the number of students hospitalized for alcohol-related problems has doubled since last year. Three students recorded blood-alcohol levels of .30 percent (.10 percent is legally drunk in Massachusetts) and two more were reportedly near death from alcohol poisoning this fall. At the University of Massachusetts at Amherst, 80 percent of weekend visits to health services are alcohol related. "You see the ambulances on college campuses all the time," says Julie Dent, 21, a student alcohol educator at Mount Holyoke.

Alcohol consumption is down throughout the country, but "this news has not reached the college campuses yet," says Dr. Henry Wechsler, a professor at Harvard School of Public Health. He surveyed the drinking habits of 1,600 freshmen at 14 Massachusetts colleges and found that among those who drink at least once a week, 92 percent of the men and 82 percent of the women consume at least five drinks in a row. Fully half said they wanted to get drunk.

Some officials blame the return to the 21-year-old minimum drinking age. Students have been forced to move their parties off campus where they lap up dangerous spiked punches rather than beer. "We want to try to bring the problems back on campus where our staff can monitor them," says Robert Sherwood, Boston College's dean for student development, who supports a return to the 18-year-old minimum.

It's not that the "just say no" message has bypassed college campuses entirely. Teetotalers have quadrupled their ranks since Wechsler first studied student drinking habits in 1977. In addition, use of all other drugs on campus—from cigarettes to marijuana and cocaine—has reportedly been cut in half over the last decade.

The alcohol problem on campus remains so widespread that 56 colleges met last week at Harvard University to discuss strategies for more aggressive education and counseling programs. But colleges really have little idea what will work. Some have even resorted to a once unimaginable option—having students arrested for minor offenses. Harsh perhaps, but preferable to waiting for one of the partygoers to end up in the morgue.

College Women and Alcohol: A Relational Perspective

Nancy A. Gleason, MSW, LICSW, BCD

A day or two after a first-year female student arrives at college, she will be invited to a fraternity party or other mixer to meet men, and her college involvement with alcohol will begin. Whether served legally or not, alcohol will be available, and her new dormitory friends will most likely be drinking. Feeling anxious, uncomfortable, and somewhat overwhelmed, the new student will find it difficult to refuse to drink—even if she wants to refuse.

Here, on a superficial level, are ingredients for drinking—peer pressure, the wish to feel more relaxed and to appear sophisticated, perhaps even seductive. If our student has had no experience with alcohol, it won't take much persuasion to get her to try it. If she feels shy, she will be told that a drink will help her relax and feel less inhibited. If she is used to drinking, she will feel right at home. The evening's activity may produce no more than a hangover or a decision never to go to another mixer, but it could also influence her future social or drinking life.

During her college years, a student will encounter a variety of hurdles and stresses that will challenge her coping skills. At the same time, there will be many opportunities to party, to unwind, or to celebrate, and she may find that alcohol is easily available and provides an adjunct to most occasions. And college has the reputation of being the "best years of our lives," perhaps a last fling before taking on adult responsibilities.

Is something wrong with this scenario?

Despite growing research and media attention to alcohol abuse during the college years and to the consequences of alcohol consumption for young women, the role that alcohol plays in the psychology of college-age women has received limited consideration. We are finally acknowledging that men and women use and abuse alcohol for different reasons—and with different results. New theories about the psychology of women stress the importance of relational competence in their healthy development and the distress created by lack of success in relationships. These insights can help us understand why and how women use and abuse alcohol and the variety of consequences to which alcohol use makes women vulnerable.[1]

The Problem

Although rates of illicit drug use in college have decreased since 1980, women's alcohol use has remained relatively constant.[2] Ninety percent of both college men and women consistently state they have used alcohol during the previous year. Although the number of college women who drink heavily has increased in the last 20 years,[3,4] only half as many women as men in college drink daily (3% of the women *v* 6% of the men). Thirty-five percent of the women describe "occasions of heavy drinking" (five or more drinks in a row) within the past 2-week period, compared with 52% of the men.[5] Wechsler and Isaac[6] expressed concern about binge drinking (also described as five drinks in a row), finding that it is generally on the increase. They found that more than twice as many college women were getting drunk in 1992 as were doing so in 1977 and that more of the women were drinking to get drunk. Men were still drinking more than women each time they drank (close to twice as much), and men drank to intoxication nearly twice as often.[3,7,8] Analyzing the results of the Fund for the Improvement of Post-Secondary Education (FIPSE) Core Survey, which included 54,361 students from 78 colleges and universities, Presley and Meilman found women binge drinking less frequently than men did, but nevertheless found that 36% of the women had binged in the previous 2 weeks.[9] Fourteen percent of those surveyed at a woman's college in 1988 had been intoxicated five or more times in the previous 30 days (N.A.G., unpublished data, 1990). Berkowitz and Perkins[10] still found that men drank more on each drinking occasion, although not necessarily more frequently than did women. They concluded that 29% of male college students have drinking problems, compared with 11% of college women.

Statistics do not tell the whole story. Perhaps because women are less likely than men to engage in destructive behavior or to get into trouble with authorities,[11] the women's drinking problems have not received adequate attention. Perkins,[12] who analyzed studies done over a

→

10-year period, confirmed the gender differential in destructive actions associated with binge drinking in college but emphasized other consequences in which drinking women reach close to equal incidence with men: unintended sexual activity, memory loss, damaged relationship, and physical injury to themselves.

In addition to the risks everyone faces when abusing alcohol (addiction, driving accidents, and alcohol poisoning), women confront risks that appear to be different from those faced by men. These risks may result from the use of alcohol, and they may lead to increased drinking. They include depression and failure in relationships. Not least is the risk of sexual victimization, which is so destructive to women's self-esteem and so intimately connected to the use of alcohol, both as a factor leading to abuse[13] and as a coping mechanism following abuse.[14]

In this context, perspectives in the psychology of women can help us understand college women's alcohol use and resulting problems. This is a new inquiry. Interest in gender issues is increasing rapidly as recognition of gender differences gains acceptance in the psychological arena and in the popular press.[15] Researchers are studying moral development, learning styles, relationship patterns, concepts of mutuality, and more. At the same time, attention is now being paid to female alcoholics and their treatment. Research on college women's use of alcohol has focused to a large extent on such negative consequences as susceptibility to rape. Several studies have investigated how personality factors are related to alcohol abuse and have identified issues of power, dominance and dependence,[16] fear of failure and sensation seeking,[17] and assertiveness and self-expression.[18] In an earlier study, Jones[19] found that women who drank moderately were socially isolated and depressed. Jones did not make clear whether drinking was the result or the cause of the isolation. These studies failed to examine the importance to women of their sense of capacity in making meaningful connections with others. Research into the link or correlation between the relational needs of women and their use of substances is remarkably rare.

Relational Theory

With recent explorations of gender differences, psychologists, sociologists, educators, and other researchers are recognizing that traditional psychological theories have undervalued women's attributes and skills and have had a negative impact on women's self-esteem.[20–22] Qualities such as sensitivity, empathy, dependence, emotionality, and putting the needs of others before one's own have traditionally been seen as "female" and therefore as deficiencies—suggesting the conclusion that women may be inherently less competent and that these qualities are roadblocks on the path to success.[20] Women are described as inadequate in academia and the marketplace if they are not clear thinking, rational, capable of simplifying ethical problems into rights and wrongs, competitive, ambitious, and career-oriented.[21] American society, Western culture, and some feminists have reinforced these messages. To date, women have not had the societal support and acknowledgment that help them feel good about who they are.

At the same time, women are encouraged to be good caretakers, mothers, and nurturers of others. They are supposed to be self-effacing yet attentive to their bodies, their clothes, their makeup, and their behavior so that they are attractive to others, especially to men. No womder women are confused about who they are and what is expected of them. They are continually re-

→

minded of their failure to achieve the expectations set for them—expectations they often incorporate as their own.

Women's psychological development does not appear to move toward the traditionally accepted goal of independence, autonomy, and separation. Recent theoretical formulations, sometimes referred to as "self-in-relation,"[23] suggest that a woman's sense of self is organized around her capacity to make and maintain relationships built on mutuality in connection, recognizing and valuing one's impact on another as well as that other's effect on oneself. The relational framework suggests responsiveness and openness to the other and activity to engage the other. Miller describes the components of "growth-fostering relationships" as "zest" and empowerment to act, leading to a more accurate image of the self and of the other, an increased sense of worth, and a greater connection to the other, with the motivation then to connect more fully to people in general.[24]

Mutuality is a key component to satisfying relationships within this framework. Jordan defines a "mutuality exchange" in which "one is both affecting the other and being affected by the other. . . . There is openness to influence, emotional availability and a constantly changing pattern of responding to and affecting the other's state."[25] Genero et al further describe a "bidirectional movement of feelings, thought, and activity between persons in relationships"[26] and demonstrate the connection of mutuality to relationship satisfaction and to social supports. Where mutuality is lacking, the individual experiences a sense of isolation and increased susceptibility to depression.

The study of friendship provides another approach to understanding how relationships work for women. Research on adult friendships has produced limited results, especially when the research seeks to evaluate the interaction between friends and the experience of friendship. In general terms, researchers have found that women tend to relate in a more personal and "expressive" way, whereas men tend to be more "instrumental."[27] Although Duck and Wright[28] do not confirm that women are less instrumental, they have found that women are more affective in their relational style and that they value their friendships more and invest more in them than men do. DeVries and Parker[29] expand the discussion of difficulties in studying friendships to include the failure in most research to discuss both the giving and receiving inherent in close relationships. Looking at the contribution of both self and other in relationships, their findings suggest that women experience themselves as giving more and that both men and women find more empathic understanding and connectedness from their women friends.

It is not our purpose here to examine men's styles of relationships or to contrast them with those of women, but some comparison is unavoidable. All who do research on the subject are careful to point out, and it needs to be stressed, that their findings offer the possibility for generalizations that do not account for a wide variety on all measures within each gender.

Some people have been studying friendships, whereas others have looked at communication styles, especially as they may create difficulties in communication between men and women.[30] Surrey[31] described a couple's problems with communication:

> When she spoke of her own needs and perceptions, she wanted him to
> listen actively, playing a part in the developing movement of ideas to a stage

→

of increased focus and clarity. He was ready for debate. "When I argue and debate with her, it is because I treat her like an equal who knows what she feels and can argue effectively on her own position." She found that his position created confusion, disorganization and a feeling of disconnection, rather than fostering her idea of communication. She was asking from him what she feels she does for him—going "with him" on his line of thinking at that time, temporarily taking herself "out of the picture." Each had difficulty understanding the other's model of relationship. (pp. 62–63)

Describing the different communication styles of men and women, Deborah Tannen[32] wrote

Intimacy is key in a world of connection where individuals negotiate complex networks of friendship, minimize differences, try to reach consensus, and avoid the appearance of superiority, which would highlight differences. In a world of status, *independence* is key, because a primary means of establishing status is to tell others what to do, and taking orders is a marker of low status. Though all humans need both intimacy and independence, women tend to focus on the first and men on the second. It is as if their lifeblood ran in different directions (p. 26). . . . If women speak and hear a language of connection and intimacy, while men speak and hear a language of status and independence, then communication between men and women can be like cross-cultural communication, prey to a class of conversational styles. (p. 42)

Studying patterns of intimacy can offer another route to exploring the relational process. Reis and Shaver,[33] doing so in detail (their analysis closely resembles that of Miller[24]), emphasize that "intimacy is a dynamic process whose operation is best observed in the pattern of communication and reaction between two people."[33] Their interactional model omits one important dimension—the sense of agency and empowerment that each person achieves in finding the capacity for giving as well as receiving in a relationship, contributing to the process as well as responding.

Looking at intimacy in terms of emotion and activity, Orosan and Schilling[34] found that

When women described their impressions of intimacy within their relationships, they spoke first about trust, dependency, closeness and self-disclosure, and secondarily about sharing experiences and doing things with the other person. . . . Men in this study tended to describe their experiences of intimacy in their personal relationships primarily by talking about activities and experiences they engaged in with one or more others, and secondarily by describing intimacy as involving trust and closeness. (p. 209)

Bergman,[35] writing about "self-in-relation" from a male perspective, notes that men may strive to be relational and search for intimacy, but that societal messages and developmental hurdles have made it particularly difficult for men to allow themselves to move away from the competitive and hierarchical stance they know.

In sum, these studies lend credence to the theory that women expect to give more in their relationships, that they value their friendships more, that they are capable of giving and receiving in mutual relationships, that they are capable and desirous of greater intimacy.

Yet when a woman strives for intimacy and mutuality, she may be disappointed, whether because her problems interfere with her capacity for intimacy or because she is in a relationship with someone who cannot reciprocate. One can wonder also if women of college age, in late adolescence, carry concepts of intimacy and mutuality that come more from an idealized wish than from genuine experience. What they search for in their relationships, whether intimacy or mutuality, is an elusive quality most often found lacking. And because women's identified role, as society has claimed it, is to be responsible for relationships, women absorb the blame when relationships fail.

Women's Normal Psychological Development

Theorists of this recent relational perspective identify self-esteem and identity for women as growing out of engaging in and facilitating mutual relationships. From birth onward, women grow by and through their connections with other people. "Self-in-relation" theory stresses the interaction between infant and mother and the empowerment that results from feeling one has an impact on the other.[36] It suggests that the infant experiences her effect on her mother, that she already finds the interaction and connection enhancing, and that the engagement is not merely a means to an end but is an end in itself.

Girls are especially encouraged to be sensitive to their emotional interplay with others—mother first, then father and other family members, and ultimately peers. It is not clear how much expectations create the kind of responsiveness seen in infants, toddlers, and young girls, but that kind of sensitivity is seldom encouraged in boys, and those boys who do develop these qualities may be characterized as "Momma's boy," or, in later life, perhaps as "effeminate." Traditionally, boys have been expected to engage in active behavior that demonstrates their independence, and they have been rewarded for taking risks. Girls tend to be more collaborative.[37]

Adolescence is a complex time for a woman. She sees pleasing others as a way to feel affirmed, to be popular, even at the expense of her freedom of expression or achievement.[38] For instance, when a young woman feels that her striving for academic excellence conflicts with her relational needs, she may not yet have the ability to modulate the conflict and will instead opt out of the race. This is the time when girls cease to excel in math and science—fearing that competition with their male classmates will interfere with their friendships, bringing disapproval and, perhaps, rejection.[39]

New research by Gilligan and her colleagues has outlined a major crisis period for girls' entry into adolescence. Adolescent girls are under increased social pressure to accept a view of the world that may contradict their own experience. "If girls know what they know and bring themselves into relationships, they will be in conflict with prevailing authorities. If girls do not know what they know and take themselves out of relationships, they will be in trouble with

→

themselves."[40] Peer pressure on girls emphasizes actions that lead to greater acceptance by boys (or men), and teenage girls are expected to accept the male view. Now, perhaps for the first time, girls discover that the world is not defined by their experience but by a male model. Even more, they find they must submerge those parts of themselves that do not fit the expectations that they sense others have for them. The conflict between what they "should" be and how they see themselves may end with the "suppression of the full participation of the woman's way of seeing and acting."[40] Jack[41] confirms that this loss of voice is experienced by women in adulthood and that it is a major factor in depression. . . .

College Women and Drinking—Facilitating Relationships

The relational model of psychological development can help us understand how and why women's search for mutual and intimate relationships can sometimes go awry. The model can help us understand peer influence on drinking patterns, as well as the external and internal pressures women students encounter in making responsible choices about using alcohol.

In women's attempts to create or find satisfying relationships, especially in their search for intimacy, alcohol may become a vehicle that is readily available and offers the promise of being helpful. As Kilbourne[47] points out, women are constantly bombarded by messages from the media that alcohol is necessary if one is to achieve happiness and success and be attractive to men.

Drinking may start as a way of being with others. For teenagers, peers and peer culture are particularly important—probably more important than family.[10] The need to be accepted does not stop when the young person enters college. The wish to fit in leads most people to adapt to the cultural norms. One college norm may be a certain level of drinking, another may be popularity through cliques or subgroups.

Peer pressure may be overt—a direct request, invitation, or challenge to drink—or it may be covert—the subtle sense that to "belong" means going along with others. A drink or two may make one feel sophisticated, relaxed, and better able to fit in. Relationships may be formed through drinking at parties and other social events. When alcohol is not involved, some relationships survive, others do not.

If a student is with a drinker, she may choose to drink to be companionable. And if she does not drink when others are drinking, she may not only feel isolated or disgusted, but she may also fear ridicule that those who are drinking may think she is a "goody-goody."

To some extent, gender differences in the way peers influence each other's alcohol use follow traditional role delineations. Downs,[48] studying adolescents aged 13 to 17, found

adolescent males exerting control over their social environment, while females are influenced by the environment. These sex differences reflect underlying sex roles in our society. While males are taught to be active, to be independent, and to influence others, females are taught to be passive, to be dependent, and to be influenced by others. These sex differences also reflect the view that females in our society are more sensitive and attentive to interpersonal relationships than are males. Consequently, these sex differences

→

indicate that the present generation of adolescents has not rejected traditional sex roles, at least in regard to peer pressure and alcohol use. (p. 484)

Putting it slightly differently, Berkowitz and Perkins stated that "because of a greater interest in group harmony and cohesion, women may be likely to accommodate group norms and less willing than men are to assert their personal viewpoints and values in group situations."[49] Both of these statements, although they value women's sensitivities, suggest a "weakness" in women that causes them to compromise to maintain the community.

Certainly friendships and affiliation are important, and success in making peer relationships enhances the female student's sense of herself. An additional concern about the young adolescent girl's suppression of her independent voice as she conforms to the expectations of the larger world is sounded by Miller[36] and by Brown and Gilligan's[38] description of girls' entry into adolescence. As they might describe it, she is caught in the struggle to deny unacceptable thoughts and feelings as she makes an effort to appear "nice and kind." It is possible that drinking not only brings a young woman together with others, but that it also helps ease her discomfort with the alienation she may be feeling with herself. In this way, alcohol offers the promise of alleviating the pain.

College Women and Drinking—Hampering Relationships

A woman may start to drink as she seeks to enhance her sense of herself as attractive and as successful in her relationships. If she drinks too much, she achieves the opposite result. It is not easy to understand, or accept, that one's drinking is disturbing to others. It may be more difficult for the drinking woman to admit the impact her drinking has on her relationships. She may drink, or may have started drinking, to facilitate her relationships, so she cannot easily recognize that her drinking interferes with them. Because of the difficulty in acknowledging her responsibility, the drinker may work out another rationale for disconnection or abandonment. If she senses failure in the relationship, she cannot help but feel worse about her relational self as she experiences increasing isolation.[46] Allowing others to see these "failures" is likely to lead her to believe that she will, indeed, be abandoned as completely unworthy.

Surrey[50] describes four components to women's drinking from a relational perspective. Although she may start to drink as a way of feeling energized, loved, or loving, a woman is also likely to turn to alcohol to help her cope with "the impact of nonmutuality, the effects of abuse and violence, the effects of isolation and shaming, and/or the impact of distorted images of self and of relationships." As Surrey describes it, the culture tells her what she should look like, how she should behave, and how she should feel to be "worthy of connection." Alcohol becomes a way to manage or alter the way she believes she looks, acts, and feels.

Popular belief has it that drinking reduces inhibitions. Superficially, alcohol may make communication easier by helping people feel that they are relating better. If a woman feels shy or inhibited in social situations, she may drink too much as she seeks to relax. If a student feels more attractive when she has had a drink, she is also saying that she does not feel at ease with herself when she is sober.

→

Alcohol may help her overcome sexual inhibitions, reduce guilt and conflict over sexual activity, feel more seductive, and believe that she can enjoy sex more. Intoxication usually reduces sexual responsiveness, however, and may confuse cues. Drinking women may have more difficulty distinguishing between real and fantasied feelings of warmth and affection and physiological arousal.[51] Using alcohol to enhance sexual responsiveness is clearly risky. In her search for intimacy or heightened sexuality, a woman may find that too much alcohol dampens her responsiveness and interferes with her judgment. There is a sense, as Sandmaier[52] states, that it is okay to take advantage of a drunk woman. After all, everyone knows that drunk women are sexually "irresponsible."

Sexual overtures are a part of college life and frequently occur when alcohol is present. Women at mixers, fraternity parties, and other social occasions receive many invitations, overt and covert, for sex. Men may find sexual activity without intimacy acceptable, with or without the involvement of alcohol.[53] Women who are in relationships with men may also feel pressure for sex before they are ready. Some will consent, believing it is the only way to keep the man involved. Others will be confused when their intimacy-seeking behavior is misinterpreted as seductive; a man may interpret a woman's desire for a relationship as an invitation to sex—his way of expressing intimacy. Bergman states that "men may use sexuality to try to connect; they can be surprised to find that women may need connection to be fully sexual."[35] Confusing sex and intimacy, a problem for both men and women, is made more serious by alcohol,[13] and drinking too much makes the achievement of mutuality virtually impossible.

Sexual violence on campus is well documented. Benson et al,[54] in a thorough discussion of acquaintance rape, review the statistics, myths, and social expectancies that connect alcohol use and rape. One study of date rape and sexual aggression among college students found that more than 77% of the women (65% during college) and 57% of the men (51% during college) had been involved in some form of "male-against-female sexual aggression," and that 15% of the women had had unwanted sexual intercourse.[55] Risk factors for date rape and sexual aggression were identified as unfamiliar partners; power differential, including age, who paid, and who drove; miscommunication about sex; alcohol or drug use; dating activity or location; and popular myths that assert that women ask for and/or enjoy rape. Ogletree[56] broadening the definition to "sexual coercion" and adding "menacing verbal pressure and misuse of authority" to the normal definitions of rape and attempted rape, found that 42% of the college women sampled had experienced sexual coercion. Alcohol was involved in 31% of these situations. In addition, when a woman has been drinking, her behavior is considered suspect, and she is less likely to be taken seriously if she complains.[57]

Ehrhart and Sandler[58] stress the damage that acquaintance rape has on a woman's ability to trust others and on her own capacity to distinguish who is safe and who is not. Her youth and inexperience increase her vulnerability and offer some men an opportunity to establish their masculinity, they maintain.

Berkowitz[59] discussed the multiplicity of factors involved in the man's role and, like Bergman,[35] found that social factors have had a major impact on how men perceive the use of power and sexuality. Looking more closely at the techniques used by men to obtain sex from an unwilling partner, Gray et al[60] found that lying, or "sexual manipulation," including threats to

→

end the relationship and continuing arguments, were more frequently used than was physical force.

Date rape is an extreme example of relationships gone awry. It is easy to see how good intentions can lead to bad results—how a woman's attempts to make a relationship mutual or intimate can lead to her being abused—or how, whether drinking or not, a woman may stay in a destructive relationship with the hope that, if she can just be a better partner, the other person will stop abusing. It is also natural to assume that she will, subsequently, have far more difficulty in trusting others or engaging in the "relational authenticity" and mutuality described earlier.

Traditionally, it has often been concluded that a woman, whether drinking or not, encouraged or seduced the man she claims raped her. If she was drinking, one can say the rape victim was not thoughtful or prepared and that her judgment and her capacity to resist were diminished. That she may have got high in response to his encouragement seems just another indication of the lengths to which a woman will go to be attractive to a man or to make a relationship work. It is ironic that we risk blaming women for what we want them to be good at. . . .

Summary

Recent theory about women's psychological development contradicts the male-oriented view that autonomy and separation are the signposts of maturity. Instead, we stress the importance of the capacity for creating authentic, mutual relationships in establishing women's identity and self-esteem. These gender distinctions are important in understanding women's use of alcohol.

For college women, drinking is often a way of making friends and of lubricating social interactions, and may also seem helpful in establishing more intimate relationships. Peer influence is a strong persuader. As a woman's sense of herself is organized around her capacity to enter into meaningful, mutual relationships, so her failure to be able to find and maintain such relationships creates pain that, in turn, may lead to depression and/or to the abuse of alcohol. The wish to belong, combined with the avoidance of subjective pain, may push women into excessive drinking.

At the same time, alcohol contributes to many relational failures, and college women who are careless in their use of alcohol may encounter additional problems.

References

1. Gleason N. Prevention of alcohol abuse by women in college: A relational perspective. *J Am Coll Health.* In press.
2. Wilsnack SC, Wilsnack RW. Epidemiology of women's drinking. *J Subst Abuse.* 1991;3:133–157.
3. Engs R, Hanson D. The drinking patterns and problems of college students. *J Alcohol Drug Educ.* 1982;35:65–83.
4. Gomberg ES. *Alcohol and Women.* New Brunswick, NJ: Rutgers University Center of Alcohol Studies Pamphlet Series; 1989.
5. Johnston LD, O'Malley PM, Bachman JG. *Smoking, Drinking, and Illicit Drug Use Among*

⟶

American Secondary School Students, College Students, and Young Adults, 1975–1991. Washington, DC: National Institute on Drug Abuse; 1992.

6. Wechsler H, Isaac N. "Binge" drinkers at Massachusetts colleges: Prevalence, drinking style, time trends, and associated problems. *JAMA.* 1992;267(21):2929-2931.

7. Meilman PW, Stone JE, Gaylor MS, Turco JH. Alcohol consumption by college undergraduates: Current use and 10-year trends. *J Stud Alcohol.* 1990;51(5):389-395.

8. O'Hare TM. Drinking in college: Consumption patterns, problems, sex differences and legal drinking age. *J Stud Alcohol.* 1990;51(6):536-541.

9. Presley CA, Meilman PW. *Alcohol and Drugs on American College Campuses: A Report to College Presidents.* Carbondale: Southern Illinois University; 1992.

10. Berkowitz AD, Perkins HW. Problem drinking among college students: A review of recent research. *J Am Coll Health.* 1986;35(1):21-28.

11. Wechsler H. Summary of literature. *Alcoholism and Alcohol Abuse Among Women: Research Issues.* Research Monograph No. 1. Rockville: US Dept of HEW, ADAMHA; 1980.

12. Perkins HW. Gender patterns in consequences of collegiate alcohol abuse: A 10-year study of trends in an undergraduate population. *J Stud Alcohol.* 1992;53(5):458-462.

13. Abbey M. Acquaintance rape and alcohol consumption on college campuses: How are they linked? *J Am Coll Health.* 1991;39(4):165-169.

14. Stewart M. *Women, Addiction and Trauma: A Model for Recovery.* Northampton, MA: Smith College School for Social Work; 1986. Thesis.

15. *Time Magazine,* January 20, 1992; *Mademoiselle,* February 1992; and many more.

16. Canetto SS. Gender roles, suicide attempts, and substance abuse. *J Psychol.* 1991;125(6):605-620.

17. Johnson PB. Personality correlates of heavy and light drinking female college students. *J Alcohol Drug Educ.* 1989;34(2):33-37.

18. Bailly RC, Carman RS, Forslund MA. Gender differences in drinking motivations and outcomes. *J Psychol.* 1991;125(6):649-656.

19. Jones MC. Personality antecedents and correlates of drinking patterns in women. *J Couns Clin Psychol.* 1971;36(1):61-69.

20. Miller JB. *Toward a New Psychology of Women,* 2nd ed. Boston: Beacon Press; 1986.

21. Gilligan C. *In a Different Voice: Psychological Theory and Women's Development.* Cambridge: Harvard University Press; 1982.

22. Belenky MF, Clinchy BM, Goldberger NR, Tarule JM. *Women's Ways of Knowing: The Development of Self, Voice and Mind.* New York: Basic Books; 1986.

23. Jordan JV, Kaplan AG, Miller JB, Stiver IP, Surrey JL. *Women's Growth in Connection.* New York: Guilford Press; 1991.

24. Miller JB. What do we mean by relationships? *Work in Progress #22.* Wellesley, MA: Stone Center; 1986.

25. Jordan J. The meaning of mutuality. In: Jordan JV, Kaplan AG, Miller JB, Stiver IP, Surrey JL, eds. *Women's Growth in Connection.* New York: Guilford Press; 1991:81-96.

26. Genero NP, Miller JB, Surrey J, Baldwin LM. Measuring perceived mutuality in close relationships: Validation of the Mutual Psychological Development Questionnaire. *J Fam Psychol.* 1992;6(1):36-48.

27. Bell RR. Friendships of women and men. *Psychol Women Q.* 1981;5(3):402-417.

28. Duck S, Wright PH. Re-examining gender differences in same-gender friendships: A close look at two kinds of data. In: Duck S, Wright PH, eds. *Sex Roles.* 1993;28:709-727.

⟶

29. De Vries B, Parker S. Men's and women's friendships with men and women. Presented at the International Network Conference on Personal Relationships. Vancouver, BC; 1991.

30. Brehm SS. *Intimate Relationships.* New York: Random House; 1985.

31. Surrey JL. The "self-in-relation": A theory of women's development. In: Jordan JV, Kaplan AG, Miller JB, Stiver IP, Surrey JL, eds. *Women's Growth in Connection.* New York: Guilford Press; 1991:51–67.

32. Tannen D. *You Just Don't Understand: Women and Men in Conversation.* New York: Morrow; 1990.

33. Reis HT, Shaver P. Intimacy as an interpersonal process. In: Duck S, ed. *Handbook of Personal Relationships.* New York: Wiley; 1988:367–390.

34. Orosan PG, Schilling KM. Gender differences in college students' definitions and perceptions of intimacy. *Women & Therapy.* 1992;12(1/2):201–212.

35. Bergman S. Men's psychological development: A relational perspective. *Work in Progress #48.* Wellesley, MA: Stone Center; 1991.

36. Miller JB. The development of women's sense of self. In: Jordan JV, Kaplan AG, Miller JB, Stiver IP, Surrey JL, eds. *Women's Growth in Connection.* New York: Guilford Press; 1991:11–26.

37. Lever J. Sex differences in the complexity of children's play and games. *Am Sociol Rev.* 1978;43:471–483.

38. Brown LM, Gilligan C. The psychology of women and the development of girls. Presented at the Laurel-Harvard Conference on the Psychology of Women and the Education of Girls. Cleveland, OH; April 1990.

39. Balkin J. Contributions of friends to women's fear of success in college. *Psychol Rep.* 1987;61:39–42.

40. Gilligan C. Joining the resistance: Psychology, politics, girls and women. *Mich Q Rev.* 1990;29(4):501–536.

41. Jack DC. *Silencing the Self: Women and Depression.* Cambridge: Harvard University Press; 1991. . . .

46. Kaplan AG. The "self-in-relation": Implications for depression in women. In: Jordan JV, Kaplan AG, Miller JB, Stiver IP, Surrey JL, eds. *Women's Growth in Connection.* New York: Guilford Press; 1991:206–222.

47. Kilbourne J. *Calling the Shots: The Advertising of Alcohol* [film and videotape]. Cambridge, MA: Cambridge Documentary Films; 1982, 1991.

48. Downs WR. Using panel data to examine sex differences in causal relationships among adolescent alcohol use, norms, and peer alcohol use. *J Youth Adoles.* 1985;14(6):469–486.

49. Berkowitz AD, Perkins HW. Recent research on gender differences in collegiate alcohol use. *J Am Coll Health.* 1987; 36(2):123–129.

50. Surrey J. Women, addiction and codependency. Presented at the Stone Center Colloquium, Wellesley, MA, February 6, 1991.

51. Wilsnack SC. Drinking, sexuality, and sexual dysfunction in women. In: Wilsnack SC, Beckman LJ, eds. *Alcohol Problems in Women.* New York: Guilford Press; 1984:189–227.

52. Sandmaier M. *The Invisible Alcoholics—Women and Alcohol Abuse in America.* New York: McGraw-Hill; 1980.

53. Leigh BC, Aramburu B, Norris J. The morning after: Gender differences in attributions about alcohol-related sexual encounters. *J Appl Soc Psychol.* 1992;22(5):343–357.

⟶

54. Benson D, Charlton C, Goodhart F. Acquaintance rape on campus: A literature review. *J Am Coll Health.* 1992;40(4):157–165.

55. Muehlenhard CL, Linton MA. Date rape and sexual aggression in dating situations: Incidence and risk factors. *J Couns Psychol.* 1987;34(2):186–196.

56. Ogletree RJ. Sexual coercion experience and help-seeking behavior of college women. *J Am Coll Health.* 1993;41(4):149–153.

57. Norris J, Cubbins LA. Dating, drinking, and rape: Effects of victim's and assailant's alcohol consumption on judgments of their behavior and traits. *Psychol Women Q.* 1992; 16(2):179–191.

58. Ehrhart JK, Sandler BR. Campus gang rape: Party games? *Project on the Status and Education of Women.* Washington, DC: Association of American Colleges; 1985.

59. Berkowitz A. College men as perpetrators of acquaintance rape and sexual assault: A review of recent research. *J Am Coll Health.* 1992;40(4):175–181.

60. Gray MD, Lesser D, Rebach H, Hooks B, Bounds C. Sexual aggression and victimization: A local perspective. *Response.* 1988;11(3):9–13.

Questions for Analysis

1. Describe the use of alcohol at your college. Is it widespread? Is it excessive? Have you had any personal experience with alcohol at college?

2. Using these articles and your own experience as resources, analyze the reasons that many college students drink too much.

3. Identify three approaches that you believe would be most effective in solving this problem, and explain the reasons why you suggested them.

4. According to some college administrators alcohol is still the No. 1 source of discipline problems and other emotional or physical problems on campus. Describe some of the negative effects of drinking that you have observed at your college.

Learning to Learn

Learning Over Time
Cramming

Linguistic
Visual
Experiential

Inductive
Deductive

Detail-oriented
Pattern-Seeking

YOUR LEARNING PERSONALITY

Careful Preparation
Immediate Action

Traditional
Innovative

Authoritative
Individualistic
Collaborative

Systematic
Spontaneous

Thinker's Guide to Successful Learning

Stage 1: Learning Goals
Stage 2: Learning Environment
Stage 3: Learning Schedule
Stage 4: Learning Approaches

From before the time you took your first step and said your first word, you have been learning. Your learning experiences have continued throughout your life. For example, describe on the lines below something that you learned in the last several days. Be specific.

_____

_____

_____

_____

Now think about *how* you learned this. Was it information that someone told you or that you read—for example, a new topic presented in one of your classes? Was it an event that you witnessed—someone you don't know well doing an unexpectedly thoughtful favor for you? Was it an activity that you learned by doing—a new dance step or basketball shot? Was it an idea that you understood through a discussion with someone else—developing new insight into the concept of "freedom"? Explain in the lines below exactly *how* you learned what you described above:

_____

_____

_____

_____

While the instruction of knowledgeable people is essential, you also need to learn independently by thinking, reflecting, and experimenting on your own.

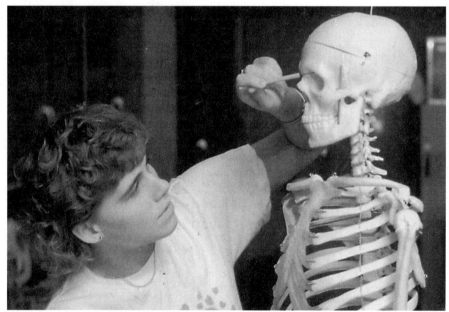

Although human beings are natural learners, most of us have spent little time trying to understand exactly how we learn best. Yet in order to be successful in college and your career (as well as in your personal life), it is essential that you become the most effective learner possible. You can accomplish this goal by *thinking critically* about the learning process in order to understand how it operates, and then *practicing* the principles you have learned in order to improve your performance. Begin this investigation by reflecting on your history as a learner. Think about the most stimulating and satisfying learning experiences that you have ever had. In the space provided below, briefly identify three such memorable learning experiences in the areas of education, skills, and human relationships.

Education learning experience: _____

_____

Skills learning experience: _____

_____

Human relationship learning experience: _____

_____

Thinking Activity 4.1

1. For each of the learning experiences that you identified, describe the experience from the moment that you first began your learning efforts to the point when you completed your goal or developed a proficiency.

2. For each of the learning experiences that you identified, analyze your learning process. What strategies or approaches did you use? Did you learn from reading or watching video? Did you do a lot of experimenting, using "trial and error"? Did other people help you? If so, what approaches did they use to help you learn? Once you began the learning process, how did you continue to improve your skills or refine your performance?

Your Learning "Personality"

The learning experiences that you described in the Thinking Activity reveal not only areas in which you enjoy learning; they also express the *approaches* to learning that you are inclined to take. In the same way that each of us has our own unique personality, we each have our own distinctive approaches to learning. Although there are general principles for effective learning that are valid for almost everyone, we must also recognize our own individual learning "personality." By combining well-established learning principles with an understanding of your own distinctive learning personality, you are able to maximize your effectiveness as a learner.

Teachers are extraor-
dinary learning
resources who are
devoted to helping
students develop
important insights
and abilities. In addi-
tion to taking their
courses, you should
speak with them, ask
questions, and seek
their counsel.

*Thinking
Activity
4.2*

Carefully review your analysis of the learning experiences that you described
above, and think about your *learning approaches* that characterize you as a
learner. The following statements reflect examples of various learning
approaches. Check the statements that most directly apply to you. For each
statement checked, provide an example from the learning experiences you
described above.

1. I learn best using language: reading appropriate material or having
    people explain things to me. *Example:* _____

    _____

2. I often need pictures, illustrations, or diagrams to really grasp what I am
    trying to learn: "A picture is worth a thousand words!" *Example:* _____

    _____

3. I learn best by actually *doing* things, using my hands and body to get
    totally involved in the learning process. *Example:* _____

    _____

4. Before I get started in a learning situation, I like to carefully prepare by
    gathering information and researching the task. *Example:* _____

    _____

    ⟶

5. I like to plunge into a learning situation as soon as possible and learn as I try things out. *Example:* _____

_____

6. I tend to work through learning situations in a very systematic, well-organized way, developing a logical plan of action. *Example:* _____

_____

7. I generally approach learning situations in a very spontaneous and flexible way, working through things in a thoughtful but not always logical sequence. *Example:* _____

_____

8. I enjoy having someone who is very knowledgeable teach me something new. *Example:* _____

_____

9. I enjoy teaching myself new things, learning through my own trial and error. *Example:* _____

_____

10. I like to work collaboratively with other people in learning situations so that we can all learn from one another. *Example:* _____

_____

11. When I learn something new, I like to use well-established methods that have been proven effective and are guaranteed to get the job done. *Example:* _____

_____

12. In learning situations, I am always trying to think of new or more effective ways to accomplish the task at hand, even though it means I sometimes make mistakes. *Example:* _____

_____

13. When learning something new, I pay a great deal of attention to the details of what I am learning, and I am very precise in the understanding I develop. *Example:* _____

_____

14. I approach learning situations in a very conceptual way, looking for general patterns, exploring various possibilities, and trying to develop novel strategies. *Example:* _____

_____

→

15. I prefer to learn in shorter time blocks, beginning well in advance of the exam or project due date. *Example:* _____

_____

16. I learn best by concentrating my efforts at the last minute, working intensely just before the exam or project due date. *Example:* _____

_____

17. I like to master the facts and examples of a situation before I reach a general conclusion. *Example:* _____

_____

18. In learning situations, I like to develop a general hypothesis as soon as possible and then test it out with specific examples. *Example:* _____

Your responses reveal the nature of your learning personality, your particular approach to learning situations. By understanding the approach you use to learn most effectively, you can refine your approach and consciously apply it to new, challenging situations. Just as important, you can become more familiar with other learning approaches that you tend *not* to use and make a conscious effort to employ them in appropriate situations in order to become a more versatile, flexible learner. Similarly, increasing your knowledge of the diverse array of learning approaches helps you better understand the various approaches other people use to learn—their unique learning personalities. This knowledge is particularly important if you are working collaboratively on a project or trying to teach someone else.

Using your responses to the statements in Thinking Activity 4.2 as a guide, create a learning portrait of yourself by describing yourself as directed.

Learning Portrait

I am the kind of learner who _____

_____

_____

_____

_____

_____

If you examine the statements in Thinking Activity 4.2 carefully, you can see that they all reflect important approaches to learning. Although we each have our own individual learning personality that reflects our learning preferences and habits, the fact is that we use all of the approaches described above, depending on the learning situation in which we are involved. Let's take a closer look at these various dimensions of the learning process.

Linguistic Versus *Visual* Versus *Experiential (Kinesthetic) Learning*

1. I learn best using language: reading appropriate material or having people explain things to me.

2. I often need pictures, illustrations, or diagrams to really grasp what I am trying to learn: "A picture is worth a thousand words!"

3. I learn best by actually doing things, using my hands and body to get totally involved in the learning process.

Although each of us has preferred approaches to learning, the most successful learners are able to use a variety of learning techniques. The same is true with the learning approaches embodied in these three statements. The most effective learning involves using language, visual media, and "hands-on" experiences in an integrated way. For example, imagine that you are faced with the task of negotiating a biology course that contains a great deal of factual material, challenging concepts, technical vocabulary, and complex models describing the way biological systems function. How should you approach it? For most people, the most successful approach will involve using an integrated set of language, visual, and hands-on methods that might include the following:

- Completing all reading assignments on time, making annotations in the book, and taking notes that highlight important points and identify unanswered questions (linguistic).

- Listening carefully to classes; taking precise, well-organized notes; participating in class discussions; and asking questions that arose during the reading (linguistic).

- Creating thinking maps that illustrate the relationships between important concepts in the course (visual).

- Creating diagrams that illustrate the functioning of various biological systems (visual).

- Reading and studying in conjunction with examining photographs and illustrations (visual).

- Creating physical models of various biological systems with cardboard or household materials, and recording technical vocabulary on the models (experiential).

- Spending extra time in the biology laboratory exploring actual specimens (experiential).

Using these learning modalities in combination is synergistic, because the different approaches enhance and strengthen each other. For example, I took a course several years ago in cardio-pulmonary resuscitation (CPR), scheduled for

Approaches to Learning:
Although every person has preferred approaches to learning, the most successful learners are able to use a variety of learning techniques, including language, visual media, and "hands-on" experiences.

two 3-hour sessions. The first session was very linguistically and visually oriented. We listened to a lecture, saw a film, and took reading material home that explained the details of CPR. After studying the materials, I was convinced that I knew everything I needed about CPR. When we walked in for the second session, we saw a number of rubber human dummies on the floor. During this session, we were presented with various scenarios, then were expected to *perform* the appropriate CPR procedure on our dummy. It wasn't long before there were a number of living human dummies down there with the rubber dummies, for the "knowledge" that we thought we had evaporated when we needed to apply it to actual situations. The lesson I learned was that there are often different forms of knowledge of the same thing, in this case an analytical knowledge of CPR and a practical knowledge of CPR. To really know something we have to learn it in all of its various forms: linguistic, visual, experiential.

In your academic studies you should also seek to learn by using a variety of different forms. For example, if you are studying molecular structures in chemistry, you could use physical models of the molecules to supplement textbook and lecture study. By manipulating these models to simulate the various molecular structures and transformations, you could tie them into your knowledge framework in diverse ways, not just analytically. Biology professor Fred Janzow, of Southeast Missouri State University, actually uses students in the class to replicate organic compounds, and then has the students "dance" to simulate the chemical transformations. This sort of multisensory approach to learning is extremely effective, an approach expressed in the statement by the ancient Greek playwright Sophocles: "Knowledge must come through action."

Thinking Application

Focus your attention on this section (pages 121-137), which deals with various approaches to learning. Design a plan for learning these ideas that uses all three learning modalities: linguistic, visual, and experiential.

Careful Preparation Versus *Immediate Action*

4. Before I get started in a learning situation, I like to carefully prepare by gathering information and researching the task.

5. I like to plunge into a learning situation as soon as possible and learn as I try things out.

Although you may find that one of these statements expresses your preferred mode of approaching learning situations, being comfortable with both of these is valuable. For example, if you are trying to decide whether you should undergo elective surgery for chronic back pain, it makes sense to learn as much as possible before reaching a decision. On the other hand, if you are confronted with a medical emergency, such as someone who is not breathing, there is no time to do research—you have to jump in and try to learn as you act. Similarly, in college, there will be learning situations in which you will want to take your time gathering information—such as working on a research paper. There will also be times in which you will need to plunge into the task and learn as you try things out—for example, developing a procedure in chemistry lab or writing a computer program. As a critical thinker, you will need to determine which of these approaches is most appropriate and then use it.

Thinking Application

Decide whether you tend toward "careful preparation" or "immediate action" in learning situations. Then select a learning situation you will be involved in during the next several days, and consciously use the approach you are less familiar with.

Systematic Versus *Spontaneous*

6. I tend to work through learning situations in a very systematic, well-organized way, developing a logical plan of action.

7. I generally approach learning situations in a very spontaneous and flexible way, working through things in a thoughtful but not always logical sequence.

Although most people tend to approach learning situations from one of the two directions embodied in these statements, the most powerful learners integrate these approaches. For example, when you are preparing for an exam, it makes sense to approach this task in a systematic, organized way. Your plan of action should include the following:

■ Identifying the information/skills that you will be responsible for.

■ Prioritizing the material: identifying which content is essential, very important, fairly important, marginal, and unimportant.

■ Developing a study plan that involves reviewing course material as well as creating study notes summarizing the material and reorganizing it into an intelligible form.

■ Creating a study schedule that gives you the opportunity to learn the material over a period of time, not "cram" it all in at the last minute.

These guidelines represent a very sound and well-organized approach to studying for exams. However, the most effective learners use an organized plan like this as a foundation, but approach it in a flexible and more spontaneous way. For example, in arranging material for study, they might develop innovative diagrams that personalize the material. Or instead of reviewing the material and study notes in a strict order, they might move around in a more flexible way, return to particularly challenging areas, devise revised notes and diagrams, and create unusual study strategies (such as making study tapes to listen to when commuting to and from school). In other words, an effective learner *thinks critically* about the learning task—devising a thoughtful study plan, but using it in a creative way that fits into the specific task. These study issues will be explored more thoroughly in other chapters, such as Chapter Five, "Mastering Tests."

Thinking Application

Select a quiz, text, or project that you have to prepare for during the next week. Follow the general study approach described above as a foundation, but make a conscious effort to adapt it in creative and spontaneous ways.

Authoritative Versus *Individualistic* Versus *Collaborative*

8. I enjoy having someone who is very knowledgeable teach me something new.

9. I enjoy teaching myself new things, learning through my own trial and error.

10. I like to work collaboratively with other people in learning situations so that we can all learn from one another.

Learning can be a very social or a very solitary activity, depending on the learning situation and learning personality. As children, we experienced all the basic ways of learning. Our parents and other authority figures were enormously influential in shaping our knowledge of the world. We also learned on our own, learning to walk, along with countless other discoveries developed through trial and error. As we got older, we spent more time with people our own age, and these peer relationships played an increasingly dominant role in our education. Each of these forms of learning is important; as we matured, however, we may have developed a preference for one or the other.

Learning from authorities, people who are particularly knowledgeable in a given area, is invaluable. The whole idea of a college education is based on the concept that people who have devoted their lives to mastering a certain area of knowledge or skill can communicate their insights to their students. In this sense, teachers are extraordinary resources. Most are devoted to helping

When people are working together as a group—a "learning community"—they all learn much more than will a group of isolated individuals trying to learn solely from the professor and the textbook.

students learn important things, and you should not only take their courses, but speak with them, ask questions, and seek their counsel. Of course, you should not accept the opinions of authorities without question. Experts often have contrasting perspectives and disagree with one another. In the final analysis, you need to *think critically* about the information being presented to you and then reach your own well-reasoned conclusions. This is true whether the source of the information is a parent, a teacher, an employer, a friend, a doctor, or a person telling your fortune!

Individual learning should play an important part in your life as well. While the instruction of knowledgeable people is essential, you also need to learn by thinking, reflecting, and experimenting on your own. If you are too dependent on the instruction of others, then you risk not developing your own well-formed, independent perspective on the world. On the other hand, if you are too individualistic in your learning approach, then you risk having a perspective that is limited and narrow, lacking the richness provided by others' knowledge and experience. The synthesis you should be trying to achieve is the result of learning all you can from others, but then thinking through things in order to develop a perspective that is truly your own.

The final piece of this particular puzzle is the learning that you can achieve from your peers. While we are generally willing to listen to our peers in informal situations, we often tend to disregard their opinions in the classroom setting, preferring to focus our attention on the teaching of the professor. However, the informed opinions of your peers represent a valuable source of learning. Your peers often have expertise, pertinent experiences, and insights that you can profit from. Be prepared to listen seriously and consider their views, relating their comments to the course material and your own perspective—and be willing to share your views and experiences as well. When people are working together as a group (a "learning community"), they all learn much more than will a group of isolated individuals trying to learn solely from the professor and the textbook. There is extraordinary energy and focus created when people work as a team, with the resulting whole being much greater than the sum of the individual parts. Of course, specific skills and strategies are required to best learn in a collaborative fashion, and we will be exploring these more fully in such subsequent chapters as Chapter Eight, "Discussing and Debating."

Thinking Application

Identify a course that you are currently taking which you find very challenging. How have you been approaching the course material? Focusing on the lectures and readings? Trying to think through the course material on your own? Working collaboratively with others? Develop a plan to strengthen the modes of learning that you are not fully using.

Traditional Versus *Innovative*

11. When I learn something new, I like to use well-established methods that have been proven effective and are guaranteed to get the job done.

12. In learning situations, I am always trying to think of new or more effective ways to accomplish the task at hand, even though it means I sometimes make mistakes.

Once again, these two approaches to learning are not in competition with each other, but instead work better when integrated in a harmonious partnership. On the one hand, there are many established insights regarding the learning process that are based on research and the experiences of people in diverse contexts. This book is a guide to knowledge about successful learning, and in this sense there is no point in "reinventing the wheel."

On the other hand, each person and each learning situation are unique, to which general learning principles must be custom tailored if they are to fit properly. And *you* are the "tailor," the individual who must think critically about yourself, the learning task, and your acquired knowledge about the learning process. By thinking critically about your unique situation, you can create the most effective approaches to mastering the challenge that is required. No predetermined recipe supplied by someone else can do this for you. You are responsible for planning your approaches to learning, evaluating their effectiveness, and continually trying to improve or refine your success.

Of course, whenever you try new ideas, there are bound to be mistakes, in the same way that departing from established recipes may sometimes lead to surprise results in the kitchen. But as critical thinkers, we can learn from our mistakes and end up with innovative results that significantly improve on traditional approaches.

Thinking Application

Carefully review the study approaches that you are using in your classes. Are they yielding the most successful results? If not, see if you can devise creative modifications for improving their effectiveness. Don't be afraid to try out new, untested ideas.

Detail-Oriented Versus *Pattern-Seeking*

13. When learning something new, I pay a great deal of attention to the details of what I am learning, and I am very precise in the understanding I develop.

14. I approach learning situations in a very conceptual way, looking for general patterns, exploring various possibilities, and trying to develop novel strategies.

One difference between successful and unsuccessful students lies in mastering the details of learning situations. Since learning the details is usually time-consuming and frustrating, many students simply don't bother. For example, when successful students complete essay exams or write papers, their responses are knowledgeable, articulate, and specific. On the other hand, the responses of less successful students are typically vague and unsubstantiated. To succeed at college, it is important to learn the course material in a deep and meaningful way, then express your understanding clearly and specifically. These are skills that we will be exploring in Chapter 7, "Writing Effectively."

Although mastering the details of a learning situation is vital, it is not sufficient. We also need to understand how these details are related, the overall context in which they exist. This is the meaning of the expression "You can't see the forest for the trees." Sometimes we can become so immersed in the details of a situation that we fail to see the overall patterns that relate these details, a perspective that can only be achieved by stepping back and examining the whole. For example, students often spend time trying to learn the facts of a course such as history, but they fail to understand how these facts were developed. Every discipline is a thinking activity, a dynamic structure of concepts and methods of inquiry used to organize experience, approach problems, and give explanations. From this perspective, instead of simply learning the facts and theories of history, students should seek to understand how a historian perceives the world. In other words, rather than simply trying to memorize the important facts about the immigration of people from various cultures to the United States, or the changing structure and role of the family in the last fifty years, students should try to understand the ways that historians view the processes that they believe caused these events to occur. By embedding historical facts in this sort of conceptual framework and developing the critical thinking skills that historians use, students learn history in a deep and meaningful way, not simply to "get the facts." And when you learn history—or any subject—in this way, it is much easier to learn the facts, because the facts are a part of an overall picture that makes sense to you. For example, you can remember many facts about the history of your family, because these facts are part of a general picture with which you are familiar. However, it would be much more difficult for someone unfamiliar with your family history to learn and remember this information, because it is not connected to the same framework. One modern historian summed up this perspective on learning history with the statement "If you can memorize it, it isn't history!"

In addition to understanding how individual disciplines function, you need to develop insight into the interrelationships among the various disciplines. For example, making sense of a historical event is enriched by bringing in the perspectives of other disciplines—for example,

- ■ theories of group motivation from social psychology
- ■ the literature, art, and music produced during this period

- the philosophical/religious ideas that influenced people's concepts of themselves and their relationships with others
- the influence of the natural environment and physical events
- the economic context and political situation

In short, much of your higher education has to do with using the analytical power of the academic disciplines to understand relationships among people, ideas, and the natural world.

Thinking Application

When you read the article and answer the related questions at the end of this chapter, pay particular attention to the facts in the article and the larger patterns that connect the facts. Apply this same approach to the courses that you take: always try to place facts and details within the context of larger thinking patterns that relate the facts to one another and give them meaning.

Learning Over Time Versus Cramming

15. I prefer to learn in shorter time blocks, beginning well in advance of the exam or project due date.
16. I learn best by concentrating my efforts at the last minute, working intensely just before the exam or project due date.

These two statements reflect an age-old debate among college students: Is it better to learn gradually over time, or "cram" it all in right before the exam is to be taken or the project is due? Most people will acknowledge that learning over time is a more effective approach, but the truth is that most of us spend a lot of time cramming at the last minute. Why does this occur? For starters, there is the widespread inclination of people to procrastinate, putting off unpleasant or challenging tasks until the last possible minute. In addition, there is the sense that concentrating our learning right before the deadline is more efficient: the knowledge is "fresher," and the amount of time we spend may be less than the total spent studying over time. Sometimes cramming is unavoidable when exams and project deadlines are concentrated together or when you encounter unexpected difficulties that affect your schedule.

There is no question that cramming is successful to a certain degree. You often are able to learn much of what you are supposed to, or produce a fairly decent paper, by focusing your energies right before the deadline. However, there are serious drawbacks to cramming as well. To begin with, the "knowledge" that you gain through cramming is generally in your possession for only a very short time because it hasn't been truly integrated into your

Cramming vs. Learning Over Time:
Instead of cramming, the most effective learning and highest quality work takes place over time, when our minds have an opportunity to process what we are learning and to produce our most thoughtful and polished work.

framework of understanding in a deep, meaningful fashion. Instead, what you have "learned" is attached in a superficial way, and your ability to recall and use the material quickly erodes. Because you haven't really learned the material deeply and significantly, you cannot use it in other courses or in your life in general.

A second disadvantage to cramming is that you rarely produce your best work when you have saved things until the last minute. Although you may be working with fierce concentration and adrenaline-fueled energy, you almost always are left with the feeling that you could have done better if you had more time. The most effective learning and highest quality work take place over time, when our minds have an opportunity to process what we are learning and to produce our most thoughtful and polished work.

Thinking Application

Select a quiz, exam, or project that is due in the next several weeks. Begin preparing much earlier than you would normally, and continue to work for at least a short period of time each day until the project is complete or you reach the deadline. Evaluate the results of this approach, and compare it to your normal study approach.

Inductive Versus *Deductive*

17. I like to master the facts and examples of a situation before I reach a general conclusion.

18. In learning situations, I like to develop a general theory or hypothesis as soon as possible and then test it out with specific examples.

The learning approaches expressed in these two statements are partners, working together to help you make sense of the world. Whether you begin with the general idea and try to identify specific examples, or start with specific instances and work toward a general idea, you need to deal with both learning dimensions. For example, imagine that in one of your courses over half of the students are failing. What's going on? Two different approaches should lead to a comparable understanding. You could use inductive reasoning by interviewing all of the failing students and then developing a general hypothesis that explains the high failure rate. Or you could use deductive reasoning by beginning with a general hypothesis—for example, "many students did not have the academic preparation required for this course"—and then interviewing students to see if your hypothesis is accurate. If your hypothesis does not explain the data, you can develop a different hypothesis and then test it by using the same approach.

This reasoning process will be explored in more depth in Chapter 9, "Reasoning Logically."

The point is that learning in this fashion involves both developing a general hypothesis *and* looking for specific examples to prove (or disprove) your hypothesis. Where you begin depends upon your critical analysis of the situation as well as your individual learning personality. Similarly, much of your academic study is involved with learning new concepts ("entropy," "ambivalence," "existentialism," "factor," "hypercard"). Learning a new concept involves both the inductive process of *generalizing,* in which you try to determine the general qualities that define the concept by examining examples, and the deductive process of *interpreting*, in which you look for specific examples of a general concept. For instance, you could try to understand the concept of "ambivalence" by examining examples of ambivalent situations and then *generalizing* the common qualities these examples exhibit. Or you could begin with what we believe is a general quality of this concept—"simultaneously experiencing two or more conflicting emotions towards someone or something"—and then look for examples that illustrate this general quality (*interpreting*). Whether we begin with the process of *generalizing* or *interpreting*, we ultimately have to involve both of these processes interactively in order to develop a clear and comprehensive concept. We will examine this process of "conceptualizing" more thoroughly in Chapter 6, "Reading Critically."

Thinking Application

To see the conceptualizing process in action, read the short essay titled "College Friends," which begins on page 150, and then answer the following questions, using the processes of generalizing and interpreting.

List the general defining qualities of the concept of "friend."

Identify some examples of friendships in your life.

1. _____   1. _____
2. _____   2. _____
3. _____   3. _____
4. _____   4. _____

Creating a Learning Portrait

Carefully examine the diagram on page 136 that illustrates the various learning approaches we have been exploring in this section. Using your responses to the questions in Thinking Activity 4.2 as a guide, fill in the appropriate circles to best describe your approach to learning.

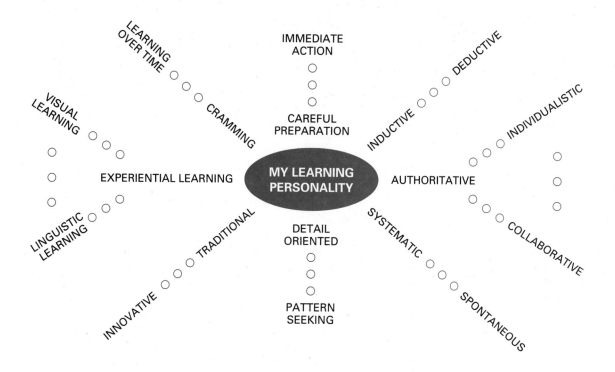

Thinking Activity 4.3

Write a two-page paper in which you thoughtfully consider your approach to learning. Identify the specific learning approaches that you are most comfortable with, and provide some examples of how you use them to learn in different areas of your life. Then identify the specific learning approaches that you are least comfortable with, and describe strategies you can use to improve your proficiency with these approaches. Provide some specific examples.

In the quest to become an expert learner, getting familiar with your learning personality is only part of the answer. You also have to develop an understanding of the general learning principles that are effective for most people. By integrating your unique learning personality with these general learning principles, you can become the most powerful learner possible. This means that you have to *think critically* about each learning situation and devise the most effective approach for yourself in that circumstance. Let's explore a powerful and flexible model for studying that you can adapt successfully for use in a wide variety of learning situations.

The Thinker's Guide to Successful Learning

"Why do I have to improve my learning methods? After all, I did all right in high school with my own approach to learning." This is a very reasonable question, but the fact is that college is a very different place from high school. The caliber of the students in your classes is probably better than you encountered in high school, and the expectations of your professors are higher. The students who are most interested in learning and developing their minds are naturally the ones who typically enroll in college, making the competition stiffer than you previously experienced. And you will likely find that your college courses are more challenging than those you took in high school. Not only will you be expected to do *more* work in your courses; you will also be expected to do this work at a higher level: to read more insightfully, to write more analytically, to think more critically. It makes sense to develop the study and learning approaches that will help you meet these new challenges.

The learning model that we will be using is both effective and versatile, since it can be applied to a wide variety of learning situations. It is based on substantive research in the field of human learning, and it incorporates the key learning insights that we have been analyzing in this chapter. "The Thinker's Guide to Successful Learning" consists of four stages, illustrated below. It is designed to help you achieve the maximum results from your natural learning talents. Naturally, this model is not a recipe or a formula. Instead, it is a dynamic approach designed to be used in an integrated and flexible way, as you think critically about your learning goals and devise strategies for meeting these goals.

The Thinker's Guide to Successful Learning

Stage 1—**Learning Goals:** What do I need to know or learn to do, and how can I motivate myself?

Stage 2—**Learning Environment:** Where will my learning take place?

Stage 3—**Learning Schedule:** How will I organize my learning preparation?

Stage 4—**Learning Approaches:** What learning approaches will I use?

Stage 1. Learning Goals: What do I need to know or learn to do, and how can I motivate myself?

This stage represents the first fork in the road that sends successful and unsuccessful learners in different directions. Successful learners specify the learning goals that they are trying to achieve. By detailing your goals, you are better able to stay on course, use time efficiently, and avoid wasted efforts. The place to begin establishing goals is with your professor. If you are preparing for a quiz or exam, you want to ask questions like these:

- What material will I be held responsible for, and in what detail?
- How will the quiz/exam be structured?
- What are sample questions and examples of exemplary responses?
- What criteria will be used to evaluate responses?

The answers to these questions will determine the nature of your preparation. There is no point in preparing for an essay exam if the test is going to require short answers or multiple choice. And it doesn't make sense to spend a lot of time studying material that will be dealt with only marginally on the exam. Instead, you want to focus your attention on the areas that will form the core of the exam. Although these points seem obvious, many students waste countless hours and perform less successfully than they should because they don't establish clear and appropriate learning goals. We will be examining the whole area of test taking in depth and detail in Chapter 5, "Mastering Tests."

Similarly, when you are preparing for a paper or an oral presentation, you need to ask questions like these:

- What is the suggested length?
- How should the paper/presentation be structured?
- What are examples of papers/presentations that the professor considers exemplary, and what accounts for their high quality?
- What approaches does the professor recommend in writing the paper or preparing for the oral presentation?

If professors do not volunteer this sort of information, then you should ask them either in class or after. Most professors are responsive to intelligent questions as long as they don't sink to the level of "What's going to be on the exam?" The subjects of writing papers and making oral presentations are addressed extensively in Chapter 7, "Writing Effectively," and Chapter 8, "Discussing and Debating."

Although it certainly makes sense to begin connecting your learning goals to the professor's expectations, you should also consider what *your* real learning goals are. After all, the ultimate purpose of your education is not simply to earn good grades, but to acquire the knowledge and develop the abilities you will need to be successful in your career and life in general. These aims may go beyond what the professor expects, but that should not prevent you from working to achieve these significant personal goals. And in many ways, your becoming aware of your real goals is one of the keys to studying with optimal motivation and enthusiasm. You can even go to the extent of visualizing your life in the future and envisioning how what you are learning will contribute to your success.

Thinking Activity 4.4

Think carefully about the courses you are currently taking. For each course, describe your personal learning goals that go beyond "learning the material" or "getting an A." Consider, for example, how your experiences in the course could be meaningful and useful to you in the years ahead, in your career, your personal life, or the general quality of your thinking.

Stage 2. Learning Environment: Where will my learning take place?

Where you learn plays a crucial role in *how well* you learn. You can think of your mind as a highly sophisticated, precision machine that requires a suitable environment in order to ensure optimal performance. Although your mind can

For optimal learning, you need to study in an environment where you can concentrate all of your mental powers on the learning at hand, without distractions or interruptions.

function in the midst of distractions, the truth is that it will not usually function very well. For optimal performance, you need to study in an environment where you can concentrate all of your mental powers on the learning task at hand, without distractions or interruptions. My preference has always been to work in the library: it is quiet; the chairs are not very comfortable (making it more difficult to doze or daydream); you are surrounded with other people who are engaged in similar pursuits; and there are a limited number of ways in which you can waste time. Home, on the other hand, is a den of temptation and distraction. Often there are other people to engage our attention, a more pleasurable alternative to working our brain. Then there is the television, filled with programming that appears irresistible when compared to the rigors of learning. (You can never tell what bargains you might be missing on the Home Shopping Network!) The telephone is sort of an electronic Venus's-flytrap, connecting us to virtually everyone we have known in our lives. And when we start to get a little sleepy, a typical effect of studying for fifteen or twenty minutes, we can always escape to our beds.

In the space provided below, identify three potential learning environments that you can use, and describe the advantages and disadvantages of each. After thinking about your analysis, select the best environment for optimal learning.

Learning Environment 1: _____

Advantages	*Distractions*
1. _____	1. _____
2. _____	2. _____
3. _____	3. _____

Learning Environment 2: _____

Advantages	*Distractions*
1. _____	1. _____
2. _____	2. _____
3. _____	3. _____

Learning Environment 3: _____

Advantages	*Distractions*
1. _____	1. _____
2. _____	2. _____
3. _____	3. _____

Of course, placing yourself in an optimal learning environment doesn't guarantee that you will learn effectively; it simply provides the conditions to make learning possible. You also need to train your mind to focus intensely in order to operate at peak mental effectiveness. Developing the ability to concentrate in this deep, absorbed way is one key to unleashing your thinking and learning powers, and it can be achieved in a variety of different ways:

■ *Conditioning:* In the same way that we are conditioned to act reverently when we enter a place of worship, we need to associate our selected learning environment(s) with focus and concentration. For example, select a favorite location in the library to use consistently so that when you sit down there, you are already beginning to get into a focused frame of mind.

■ *Habits of mind:* Our personalities contain a great deal of habitual behavior: some positive, some negative, and much of it neutral. Creating the habit to focus and concentrate when sitting down to study may require an initial extra effort, but the more that we do it, the more natural and automatic it becomes.

■ *Mindfulness:* Our minds are typically filled with thoughts, feelings, memories, plans—all of which are vying for our attention. In order to concentrate on your learning task, you need to clear a lot of this stuff out. One strategy to achieve this state of "mindfulness" is the following:

Meditating for Mindfulness

When you sit down to study, take about five minutes to get in the proper frame of mind. Sit comfortably in your chair, close your eyes, and take turns at first clinching and then relaxing each part of your body. Work especially at releasing the tension that has built up in various areas. After relaxing your body, turn your attention to relaxing your mind. Visualize your mind as a container crammed with thoughts and feelings, and gradually empty these contents till there is nothing left. Imagine that you are in a pitch-black room, so dark that you cannot see anything. Sink into that feeling of relaxed darkness, letting all of the worries and anxieties drift away. After a while, gradually bring yourself back to your situation, finally opening your eyes. Then focus all your attention and energy on your learning project.

Stage 3. Learning Schedule: How will I organize my learning preparation?

As we discovered when we evaluated the advantages and disadvantages of "cramming" (page 133), successful learning is best achieved progressively over time. Learning involves gradually integrating new information into your existing framework of knowledge. Your mind creates complex connections with what you already know, a process analogous to weaving individual pieces of yarn into an existing fabric. This process of "mental weaving" takes time, and it is aided by sleeping (which consolidates memories into permanent patterns) and your subconscious, which continues to integrate new information even when you are involved in other activities. Let's examine the way that you can use effective scheduling to achieve learning success.

Imagine that you are preparing for an important exam schedule one week from today. Instead of waiting until the day or two before the exam to begin serious study, do just the opposite. Begin to study well in advance of the exam by reviewing the readings and lecture notes, and begin creating study notes that summarize and organize the material in a personalized form. If the course involves problem solving or analysis, create sample problems and case studies that illustrate the principles to be learned. Once your study notes are complete, review them quickly for a short period each day. The night before the exam, review your notes right before you go to sleep, and be sure to get enough rest! Research indicates that the things we think about immediately before sleep receive special attention by our subconscious. On the day of the exam, be sure to reserve an hour or so to review your notes one final time, preferably just before the exam.

By following a learning schedule similar to this, you will find that you will learn the course material in a way that is deeper, more meaningful, and more lasting than cramming. You will also be more relaxed and rested, having attuned yourself to the natural process of learning instead of trying to accelerate it artificially. It's a little like watching a video on fast-forward: it simply isn't the same quality experience as watching it at normal speed. Ironically, by distributing your learning in this way, you will probably find that you actually spend fewer total hours studying than you did under the last-minute approach, desperately trying to jam information into a resistant and tired brain.

Here is an outline of the study schedule we explored, which you can adapt to each new learning situation. A Study Schedule Worksheet is located on page 144.

Learning Schedule

- *Days 7 and 6:* Review readings and lecture notes, and create study notes that summarize and organize the material in a personalized form.

- *Days 5, 4, and 3:* Review study notes and related material for an hour or so each day.

- *Day 2:* Review study notes immediately before going to bed, getting a good night of sleep.

- *Exam Day:* Review study notes—if possible, just before the exam.

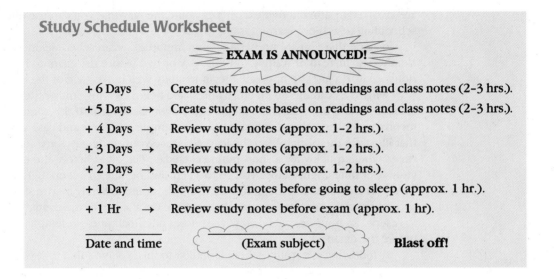

Study Schedule Worksheet

EXAM IS ANNOUNCED!

+ 6 Days →   Create study notes based on readings and class notes (2–3 hrs.).

+ 5 Days →   Create study notes based on readings and class notes (2–3 hrs.).

+ 4 Days →   Review study notes (approx. 1–2 hrs.).

+ 3 Days →   Review study notes (approx. 1–2 hrs.).

+ 2 Days →   Review study notes (approx. 1–2 hrs.).

+ 1 Day →   Review study notes before going to sleep (approx. 1 hr.).

+ 1 Hr →   Review study notes before exam (approx. 1 hr).

_____

Date and time   (Exam subject)   **Blast off!**

Stage 4. Learning Approaches: What learning approaches will I use?

The final stage of our Thinker's Guide to Learning involves the general approaches we should use to learn most effectively.

Develop the appropriate learning attitude. It is essential to develop a positive, realistic, and problem-solving attitude toward learning. Many students undermine their own learning efforts because they let negative, self-critical attitudes creep into their thinking: "I'll never be able to learn this." "This course is too difficult." "I was never a very good student anyway." These and other similar attitudes have the potential to become "self-fulfilling prophecies" in the sense that we predict failure for ourselves, and then we act in a way that ensures that failure will occur. If we adopt the attitude "I'll never be able to learn this," then we are unlikely to put forth our best effort or may simply give up. When we perform poorly, we can then cite this as "proof" that our negative prediction was accurate.

The way to counter this attitude is by a realistic appraisal of your abilities and a commitment to intelligent learning approaches. You need to adopt the attitude that you *will* be successful, then devote your efforts to making this prediction come true. Although you may not realize it, you have the power to influence your own thoughts, to "train" your thinking so that it is more positive and focused. Most students are certainly capable of doing passing work in most courses. Poor performance usually results from other factors: lack of effort, ineffective study approaches, or personal problems. By developing the realistic confidence that you can be academically successful, you can focus your attention on solving the practical problems posed by a given situation. And helping solve these academic problems is one of the main purposes of this book.

Use the appropriate learning resources. The administrators and faculty at your college want you to succeed, and they provide many resources to assist you. Your professors are not only experts in their fields of specialization; they are also teachers who are interested in helping you learn. However, it is your responsibility to reach out and let them know what sort of help you need. For example, often a professor will ask the class: "Are there any questions?" "Is everything clear?" "Is there anybody who doesn't understand?" Typically, a deafening silence follows these questions, even when students have questions, are confused, and don't understand the ideas being presented. Students mistakenly believe that by acknowledging these difficulties, they will appear stupid and uninformed. However, the reverse is actually the case. One mark of an expert learner with an active mind is a willingness to admit a lack of understanding and to ask intelligent questions in an effort to learn. Ironically, it is often the best students who seek out professors for their assistance, but students having difficulties often avoid professors like the plague. Achieving your potential as a college student means that you must develop your active learning qualities.

Similarly, your college probably offers an array of support services in the form of academic advisement, counseling, writing and reading laboratories, and academic support courses and personnel. However, these are of little help to you if you don't think critically about your needs and then take the initiative to use the appropriate resources.

A third resource at college is your classmates. Many research studies have demonstrated that students learn most effectively in collaboration with one another. By pooling your efforts with others, you can learn in a deeper and richer way. Also, working with others helps you maintain motivation. And by "teaching" others what you know, you yourself learn the material in a more meaningful way. So it makes sense for you to form study groups with people who are as interested in succeeding as you are.

Reorganize the material to be learned to match your knowledge framework. The information presented in your textbooks and your professors' lectures is organized in a way that reflects a knowledge framework. In order for you to learn this information in a meaningful way, you have to integrate it into the way you make sense of things—your own knowledge framework. In other words, you have to connect this new information with what you already know and then organize it into a form that expresses the ideas in a clear way.

For example, imagine that you have spent the last unit in your World Civilization course studying four early civilizations: Roman, Persian, Han (China), and Mauryan (India). For the upcoming examination, you are responsible for a staggering amount of information: several hundred pages of text filled with confusing details, not to mention voluminous notes from class lectures. How in the "world" are you going to remember all of this? Many students would approach this challenge by plowing through the text and notes, trying to learn all of the material and keep it straight. Although a common approach, this is perhaps the least effective way to learn.

Instead, a more productive approach is to begin by creating a comprehensive set of study notes that summarize the information contained in the text and lectures. You might try to create a general framework that organizes the information, including the important details, into categories that make sense. For instance, you might look at each of the civilizations in terms of

- political system
- bureaucracy
- quality of life for the average citizen
- military
- economic base
- religious/philosophical synthesis

Using these categories as lenses, you can analyze the structure of these civilizations and compare and contrast them with one another, as well as with current civilizations. By your creating this kind of general framework and making these sorts of connections, the facts and details of these civilizations are embedded in a meaningful context that makes them easier to remember and keep straight.

Although creating these study notes is time consuming, by actively reorganizing the information into a form that makes sense to you, and writing this information down, you are engaged in the process of integrating this material into your thinking and memory bank. And once you are done, you can review these notes relatively quickly, using a study schedule similar to the one described on page 144. As a further step, you could create a visual chart or diagram to summarize the key points from your study notes. This chart enables you to keep the general organization clearly in mind, and it acts as the "tip" of your "knowledge iceberg," representing all the information you have learned. A sample chart is located on page 147.*

Use all learning modalities: linguistic, visual, and experiential. As we have discussed, the most effective learning involves using language, visual media, and "hands-on" experiences in an integrated way. For example, preparing for the World Civilization examination described in the previous section specifically involves language: reading the textbook in an active fashion, listening carefully to the lectures and taking clear notes, and creating a comprehensive set of study notes.

However, successful learners use other learning modalities as well. The chart we used to organize our study notes is an example of a visual medium. You could also, for instance, create diagrams that illustrate the bureaucratic structure or the religious/philosophical synthesis. Photographs of art, architecture, and artifacts from these civilizations would also enhance the knowledge fabric that you are weaving.

In addition to language and visual media, experiential activities are also

*The chart on pages 147–148 was developed by Jessie Chaffee.

	RULER	MILITARY	BUREAUCRACY	ECONOMIC BASE	WHAT PEOPLE THINK	OTHER
ROMAN	1. Strong, loyal subjects 2. Controlled bureaucracy and army 3. Pomp and ceremony—regalia 4. Semi-divine 5. Not a good way of passing power—didn't want to admit to empire. Finally for a while used heirs	1. Enough soldiers—supp. by spoils 2. Loyal and committed—needed to keep adding 3. High wages, good weapons 4. Leaders—often corrupt 5. Soldiers: well-trained, high disciplined, good punish every 10th kept peace	1. Fair taxes—collectors checked on 2. Leader had control 3. Officials could be corrupt 4. Laws: enforced, disputes settle by local leaders 5. Communication—roads, census and survey 6. Loyal officials 7. Jobs given eventually by talent.	1. Money for poor and buildings 2. Fair taxes 3. Coined money 4. Trade: geography through Alexandria Large pop—7 mil produced tax traders Military protects merchants Navy and Legion Roads—bridges—aque. Latin Language	1. Loyal and proud 2. Jobs provided 3. Welfare system 4. Tolerant of diverse 5. Rules enforced fairly: adapted locally 6. Latin 7. Fair taxes 8. Slaves and army do corvee 9. Army in own area and emot religious base	Downfall: *Disease*—pop↓, ↑taxes, inflation, x trade, rebel military, rebel, badini *X expand*—$soldiers and tax, ↑bureaucracy, $bureaucracy *X succession*—generals power base, civil war, no one notices what goes on, poor→landowners, lat fundia, won't $ tax, confrontation, self-sufficient *Christianity*—breakdown *X expand*—nomads in
HAN	Ch'in Shi Huang Ti 1. Inherited throne at 13 2. Trusted no one Study analects to be in leadership position—chosen by test Lead by example Mandate of T'ien Chosen rulers—moral characteristics	1. Conquered states 2. Powerful army, fighting tech. 3. Easy switch to cavalry (raised horses) 4. People in 5/10 families severe punishment well-field system 5. Spies Protection: Great Wall cavalry/army	1. Ends feudalism—kills nobility 2. Heavy taxes Organization: 18 provinces, central bureaucracy, central rule	Family: education, religion, economy, social, health	Unhappy: heavy taxes forced labor forced military service ruthless tactics tried to overthrow him burn confuciunist books Safe	Reforms: roads, axles, read/write simplified Chinese characters, standardized writing
MIAURYAN	Chandrogupta 1. Strong—ruler by military 2. Controlled bureaucracy and military 3. Beautiful clothing and ceremonies 4. Fair ruler (men punished if cruel to wives) 5. People speak to ruler—petitioners 6. Worried about assass.	Fairly strong army 1. Supported soldiers—free time 2. Loyal soldiers—well treated 3. Armed and fed soldiers 4. High walls: strong or weak?	1. Elected council to work on govern. plans 2. Ran economic life 3. Not too much power 4. Great communication post for letter/package	1. Lot of good trading and wealth 2. Not too high taxes	1. Loyal 2. Much diversity 3. Satisfied ARTHA	
PERSIAN (Darius)	1. Just, tolerant ruler 2. Imperial government and controlled strong army 3. Ahura Mazda worshipped 4. Passing power—hereditary	1. Mercenaries 2. Large numbers Delian League: created for defense—Athens controlled Forced members—Athens overextended—treasury used to rebuild Athens moved from Delos Is.	1. Responsible satrapies (20) and tribal leaders 2. 5 made effective control possible 3. Leaders by area 4. Collected taxes leaders military and adminis. 5. Good comm. (spies for ruler) 6. Darius selected	1. Good trade 2. Fair taxes	1. Loyal (tolerant—no revolt) 2. Diversity 3. Satisfied w/ruler	Hellenistic Age: Greek important Slaves trade→mater. poss. Wealth important Private buildings

SYNTHESIS

HELLENISTIC (Persia)	HINDU (Mauryan-India)	HAN (Mk)	ROME (A Synthesis)
"One world" Persians values flow East Loyal to world—not polis *Persian leaders:* divine and absolute power Seleucid: pomp and ceremony king appointed nobles *Spoke Greek:* Greek ideals, plays—upper-class 85% didn't speak *Hellenic and Persian:* slavery citizens of diversity 21,000 citizens 10,000 resident aliens 400,000 slaves *Hellenic:* Few material possessions—changed wealth important *New:* Alex. opened trad routes—trade— Hellenic currency— Greek language Sculpture became realistic Private buildings Small families Moral political legitimacy Rise of Rome 800BCE–150 I. Geography—fertile plain—dense pop—main road Tiger River—began as market town—sacred bridge	4 Goals of Life: Everyone start w/ Dharma, Karma, Samsara, Branman, lila, cast doesn't change Artha—success and survival Kama—pleasure Dharma (Phamma)—caste, respect life, be just, ceremonies, honor others 4 Goals: 1. Students Dharma 2. Household, Dharma, Kama, Artha (Armathastra) 3. Don't like others—want way out—drop out (forest), seek moksha. No goals if go back 4. Holy man/woman don't exist. Remind others it's possible	I. Legalism A. Wall—army at wall B. Communic.: weights, measures, language, axle C. Organization: no feudalism, family supp. members D. Wutiiiked legalists exams, but leaned to legal II. Taoists A. Relaxation—time off B. Harmony w/nature—don't try to control—let universe C. No war—causes destruction only defensive—art of war D. Ruler—low—appear not to rule III. Confuciunists—official philosophy A. Spirit—li-action and jen B. Family—central—no priests—father C. Hierarchy learned—respect learned—farmers after scholars D. Anyone in bureaucracy—standardized test—sentry E. Emperor like father F. Filial piety G. No war—don't need it IV. Old China A. Ruler (relatives or friends) B. Ancestor worship—main religion, past not future, ancestral altars C. Mandate of T'ien D. Important written language V. New A. 18 provinces, 6 ministries—appoints w/govern. post—collect taxes—ceremonies B. Price control system prosperity—food stored C. Breakdown pwr—middleman D. Everyone register—income Public works—bureaucracy of scholars	soldiers—spoils senate—debate I. Roman values 1. military • legions • reliance on • respect for law 2. Religion • worship Rome • 82 temples rebuilt • household sacrifices 3. Political leadership—Senate losing power—and put own friends in II. Hellenistic 1. loyalty to Rome—citizens 2. Religion—Greek God—human charact.—Dionysus 3. end factionalism 4. military reliance and importance of law III. Persian 1. government • friend of ruler in senate • ruler absolute—sub. 2. Religion—some Zoroastrians are • Mithra • Tauroboliun • Maunicholism 3. Troops on front 4. Emperors divine 5. Reliance on military 6. Respect in values, wealth Praetorian guard—guard empires like Macedonia IV. Egyptian God Isis V. Army—spoils of war obedient—phalanx switched to legions, well-trained VI. Why successful in expand? *Political* enemies, allies Communic: main roads Civil engin: sewer and aqueduct VII. Carthaginians trade rivals—Phobeus Messina—go after traders—good for trade VIII. Result of 3 Punic Wars 1. Get Corsica part of Spain. Build empire, don't realize 2. Hannibal 3. destroy Carthage IX. How Rome changed *Army:* Navy doesn't use phalanx—job fight for spoils *Contact w/cultures:* fashion and luxury *Values:* breakdown of family wealth *Conspicuous Census* luxuries, vomitoria Caesar—gladiators rally people. Art: mot. paintings, advert., beauty Archit spec build Farmers—debt—sell poor—slaves—kill rich land to poor—Generals—civil war
II. Virtues Respect tradit, responsible Gravitas—sober Vira—manliness Patriarchal III. Early Govern IV. Patrician—wealthy aristocrat 2 consuls Senate—legislation 12 Tablets Plebeian assemble— Tribunes—could sit in senate 440 V. Classes Patricians—rich Army—own equipment to supply Proletariat—landless poor, no taxes, no rights Plebeians—small farmers, artisans, etc.—army service debt—slavery. Needed by Patricians			

effective learning vehicles. For example, you could visit museums that dramatize aspects of these ancient civilizations or reenact ritualistic dances that were integral to the culture. In a sense, learning about world civilizations is like painting a mental picture. The more colors, textures, and techniques you use to create the picture, the more realistic and familiar your painting will be.

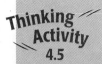

Create your own comprehensive guide for learning, based on The Thinker's Guide to Learning. A worksheet is located below to help you organize your ideas.

Learning Worksheet

Stage 1 Learning Goals: What do I need to know or learn to do, and how can I motivate myself?

Exam/Quiz:

- What material will I be held responsible for, and in what detail?
- How will the exam/quiz be structured?
- What are sample questions and examples of exemplary responses?
- What criteria will be used to evaluate responses?

Paper/Oral Presentation:

- What is the suggested length?
- What are examples of papers/presentations that the professor considers exemplary, and what accounts for their high quality?
- What approaches does the professor recommend in writing the paper or preparing for the oral presentation?

Stage 2 Learning Environment: Where will my learning take place?

- Identify the most productive study location.
- Use strategies to develop focus and concentration.
- Meditate for mindfulness.

→

Stage 3 Learning Schedule: How will I organize my learning preparation?

■ Develop a study schedule.

Stage 4 Learning Approaches: What learning approaches will I use?

■ Develop the appropriate learning attitude.

■ Use the appropriate learning resources.

■ Reorganize the material to be learned to match your knowledge framework.

■ Use all learning modalities: linguistic, visual, and experiential.

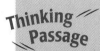

"College Friends"

Learning to cultivate productive friendships is an important part of success in college and elsewhere in life. In the following selection, Jennifer Crichton offers advice that is both philosophical and practical, while sharing her own friendship experiences. As you read the passage, think about your own successes and failures in the realm of friendships, and then complete the questions that follow the selection.

College Friends

Jennifer Crichton

As far as I'm concerned, the first semester away at college is possibly the single worst time to make friends. You'll make them, but you'll probably get it all wrong, through no fault of your own, for these are desperate hours.

Here's desperation: standing in a stadium-like cafeteria, I became convinced that a thousand students busy demolishing the contents of their trays were indifferent to me, and studying me with ill-disguised disdain at the same time. The ability to mentally grasp two opposing conceptions is often thought of as the hallmark of genius. But I credit my mind's crazed elasticity to panic. Sitting alone at a table, I see the girl I'd met that morning in the showers. I was thrilled to see her. The need for a friend had become violent. Back at the dorm, I told her more about my family's peculiarities and my cataclysmic summer fling than I'd ever let slip before. All the right sympathetic looks crossed her face at all the right moments, whereupon I deduced that through the good graces of the housing department, I'd stumbled upon a soulmate. But what seemed like two minds mixing and matching on a cosmic plane was actually two lonely freshmen under the influence of unprecedented amounts of caffeine and emotional upheaval. This wasn't a meeting of souls. This was a talking jag of monumental proportions.

By February, my first friend and I passed each other in the hall with lame, bored smiles, and now I can't remember her name for the life of me. But that doesn't make me sad in the least.

Loneliness and the erosion of high school friendships through change and distance leave yawning gaps that beg to be filled. Yet, I never made a real friend by directly applying for the position of confidante or soulmate. I made my best friendships by accident, with instant intimacy marking none of them—it wasn't mutual loneliness that drew us together.

I met my best friend Jean in a film class when she said Alfred Hitchcock was overrated. I disagreed and we argued out of the building and into a lifelong friendship where we argue still. We became friends without meaning to, and took our intimacy step by step. Deliberate choice, not desperate need, moved us closer. Our friendship is so much a part of us now that it seems unavoidable that we should have become friends. But there was nothing inevitable about it. It's easy to imagine Jean saying to me in that classroom, "Hitchcock's a hack, you're a fool, and that's all I have to say." But that was not all she had to say. Which is why we're friends today. We always have more to say.

Friendship's value wasn't always clear to me. In the back of my mind, I believed that platonic friendships were a way of marking time until I struck the pay dirt of serious romance. I'd managed to digest many romantic notions by my first year of college, and chief among them was the idea that I'd meet the perfect lover who would be everything to me and make me complete. I saw plunging into a relationship as an advanced form of friendship, friendship plus sex. Lacking sex, platonic friendships seemed like a lower standard of living. As long as my boyfriend offered me so much in one convenient package, women friends were superfluous. I thought I was the girl who had everything.

But what made that relationship more—the sex—made it a bad replacement for friendship. Sexual tension charged the lines of communication between us. White noise crackled on the wire as desire and jealousy, fear of loss, and the need to be loved conspired to cloud and distort expression. Influenced by these powerful forces, I didn't always tell the truth. And on the most practical level, when my boyfriend and I broke up, I had lost more than my lover, I lost my best friend.

"You can't keep doing this," Suzanne told me later that same year.

"What?"

"Start up our friendship every time your relationship falls apart."

"I don't do that," I said. It was exactly what I did.

"Yes, you do, and I'm sick of it. I'm not second best. I'm something entirely different."

Once you see that relationships and friendships are different beasts, you'll never think of the two things as interchangeable again, with friendships as the inferior version. . . .

Friendships made in college set a standard for intimacy other friendships are hard-pressed ever to approach. "I've become a narrow specialist in my friendships since graduation," says Pam. "With one friend I'll talk about work. With another, we're fitness fanatics together. But I don't really know much about them—how they live their lives, what they eat for breakfast, or if they eat breakfast at all, who their favorite uncle is, or when they got their contact lenses. I don't even know who they voted for for President. There will be a close connection in spots, but in general I feel as if I'm dealing with fractions of people. With my college friends, I feel I know them *whole*."

→

In college, there's time to reach that degree of intimacy. One night, my best friend and I spent hours describing how our respective families celebrated Christmas. My family waited until everyone was awake and caffeinated before opening presents, hers charged out of bed to rip open the boxes before they could wipe the sleep out of their eyes. We were as self-righteous as religious fanatics, each convinced our own family was the only one that did Christmas right. Did we really spend an entire night on a subject like that? Did we really have that much time?

Operating on college time, my social life was unplanned and spontaneous. Keeping a light on in our rooms was a way of extending an invitation. We had time to hang out, to learn to tell the difference between ordinary crankiness and serious depressions in each other, and to follow the digressions that were at the heart of our friendships. But after college, we had to change, and in scheduling our free-form friendships we felt, at first, self-conscious and artificial.

When I had my first full-time job, I called my best friend to make a dinner date a week in advance. She was still in graduate school, and thought my planning was dire evidence that I'd tumbled into the pit of adult convention. "Why don't you have your girl call my girl and we'll set something up?" she asked. Heavy sarcasm. While the terms of the friendship have shifted from digressive, spontaneous socializing to a directed, scheduled style, and we all feel a certain sense of loss, the value of friendship has, if anything increased.

If my college journals were ever published in the newspaper, the headline would most likely read, "FEM WRITER PENS GOO," but I did find something genuinely moving while reading through my hyper-perceptions the other day. Freshman year I'd written: "I am interested in everything. Nothing bores me. I hope I don't die before I can read everything, visit every place, and feel all there is to feel."

The sentiment would be a lot more poignant if I'd actually gone ahead and died young, but I find it moving anyway because it exemplifies what's good about being young: that you exist as the wide-eyed adventurer, fueled by the belief that you might amount to something and anything, and that your possibilities are endless. When I feel this way now, I'm usually half-dreaming in bed on a breezy Saturday morning. Or I'm with a college friend—someone with whom I'd pictured the future, back when the future was a dizzying haze viewed with the mind's eyes from the vantage point of a smoky dorm room. Together we carved out life with words and hopes. When I'm with her now, I remember that feeling and experience it all over again, because there's still a lot of hazy future to imagine and life to carve. With my friend, I can look to my future and through my past and remember who I am.

Questions for Analysis

1. Think about the lasting friendships in your life. How did they get started? How did you sustain them over the years? What have you learned about friendship?

2. Crichton states that we should take care to develop friendships that are independent of romantic relationships. Do you agree with this advice? Why or why not?

→

3.　Think about the friendships you have formed since coming to college. What are some of the opportunities and difficulties in forming college friendships? What will be the special challenges of maintaining your college friendships *after* college?

4.　Crichton concludes her essay as follows: "With my friend, I can look to my future and through my past and remember who I am." Explain what you think she means by this, and provide examples from your life that illustrate her meaning.

5
Mastering Tests

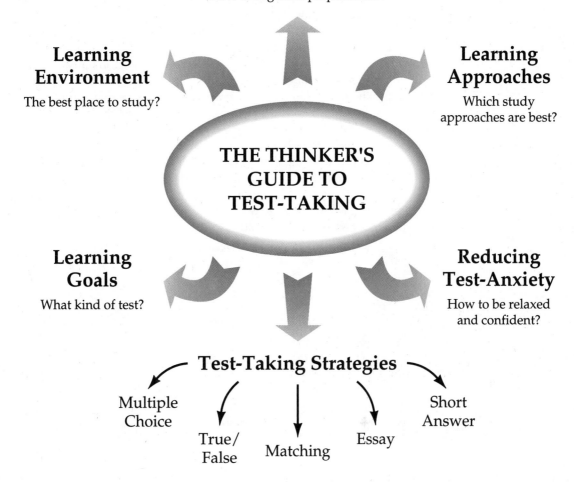

Learning Schedule
How to organize preparations?

Learning Environment
The best place to study?

Learning Approaches
Which study approaches are best?

THE THINKER'S GUIDE TO TEST-TAKING

Learning Goals
What kind of test?

Reducing Test-Anxiety
How to be relaxed and confident?

Test-Taking Strategies

Multiple Choice

True/ False

Matching

Essay

Short Answer

My first set of final exams at the conclusion of my first semester at college was painfully memorable. I was scheduled for six exams over three days, and since I had not prepared adequately in advance, I spent virtually all my time studying frantically, carefully reserving two hours a night for sleep. Because of my fatigue and mental overload, my performance progressively declined with each exam. By the time I stumbled in to take my sixth and final exam, I was a total wreck. The true/false and matching questions seemed to be written in some ancient, forgotten language. I completed them randomly, without thought. Writing organized, coherent responses to the essay questions seemed like an impossible task, and for me it was indeed. I "finished" before anyone else, staggered home, and went to bed. When I became conscious, I promised myself that I would never permit a disaster like that to occur again. Four years later I graduated in the top of my class and as a member of the Phi Beta Kappa Honor Society, proof that I learned my lesson well!

Tests often bring out the worst in us. They inspire a collection of unpleasant emotions, including anxiety, fear and dread. Just thinking about upcoming tests can knot up your stomach, make you perspire in unusual places, and result in a loss of sleep and appetite. Tests can really take the fun out of college, and if you don't perform well, they can take *you* out of college as well. That's the bad news. The good news is that you have the potential to overcome much of the negative power tests seem to hold. In order to slay the test "dragon," you need to use the critical thinking and problem-solving abilities that you have been developing in this course. Thinking critically about tests can enable you to approach them confidently, knowing that you are prepared, relaxed, and ready to perform at your peak. Although preparing for and taking tests will probably still not be exactly enjoyable, at least tests won't cause near-death experiences when you have to deal with them.

Thinking Activity 5.1

1. Think back to a time when you had a very difficult time taking a test, and describe the experience in detail, including how you felt. In retrospect, what were the reasons that you did poorly on the test?

2. Now think back to a time when you did exceptionally well on a test, and describe this experience in detail, including how you felt. In retrospect, what were the reasons that you did so well on the test?

Fear of Tests:
Although tests often inspire anxiety, thinking critically about tests can enable you to approach them
confidently, knowing that you are prepared, relaxed, and ready to perform at your peak.

Why Tests?

"What diabolical sadist invented tests, and for what possible purpose other than to ruin our lives and take the joy out of learning?" It's likely that some version of this question has occurred to you at one time or another, probably late at night when you were in the throes of studying a mountain of hopelessly incomprehensible material, or sitting at a desk on exam day with the sinking realization that you studied the wrong things, or experiencing the blinding test panic that erases all trace of what you thought you had learned. Although it may be difficult for you to accept during these moments of emotional devastation, tests *do* serve a number of useful functions, particularly when they are thoughtfully constructed and fairly evaluated.

To begin with, tests act as great motivators for learning. If you knew that you were *not* going to be tested on the subjects that you were taking, you probably would not study with the same seriousness and intensity. Tests also let you know how your learning is progressing and how well you are doing in the course. A research study at my college found that students tend to think that they are doing better than they actually are, so tests serve as an important "reality check." And if a test is skillfully designed—so that you are stimulated to think and apply the course material, instead of simply re-presenting information—then the test itself can become a learning experience.

Why do tests inspire such fear and loathing in us? One reason is that the stakes *are* significant. Although your performance on any one test may not say a great deal about you as a person, the overall *pattern* of your results on tests says a great deal about you—not just your talents and abilities, but your determination and work ethic as well. The truth is that the world sees an "A" student differently than it views a "C" student, so if you are serious about being successful in life, you should work to achieve the best grades you are capable of. Many students believe that they can cruise through college working at a 50 or 75 percent level of efficiency. However, if you are hoping to achieve significant goals in a desirable career, you really can't afford to give much less than 100 percent. There is simply too much competition, too many talented people who *are* willing to give 100 percent! You should be concerned about your *overall* level of performance on tests, but you should not get excessively anxious about any *one* test, particularly since anxiety tends to undermine your performance. In this book, I emphasize an approach that encourages you to take your tests and academic work seriously, but helps you reduce unnecessary anxiety and panic.

The Thinker's Guide to Successful Test Taking

In retrospect, the disaster that I experienced during my first set of final exams resulted because I did not have an effective plan of action. This plan would have included strategies for the following:

- preparing useful study notes and materials
- creating and following an intelligent study schedule
- developing a clear understanding of what will be expected on the exam
- approaching the exam with a relaxed and confident attitude
- thinking critically during the exam
- controlling test-anxiety

The truth is that performing well on exams means developing *all* the qualities involved in becoming a successful student who *thinks critically.* If somebody suggests that there are a specific number of sure-fire techniques that will guarantee success on exams with a minimum of effort, that person is misleading you. Unfortunately, many students come to this realization after the damage has been done and their academic lives are in jeopardy. In Chapter Four we developed "The Thinker's Guide to Successful Learning" as a general approach to the learning process.

The Thinker s Guide to Successful Learning

Stage 1. **Learning Goals:** What do I need to know or learn to do, and how can I motivate myself?

Stage 2. **Learning Environment:** Where will my learning take place?

Stage 3. **Learning Schedule:** How will I organize my study preparation?

Stage 4. **Learning Approaches:** What learning approaches will I use?

We can apply this comprehensive learning approach to the subject of this chapter in order to create "The Thinker's Guide to Successful Test Taking."

The Thinker s Guide to Successful Test Taking

Stage 1. **Learning Goals:** What kind of test will be given, and how will it be structured and evaluated?

Stage 2. **Learning Environment:** Where can I best study for the test?

Stage 3. **Learning Schedule:** How will I organize my preparation for the test?

Stage 4. **Learning Approaches:** What learning approaches should I use to prepare for the test?

Stage 5. **Test-Taking Strategies:** What general and specific strategies should I use when taking tests?

Stage 6. **Reducing Test Anxiety:** How can I solve the problem of test anxiety and stress?

Stage 1. Learning Goals: What kind of test will be given, and how will it be structured and evaluated?

As we saw in Chapter 3, the first step in solving problems is to define the problem as clearly and specifically as possible. In order to perform optimally on tests, you have to tailor your study effort to the test itself. It doesn't make sense to simply "study in general" because you will not be making the most effective use of your time. Instead, you have to *think critically* about the precise nature of the test and what will be expected of you. With this information in hand, you can then create a study plan specifically designed to meet the challenges posed by this specific test. Here is a checklist of questions that you should try to answer before creating your study plan:

Test Checklist

Test Format

■ What *form* will the test be? Essay? Short answer? Multiple choice? Matching? True/false? Fill in the blanks? Other? Some combination of forms?

■ How many *questions* will there be, and how much will each question be worth?

■ How much *time* will be allowed to complete the test (not including passing out the test, preliminary instructions, and collecting the papers)?

Test Content

■ What specific course *materials, areas,* or *skills* will the test cover?

■ In addition to knowing the course material, what *thinking operations* will I be asked to perform (for example, analyze, compare and contrast, exemplify, solve, apply, evaluate, discuss)?

■ What specific suggestions does the instructor give for preparing for the test? Can the instructor provide a *study guide* to help focus my preparations?

Test Evaluation

■ What criteria will the instructor be using to evaluate the responses?

■ What are some sample responses that meet these criteria?

You may be asking yourself, "Where in the world am I going to get all this information?" The best place to begin is with your instructor. This suggestion may surprise you, but the fact is most instructors are more than willing to respond to intelligent, specific questions like those included above. It's uninformed questions ("What's going to be on the test?" "What are the questions going to be?") that may evoke annoyed responses. Remember, most instructors are trying to construct a fair evaluation of your learning, not attempting to sabotage your efforts in some sneaky, underhanded way.

In addition to your instructor, other sources of information include previous tests (faculty tend to use the same test forms and often the same questions!), which you can secure from students who have already taken the course. But a word of caution: don't assume that the questions from previous tests will be repeated, because you may be unpleasantly surprised. Instead, use this information to guide your general preparation. If previous tests are not available, then you can interview students regarding what they recall about previous test questions.

In addition to determining the *form* of the test, the *nature* of the questions, and the *content* that you will be responsible for, it is also important to determine how your instructor plans to *evaluate* the responses. On one level, this means finding out how much the various questions will be worth. This is useful information for budgeting both your study time and your test-taking time. On a deeper level, however, you need to determine the criteria that your instructor is using to evaluate the quality of your answers. In the case of objective questions—multiple-choice, true/false—this task should be pretty straightforward. However, in the case of short-answer and essay responses, the criteria are often unstated, complex, and confusing. Although your instructors may have a clear idea of what they are looking for, they don't always communicate this information to students in advance. And sometimes instructors themselves are not clear on the criteria they are using. Although they are able to discriminate between A, B, C, D, and F responses, they may have difficulty specifying exactly what criteria they are using to make their evaluations. In these situations, it's difficult for students to study and perform effectively. As a result, you should ask your instructors to detail their evaluation criteria and to provide you with sample responses to analogous questions that illustrate the differences between A, B, and C responses.

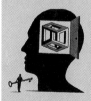

Identify an upcoming test or quiz in one of your courses, and use the Test Checklist to gather information about it. Use this information to help you study more effectively, and evaluate how this approach was different from the way you normally approach studying for tests.

Stage 2. Learning Environment: Where can I best study for the test?

It is essential that you identify an appropriate study location where you can concentrate without distractions or interruptions. Review the Learning Environment section in Chapter Four (page 140) to help you identify the best study location. Also, be sure to work at the other dimensions of creating a productive learning environment explored in that section:

- ■ **Condition yourself** to begin studying as soon as you reach your study location.
- ■ **Develop the habits of mind** to focus and concentrate at your study location.
- ■ **Develop mindfulness** as an integral part of your study environment.

If you are able to create and consistently use a learning environment, you will find that you are learning more efficiently and effectively than you ever have before.

Stage 3. Learning Schedule: How will I organize my preparation for the test?

As we saw in Chapter Four, the most effective and lasting learning takes place gradually over time. Although probably everyone engages in "cramming" at the last minute to a certain degree, the experience is stressful and you generally don't retain what you have "learned" for long after the test. Cramming results in a superficial understanding because you have not had the opportunity to integrate the material deeply and thoroughly. And although cramming is successful to a certain degree, disasters *do* sometimes occur. For example, I was once studying for an art history midterm exam, and I was responsible for knowing nearly 2,000 works of art and architecture, including the artist/designer, date, cultural context, and stylistic characteristics of each piece. Regrettably, I waited until several days before the exam to begin studying. For three days I ate, drank, and breathed (there was no time for sleep) those 2,000 works of art, and by the exam I had them all crammed in, existing in a rather delicate balance. When the first pair of slides was projected onto the screen, some irrational urge prompted me to ask myself, "What would you do if you forgot everything that you just crammed in?" This is exactly what I proceeded to do! It was as if an eraser had completely wiped clean all the "facts" that I had so desperately crammed in, and there was nothing left.

Unfortunately, I was not aware of the research findings which show that much of what we learn is consolidated during sleep, a process that takes place over time. Even when you are awake, learning continues to take place on subconscious levels, providing that you continue to make contact with the material or tasks you are trying to learn. Even though cramming will continue to be the preferred learning choice for many students, the most successful students will avoid it if at all possible, preferring instead to learn gradually, meaningfully, and more permanently.

The most productive approach to successful and lasting learning is to stay current with your class readings and assignments, and then to create a study schedule that begins well in advance of the test. After creating a comprehensive set of study notes based on your class notes, readings, and related course materials, plan to review these several hours a day over a period of five to seven days before the test. Of course, the process of creating your study notes is a powerful learning aid—reviewing the notes simply embeds them more firmly into your knowledge framework. This repeated review will enable you to "over-learn" the material, which research has shown results in progressively greater retention. When studying, take short breaks every hour or so, and longer breaks every two to three hours, in order to stay mentally and physically fresh. The night before the test, review your notes just before you go to bed, which should be early enough for you to get a good night's sleep. If time permits, review your notes first thing the next morning and right before your test. You'll be amazed at how clearly you remember all you have studied. The sample learning schedule that we developed in Chapter Four is included below, and you can review the Learning Schedule section (page 142) to underscore the points made here and use the Study Schedule Worksheet on page 144.

Learning Schedule

- *Days 7 and 6:* Review readings and lecture notes, and create study notes that summarize and organize the material in a personalized form.

- *Days 5, 4, and 3:* Review study notes and related material for an hour or so each day.

- *Day 2:* Review study notes immediately before going to bed, getting a good night's sleep.

- *Exam Day:* Review study notes—if possible, just before the exam.

Stage 4. Learning Approaches: What learning approaches should I use to prepare for the test?

The key learning approaches points that we identified in Chapter Four are naturally vital for successful test taking. They are summarized below, although you can review them in their entirety (pages 144–149) if needed.

- ***Develop the appropriate learning attitude.*** Approaching your test taking with confidence will encourage you to commit yourself fully to preparing for your tests, and it will also help reduce your anxiety and negative personal judgments, which are debilitating obstacles to successful performance.

■ *Use the appropriate learning resources.* We have already explored the central role that instructors play in providing information and study suggestions for your test taking. Your classmates are also potentially important resources. You can exchange class notes, discuss particularly difficult concepts or problems, and form study groups to help prepare for your tests. Working with others can make studying more interesting, sustain your motivation, and help you see the material from fresh perspectives. Also, "teaching" others is an important learning strategy.

■ *Reorganize the material to be learned to match your knowledge framework.* The material you need to study for your test is probably contained in a variety of sources: textbook, class notes, course handouts, primary sources, video, and software. It is not practical or efficient to review all these materials as you prepare for a test. Instead, you need to reduce all of this material to a manageable form that you review a number of times. How do you accomplish this? By creating a comprehensive set of study notes that includes all the important information that is likely to be covered on the test and organizing these notes in a personalized form. In this regard, it is often helpful to use charts, mental maps, and other graphic organizers that present the material in a clearly organized, visually engaging format. This process results in valuable, in-depth learning. In addition, condensing your text and lecture notes enables you to review the most important and difficult material without reviewing all your notes. For example, you can use condensed note cards as "flash cards," integrating your other senses in the learning process.

Stage 5. Test-Taking Strategies: What general and specific strategies should I use when taking tests?

Imagine it: test day arrives, and if you have followed the first four stages of "The Thinker's Guide to Successful Test Taking," you should be well prepared and confident. However, your job is not finished. You still must perform well on the test that the professor has devised, accurately displaying all that you have learned. Sometimes students study seriously and are well prepared, but they do poorly on the test. How can this happen? Because they have not mastered the strategies required for performing well on tests. Of course, these strategies are not a *substitute* for being well prepared—they simply provide you with the tools to excel once you *are* well prepared. Let's explore these important test-taking strategies.

General Test-Taking Strategies

Critically analyze the entire test. Students are often so anxious to get started on tests that they put their heads down and just start working from the beginning. Although this "straight ahead" approach is understandable, it is not effective. Instead, you need to *think critically* about the test as a whole:

- Look through the entire test and examine the way it is structured.
- Carefully read the directions for each section.
- Carefully review the essays or short-answer questions so that you can begin thinking about them as you work on the objective portions of the test.
- Note the point values of the various sections and questions.
- If there is anything that is not clear, ask your instructor for clarification right away.

The few minutes that you invest to analyze the test as a whole will pay big dividends, because it will enable you to see the "forest," not just the individual "trees."

Create a test-taking plan. Because you can see the entire "forest," you are in a position to quickly create an intelligent test-taking plan, a path that will guide you through the "trees" without serious mishaps. Determine the point values of each section, and budget your time accordingly. For example, if a test scheduled for 45 minutes contains an objective section that is worth 30 points and two essay questions that are worth 35 points each, you should budget approximately 15 minutes for the objective section and an additional 15 minutes for each of the essay questions. Of course, if you are able to complete the objective section in less than 15 minutes, which is very likely since objective questions generally require only recognition and recall, then you will have additional time for the more complex thinking required in the essay questions.

However, the problem many students encounter is that they spend *too much* time on a section or question, thereby reducing the time available for other questions. For instance, on a test consisting of three essay questions scheduled for 60 minutes, I regularly see students spend most of their time on the first question or the first two questions, leaving virtually no time for the third question. This is a serious mistake, since there is a limit on the number of points you can earn for any one question. So even if you earn the maximum credit for the first two questions but don't complete the third, then you will do poorly on the test.

The solution is to budget your time *and then stick to your budget.* It's very difficult for students to move from a question if they haven't completed it, but it's often necessary. If you have time at the end of the test, you can return and finish up your response. But you have to be tough with yourself. Even though I tell students how much time is remaining at various intervals and then urge them to move on to the next question, many times they simply ignore my advice. Since you can't count on your instructor letting you know the time, be sure to bring your own watch, and then pay attention to it!

Write down key information. If you have reviewed your notes just before the test, the key information should be fresh in your mind. As soon as the test papers are handed out, write down important formulas, concepts, and notes you are likely to need. Once you get involved in actually answering the questions, you may forget some of this key information. If you have done an effective job of creating your study notes, the key ideas you write down should be threads that are tied to all of the other important information in your knowledge fabric.

Multiple-Choice Test Strategies

1. When you first review a multiple-choice test, you should
   a. give preference to long answers, particularly those that use such qualifiers as *some, usually, probably, many.*
   b. use the process of elimination to narrow down choices.
   c. be suspicious of answers that contain such absolute terms as *always, never, everyone.*
   d. read all the answers before making a choice.
   e. do all of the above.
2. When taking a multiple-choice test, if you have absolutely no idea what the correct answer is, you should
   a. estimate the number of a, b, c, d, and e answers on the test and put down the letter least selected, since instructors tend to balance out answers in a test.
   b. always make a guess, even if you are penalized for incorrect answers.
   c. select one of the middle answers, since instructors generally avoid making the first and last answers the correct ones.
   d. don't waste time reading the question as you consider each of the answers.
   e. scream.

You may have found these questions somewhat puzzling, but the fact is there are certain principles that influence the design of multiple-choice tests. By understanding these principles, you can improve your overall performance on these types of exams. Each of the question options illustrates one of these principles, but be sure to remember that these principles are *guidelines,* not *rules.* They are to be used as tools for analysis in conjunction with your knowledge of the subject, not recipes to be followed blindly.

1. When you first review a multiple-choice test, you should
   a. *give preference to long answers, particularly those that use such qualifiers as some*, *usually*, *probably*, *many*. In Chapter Three we quoted H. L. Mencken, who once said "To every complex question there's a simple answer—and it's wrong!" There's a great deal of truth in this insight. The world is a complicated place, and there are few issues that can be treated in a clear, unambiguous, yes-or-no fashion. As a result, accurate statements usually require longer explanations and more qualifications. Don't forget this principle is *usually (not always)* the case in *many (not all)* instances.

b. *use the process of elimination to narrow down choices.* If you are not sure about the answer to a question, use the process of elimination to narrow down your choices. Begin with the most obviously false answers, and work your way to those most likely to be true. Then use your best "educated guess." If two answers contradict each other, then it is very possible that the correct answer is one of these two choices, since instructors often include slightly different versions of the correct answer.

c. *be suspicious of answers that contain such absolute terms as* **always**, **never**, **everyone**. This is the companion principle to the one embodied in answer "a." For the same reasons that you should give preference to answers with qualifiers, you should be suspicious of answers with absolute terms such as *always, never, everyone.* Of course, this is not *always* the case, but there are comparatively few accurate statements that can be stated in such absolute terms.

d. *read all the answers before making a choice.* Don't make the mistake of selecting the first correct answer you come across. First, one of the answers you don't get to may be "more correct" than another, and although you can always argue the point with your teacher, it's easier to choose the best response. Second, some questions may give you the option of selecting "all of the above," but you might not realize it if you don't complete your reading of the answers. Third, some of the answers may contain clues that assist you in identifying the correct answer.

e. *do all of the above.* In analyzing a question of this type, remember that you only need to be certain that at least *two* of the answers are correct. Once this happens, you know that the question is not a single answer type, and "all of the above" is the only appropriate response.

2. When taking a multiple-choice test, if you have absolutely no idea what the correct answer is, you should

a. *estimate the number of* a, b, c, d, *and* e *answers on the test and put down the letter least selected, since instructors tend to balance out answers in a test.* Although this seems logical, it is *generally* incorrect. Most teachers follow patterns for placing correct answers, as we will see below, but they don't usually try to balance their answers out. One exception to this is when the test items have been distributed randomly by a computer, but even in this case, it could take hundreds of questions for a balanced distribution to show up.

b. *always make a guess.* Again, this answer seems to make sense, but the absolute term *always* should make it suspicious to you. *Most* multiple-choice tests don't penalize you for incorrect answers, but *some* do. If there is no penalty, then you have nothing to lose by guessing. However, if there is a penalty for wrong answers, then blind guessing, where your chance for a correct response is 20 percent, will end up costing you points. However, even when a penalty is in effect, you should still make educated guesses between two possible answers; here, your chances for a correct answer are 60 percent.

c. *select one of the middle answers, since instructors generally avoid making the first and last answers the correct ones.* For whatever psychological reasons, teachers *do* tend to position the correct answers toward the middle of the list of choices. Perhaps they feel that the correct answer is better "disguised" in the middle of the answers than at the extremities, or perhaps they begin with the correct answer and then "build" around it. In any case, it makes statistical sense to guess from the middle choices rather than the first and last.

d. *don't waste time reading the question as you consider each of the answers.* Actually, it makes sense to read each of the answers in conjunction with the initial question. Since the question and the correct answer together form a complete sentence, by reading them together you are better able to grasp the entire meaning of that particular combination and thus better assess its accuracy. Also, there are sometimes subtle grammatical clues that make some answers "sound" better than others. For example, this particular answer ("don't waste time reading the initial question as you consider each of the options") does not fit grammatically with the question ("When taking a multiple-choice test, if you have absolutely no idea what the correct answer is, you should"). That information alone should tell you that this answer is incorrect. As an alternative to rereading the question for each answer, you can try reading the question several times and then constructing your own answer before reading the options.

e. *scream.* Foolish and far-fetched answers are a gift to you, because you can quickly discard them. Don't waste time trying to figure out why your teacher included them—probably only to get a laugh—just cross them off and move on. You can laugh later.

Multiple-Choice Test Study Guide

1. Read all the answers before making a choice, and combine each of the answers with the question to see how well they go together.

2. Use the process of elimination to narrow down choices, discard frivolous answers quickly, and make educated guesses when you're not sure.

3. Give preference to long answers, particularly those that use such qualifiers as *some, usually, probably, many.*

4. Be suspicious of answers that contain such absolute terms as *always, never, everyone.*

5. If you have no idea which is the correct answer, select one of the middle choices rather than the first or last.

True/False Test Strategies

1. T F If you don't know the answer to a T/F question, choose "True."
2. T F If an answer is mostly false, then you should mark it "False."
3. T F If an answer is mostly true, then you should mark it "True."
4. T F Be careful of the use of negatives (and double negatives) in T/F statements.
5. T F Be suspicious of long and complex statements on T/F tests.
6. T F Statements that include such qualifiers as *always, never, everyone* are usually false.
7. T F Statements that include such qualifiers as *some, usually, probably, many* are often true.

As with the multiple-choice examples we examined above, each of these guidelines demonstrates important principles about successfully taking True/False tests.

1. T F *If you don't know the answer to a T/F question, choose "True."* Statistically speaking, this statement is true. Instructors tend to make the majority of statements on a T/F test true. Perhaps it is the instructors' habit of trying to make accurate statements in class that carries over into making up the tests. Or perhaps they want to leave true statements embedded in students' minds. Whatever the reason, if you have no idea about the truth or falsity of a statement, your best chance is to go with the odds and pick "True."

2. T F *If an answer is mostly false, then you should mark it "False."* If even the slightest detail of a statement is false, then the entire statement must be marked false. Just like a woman can't be "a little bit" pregnant, on a True/False test a question can't be just a little bit false—either it's completely true or it's false.

3. T F *If an answer is mostly true, then you should mark it "True."* Based on what we just found out about the previous statement, the answer to this question should be obvious. It's false! Even if a statement is 99% true, on a True/False test that 1% of falsity dooms it to be a false statement. Also, this situation illustrates the way some test questions can provide clues to the correct answers of other test questions. Be sure to look for these kinds of connections as you are taking a test.

4. T F *Be careful of the use of negatives (and double negatives) in T/F statements.* True! In many instances, teachers slip negatives and sometimes even double negatives into T/F statements, and if you *don't* stay on your toes, then you might *not* have any toes left! (In other words, since two negatives make a positive, "stay on your toes in order to keep your toes.") For example, the previous *false*

statement "If an answer is mostly true, then you should mark it 'True'" becomes a *true* statement by simply changing *should* to *shouldn't:* "If an answer is mostly true, then you *shouldn't* mark it 'True.'" Be careful—it's a confusing True/False jungle out there!

5. T F   *Be suspicious of long and complex statements on T/F tests.*
Although a generality with many exceptions, this statement is true. Since a statement must be 100 percent true in order to be considered true on a T/F test, the more information or the more complex the structure, the greater the opportunity for the statement to be false. Also, many teachers delight in cleverly inserting some false detail in the midst of accurate information in order to test how well you know the course material.

6. T F   *Statements that include such qualifiers as **always, never, everyone** are usually false.* Based on the same reasoning we used in the multiple-choice test section, this statement is true. Most absolute statements about the world are false, because there are almost always exceptions or special circumstances. Absolute terms should sound alarm bells in your mind, and you should evaluate these questions with special care. Teachers often want to test how precise your knowledge is by presenting statements that are *generally* true but for which there may be a few specialized exceptions. Of course, like any general statement, this one has exceptions as well, which is why we use the term *usually.*

7. T F   *Statements that include such qualifiers as **some, usually, probably, many** are often true.* As the flip side of the previous guideline, this statement is true. Qualifying terms give a statement much more opportunity to be true than do absolute terms. Of course, finding one of these qualifiers is no guarantee that a statement is true, which is why we include the qualifier *often,* but it does increase the odds. For example, if the statement had read "Statements that include such qualifiers as *some, usually, probably, many* are *always* true," it would be clearly false. Even if it included the qualifier "*almost always* true," it would be false. Qualifiers need special attention, so be sure that you provide it.

True/False Test Study Guide

1. If you don't know the answer to a T/F question, choose "True."

2. All parts of an answer must be completely true in order for the answer to be true. Otherwise, it is false.

3. Be careful when you see negatives (and double negatives) in T/F statements.

4. Be suspicious of long and complex statements.

5. Statements that include such qualifiers as *always, never, everyone* are usually false.

6. Statements that include such qualifiers as *some, usually, probably, many* are often true.

Matching Test Strategies

Match the following types of tests to the *best* description of that particular test.

_____	1. multiple-choice	a. particularly important to mark sure things first
_____	2. true/false	b. requires not just recall of information, but also organization and critical thinking
_____	3. matching	c. important to pay close attention to language, especially qualifiers and negatives
_____	4. short-answer	d. requires recognition of correct response, not recall and expression
_____	5. essay	e. requires concise, specific answers

Although less frequent than multiple-choice and true/false tests, matching tests do occur, and they require a special approach. Let's explore the strategies for success.

1. *Read both lists through completely and develop an overall plan.* The *least* effective way to approach a matching test is to start at number one and simply work your way through the test a question at a time. Instead, it is essential to read the entire lists of items, look for patterns, and develop an overall plan. For example, in the first example in the "test" above, it would be possible to select answer a, c, or d. However, the directions instruct us to select the *best* description of each type of test, and if you choose either a or c instead of d, then you will upset the entire pattern of the test and set off a chain reaction of incorrect responses. That's why you need to read the entire test over completely and approach the questions as a whole, not just individually.

2. *Select the sure matches first and mark them off as you complete them.* After reviewing the entire test, begin by matching the items you are absolutely certain of. *Use pencil* in case you have to make changes. As you match a pair, put a line through each of the items. This will prevent you from rereading them as you review columns for the remaining matches.

3. *Move from the most-sure matches to the least-sure matches.* After matching the items you are most sure of, then match the items you are next most sure of, gradually working your way to those you are least sure of.

Once you have completed your matches, resist the impulse to start second-guessing yourself. There is often a built-in ambiguity in matching tests that would permit you to spend the rest of your life working on finding the perfect matches.

Matching Test Study Guide

1. Read both lists through completely, look for patterns, and develop an overall plan.
2. Select the sure matches first and mark them off as you complete them. *Use pencil.*
3. Move from the most-sure matches to the least-sure matches.

Short-Answer Test Strategies

1. In the space provided, define the concept of critical thinking and include the five qualities of a critical thinker.

   _____

   _____

   _____

   _____

2. Explain why it is important to use an organized approach to solving complex problems, and identify the major steps in the problem-solving process.

   _____

   _____

   _____

   _____

3. Identify five kinds of tests, and briefly define each one.

   _____

   _____

   _____

   _____

These questions are examples of short-answer questions. The key to answering short-answer questions is to be concise and specific. Get right to the point, and then move on. Short-answer questions are generally of limited point value, and you won't get additional points for elaborate responses. On the other hand, if you don't know the answer, there is little point in wandering around, trying to create the illusion that you know something.

How concise and specific should you be? Ask your teacher. Additional clues include the point value of the questions and the amount of space provided for your response. For instance, here is a sample response to the first question:

> Critical thinking is the process of thinking about our thinking, carefully examining the thinking process in order to clarify and improve our understanding of the world. A critical thinker is someone who thinks actively, carefully explores situations with questions, thinks independently, views situations from different perspectives, and discusses ideas in an organized way.

Essay Test Strategies

1. *Analyze* the various forms of testing people's knowledge by addressing the following issues:

   a. *Define* objective tests, *discuss* their purpose, and *describe* the best way to prepare for them.

   b. *Define* essay tests, *discuss* their purpose, and *describe* the best way to prepare for them.

   c. *Compare* and *contrast* objective tests and essay tests, *evaluating* their strengths and weaknesses and *explaining* which type of test you prefer. Be sure to *support* your answer with reasons and to *illustrate* your point of view with examples.

For many students, encountering essay questions like this is their worst nightmare. Essay questions can appear to be overwhelming: complicated, confusing, and phrased in an alien language. Students are often unsure how to go about approaching these questions and are uncertain what criteria the instructor will use to evaluate their answers. All in all, a sure-fire recipe for disaster!

Yet, properly understood, essay tests may end up becoming your *favorite* kind of examination! Unlike objective tests, they allow you to express your knowledge and thinking in an open and developed fashion. Freed from the burden of deciphering each objective question and searching for the "best" answer, you can concentrate on organizing your ideas and communicating them in a clear, articulate way. Once you become confident with essay tests, you may discover that you prefer them to the rigid confines of objective tests. Let's use the sample question above to explore the strategies required to master essay tests.

Read the question very carefully and be sure to explicitly respond to each of its parts. This may seem like common sense, but the sad truth is many students get off on the wrong path from the start. For example, they read the questions quickly, pick out a few familiar words, and then mentally compose their own question, which they proceed to address. The problem is that the question they compose is not the same one that the instructor has provided. And even though their response may be knowledgeable and well reasoned, it addresses the wrong question.

Another common mistake that students make is to answer only some of the essay question parts, either ignoring the other parts or trying to incorporate them into the parts they are answering. Students may get caught up in answering the initial parts and either "forget" about the other parts in the heat of the moment, or run out of time for the remaining sections. Whatever the reason, it is essential to respond to every part of the question, and do so explicitly.

Organize your answers in the same outline format as the question so the instructor can see that you are addressing each part. Begin each response with a rephrasing of the question, and be sure to budget your time so you can respond to each aspect of the question.

For example, let's critically examine the essay question on page 173. You should note immediately that although it is technically "one" question, it is composed of three different parts, and each of these parts has different elements as well. Unfortunately, instructors don't always articulate their questions this clearly, although they expect you to address all the issues. For instance, the question above might appear as

1. Discuss objective tests and essay tests: their similarities and differences, their strengths and weaknesses, and the best way to excel at them.

When this happens, it's up to you to provide the missing structure, similar to that expressed in the original phrasing of the question.

1a. Objective tests can be defined as tests that. . . .
   The purpose of objective tests is to. . . .
   The best way to prepare for objective tests is to. . . .
1b. Essay tests can be defined as tests that. . . .
   The purpose of essay tests is to. . . .
   The best way to prepare for essay tests is to. . . .

Highlight key words *in the questions and pay particular attention to them.* Essay questions are always built around key words that tell you what thinking operations you are supposed to perform in order to respond. Objective tests are primarily focused on evaluating how much information you have learned, but essay tests expect you to make use of this information in various ways. For example, in the sample question above, you are asked to *define, discuss, describe, compare, contrast, evaluate, explain, support,* and *illustrate.* These are all thinking operations you are expected to apply to the course material you are being tested on, and they form the heart of the essay questions. In order to perform well, you need to understand the precise thinking operation you are being expected to perform, and then you have to perform it effectively. A list of the key terms and their definitions you are likely to encounter

on essay tests is located in Table 5–1. However, a definition is only the starting point, since these are complex thinking abilities that must be developed through practice and guidance, one of the central aims of this book.

Table 5–1. Key Terms Used in Essay Tests

Analyze   Break a whole into parts, explore these parts, and discuss their relationship to the whole.

Compare   Identify and discuss the similarities and differences between two or more subjects.

Contrast   Identify and discuss the differences between two or more subjects.

Define   Explain the central meaning of a term. Provide an example that illustrates the definition, if requested.

Demonstrate   Show or prove a conclusion or point of view.

Describe   Provide a detailed account.

Discuss   Explain and debate the various points of view on an issue.

Enumerate   Identify and list the main points.

Evaluate   Judge the value of something by identifying the evaluative criteria and supporting evidence.

Explain   Provide a clear and coherent description of why something happened, including reasons and rationale.

Identify   List and describe.

Illustrate   Provide concrete examples that illustrate a general point or idea.

Interpret   Explain a complex meaning in clear, well-reasoned terms from your own point of view.

Outline   Describe the main ideas or events and show how they are related.

Prove   Support a conclusion with relevant facts, evidence, and reasons.

Relate   Explain the connections between ideas or events.

Solve   Analyze a problem; identify various alternatives; come up with a solution based on your evaluation.

State   Explain the main points precisely.

Summarize   Provide a brief, condensed account that preserves the main points while excluding less significant details.

Support   Back up a point of view with relevant facts, evidence, and reasons.

Trace   Describe the history of a process or the order of events.

Although the key words in the essay question on page 173 are italicized, you won't find this to be the case on most essay exams. As a result, when you first read the essay question, you should underline or circle the key words to help you clearly understand what is being asked and to focus your response. Paying particular attention to the key words, answer the questions 1a and 1b in the space provided below.

1a. Objective tests can be defined as tests that _____

_____

_____

_____

The purpose of objective tests is to _____

_____

_____

_____

The best way to prepare for objective tests is to _____

_____

_____

_____

1b. Essay tests can be defined as tests that _____

_____

_____

_____

The purpose of essay tests is to _____

_____

_____

_____

The best way to prepare for essay tests is to _____

_____

_____

_____

After completing your responses, *compare* and *contrast* your answers with those of the other students in the class, and record additional relevant points they included that you didn't. Remember, it's the *quality* of your responses that determines your grade, and the more comprehensive and thoughtful your answers, the better the response from the instructor.

Brainstorm *ideas for addressing the topic and then* **organize** *the key ideas into a plan for your essay, using a mapping or outline format.* After reading (and as we noted, often *mis*reading) the essay question, many students begin writing immediately. This is generally a mistake. Although you may feel the pressure of time, you should not begin before planning your answer. The few minutes that you invest in planning your response will pay large dividends: your answer will be better organized and more likely to stay focused, and you will be less likely to forget important points or details. Let's explore the best way to create a test plan, using the last part of our sample essay question as an example.

    c. *Compare* and *contrast* objective tests and essay tests, *evaluating* their strengths and weaknesses and *explaining* which type of test you prefer. Be sure to *support* your answer with reasons and to *illustrate* your point of view with examples.

By applying our first essay test strategy, "Read the question very carefully and be sure to explicitly respond to each of its parts," we note that this main question is actually composed of two different subquestions. Describe each of these question parts in the space provided below.

Main question: _____

_____

Subquestion 1: _____

_____

Subquestion 2: _____

_____

The second test strategy, "Highlight *key words* in the questions and pay particular attention to them," alerts us to the fact that the question is asking us to perform a number of thinking operations. Define these thinking operations in the space provided below:

compare/contrast: _____

evaluate: _____

explain: _____

support: _____

Having carefully read the question and highlighted the key words, the third essay test strategy is to "*Brainstorm* ideas for answering the question and then *organize* the key ideas into a plan for your essay, using a mapping or outline format." Your first response to this suggestion may be "Are you crazy? I usually don't even have enough time to complete my answer—how do you expect me to take time to generate ideas and create an outline?" Although this reaction is understandable, the fact is that, properly implemented, this strategy is nearly guaranteed to improve your performance. How is this possible?

To begin, think about what qualities your teacher is looking for in your essay. In most cases, teachers are looking for responses that are comprehensive, well organized, and to the point. When you begin writing your essay without planning or preparation, you are reducing the chances that you will meet these criteria, and the following are more likely:

- you will forget to include some relevant knowledge that you possess as you become involved in writing your response.
- your essay will be less well organized as you move from idea to idea, instead of working from an overall plan.
- your answer will "wander" around instead of staying focused.

Taking a few minutes for planning and preparation will help you create essays that are more comprehensive, better organized, and more focused. In addition, these preliminary activities can be accomplished quickly and will enable you to work more efficiently once you begin writing. The result is that you will probably *save* time in completing your answer. Let's see how this works by generating ideas relevant to answering the question we are considering:

c. *Compare* and *contrast* objective tests and essay tests, *evaluating* their strengths and weaknesses and *explaining* which type of test you prefer. Be sure to *support* your answer with reasons and to *illustrate* your point of view with examples.

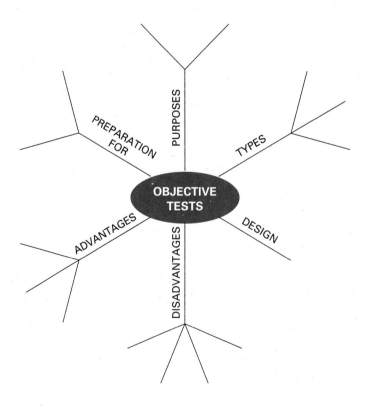

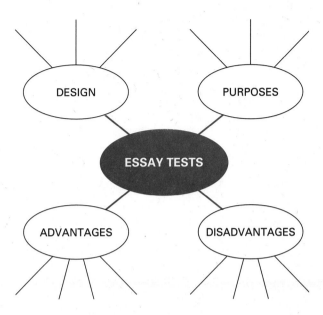

Mapping is a particularly effective approach for generating ideas and illustrating the relationships between them. Use the beginning maps displayed above as a starting point, and then record as many ideas as you can about objective and essay tests. Once your maps are complete, compare them to those developed by other students, and add relevant points that you may have overlooked.

After generating relevant ideas and articulating some of the key relationships between them, the next step is to create a rough outline that expresses the organization of your essay. Create a brief outline that incorporates the points that you consider most important. A sample outline is illustrated below.

Sample Outline for Essay Question

Objective Tests

Types: MC, T/F, MATCH

Purpose: determine mastery of course material

Design: manipulation of information

Preparation: recognition vs. in-depth understanding

Advantages:
   clear idea what to expect
   clear-cut "right" answer—no teacher bias
   graded quickly

→

Disadvantages:
   may not ask what you know
   responses limited by questions
   can't express your own opinion
   questions can be tricky

Essay Tests

Purpose: recall, produce, think

Design:
   analyze, relate, evaluate large issues and broad themes
   express your own view

Advantages:
   can express what you have learned—not limited by questions
   straightforward questions
   usually more interesting
   opportunity to think and express your ideas

Disadvantages:
   too general sometimes
   grading more subjective
   not always clear what teacher wants
   handwriting may affect grade

Having completed these preliminary activities, you are now ready to compose your essay. Once you become accustomed to these thinking strategies, you will be able to complete them in just a very few minutes.

Build your essay around clearly defined points and support your points with thoughtful reasons. The brainstorming, mapping, and outlining of the previous strategy are the best preparation for an intelligent, well-organized essay. Begin your answer with a restatement of the question to ensure that you start at the right point, and then follow the outline you have prepared. Every point needs to be supported with relevant reasons, evidence, and examples. To make the structure of your answer clear, use such terms as these:

first, second, third

to begin with, also, in addition

on the one hand, on the other hand

because, as a result

in summary, in conclusion

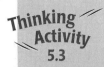

Thinking Activity 5.3

Using the map and outline that you developed, write an essay in response to the topic that we have been working on:

    c. *Compare* and *contrast* objective tests and essay tests, evaluating their strengths and weaknesses and *explaining* which type of test you prefer. Be sure to *support* your answer with reasons and to *illustrate* your point of view with examples.

There is a sample student response to this question included below, but you should write your answer *before* you read this student's response. After you complete your answer, compare and contrast it to this sample response, as well as to others in your class. What are the similarities? What are the differences? How could you strengthen your answer?

Sample Student Response

There are a number of important differences between objective tests and essay tests, and each format has its own purposes, strengths, and weaknesses. Objective test formats include multiple choice, T/F, matching, and short answer. The major purpose of these tests is to determine to what extent you have mastered the basic course material. Objective tests present you with information that you are expected to manipulate in some way: choose the correct response, determine the truth or falsity, or match the correct items. As a result, when preparing for objective exams, you should concentrate on *recognition* knowledge rather than in-depth understanding. It's more important to be familiar with all of the course material to a certain extent than to focus on fewer topics in more depth. The type of material tested is usually factual in nature, rather than dealing with large issues or broad themes.

    There are a number of advantages to objective tests. You have a pretty clear idea what to expect and how to prepare for them. In most cases there is a clear-cut right answer, and your grade won't be affected by a teacher's personal biases. If your teacher doesn't like you, a correct answer is still correct! Because objective tests can be scored quickly, you get back your test results in a timely fashion. On the other hand, there are some disadvantages to objective tests as well. Often there is a lot of knowledge that you have learned that is not tested, and there is no way to communicate what you know to the teacher. You are limited to the specific information that the questions ask for. Also, you are not able to express your own opinion about the course material; you simply respond to the question as it is presented. And sometimes these questions are very tricky. They are intentionally

→

designed to be ambiguous or to have a number of "almost correct" responses. In fact, sometimes the "almost correct" responses seem just as defensible as the designated "correct" answers.

Essay tests are much different. Instead of testing your recognition of course material, they require you to *recall* and *produce* information you have learned, and then *think* about it in some way. Usually the questions deal with large issues and broad themes that you are expected to analyze, relate, or evaluate in some way. In addition to expressing what you have learned, you are also expected to express your own viewpoint or evaluation. In preparing for essay exams, it's more important to understand the important issues and overall themes than to concentrate on learning every last detail like you do for objective tests.

There are a number of advantages to essay tests. First of all, they give you an opportunity to express a lot of what you have learned, since you are not being limited to specific objective questions. Second, the questions are general but usually fairly straightforward, unlike the "tricky" questions of objective tests. Third, the questions are usually more interesting, since they are dealing with larger issues that you have studied and discussed in class. Finally, essay questions give you an opportunity to really think about things and express your own viewpoint. You really feel that you are writing about important issues in your education.

However, there are some disadvantages to essay tests. To begin with, the questions are sometimes so general that you're not sure exactly what the teacher wants for an answer. Also, the grading of the answers is more subjective than objective tests. It's not always clear what criteria the teacher is using to evaluate the responses. And there is always the possibility that the teacher may be influenced by who you are or how neat your handwriting is!

In summary, I would say that I prefer essay tests, although they have some disadvantages. I find that they challenge my mind and give me an opportunity to really think and express my ideas. This is the sort of thing that education is supposed to be about: learning important ideas, discussing them, and expressing your own views about them. Also, essay questions accommodate the fact that the world is a complicated place, and there aren't always simple, cut-and-dried answers to things. Many times there is more than one side to an issue, and to become a truly educated person, you need to be able to see all of these different sides and arrive at your own thoughtful conclusion. Essay tests scare me sometimes, but I think that's what education is all about.

Essay Test Study Guide

1. Read the topic very carefully and be sure to explicitly respond to each of its parts.

2. Highlight key words in the topic and pay particular attention to them.

3. Brainstorm ideas for addressing the topic and then organize the key ideas into a plan for your essay, using a mapping or outline format.

4. Build your essay around clearly defined points and support your points with thoughtful reasons.

Reducing Test Anxiety: How Can I Solve the Problem of Test Anxiety and Stress?

I encountered the paralyzing effects of test anxiety a number of years ago when administering an examination in my Introduction to Philosophy class. Halfway through the exam, I looked up and noticed that one of my better students was sitting motionless. When I walked over to her desk, I found she had not written anything in her examination booklet. I tried to speak with her, but she was frozen, almost unable to utter a word. After class, I arranged for her to take the test in the less-pressured environment of the department office, and I worked with her to help her relax. She performed well on the test.

It's natural to be somewhat anxious before a test, and some anxiety is actually beneficial: it serves to motivate you to prepare effectively, and it can help you perform at peak efficiency by sharpening your focus and fueling you with adrenaline energy. However, too much anxiety has just the opposite effect: it can inhibit your study efforts because you are preoccupied with worry and paralyze your thinking process as it did with the student described above. However, the negative effect of stress is not restricted to test taking—excessive stress is a destructive threat that intrudes into many aspects of your life, and it makes sense for you to develop strategies for coping with it. To accomplish this, we will use the problem-solving method that we explored in Chapter 3, in order to analyze the dynamics of stress and to develop productive approaches to reducing it.

Accepting the Problem

Stress is a common part of life that can interfere with your performance and your happiness. Often, however, people are reluctant to fully acknowledge that they are experiencing stress, preferring instead to minimize its effect or deny its existence altogether. Unfortunately, these responses usually succeed in only making things worse, since stress doesn't go away merely because you don't recognize it, and you can't solve a problem that you don't acknowledge exists. So the place to begin dealing with stress is by fully acknowledging its reality and then committing yourself to controlling its effect. Don't feel embarrassed to admit that you are experiencing anxiety—it's a universal emotion. By acknowledging its existence, you are in a position to address it openly and assertively. On the other hand, anxiety and stress thrive when you try to pretend that they don't exist or when you just give into them and let their growing emotional power overwhelm you. If you find that you have difficulty in accepting this problem in your life, review the Acceptance strategies described in Chapter 3 on pages 81–82 and use those that are most appropriate to your situation.

Step One: What Is the Problem?

Stress is caused by circumstances that threaten our sense of control. Sometimes we choose to place ourselves in stressful circumstances because we want to experience the excitement that can accompany a loss of control. For example, you may choose to ride a roller coaster or go skydiving for the "thrill" of the experience. However, even in these situations, the reason you can enjoy the excitement is because you are confident that although you feel in danger, you are actually reasonably safe. But if the roller coaster starts to go off the track or if you have trouble opening your parachute, your "excitement" quickly becomes desperate terror!

When you are not deliberately seeking excitement, stress can be an extremely unpleasant and disruptive force in your life. It can paralyze you into inaction, keep you awake at night, inhibit you from doing your best, create a sense of panic or hopelessness, mire you in depression, and cause a variety of physical symptoms ranging from headaches to ulcers. We are all susceptible to the debilitating effects of stress, but some people are better at dealing with stress than others because they have developed effective coping strategies. Let's explore how you can better deal with the problem of stress.

What Do I Know About the Situation? Managing stress begins with developing a thorough understanding of the situation that is causing the stress. As you become familiar with the dynamics of the situation, you can then devise a plan of action to deal with it. In your analysis it's important to distinguish the "symptoms" of the problem from the situation that is actually causing the problem. For example, imagine that you are supposed to make a major oral presentation in class on Thursday. When you think about standing up in front of all those people and speaking for fifteen minutes, your throat constricts and your mouth goes dry, your breathing becomes shallow and difficult, and you

Being Well Prepared:
Effective performane is the result of being well prepared, using practical strategies to overcome anxiety, and creating a confident attitude.

feel as if your wildly beating heart is going to erupt through your chest. When you try to practice your presentation in front of a mirror or friends, your voice comes out like a strangled croak and your mind goes blank. Yet as bothersome as these reactions are, they are not the problem—they are *symptoms* of the problem.

The "problem" lies in your fear of speaking in front of a group (a very common fear, by the way). Where did this problem originate? Perhaps it stems from your dislike of being placed in a vulnerable position in front of people you don't know that well. Will they ridicule and insult you? Or perhaps it expresses your fear of appearing inept and foolish, as you imagine your tongue-tied presentation degenerating into a series of unintelligible croaks. In either case, your stress originates from the prospect of being placed in a situation in which you fear losing control, with disastrous results. And it is this problem that is responsible for the stress symptoms that you are experiencing.

Thinking Activity 5.4

Describe a situation in your life that is currently causing you stress. Begin with a description of the stress symptoms. Are you feeling tense, panicked, depressed, anxious, worried, unfocused, preoccupied, or afraid? Are you having difficulty sleeping, eating, concentrating, or getting things accomplished? Are you experiencing a physical symptom such as a headache, an upset stomach, or muscular tension or pain?

After giving a comprehensive description of the stress symptoms, explain the situation that you believe is causing the symptoms. Be as specific as you can. Distinguish events in reality ("I have to give an oral presentation on Thursday") from those in your mind ("I know that I will make a fool of myself").

What Results Am I Aiming for in This Situation?   Think about the stress situation that you wrote about in Thinking Activity 5.4. Although it would be nice to completely eliminate the stress from that situation, doing so may not be possible. With this in mind, the next step is to describe the *realistic* goals that you would like to achieve. It is important to be as specific and concrete as possible, for this will help you develop approaches for meeting these goals. For example, if you are anxious about making an oral presentation, your goals might include the following:

1. Not being so worried about it that you have trouble sleeping

2. Being able to speak in a voice loud and clear enough for everyone to hear

3. Being able to remember your main points

For each of these goals there are strategies that can help you. For instance, relaxation techniques can help you get the sleep you need. There are voice and breathing exercises that will prepare you to speak clearly and with sufficient volume. And there are note formats you can use to help you remember the main points you are speaking about.

Identify below the results you would like to achieve in solving your problem with stress.

1. _____

2. _____

3. _____

How Can I Define the Problem?   Using the analysis you have completed, summarize your stress problem in the space below. The strategies on pages 85–86 can help you in this regard.

_____

_____

_____

_____

_____

Step Two: What Are the Alternatives?

Many people act as if stress is a curse that they cannot escape, but the truth is there are many approaches that you can use to reduce and sometimes even eliminate stress. Some strategies are designed to address the physical dimensions of stress, and others are intended to focus on the psychological and emotional dimensions. Because the physical and psychological are closely inter-related, addressing one dimension also influences the other in a positive way. After reviewing the strategies described below, write down additional alternatives that are appropriate to your own individual situation. Use one or more of the approaches described on page 86 in Chapter Three to help you think about your problem in new and creative ways.

Alternative 1: Enhance the _Voice of Confidence_ and banish the _Voice of Panic._   Each of us has voices inside our minds that speak to us with what psychologists describe as "self-talk." Sometimes these voices are positive and constructive, bolstering our self-esteem and increasing our confidence with such messages as "I will be successful on this test" and "I am intelligent, talented, and creative." Often, however, these voices are negative and destructive, undermining our self-esteem and shattering our self-confidence with such messages as "I am going to fail this test," "I am not as intelligent as other students," and "I am mediocre and have a dull personality." The stress that you experience increases as the Voice of Panic grows stronger and diminishes as the Voice of Confidence takes over. In order to influence these voices, you first need to become aware of them, for they usually operate without your conscious knowledge. A daily journal devoted entirely to these voices is a good way to start becoming aware of them. When the Voice of Panic shows up, you need to get tough with it and banish it from your mind. On the other hand, you need to make conscious efforts to send positive messages to yourself through your Voice of Confidence. Build on the successes you have already achieved, and remind yourself that since you succeeded before, you can succeed now.

Alternative 2: Analyze the reality of your anxiety-provoking situation as objectively as possible.   Much of the stress that you experience is needless in the sense that it is not grounded in reality. For example, the anxiety you may be feeling about an upcoming oral presentation is fueled by fantasies of humiliating yourself while your classmates laugh uproariously at your difficulties. Yet these fantasies are just that—fantasies. The reality of the situation is you are unlikely to humiliate yourself in the way you fear. If you prepare carefully, your presentation at the very least will be adequate. And it is even more unlikely other students will be so cruel and insensitive that they will want you to feel worse than you already do. They are much more likely to empathize with your difficulties, since they are painfully aware of how it feels to be in a vulnerable situation like that. And your instructor is likely to create a mature and supportive environment in the class. Analyzing the facts of the situation in a clear and objective fashion should help reduce the stress that you feel, because the way that you *think* about a situation influences how you *feel* about the situation. It is also useful to have others give you "reality checks" to prevent your fantasies from spiraling out of control.

Alternative 3: Seek the support of other people. In the same way other people can provide reality checks to help us keep things in perspective, they can also provide positive support to help us deal with stressful situations. You shouldn't be reluctant to express fears and anxieties to others, since they are probably experiencing similar feelings of their own and will welcome someone to talk to. This connection also underscores the importance of choosing friends who have caring and supportive attitudes toward others.

Alternative 4: Create a plan of action and implement it. Since stress is caused by circumstances that threaten your sense of control, you can reduce stress by working to take control of the situation that you are in. In order to do this, you first have to accept responsibility for your situation, believing that you *can* exert meaningful control, instead of simply giving in to your panic and fear. Next, you have to create an intelligent plan of action designed to help you control the stress situation. As you see yourself making progress in taking control and diminishing your stress, this will increase your confidence and determination. For example, by following the test-taking strategies that you have been exploring in this chapter, you have good reason to feel confident about your performance on most tests. If you combine these academic strategies with some of the stress-reducing approaches that you are exploring in this section, you should find yourself dealing with stress more effectively, which will bolster your confidence and sense of control.

Alternative 5: Seek professional help. There are times when the stress in our lives becomes so overwhelming and debilitating that we simply cannot cope with it, whether through our own efforts or with the assistance of friends. On those occasions, it makes sense to seek the assistance of a professional who has been trained to help people in just these circumstances. If the source of your anxiety is a specific course, it makes sense to speak with the instructor about your fears and to get his or her advice. If your concern is other than a specific course, there are usually counselors or support staff on your campus who can be helpful. When you feel overwhelmed, you shouldn't be reluctant to admit that things are getting out of control, and you shouldn't be ashamed to have a trained professional help you regain control and get back on track. Virtually everyone is in this position at one time or other in life. After all, you don't feel ashamed to seek medical help when you have a physical ailment; there is also no need to feel ashamed when you need psychological or emotional healing.

Meditation is a powerful tool for helping you relax and concentrate, enabling you to let go of the irrational fears that are crowding in on your consciousness.

Alternative 6: Practice meditation. You don't have to be a practicing Zen Buddhist to enjoy the beneficial effects of meditation. Meditation is a powerful tool for developing control over your thinking and emotions. It helps you to relax, focus, and concentrate, and it enables you to let go of many of the irrational fears and anxieties that are crowding in on your consciousness. You can practice meditation in many different situations, whether you are alone or with others, and it is easily integrated as a natural part of your life. A suggested approach for meditating can be found on page 142. Feel free to adapt this protocol in ways that work best for you.

Alternative 7: Work on your breathing. As we previously noted, stress is expressed in a variety of physical symptoms, but it's a two-way street—by addressing the physical symptoms, you can improve the way you feel. For example, when you are feeling stressed, your breathing becomes shallow and more rapid, often accompanied by a tightness across your chest. On the other hand, if you concentrate on breathing slowly and deeply, this has the effect of relaxing you and easing your tension.

Alternative 8: Use muscle relaxation. In a similar fashion, by progressively relaxing the areas of your body that have become tense as a result of stress, you can reduce feelings of stress as well as make yourself feel better physically. One effective approach is to take turns tensing and releasing various parts of your body, working from the feet up. Of course, if you can arrange for someone to give you a deep-body massage, so much the better!

Alternative 9: Follow a schedule of regular physical exercise.

There are many reasons why regular physical exercise is beneficial for you, and helping to keep stress under control is one of the most important. Stress builds up in us, both physically and psychologically, and vigorous physical exercise helps release this accumulated tension while also taking our mind off the source of the stress. Regular exercise also helps us maintain healthy sleep and eating patterns, not to mention the benefits to our muscles, appearance, and cardiovascular system. The physical and psychological aspects of ourselves are closely integrated, and we need to take care of both dimensions of our lives to achieve optimal well-being.

Alternative 10: _____

_____

Alternative 11: _____

_____

Step Three: What Are the Advantages and/or Disadvantages of Each Alternative?

Carefully review the alternatives just described, as well as those that you identified, and for each alternative describe the advantages, disadvantages, and further information needed.

Step Four: What Is the Solution?

Which Alternative(s) Will I Pursue? Your analysis of the various alternatives for managing stress should have provided you with some useful ideas that you can use in your own life. Review the strategies for selecting alternatives explained on page 92, and then identify below one or more alternatives that you plan to implement.

Alternative 1: _____

_____

Alternative 2: _____

_____

Alternative 3: _____

_____

What Steps Can I Take to Act on the Alternative(s) Chosen? For each of the alternatives that you identified, design a plan of action that specifies the steps you need to take to implement it. Don't forget to include a schedule.

Step Five: How Well Is the Solution Working?

As you implement your plan, monitor how successfully it is helping you. If you find that you need to make adjustments, then make them. If you find that a plan is not working, go back and review your list of alternatives and try another one. If you discover that your motivation to manage stress is diminishing, review the strategies that you used during the Acceptance stage of your analysis (pages 81–82) in an effort to recommit yourself to solving this problem. Additional evaluation strategies can be found on pages 93–95.

"Nurturing Physical Health"

The problem of stress affects many areas of your life at college besides tests, including your eating patterns. The two passages in this section deal with some of the psychological issues related to eating. Don't lose sight of the fact that success in college depends on having a healthy body as well as a robust mind. The first article, *Diary of an Eating Disorder* by Michelle Stacey, chronicles the disturbing experiences of a compulsive dieter, an affliction that young women are particularly susceptible to. *Dangerous Diets*, by William C. Rader, M.D., analyzes the analogous dieting problems in men. After carefully reading these articles, answer the questions that follow.

Diary of an Eating Disorder

Michelle Stacey

> Our national obsession with dieting has gotten so out of control that no one knows what normal eating habits are. Here, the chronicle of one compulsive dieter.

It's eight o'clock on a cool spring evening in New York, and Laurel Schiller (not her real name) is making herself a dinner only an obsessive could love. Here, in perfect profile, is what the ascetics of the 90s are eating—all roughage and renunciation, no fat of any kind. As she tosses together the ingredients, her mind automatically clicks off the calorie count: 50 for the lettuce, another 50 for the cucumber, say, 40 for the tomato. Mushrooms—those are good, hardly any calories—carrots, alfalfa sprouts. Dressing—balsamic vinegar mixed with mustard—close to zero. Two hundred total.

Schiller used to consult a well-thumbed calorie counter; now the counts are internalized. But while calories are still useful—she consumes a precise 1,400 per day, including even the stray stick of gum (15 calories)—they are to an expert like Schiller the dinosaurs of dieting. *Fat* is the new last word in the weight-loss liturgy, and for that she needs no counter: Schiller is on the zero-fat plan. She can't even remember the last time she ate peanut butter or pizza. Even a skinless chicken breast and fish, those diet classics, are impossibly greasy.

→

Salad eaten, Schiller is ready for her reward, the 392-calorie dessert whose lack of sin adds perversely to its pleasure. She splits a banana lengthwise (average calories: 100), puts it in a bowl, and starts spooning over it Dutch Chocolate American Glacé frozen dessert (which has 292 calories per carton and no fat). This is Schiller's regular institutionalized binge: She knows even before she starts that she will eat the entire carton—a thought that never fails to give her a frisson of pleasure.

At the end of the carton, she knows she should be thinking about which clients she'll be seeing tomorrow at her $55,000-a-year job, but instead she's thinking about what she will eat: fat-free wheat flakes and skim milk for breakfast, a plain bagel and a salad dressed with vinegar for lunch, intermittent snacks of jelly beans or Gummi Bears or nonfat frozen yogurt from the machine at the deli. Then she's going out for dinner, where she knows, unrepentantly, that she'll be her waiter's worst nightmare: steamed vegetables, not grilled. Is there oil in that sauce? Can you put that on the side? (She might even squeeze the baked potato to be sure it doesn't have any oil or butter on it.) By the time Schiller goes to bed, she has the next day's eating mapped out. But as she turns out the light, she wishes it were morning already because she is feeling hungry again.

Laurel Schiller is proof, if any was needed, of one of the cultural realities of our age: We have become absolute experts at dieting. So expert, in fact, that the control-freak staples of Schiller's day—rigid calorie counts, constant obsessing about eating, fanatical rejection of any fats—are not examples of aberration but instead the hallmarks of something akin to a national eating disorder. Forget eating normally. Dietitians and eating disorder researchers can't even define it anymore. So many of us restrain ourselves—eating not in response to natural cues of hunger but to external cues of will and self-control—that it's become "normal" to be on a diet. Hunger is no longer the enemy but something to be courted—proof that we're doing the right thing.

What do we get in return for this Snackwell's/fat-free yogurt/Lean Cuisine mind-set? Whether we get smaller buns is debatable; we do get a reassuring sense of control and a pretty sick idea of what's pleasurable (fat-free cheese? Try rubber). We also get a new eating disorder: subclinical eating disorder, SED, which stops short of anorexia and bulimia on the obsession scale. You may not be so thin that your bones are showing, but you're enslaved all the same. Just ask Schiller.

"I used to be an enormous junk-food eater," she says. "I was never overweight, but I was never thin-thin." This mantra, *thin-thin,* comes up often in her patter about food. It denotes just the right level of thin—not natural slenderness, which is what Laurel has had most of her life (she is now in her late 20s), but which is a size 8 rather than a size 6. Thin-thin is something that works with the Alaïa dress that measures six inches across on the hanger. Once she became thin-thin, Schiller says, "I could wear all these things I'd always wanted to wear and never wore." It did not bother her that friends and family wondered about her health. "At work people were saying I was getting too thin. When I went home for Christmas, everyone was saying, 'Oh my God, you're so thin.' That made me so happy. Isn't that sick?"

Schiller became thin-thin originally on what some women call the dumped-again diet. Her fiancé, Aaron, had announced that he wasn't ready for marriage and moved out. For a while, "I

→

just didn't have an appetite, and I was always crying, always had a lump in my throat. And even when I did eat, I kept losing weight." The weight loss was one of the few bright spots in what was a very dark time.

Then Schiller found something else that made her happy: exercise. She tried a videotape home-aerobics routine, and she says, "I found that right after the exercise was the first time in such a long time that I had felt good about myself. So I got totally addicted to it. I was doing it every single day." Eventually, she got happy enough to start putting weight back on, despite the exercise. She saw thin-thin slipping away. "My clothes weren't fitting the same way anymore. I thought my legs were getting heavy—muscles were building up. I wanted to get back to the skinniness that I had been."

That was when, for the first time in her life, Schiller thought about consciously dieting. She began to diet-shop, trying one, then another. The one she eventually found was actually presented to her with a sort of antirecommendation; Schiller was immediately attracted. "A friend of mine was telling me in a very negative way about this other friend of hers who wouldn't eat any fat, not a gram of fat," she says. "And I thought, Oh, that's the best idea! Then I found a book that was all about fat-free diets, with recipes and stuff. It became my bible. It lists tons of fat-free things, with brand names and everything." At about the same time, she obtained from a magazine article a formula for figuring out the lowest number of calories you can eat per day without slowing your metabolism and came up with the magic 1,400.

Those two concepts—no fat, 1,400 calories per day—became the constructs for a new life. One of the most delightful and unexpected benefits of that life was the gratifying sense of control Schiller felt. "I remember thinking, God, I have such willpower. If I set my mind to do something, I can do it," she says. "Watching other people who said, 'Oh, I want to lose weight,' but they couldn't stop eating and start dieting, I'd think, How come I'm so strong?" Her workouts too, which she almost never skipped, made her feel strong and resilient. She sometimes felt that she could do anything.

It took a while for the dark underbelly of her new plan to show itself. She began to constrict her social life because she couldn't be sure of maintaining her regimen if she went out to a restaurant. "I'd think, I don't want to do this because there's nothing for me to eat there. So I wouldn't want to make plans, or I'd make plans not involving dinner. Or I'd just make sure we went to a restaurant where I knew there were things I could order. But I used to love to go out to good restaurants, and at a certain point I realized it was kind of weird that I was staying home just so I could eat what I wanted."

Her body, in its infinite wisdom, already knew something was very weird. The first sign was the disappearance of her period (a low calorie intake or a high level of exercise can disrupt the hormones that trigger ovulation). "I remember one morning waking up thinking that I felt really skinny," Schiller says. "I totally had lost my chest—I was completely flat-chested—and my hair was not in good shape, and I thought to myself, This is disgusting." But she stayed on the diet.

The diet's dark side finally lurched into public view at Thanksgiving. Schiller had been strictly following her diet for several months, and she went home to visit her family. She decided that for Thanksgiving dinner she would allow herself to eat what she calls "normally," that is, without restrictions. So she began—and she couldn't stop. "It was horrible," she says. "It was disgusting. It's the joke of my family now. I ate all the dinner, with about three helpings, and then dessert—I must have had 15 desserts. I was just thinking, This is so yummy. I love this. I haven't had this in so long. I never eat it. I deserve it. Even my mother, who thought I'd gotten too thin and was too restrictive, was saying, 'You have to stop—you're going to get sick.' But I couldn't control myself. It was scary."

Schiller had just had, for the first time in her life, a certifiable binge. The next day she was back on her diet.

Schiller's weight is within the normal range and she doesn't make herself vomit, but she would be the first to admit that her eating is disordered. The symptoms of SED are familiar enough: chronic undereating, overexercising, and binge eating that results from undereating. This behavior in turn can lead to scant or nonexistent periods and the effects of a low metabolic rate from undereating (fatigue, cold intolerance, depression, dizziness on standing, constipation). While only 2 to 5 percent of women fit the definition of anorexic or bulimic, one clinician who runs an eating disorders counseling group estimates that 80 to 85 percent of women fall into the category of "disordered eating—people who are obsessed with weight and body image" at some point in their lives.

What SED shares with its big sisters, anorexia and bulimia, is a search for control through food—control of one's body, one's desires, one's fate—and a simultaneous investing of food with a terrible power. Food is not a source of pleasure but a wily adversary. That leads to the kind of logic described by C. Wayne Callaway, an endocrinologist at George Washington University who has looked extensively at SED: "Someone like this will say, 'Oh, I binged yesterday.' If you ask, 'What did you actually eat?' she'll say, 'Gosh, I had a peanut butter and jelly sandwich' or 'I had three pieces of cheese.' That's somebody who's not binging but who does have a distorted view of eating."

When it comes to eating, it seems, reality has become an extremely elastic concept. Another eating disorders expert, C. Peter Herman of the University of Toronto, who was the first to propose that "normal eating" has acquired a new definition, describes what happens when dieting becomes a cherished lifestyle: "The bodies of people who don't diet tell them with reasonable efficiency when to eat and when to stop eating. A diet imposes unnatural signals—cognitive ones, not physiological—that undermine one's ability to know when one is truly hungry or truly full, so that the regulation of eating becomes entirely dependent on these fairly arbitrary mental rules of what to eat. Mostly these rules are telling you, Don't eat even though you might be tempted to."

Laurel Schiller has seen the seductive beauty and simplicity of those rules and has embraced their promise of inner strength. When we met for lunch, she warned me, laughingly, that I might be embarrassed by the way she orders her lunch. And, indeed, when the waiter came, she entered into a discussion: Could she have the mozzarella and tomato salad, except without the mozzarella and with mustard and balsamic vinegar on the side? And the steamed artichoke, could that be served with no sauce? We were at a chic little French brasserie where tables were lined up on the sidewalk to take advantage of the sunshine. The menu featured

→

many light entrées—seafood salads, chicken niçoise, grilled vegetable plate—but in Schiller's book all of these were flawed. "I never get grilled vegetables, just steamed," she confided, "because they always put oil on the grilled ones."

When her food arrived, it looked dry and stark on the huge bistro dinnerware: alternating slabs of bare tomato and purple onion on one plate, an unadorned artichoke marooned in the center of the other. But Schiller dug in happily, mixing the mustard and balsamic vinegar into a paste that she used for dipping artichoke leaves, and eating a little bread on the side. "Some people just can't stand to eat at restaurants with me," she said cheerfully, "because my ordering is so involved, and I'll send things back if I think they have any oil on them. I've found a handful of restaurants in the city where there are things I can order. For a long time I just didn't want to go out much because I was worried about what I'd eat. That's when I realized there was something a little wrong with this—that it probably had a lot to do with control. Aaron moving out was completely *out* of my control, and it was so awful. And then there I was, all of a sudden living alone in New York. This eating thing showed I really was in control. It felt good."

There was no hint of deprivation or calorie obsession in her upbringing or even in her college years, the time when an estimated 80 percent of women flirt with disordered eating behavior. Schiller was never overweight. "I guess I was normal—about a size 8. But I always felt I should be thinner. Always. I didn't think of myself as slender. But it never crossed my mind really to diet or exercise. I just thought, Oh, this is the way I am."

Now she is an aficionada of fat-free foods and cooking methods, and a veritable dictionary of calorie and fat counts. But she has substituted other indulgences for the prime ribs of the past. The premier one is sugar. "I *crave* sweet things," she says. "I live on Skimpy Treats and jelly beans and Gummi Bears." And occasionally she eats a whole cake. A fat-free cake, of course.

Schiller's largest concession to normal eating now takes the form of a planned binge. One day a week she allows herself to eat normally—whatever she wants, not thinking about the diet. Because it's her one day of free eating—a broken diet, essentially—she eats more, without regard to internal hunger cues. "I'd think, This is my one night. I'd better get it all in," she says. "So I'd eat whatever I wanted, and it wouldn't even be a question of hunger. I'd just think, I might as well have this because it's going to be another week." Every time that happens, the link between hunger and eating becomes weaker. But then, hunger is almost beside the point in Schiller's life. "I'm always hungry," she says.

The recent (slight) loosening of her rigid diet rules has coincided with the entry of a new man into Schiller's life. Now she coordinates her night of normal eating with date nights. "When we first started dating, he would pick a place where there wouldn't be fat-free food. Like one time he picked this Mexican restaurant, and I felt kind of foolish saying I can't eat there."

This is as far as Schiller will go toward eating normally. She hopes to stick with her restrictions forever, through marriage and having children. "I think it will be much harder," she admits, "but I hope I'll be able to do it." Schiller is, with thorough good humor, in love with her chains; they still feel strangely like salvation.

→

Dangerous Diets

William C. Rader, M.D.

We're all well aware of the popular media's images of physical perfection. As a physician who specializes in eating disorders, I can testify to that. And I'm seeing an increasing number of men who are as mesmerized by those models as women have been for years. They'll look in the mirror and see fat where there is none, and they'll resort to extreme methods—even surgery—to eliminate any fat they *do* have via the fastest route. I also find that, psychologically, for men the ends justify the means more than for women, and this leads them to endure diets, exercise regimens, strange foods and medical procedures which might improve their appearance (though even that's doubtful) but which will almost certainly harm their health in the process.

The Male Yo-yo

Yo-yo dieting—the repeated gain/lose, gain/lose weight-loss pattern that often persists for years—once was the exclusive province of women, but with ever-larger numbers of men either following book-based diets or enrolling in formal diet programs, more of them are falling into it as well. Yo-yoing is psychologically damaging because repeated "failures" to keep weight off injure self-esteem. It's also physically harmful: New studies show that even minor-league weight fluctuations can shorten one's lifespan.

Yo-yo dieting subjects the body to a kind of stress that is bad enough in women but is *extremely* dangerous in men. Not only does the process become self-perpetuating (you'll develop a lower metabolic rate, making it ever harder to lose weight), but more important, the yo-yo syndrome contributes to the development of abdominal-fat deposits. Men are prone to gaining weight around their midsections to begin with, and extra weight on this part of the male anatomy is a risk factor for cardiovascular disease.

So don't get involved in quick-fix weight loss, one of the leading causes of the yo-yo diet syndrome. A nutritionally sound, high–complex-carbohydrate, low-fat diet is much more effective for long-term weight maintenance. If you're extremely overweight, select an eating program with the advice of a doctor who knows you and is knowledgeable about weight loss.

Exercise Addiction

Large numbers of men have turned to aerobics, running and other cardiovascular exercise to lose weight and maintain weight loss after changing their eating habits. As a result, there's been an increase in the numbers of men who don't know when a good thing turns bad. Because of their tendency to rely more actively on exercise in combination with a diet than do women, men are especially prone to this addiction.

The situation isn't difficult to understand. A man starts using exercise intelligently to control his weight. After he achieves his weight-loss goals, he may become extremely sensitive to gaining an extra pound or two, so much so that he'll rev up his exercise routine in response to the smallest weight increase. In addition, vigorous cardiovascular exercise causes the body to up its production of endorphins, the source of the so-called runner's high, and he might

→

develop an urge for more of that pleasant experience. Along with his exaggerated perception of his body weight, this exercise benefit might move him to overtrain.

Consequently, men work out despite injuries; they neglect personal or work problems in favor of workouts designed to eliminate nonexistent excess pounds—in short, men hurt rather than help themselves.

Extreme Diets

Since sports celebrities started promoting diet programs on television, I've noticed a marked increase in the number of men who come to me after having gotten started on a variety of wacky eating programs.

Because men tend to treat any sort of diet program as they would a work project—perhaps overzealously—they make liquid and other rapid-results diets even more harmful than they would be for women who follow the (usually minimal) instructions. Men first starve themselves, making the liquid diet their only nourishment. Then, after they see that a few pounds have come off, the reservoir of hunger they've been building up overpowers them, and they start to binge. Usually, they gain even more weight than they started out with because they stick with the liquid-diet drink in addition to the food they've begun eating.

Especially in younger men, repeated fad dieting can also lead to development of full-blown eating disorders, such as anorexia (self-starvation) and bulimia (a binge/purge cycle whose victims eat obsessively, then force themselves to vomit or take laxatives to remove the food from their systems). Though still relatively rare in men, these extremely serious conditions are on the rise as more men begin to suffer from distorted body images. The possible complications can be life-threatening: extreme fatigue, kidney malfunction, erratic heartbeat and cardiac arrest. Bulimia can contribute to the worsening of an already present diabetic condition and cause hypoglycemia (abnormally low blood sugar) and stomach rupture.

Surgery to the Rescue

Because most men like the quickest route to a desired goal, they are also turning in disturbingly high numbers to surgical procedures to solve their weight-loss problems. Believe it or not, in 1991 some doctors still perform surgery that reduces the size of the stomach by literally stapling part of it shut. The procedure can work (if the stomach's smaller, you can't put as much into it), but it is dangerous in two respects: It doesn't address underlying psychological issues, and patients can—and I've seen it happen—burst their staples in a desperate bid to overeat.

Intestinal-bypass operations designed to decrease the amount of food absorbed by the body are also still being performed on men to help control extreme obesity. I don't recommend this procedure, *ever,* unless a man is so severely overweight that there is no other way out. It is a major operation, and experience tells me that the associated risks are too high.

What Does Work for Men?

Men are fast becoming familiar with the diet world's terrain—and all of its pitfalls. What we have to learn is that there are no quick routes through or around a weight problem.

⟶

After years of dealing with severe eating disorders that result in a variety of physical and psychological problems, I've decided that there's only one sure way to control weight and keep a healthy psyche. It's the classic three-pronged approach: *exercise, good nutrition* (meaning low-fat, high–complex-carb foods) and a basic *acceptance* of your own unique look.

The greatest single contributor to the growth of dangerous weight-loss methods among men is the influence of advertising messages that have men, like women, pursuing unattainably perfect body images. If you have special needs, see a physician who specializes in weight loss. But if you're just a regular guy who's concerned about his appearance, do what healthy, happy people have done about their weight since the first french fry hit a plate: Exercise caution and moderation.

_____

Questions for Analysis

1. Explain the reasons why men and women get involved in the unhealthy and dangerous dieting practices described in these articles. Why do you think eating disorders like these are so widespread in American society?

2. Compare the dieting disorders of men and women, discussing the similarities and differences between them.

3. Have you ever experienced any problems or anxieties related to eating? If so, describe your experience, the reasons why you think the problem developed, and the approaches you used to deal with it.

6
Reading Critically

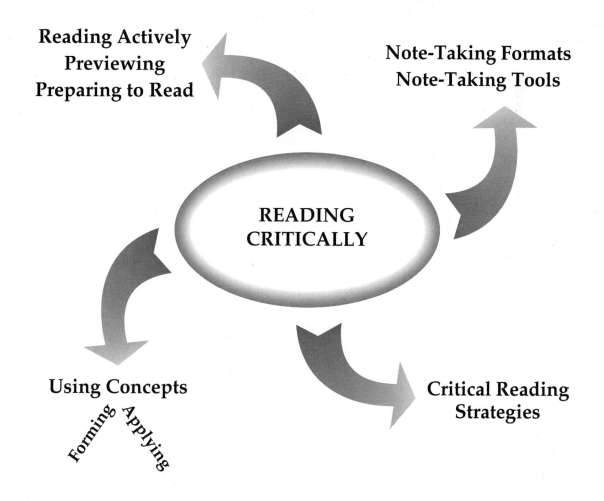

Reading Actively
Previewing
Preparing to Read

Note-Taking Formats
Note-Taking Tools

READING
CRITICALLY

Using Concepts
Forming Applying

Critical Reading
Strategies

A successful college student is both a critical thinker and a skilled user of language—someone who is "critically literate." College success requires that as you develop knowledge and advanced thinking abilities, you also develop sophisticated language skills: the ability to read critically, write effectively, and discuss ideas intelligently. In these next three chapters, we will be exploring and helping you develop the reading, writing, and discussion abilities you will need to become critically literate and academically successful.

The processes of thinking and language are closely related. When you write or speak, you are using language to express your thinking, and when you read, you are using your mind to comprehend the thinking of others and share their experiences. For example, read the following eloquent passage by Malcolm X, which describes the power of the reading process, a discovery he made as a young man serving time in prison. Nearly illiterate when he entered prison, he began to educate himself by copying—and learning—the dictionary. As you read the passage, take notice of how his words stimulate your thinking processes.

> I suppose it was inevitable that as my word-base broadened, I could for the first time pick up a book and read and now begin to understand what the book was saying. Anyone who has read a great deal can imagine the new world that opened. Let me tell you something: from then until I left that prison, in every free moment I had, if I was not reading in the library, I was reading on my bunk. You couldn't have gotten me out of books with a wedge. Between Mr. Muhammed's teachings, my correspondence, my visitors, and my reading of books, months passed without my even thinking about being imprisoned. In fact, up to then, I never had been so truly free in my life.

One of the differences between high school and college that you have probably noticed is both the *quantity* and the *quality* of the reading assignments. In general, your teachers are assigning a much greater volume of material than you were used to in high school. In addition, you are probably discovering the readings themselves are more complex, and you are expected to be more analytical and critical as you read them. The total effect of these reading assignments may be somewhat overwhelming to you, and it is not difficult to feel discouraged or even a little panicky. Let's examine effective approaches for solving the challenge of becoming a critical reader.

Think about the reading assignments that you have had during the last several years of your education, and then respond to the following questions:

- Which assignments have given you the most difficulty?
- What are some of the most prominent problems that you have with challenging readings?
- Do you get lost easily or have difficulty in concentrating for long periods of time?
- Do you have trouble understanding complex concepts and then explaining what these concepts mean?
- Do you have difficulty with questions that ask you to analyze, relate, compare, contrast, or apply the ideas you have been reading?
- After completing your assignment, do you find you can't recall what you just read?

Preparing to Read

In completing Thinking Activity 6.1, you were probably able to identify a number of problem areas in your reading. However, your difficulties probably began *before* you even began your reading. As we saw in Chapter Four, effective learning involves careful preparation, and the same is true of efficient reading.

- **Identify a suitable reading environment.** Although you may be able to read the newspaper or a novel while music or the television is on, while engaging in conversations with people around you, or while eating a snack and talking on the phone, this approach will not work for academic reading. The material in textbooks and scholarly articles is simply too complex, abstract, and densely packed to permit these sorts of distractions. This sort of "heavy duty" reading requires a learning environment that will help you focus your attention and concentrate. Review the section on Learning Environment on page 140 to help you identify an appropriate place to do your reading.

- **Create an effective reading schedule.** Reading academic material can sometimes feel like running through deep sand—it requires commitment, hard work, and pacing. (Pacing yourself allows you to avoid wearing out prematurely.) Plan to do approximately 60-90 minutes of concentrated reading at a time—probably all the reading you can effectively process. Divide this larger time block into 15-20 minute intervals. During these intervals, don't allow yourself to become distracted or your concentration to wander. Keep your head down and plow through the sand. At the end of each interval, take a mini-break of about 5 minutes, giving you an opportunity to relax a little and review what you have just read.

By maintaining this pattern of concentrated reading, interspersed with mini-breaks, you should be able to make the most efficient use of your mental resources. After 60–90 minutes of this schedule, you'll probably be ready for a break. Get some exercise, relax for 15–20 minutes, and then study a different subject to give yourself a change of pace. One word of caution: don't save up large chunks of reading to complete at one sitting. It is essential that you complete your reading over a period of time in order to achieve maximum comprehension and retention.

Sample Reading Schedule

Concentrated Reading	15–20 minutes
Relax and Review	5 minutes
Concentrated Reading	15–20 minutes
Relax and Review	5 minutes
Concentrated Reading	15–20 minutes
Break	15–20 minutes
Study New Subject	

Previewing Your Reading Assignments

Imagine that you are under time pressure to reach a destination you've never been to before and your traveling companion suggests: "Let's just jump into the car and start driving." Your response might be, quite reasonably, "Are you crazy? We have to plan where we're going! We have to look at a map!" Yet many students who would agree with this response do exactly the opposite when they are faced with an unfamiliar reading assignment. They immediately go to the beginning of the assignment and start reading, entering into this unexplored territory without a plan or a map. Paradoxically, starting at the beginning is usually the *least* effective way to approach your reading assignments. Instead, you need to *think critically* about your assignments by analyzing them as a whole and developing a plan of action. Here's how you can do this.

Examine the Table of Contents or Chapter Outline.

The table of contents and chapter outlines provide you with the general structure and organization of your reading assignment. By beginning with these elements, you can develop an overall understanding of the reading passage, the organization of the major ideas, and the way specific details fit into this overall organization. It's as if you are taking an aerial view of the territory you are going to explore, looking for key landmarks, examining the patterns of connecting roads, and developing an overall sense of the terrain. For example, review the table of contents in this book, taking particular note of the topics that are covered and the way these topics are organized. Now look at where this chapter fits in relation to the overall design of the book. Describe in the space below how the topics of this chapter relate to the other topics in the book:

_____

_____

_____

Next, examine the thinking map that opens this chapter (page 199). What is the overall design of the chapter? What are the major topics, and how are they related? Describe in the space below the general goal of the chapter, and identify some of the key topics designed to help you achieve this goal:

General goal of the chapter: _____

_____

Key topics:

1. _____

2. _____

3. _____

4. _____

5. _____

Read the Introductory Paragraphs and the Concluding Paragraphs or Summary.

After reviewing the table of contents or chapter outline, next review the opening and closing paragraphs or summary. Authors generally explain the major goals of the chapter in the introduction and then conclude by reviewing the key topics that have been explored. Reviewing these sections should help you fill in the mental map you are creating of the reading assignment and help you develop a plan for exploring the material. Review the opening and concluding sections of this chapter, and then describe what additional information you have learned about the chapter.

_____

_____

_____

_____

Scan the Reading Assignment, Taking Particular Note of Section Headings, Illustrations, and Diagrams.

The next step in creating your map is to actually scout the territory by completing a rapid scan of what lies ahead. Move quickly through the material, focusing on the section headings, boxed or shaded areas, illustrations, diagrams, and other defining features. This should help you continue to fill in and elaborate your mental map, noting key points, concepts, definitions, and relationships. For example, quickly scan this chapter, noting the features mentioned above, and then describe new information that you have learned as a result of this scouting process.

_____

_____

_____

_____

Thinking Activity 6.2

Select a difficult reading assignment from one of your courses, and before beginning your reading, apply the previewing strategies that we have been considering:

■ *Examine the table of contents or chapter outline.*

■ *Read the introductory paragraphs and the concluding paragraphs or summary.*

■ *Scan the reading assignment, taking particular note of section headings, illustrations, and diagrams.*

After completing your reading assignment, analyze and describe how the previewing activities helped you create a "mental map" of the assignment, which in turn helped you understand and remember the material in the reading.

Reading Actively

Critical thinkers are people who use their minds actively, not passively, as we discovered in Chapter 2. Using your mind actively is one of the keys to becoming a successful reader. Instead of turning the pages mechanically and using only a small portion of your mind to engage the material, you must use strenuous mental action—asking and trying to answer questions, elaborating points, reorganizing material, relating ideas to knowledge you already have. When you read actively, you are relating and reshaping the material to conform to—and s-t-r-e-t-c-h —your own mind, integrating the material into your own knowledge framework. By actively transforming the material, you are understanding what you are reading in a meaningful and lasting way. This "deep" learning—much different than the "superficial" learning many students engage in—will enable you to understand the course material effectively, participate knowledgeably in class, and prepare for tests in a relatively easy manner. Let's examine the strategies that you can use to become an expert, active reader.

Approach Reading Passages as a Whole, Instead of One Word or Phrase at a Time.

Reading is a dynamic language process that involves a variety of complex thinking activities. Unfortunately, traditional pre-college education often teaches reading as a series of decoding skills, with students learning to use the strategies of dictionary search and "sounding-it-out" in order to build their understanding one word at a time. However, expert readers approach the reading process much differently. They view the reading passage as a whole, and actively use their minds to determine the overall meaning that is being expressed. If they don't understand a particular word or phrase, they try to figure out the meaning within the context of the entire passage, using a dictionary to check their conclusions about a word. They use their thinking abilities to connect reading content to what they already know, gradually expanding their knowledge framework to include these new ideas.

For example, think about how you just read the preceding paragraph. Did you try to understand it a word at a time, or did you read through the entire passage and then try to figure out what you didn't understand? If you found yourself focusing on a word at a time, you need to work at approaching your reading as a whole. If you found you *did* try to understand the passage as a whole, connecting the ideas to what you already know, then you need to work at maintaining this approach when you are reading even more difficult textbook material.

Approach Your Reading Like a Problem Solver.

Successful readers often approach difficult reading passages with a problem-solving approach similar to the one we explored in Chapter Three.

Step 1: What is the problem? What don't I understand about this passage? Are there terms or concepts that are unfamiliar? Are the logical connections between the concepts confusing? Do some things just not make sense?

Step 2: What are the alternatives? What are some possible meanings of the terms or concepts? What are some potential interpretations of the central meaning of this passage?

Step 3: What is the evaluation of the possible alternatives? What are the "clues" in the passage, and what alternative meanings do they support? What reasons or evidence support these interpretations?

Step 4: What is the solution? Based on my evaluation and what I know of this subject, which interpretation is most likely? Why?

Step 5: How well is the solution working? Does my interpretation still make sense as I continue my reading, or do I need to revise my conclusion?

Of course, expert readers go through this process very quickly, much faster than it takes to explain it. Although this approach may seem a little cumbersome at first, the more you use it, the more natural and efficient it will become. Let's begin by applying it to a sample passage. Carefully read the passage below, and then use the problem-solving approach to determine the correct meanings of the italicized concepts and the overall meaning of the passage.

Existentialism, of which I am a representative, declares with greater consistency that if God does not exist there is at least one being whose existence comes before its essence, a being which exists before it can be defined by any conception of it. That being is man or, as Heidegger has it, the human reality. What do we mean by saying that existence precedes essence? We mean that man first of all exists, encounters himself, surges up in the world—and defines himself afterwards. If man as the existentialist sees him is not definable, it is because to begin with he is nothing. He will not be anything until later, and then he will be what he makes of himself. Thus, there is no human nature, because there is no God to have a conception of it. Man simply is. Not that he is simply what he conceives himself to be, but he is what he wills, and as he conceives existence. Man is nothing else but that which he makes of himself. This is the first principle of existentialism. . . . If, however, it is true that existence is prior to essence, man is responsible for what he is. Thus, the first effect of existentialism is that it puts every man in possession of himself as he is, and places the entire responsibility for his existence squarely upon his own shoulders. . . . That is what I mean when I say that man is condemned to be *free*. Condemned, because he did not create himself, yet is nevertheless at liberty, and from the moment that he is thrown into this world he is responsible for everything he does. . . . In life, a man commits himself, draws his own portrait and there is nothing but that portrait.

Step 1: What parts (if any) of this passage do you find confusing?

Step 2: Based on the contextual clues and the knowledge you have, what are some possible definitions of the italicized words, and what are some potential interpretations of this passage?

Existentialism: (a) _____

               (b) _____

Free: (a) _____

               (b) _____

Overall meaning: (a) _____

               _____

Overall meaning: (b) _____

_____

Step 3: What contextual clues can you use to help you define these concepts and determine the overall meaning? What knowledge of this subject do you have, and how can this knowledge help you understand this passage?

Step 4: Based on your evaluation in Step 3, which of the possible definitions and interpretations do you think are most likely? Why?

Step 5: How do your conclusions compare to those of the other students in the class? Should you revise your definitions or interpretation?

Use Metacognitive Strategies.

Although *metacognition* sounds intimidating, it's actually a process we have been working on throughout this book. While *cognition* refers to the process of thinking, *metacognition* refers to a form of thinking *about* the thinking process—an integral part of the definition of "critical thinking" we explored in Chapter Two. For example, think about what you will be doing this evening, and as you are thinking about this, make a special effort to stand outside of your thinking process and observe it while it is going on. This process of becoming an observer to your own thinking process—"reflecting" on your thinking—may feel strange, but it is well within your power if you concentrate. In the space below, describe some of the characteristics of the thinking process that you observed yourself engaging in. For instance, did you find you were talking (silently) to yourself? Did your thinking make use of still or moving visual images? Did you feel ideas were rushing through your mind like a river, or were your thoughts organized in an orderly fashion? Did you find one idea led to another idea, which led to another idea, through a series of associations?

Characteristics of My Thinking Process:

_____

_____

_____

By participating in this activity you were actually engaging in the process of *metacognition,* working to become aware of the process you use to think about something.

While the process of reading is a thinking (cognitive) activity, expert readers also engage in metacognition while they are reading. In other words, they are aware of their thinking process as they are reading, and they use this awareness to improve their thinking. This awareness can be expressed as a variety of questions:

Goals: What are my goals in reading this passage? How well am I meeting these goals?

Comprehension: How well do I understand what I am reading? What parts do I understand, and what parts am I confused about?

Anticipation: What events are going to take place following the ones I am reading about? How will the author develop and elaborate on these ideas?

Author's Purpose: What is the author's point of view, and why did she adopt this particular perspective? How has her point of view affected the information she selected and the manner in which she presented this information?

Evaluation: Is this information accurate? Do the ideas make sense? What evidence and reasons does the author provide to support her perspective?

As you work to answer these questions, you will likely find that you are *rereading* key sections, and this rereading is an essential part of the process of reading effectively.

Thinking Activity 6.3

Although developing metacognitive reading abilities is a complex process that takes place over time, you can begin using these strategies immediately. Select a chapter from one of your textbooks. As you read, make a conscious effort to ask—and to answer—the metacognitive questions noted above. Record your experience, identifying the questions that you found yourself asking, and how the process of asking—and trying to answer—these questions while you were reading affected your understanding of the material. The metacognitive questions are part of a reading worksheet located on page 210 that you can detach and use for reference later.

Annotate Your Reading.

You're sitting back in a comfortable position, and the neatly printed lines are organized like corn rows, each page looking indistinguishable from the others as you monotonously turn them one at a time. With this relationship to your book, it's easy for reading to become a passive activity, lulling you into a mental state of reduced concentration and semi-awareness. *You need to shake things up!* You need to break out of this passive state and actively engage and interact with the ideas you are reading about. How do you do this? In addition to sitting upright and placing your book on a flat surface, you need to use your pen or pencil as a tool to carry on a conversation with your book. For example, the write-on lines in this book are designed to stimulate your thinking and provide an opportunity for you to express your ideas. Similarly, you have been encouraged to *make this book your own* by customizing it with your own notes and responses. This is a productive approach to virtually all textbooks.

As we noted in Chapter 2 (page 50), there are a variety of writing strategies you can use to promote an active relationship with the material you are reading:

Metacognition:
Expert readers engage in metacognition *as they read, using an awareness of their thinking process to set goals, monitor their comprehension, ask questions, and evaluate what they are reading.*

1. *Underline and number important points.*

2. *Circle key words and draw lines between them to show relationships— for example, between the main idea and its supporting details.*

3. *Write notes in the margins that exemplify or extend the ideas being presented.*

4. *Use question marks to indicate parts that you don't understand.*

5. *Use notebook paper to record summaries, more extended responses, and diagrams to illustrate important ideas and their relationships.*

These kinds of annotations and more extended responses stimulate your thinking and help you respond to the ideas you are reading about. Using your mind in this way helps you understand and transform the material so that it can be meaningfully integrated into your knowledge framework.

Reading Worksheet

Reading Assignment: _____

Reading Environment: _____

Reading Schedule

Date Due: _____

Day   *Time Planned for Reading*

_____   _____

_____   _____

_____   _____

Reading Strategies

Problem Solving

Step 1: What is the problem in understanding the reading?

Step 2: What are the possible meanings and interpretations?

Step 3: What are the contextual clues, reasons, or evidence?

Step 4: What meaning or interpretation is most likely?

Step 5: How well is my conclusion working?

Metacognition

What are my **goals** in reading this passage, and how well am I meeting these goals?

What parts do I **understand,** and what parts are **confusing?**

How will the author **elaborate** and **develop** the ideas I am reading about?

What is the author's **point of view,** and why did she adopt this particular perspective?

Do the ideas **make sense?** What **evidence** and **reasons** support the ideas presented?

Annotation

Active Reading Strategies: Summary

- Approach your reading passages as a whole, instead of one word or phrase at a time.
- Approach your reading like a problem solver.
- Use metacognitive strategies.
- Annotate your reading.

Taking Notes

Effective note taking is central to effective reading and to your overall success as a student. There are a number of learning contexts in which taking clear and comprehensive notes is vital:

- *In your classes:* Whether your class is structured as primarily lecture or is more interactive, taking effective notes helps you relate to the material being presented and provides you with a written record for future study.

- *With your reading:* Reading textbooks and academic articles can easily deteriorate into a passive activity, with your eyes and mind glazing over. As we noted above, annotating the text and taking notes on separate sheets of paper promotes active learning, helping you understand and integrate the material you are reading.

- *Studying for tests:* As we explored in Chapter Five, creating study notes based on your classes and readings is a powerful way to process and retain course material, enabling you to perform well on tests and quizzes.

- *Writing research papers:* As we will see in Chapter Seven, taking effective notes on research texts and articles is integral to the process of writing research papers: gathering relevant information, synthesizing this information into a coherent form, citing sources, and creating a bibliography.

Taking clear and comprehensive notes is a complex activity, involving an integrated set of thinking and language abilities. Note-taking abilities develop in the same way that other complex activities do: by your engaging in the activity and then thinking critically in order to improve your performance. There are key strategies that form the core of effective note taking. By becoming familiar with these, you can develop a note-taking approach customized to fit your learning personality and the specific learning situation.

Note-Taking Materials

I suggest you use three-ring binders (one for each course or for two courses as the most). These binders provide the maximum flexibility for organizing your notes, adding supplementary handouts, and integrating your study and lecture notes.

Note-Taking Tools

- *Summarizing:* Unless you have the skills of a professional stenographer or court reporter, it is neither possible nor desirable to take notes verbatim. The essence of effective note taking is to extract the main points and key details from the material being presented. Some professors and textbooks aid this process by providing clear organization, highlighting central concepts, and offering appropriate definitions. In other instances, you will have to do more of the work yourself.

■ *Condensing:* When we write for other people in forms such as papers, letters, and memos, we typically want to use complete sentences in order to ensure that our total meaning is being communicated and also to abide by the conventions of these forms. However, when we take notes, we can eliminate many of the words we normally use, retaining only those words required to preserve the central meaning. For example, consider the following information:

Sigmund Freud suggested several different meta-psychological models to explain the functioning of the human personality. One model was built on the concepts Conscious, Preconscious, and Unconscious. A later model used the concepts of the Id, Ego, and Superego. It is possible to integrate these two models, but it involves delineating a complex set of relationships between them.

By using key terms organized in an intelligible pattern, we can communicate the same meaning in a simple, direct form:

Freud's metapsychological model of the human mind/personality

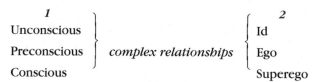

1		*2*
Unconscious		Id
Preconscious	*complex relationships*	Ego
Conscious		Superego

■ *Abbreviating:* Another way to take rapid and clear notes is to use abbreviation symbols to represent words and relationships. For example, notice how the following passage can be reduced through condensing and abbreviating:

Freud believed that the repressed contents of the Unconscious influence our thoughts, feelings and actions, in ways that we are unaware of. In other words, you may *think* that you are marrying someone as a result of a conscious and free choice on your part, but according to Freud's theory, your choice is in reality being influenced by powerful unconscious forces which probably originate in your relationship with your parents.

	Example
Contents of the Unconscious	Unconscious feelings toward parents
(influence)	(influence)
actions we think are free choices	who we choose to marry

The chart on page 213 displays some commonly used abbreviations.

Note-Taking Abbreviations

=	Equals
≠	Does not equal
"	Ditto (repeating same information)
#	Number
E.G.	For example
→	Causes
%	Percentage
‖	Parallel
∴	Therefore
{	Related items
¶	Paragraph
>	Greater than
<	Less than
+	Plus
&	And
⊃	Implies or suggests
cf	Compare
w/	with
w/o	without
p.	page
pp.	pages

■ *Illustrating:* The final note-taking tool involves using simple illustrations to communicate the same meaning in a clear, direct way. For example, the passage on page 212 about Freud's models of the human mind/personality could be illustrated as in Figure 6.1.

Note-Taking Formats

In addition to note-taking tools, there are several note-taking formats:

Outlining/Indenting. The most traditional format uses an outline structure in which the relationship between ideas is expressed through indenting (numbers and letters can be used as well). For example, information about Freud's models of the mind/personality can be recorded in the following way:

    I. Freud's models of the mind/personality
      A. Earlier model
        1. Unconscious

Figure 6.1. Freud's models in illustration format

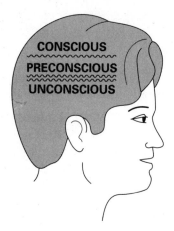 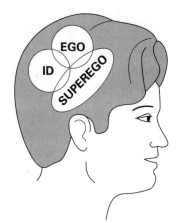

 2. Preconscious
 3. Conscious
B. Later model
 1. Id
 2. Ego
 3. Superego

With this format, ideas move from the general to the specific as you move from left to right. When using this format, as with other formats as well, it makes sense to leave space so that you can add additional information when it becomes available. For instance, after presenting an overview of these two Freudian models, your professor is likely to return to the concepts in order to provide more detail.

B. Later model
 1. Id: df . . .
 2. Ego: df . . .
 3. Superego: df . . .

Certain topics naturally lend themselves to an outline format, and you will find that many professors will explicitly organize ideas they are presenting in this fashion.

Mind Mapping. A *mind map* is a visual presentation of the various ways ideas can be related to one another, and it is a valuable tool for taking effective notes. For example, each chapter in this book opens with a diagram—a "mind map"— that visually summarizes the chapter's basic concepts as well as the way these concepts are related to each other. These maps are reference guides that reveal basic themes and chapter organization.

Because they clearly articulate various patterns of thought, mind maps are effective tools for helping us understand and represent complex bodies of information received either through reading or through listening. For example, consider the first paragraph from the essay "Our Two-Sided Brain":

> One of the most intriguing areas of scientific and educational exploration concerns the manner in which our brain processes information. It has been known for a long time that the brain is divided into two seemingly identical halves, usually termed the left hemisphere and the right hemisphere. Until recently, it was assumed that these two hemispheres were similar in the way that they operated. However, a variety of current research has shown conclusively that each hemisphere has a distinct "personality," processing information in its own unique way.

How would you graphically represent the ideas and their relationships in this passage? Take a piece of paper and pencil, and develop at least one mind map. Figure 6.2 illustrates one possible rendering.

Now review the next paragraph of the essay, which focuses on the qualities of the brain's left hemisphere:

> The left hemisphere exhibits those qualities that we normally associate with higher intellectual activities. For example, the left hemisphere functions analytically, tending to break things and processes down into component parts, like taking apart an automobile engine in order to diagnose the problem. The left hemisphere is also the seat of most of our verbal activity, decoding and encoding the bulk of our language, mathematical symbols, and musical notations. Finally, the left hemisphere tends to process information in a linear, sequential way, one step at a time. This is consistent with the verbal capacities which it exhibits, since language is spoken/heard/read one word at a time, and the meaning of the words depends in large measure on the order in which the words are placed. In short, the left hemisphere is similar to a modern, digital computer in that its individual operations unfold in an orderly, logical sequence.

Expand the mind map you developed for the first paragraph of the essay to include this additional information. Your ideas should be either written on lines

Figure 6.2
Preliminary mind map

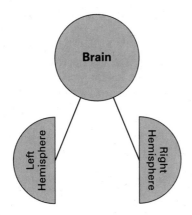

Figure 6.3
Intermediate mind
map

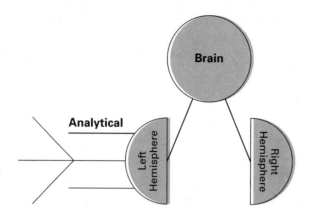

connected to other lines or written within shapes connected by lines in order to express clearly the relationship between the various ideas. Print the ideas in capital letters so that they can be easily read and referred to. Figure 6.3 is a sample of how you might begin elaborating the preliminary mind map to integrate this new information. Fill in the information that has been omitted.

Now review the next paragraph of the essay, which describes the qualities of the right hemisphere and compares these qualities to those of the left hemisphere.

The right hemisphere operates in a much different fashion. Instead of analyzing things and processes into component parts, it seeks to synthesize by organizing parts into patterns and wholes—like arranging individual flowers into a floral arrangement. The right hemisphere normally has much less to do with verbal activity. Instead, it is much more visually oriented, focusing on shapes, arrangements, and images. It also processes information based on what we personally experience with all of our senses (including touch). So, for example, while the left hemisphere might enable us to remember people by their name, the right hemisphere might enable us to recognize them by their face or the feel of their handshake. Finally, rather than processing information in a linear, sequential fashion, the right hemisphere tends to organize information into patterns and relationships which are experienced as a whole. For instance, the right hemisphere focuses on the overall melody of a piece of music rather than the individual notes, or on the pattern of play on the chessboard rather than the individual pieces. While we compared the linear functioning of the left hemisphere to a digital computer, we might compare the functioning of the right hemisphere to a kaleidoscope, as it continually works to organize information into meaningful shapes and patterns.

Using the mind map you created for the first two paragraphs of the essay as a starting point, expand your map by including this new information. In composing your map, be sure to represent the relationships between the various qualities of the two hemispheres. A sample of an elaborated map is

Figure 6.4. Final mind map

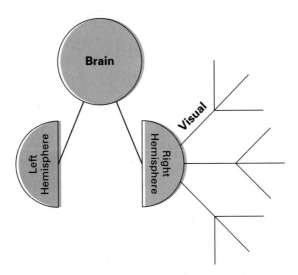

shown in Figure 6.4. Fill in the missing information in the spaces provided before you finish your map.

The final paragraph of the essay moves into a new direction, relating the information we have been reading (and thinking about) to education. Read this paragraph and then incorporate the ideas it presents in terms of the mind map you have created for the essay.

> The modern research into how our brain functions has significant implications for human learning. Much of our education is structured for left hemisphere thinking—analytical, verbal, logical, and sequential. Yet much of our understanding about the world is based on the activities of the right hemisphere—synthesizing, visual, experiential, and pattern-seeking. If education is to become as effective as possible, it must introduce teaching methods that address the right hemisphere as well as the left hemisphere.

Clearly, creating mind maps can be a useful strategy in helping us understand complex written information. However, this versatile tool is not merely a reading aid; it has other language uses as well—for example, organizing and interpreting spoken information, such as you receive in lectures. When people read and hear language, they normally do not try to interpret one word at a time, unless they are beginning to learn a new language. Instead, we typically group words together in "chunks" of meaning, trying to make sense of the *entire* meaning the words express. For instance, when you read the last two sentences, did you try to understand them one word at a time, or did you try to make sense of the complete ideas being expressed? In all likelihood, you tried to interpret the overall meaning being expressed, including the relationships among the various ideas.

The same is true when we speak. Although we pronounce the words one at a time, they form part of an entire meaning—a network of relationships that we are trying to express. Again, examine your thinking process as you attempt to explain an idea to someone. Are you thinking one word at a time, or do you find there is a complex process of examining, sorting, and relating the various words to express the meaning you are trying to communicate? Probably the latter.

Based on these considerations, we can see that a mapping approach offers some clear advantages in organizing the information you receive from oral communication. For instance, when you take notes of an instructor's lecture, you may find that you try to copy down full sentences the teacher has said. When you return later, you may find the notes are not adequate because they do not include the relationships among the ideas. Using a mapping approach to note taking will provide you with the means for identifying the key ideas and their relationships.

Mapping is also an effective aid in preparing for oral presentations. By organizing the information we want to present in this way, we have all the key ideas and their relationships in a single whole. Probably the greatest fear of people making oral presentations is that they will "get stuck" or lose their train of thought. If you have a clear map of the main ideas and their relationships either in your mind or in notes, the chances of this kind of "freeze-up" are considerably reduced.

One of the advantages of using maps is that once you have constructed them, you can place the ideas in whatever order you may need by simply numbering them or circling them in different colors. As a result, a map not only represents all the key ideas and their relationships simultaneously, but it can also be used to construct more traditional outlines or speaking notes.

Using Borders.   A final note-taking strategy involves creating borders to assist your processing of the information. For example, you can draw a horizontal line across the page two or three inches from the bottom and then use this space to summarize the content of the page. Another border strategy, used in the Cornell note-taking system developed by Walter Pauk, involves drawing a vertical line 2 1/2" from the left edge of the page. Use the remaining 6" to take notes from the lecture or reading. When you review your notes after class or reading, summarize the main points in the left column, and record any additional ideas or questions that occur to you. This format gives you the opportunity to elaborate and extend the content included in your notes by responding to the ideas being presented. Examples of these two border formats are shown in Figure 6.5.

Using Concepts in Reading and Learning

Most of your academic study involves learning new concepts, and in order to be successful, you need to master the conceptualizing process. For example, when you read textbooks or listen to lectures and take notes, you are required to grasp the key concepts and follow them as they are developed and supported. When you write papers or homework assignments, you are usually expected to

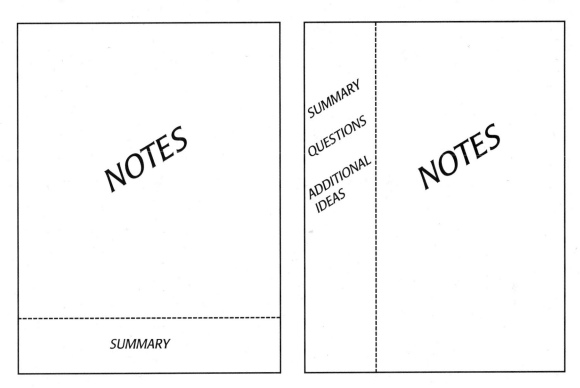

Figure 6.5 Bordered pages for note taking

focus on certain concepts, develop a thesis around them, present the thesis (itself a concept!) with carefully argued points, and back it up with specific examples. Many course examinations involve applying key concepts you have learned to new sets of circumstances.

What exactly are concepts? They are general ideas you use to organize your experience and, in so doing, bring order and intelligibility to your life. Your world is filled with concepts, and a large number of the words you use to represent your experience express the concepts you have formed. In the same way that words are the vocabulary of language, concepts are the vocabulary of thought. As organizers of your experience, concepts work in conjunction with language to identify, describe, distinguish, and relate all the various aspects of your world.

Concepts

General ideas that we use to organize experience, bringing order and intelligibility to our lives.

To become a sophisticated thinker, you must develop expertise in the conceptualizing process, improving your ability to *form, apply,* and *relate* concepts. This complex conceptualizing process is going on all the time in your mind, enabling you to think in a distinctly human way.

How do you use concepts to organize and make sense of experience? Think back to the first day of the semester. For most students, this is a time to evaluate their courses by trying to determine which concepts apply:

- Will this course be interesting? Useful? A lot of work?
- Is the teacher stimulating? Demanding? Boring?
- Are the students friendly? Intelligent? Conscientious?

Each of these words or phrases represents a *concept* you are attempting to apply so you can understand what is occurring at the moment and also anticipate what the course will be like in the future. As the course progresses, you gather further information from your actual experiences in the class. This information may support your initial concepts, or it may conflict with these initial concepts. If the information you receive supports these concepts, you tend to maintain them ("Yes, I can see that this is going to be a difficult course"). On the other hand, when the information you receive conflicts with these concepts, you tend to find new concepts to explain the situation ("No, I can see that I was wrong—this course isn't going to be as difficult as I thought at first"). A diagram of this process might look something like Figure 6.6.

To take another example, imagine that you are a physician and that one of your patients comes to you complaining of shortness of breath and occasional pain in his left arm. After he describes his symptoms, you ask a number of questions, examine him, and perhaps administer some tests. Your ability to *identify* the underlying problem depends on your knowledge of various human diseases. Each disease is identified and described by a different concept. Identifying these various diseases means that you can *distinguish* different concepts and that you know in what situations to apply a given concept. In addition, when the patient asks, "What's wrong with me, doctor?" you are able to *describe* the concept (for example, heart disease) and explain how it is related to his symptoms.

Thinking Activity 6.4

Identify an initial concept you had about an event in your life (a new job, attending college, etc.) that changed as a result of your experiences. After identifying your initial concept, describe the experiences that led you to change or modify the concept, and then explain the new concept you formed to explain the situation. Your response should include the following elements:

1. Initial concept.
2. New information provided by additional experiences.
3. New concept formed to explain the situation.

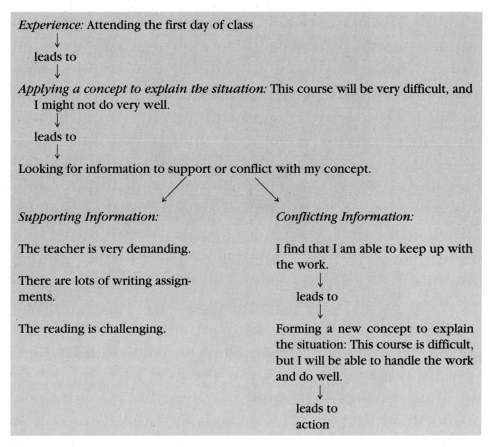

Experience: Attending the first day of class

leads to

Applying a concept to explain the situation: This course will be very difficult, and I might not do very well.

leads to

Looking for information to support or conflict with my concept.

Supporting Information:	*Conflicting Information:*
The teacher is very demanding.	I find that I am able to keep up with the work.
There are lots of writing assignments.	leads to
The reading is challenging.	Forming a new concept to explain the situation: This course is difficult, but I will be able to handle the work and do well.
	leads to action

Figure 6.6. **Conceptual analysis of a new class**

Learning to master concepts will help you in every area of your life: academic, career, and personal. In college study, each academic discipline or subject is composed of many different concepts that are used to organize experience, give explanations, and solve problems. Here is a sampling of college-level concepts: *entropy, subtext, Gemeinschaft, cell, metaphysics, relativity, Unconscious, critical thinking, transformational grammar, aesthetic, minor key, interface, health, quantum mechanics, schizophrenia.* Therefore, to make sense of how a discipline functions, you need to understand what the concepts of that discipline mean, how to apply them, and the way they relate to other concepts. You also need to learn the methods of investigation, patterns of thought, and forms of reasoning that the various disciplines use to form larger conceptual theories and methods. We will be exploring these subjects in the next several chapters of the text.

Regardless of their specific knowledge content, all careers require conceptual abilities, whether you are trying to apply a legal principle, develop a promotional theme, or devise a new computer program. Similarly, expertise in

All academic disciplines and careers are composed of many different concepts that are used to organize experience, give explanations, and solve problems.

forming and applying concepts helps you make sense of your personal life, understand others, and make informed decisions. In short, we might agree with the Greek philosopher Aristotle, who once said that the intelligent person is a "master of concepts."

The Structure of Concepts

The best way to understand the structure of concepts is to visualize them by means of a model. Examine Figure 6.7. The *sign* is the word or symbol used to name or designate the concept; for example, the word *triangle* is a sign. The *referents* represent all the various examples of the concept; the three-sided figure we are using as our model is an example of the concept *triangle.* The *properties* of the concept are the features that all things named by the word or sign share in common; all examples of the concept *triangle* share the characteristics of being a polygon and having three sides. These are the properties that we refer to when we *define* concepts; thus, "A triangle is a three-sided polygon."

Let's take another example. Suppose we wanted to explore the structure of the concept *automobile.* The *sign* that names the concept is the word *automobile* or the symbol. *Referents* of the concept include a 1963 Chevrolet Corvette and a late-model Ford Explorer truck. The *properties* that all things named by the sign *automobile* include are wheels, a chassis, an engine, seats for passengers, and so on. Figure 6.8 is a specific model of the concept *automobile.*

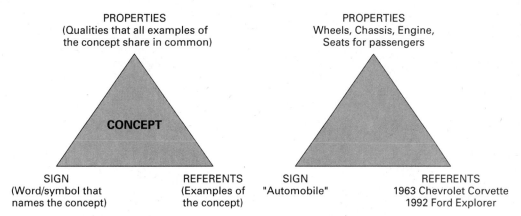

Figure 6.7. *Conceptual model*

Figure 6.8. *Conceptual model of* automobile

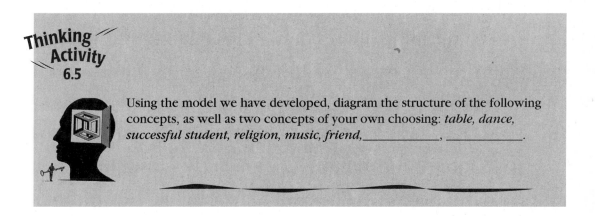

Thinking Activity 6.5

Using the model we have developed, diagram the structure of the following concepts, as well as two concepts of your own choosing: *table, dance, successful student, religion, music, friend,_____, _____.*

Forming Concepts

Throughout our lives, we are engaged in the process of forming—and applying—concepts to organize our experience, make sense of what is happening at the moment, and anticipate what may happen in the future. We form concepts by the interactive process of *generalizing* (focusing on the common properties shared by a group of things) and *interpreting* (finding examples of the concept). The common properties form the requirements that must be met in order to apply the concept to our experience. If we examine the diagram of concepts in the last section, we can see that the process of forming concepts involves moving back and forth between the *referents* (examples) of the concept and the *properties* (common features) shared by all examples of the concept. Let's explore further the way this interactive process of forming concepts operates.

Consider the following sample conversation between two people trying to form and clarify the concept *philosophy.*

A: What is your idea of what "philosophy" means?

B: Well, I think philosophy involves expressing important beliefs that you have—like discussing the meaning of life, assuming that there is a meaning.

A: Is explaining my belief about who's going to win the Super Bowl an example of engaging in philosophy? After all, this is a belief that is very important to me—I've got a lot of money riding on the outcome!

B: I don't think so. A philosophical belief is usually a belief about something that is important to *everyone*—like what standards should we use to guide our moral choices.

A: What about the message that was in my fortune cookie last night: "Eat, drink, and be merry, for tomorrow we diet!"? This is certainly a belief that most people can relate to, especially during the holiday season! Is this philosophy?

B: I think that's what my grandmother used to call "foolosophy"! Philosophical beliefs are usually deeply felt views that we have given a great deal of thought to—not something plucked out of a cookie.

A: What about my belief in the Golden Rule: "Do unto others as you would have them do unto you," because if you don't, "What goes around comes around"? Doesn't that have all of the qualities that you mentioned?

B: *Now* you've got it!

As we review this dialogue, we can see that *forming* the concept works hand in hand with *applying* the concept to different examples. When two or more things work together in this way, we say that they interact. In this case, there are two parts of this interactive process.

We form concepts by *generalizing*, by focusing on the similar features among different things. In the dialogue just given, the things from which generalizations are being made are kinds of beliefs—beliefs about the meaning of life or standards that we use to guide our moral choices. By focusing on the similar features among these beliefs, the two people in the dialogue develop a list of properties that philosophical beliefs share, including

- beliefs that deal with important issues in life that everyone is concerned about
- beliefs that reflect deeply felt views we have given a great deal of thought to

These common properties act as the *requirements* that must be met for an idea to be considered a philosophical belief.

We apply concepts by *interpreting,* by looking for different examples of the concept and seeing if they meet the requirements we are developing. In the conversation, one of the participants attempts to apply the concept *philosophical belief* to the following examples:

■ a belief about the outcome of the Super Bowl

■ a fortune cookie message: "Eat, drink, and be merry, for tomorrow we diet"

Each of the proposed examples suggests the development of new requirements for the concept to help clarify how the concept can be applied. Applying a concept to different possible examples thus becomes the way we develop and gradually sharpen our idea of the concept. Even when a proposed example turns out *not* to be an example of the concept, our understanding is often clarified. For instance, although the proposed example in the dialogue—a belief about the outcome of the Super Bowl—turns out not to be an example of the concept *philosophical belief,* examining it as a possible example helps clarify the concept and suggests other examples.

The process of developing concepts involves a constant back-and-forth movement between these two activities:

■ *Generalizing:* Focusing on certain similar features among things to develop the requirements for the concept.

■ *Interpreting:* Looking for different things to apply the concept to so as to determine if they "meet the requirements" of the concept we are developing.

As the back-and-forth movement progresses, we gradually develop a specific list of requirements that something must have to be considered an example of the concept, and at the same time, we give ourselves a clearer idea of how it is defined. This *interactive* process is illustrated in Figure 6.9.

Thinking Activity 6.6

Select a type of music with which you are familiar (for example, jazz), and write a dialogue similar to the one just examined. In the course of the dialogue, be sure to include

1. examples that you are generalizing from (cool, big band, etc.).

2. general properties shared by various types of this music (for example, jazz's audience spans many generations).

3. examples to which you are trying to apply the developing concept (the music of Miles Davis or Thelonius Monk).

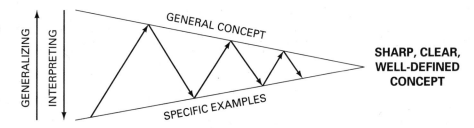

Figure 6.9. Interactive process defining of a concept

Applying Concepts

Making sense of our experience means finding the right concept to explain what is going on. To determine whether the concept we have selected fits the situation, we have to determine whether the requirements that form the concept are being met. To do so, we have to

1. be aware of the properties that form the boundaries of the concept.
2. determine whether the experience meets those requirements, for only if it does can we apply the concept to it.

Consider the concept *dog*. Which of the following descriptions are requirements of the concept that must be met to say that something is an example of this concept?

1. Is an animal
2. Normally has four legs and a tail
3. Bites the letter carrier

It is clear that descriptions 1 and 2 are requirements that must be met to apply the concept *dog,* because if we apply our "test" question, "Would something be an example of this concept if it did not meet this requirement?" we can say that something would not be an example of the concept *dog* if it was not an animal and did not normally have four legs and a tail.

However, this does not seem to be the case with description 3. If we ask ourselves the same test question, we can see that something might still be an example of the concept *dog, even if* it did not bite the letter carrier. This is because even though *some* dogs *do* bite, this is *not* a requirement for being a dog.

Of course, there may be other things that meet these requirements but are not dogs. For example, a cat is an animal (description 1) that normally has four legs and a tail (description 2). What this means is that the requirements of a concept only tell us what something *must* have to be an example of the concept. As a result, we often have to identify additional requirements that will define the concept more sharply. This point is clearly illustrated by looking at the way children form concepts. Not identifying a sufficient number of the concept's requirements leads to such misconceptions as "All four-legged animals are doggies" and "All yellow-colored metal is gold."

It is very important for us to know as many specific requirements as possible. These requirements determine when the concept can be applied and indicate those things that qualify as examples of it. When we are able to identify *all* the requirements of the concept, we say these requirements are both *necessary* and *sufficient* for applying the concept.

While dealing with concepts like *dog* and *cat* may seem straightforward, matters quickly become more confusing when we start analyzing more complex concepts that occur in academic study. For example, consider the concepts of *masculinity* and *femininity,* two of the more emotionally charged and politically volatile concepts in our culture. There are many different perspectives on what these concepts mean, what they should mean, or whether we should be using them at all. In the space below, list what you consider to be the essential requirements of the concepts as well as examples of people or behavior that illustrate these concepts. For example, you might identify "physical strength" as a property of the concept *masculinity* and name Arnold Schwarzenegger as a person who illustrates this quality. Or you might identify "intuitive" as a property of the concept *femininity* and define this term as the "ability to predict what is going to happen before it occurs."

	General Properties	*Specific Examples*
Femininity	1.	1.
	2.	2.
	3.	3.
Masculinity	1.	1.
	2.	2.
	3.	3.

Compare your responses to those of the other students in the class. What are the similarities and differences in your concepts? What factors might account for these similarities and differences?

The concepts of *femininity* and *masculinity* are two of the more complex, emotionally charged, and politically volatile concepts in our culture.

Thinking Passages

The following passages by Susan Brownmiller and Michael Norman deal with the concepts of *masculinity* and *femininity.* After reading the passages, name the properties that the authors identify for each concept, as well as the examples of the behaviors that they believe illustrate these properties. How do their perspectives on these concepts compare and contrast with your concepts and those of the other members of the class?

from *Femininity*

Susan Brownmiller

It is fashionable in some quarters to describe the feminine and masculine principles as polar ends of the human continuum, and to sagely profess that both polarities exist in all people. Sun and moon, yin and yang, soft and hard, active and passive, etcetera, may indeed be opposites, but a linear continuum does not illuminate the problem. What, then, is the basic distinction? The masculine principle is better understood as a driving ethos of superiority designed to inspire straightforward, confident success, while the feminine principle is composed of vulnerability, the need for protection, the formalities of compliance and the avoidance of conflict—in short, an appeal of dependence and good will that gives the masculine principle its romantic validity and admiring applause. Femininity pleases men because it makes them appear more masculine by contrast; and, in truth, conferring an extra portion of unearned gender distinction on men, and unchallenged space in which to breathe freely and feel stronger, wiser, more competent, is femininity's special gift. One could say that masculinity is often an effort to please women, but masculinity is known to please by displays of mastery and competence while femininity pleases by suggesting that these concerns, except in small matters, are beyond its intent. Whimsy, unpredictability and patterns of thinking and behavior that are dominated by emotion, such as tearful expressions of sentiment and fear, are thought to be feminine precisely because they lie outside the established route to success.

from *Standing His Ground*

Michael Norman

From analyst's couch to tavern booth, the message is the same: The male animus is out of fashion. The man of the hour is supposed to be gentle, thoughtful, endearing and compassionate, a wife to his woman, a mother to his son, an androgynous figure with the self-knowledge of a hermaphrodite. He takes his lumps on the psyche, not the chin, and bleeds with emotion. Yes, in the morning, he still puts on a three-piece suit, but his foulard, the finishing touch, is a crying towel. He is so ridden with guilt, so pained about the sexist sins of his kind, he bites at his own flanks. Not only does he say that he dislikes being a man, but broadly proclaims that the whole idea of manhood in America is pitiful. He wants to free himself from the social conditioning of the past, to cast off the yoke of traditional male roles and rise above the banality of rituals learned at boot camp or on the practice field. If science could provide it, he would swallow an

→

antidote of testosterone, something to stop all this antediluvian thumping and bashing. But the fashion for reform, the drive to emasculate macho, has produced a kind of numbing androgyny and has so blurred the lines of gender that I often find myself wanting to emulate some of the women I know—bold, aggressive, vigorous role models.

Reading and Evaluating

Up to this point in this chapter we have been concentrating on the thinking and language abilities required to understand what an author has written. However, becoming an expert reader also involves *evaluating* what you are reading: Does it make sense? Is it accurate or inaccurate? Is it biased or objective? Is the information supported by evidence and reasons, or does it consist of unsubstantiated assertions? Is the author credible, or should you be suspicious about his or her believability? In other words, becoming an expert reader involves

Perceiving Lenses:
Each of us views the world through unique "lenses" that shape and influence the way we perceive the world, process information, and decide to act. These lenses reflect our values, past experiences, interests, biases— everything that is a part of our individual personalities, and we need to become aware of these lenses in order to think critically.

applying your abilities as a critical thinker to the material that you are reading, not simply accepting it at face value.

In order to perform this type of evaluation, you need to understand the perspective of the author, as well as your own reaction to the ideas being presented. For example, one of the important qualities of becoming a critical thinker that we explored in Chapter Two was the ability and willingness to view situations from different perspectives. Each of us has a unique perspective on the world, a perspective that reflects our entire life history: our sex, age, race, economic class, family, schooling, and all of the other countless experiences that have a part in making up who we are. A useful analogy to understand this idea of "perspective" is to consider that each of us views the world through a unique pair of "lenses" that shape and influence what we perceive, how we process information, and how we decide to act. These lenses include our values, past experiences, interests, biases—everything that is a part of our individual personalities. However, in most instances, we are unaware that we are viewing the world through these lenses; instead, we believe that the way we view things is the way things *are*, and if people see things differently than we do, then they must be *wrong.*

Becoming a critical thinker requires becoming aware of our "lenses" (and those of others) by examining various viewpoints on issues and situations, and understanding how we and others have developed these perspectives. For example, people often argue over such issues as "The chili you made is too spicy," which is a pointless argument since our taste in chili simply reflects the taste we have become accustomed to—our "food lenses." These sort of "uncritical" disagreements take place all of the time: Was the party dull or exciting? Was the movie entertaining or boring? Is the class we are taking too demanding or simply challenging? Is that stuff you are listening to music or noise? Is the person we are discussing sincerely friendly or untrustworthy and manipulative? In order to answer any of these questions, we need to understand the lenses that are shaping and influencing the experience—our lenses and those of others. For example, consider the contrasting perceptions of the various characters shown in Figure 6.10. How do you think each individual arrived at his or her description?

The most effective way to become aware of our own perceiving lenses is to come into contact with people who have lenses *different* from our own. For example, it would be normal for each of the individuals in "The Investigation" to be convinced that his or her description is accurate. Only if they were confronted with differing descriptions would they be stimulated to analyze to what extent their descriptions reflect their own personal lenses. Similarly, when we get information from other people—whether through reading, listening, or watching television—we should always strive to find a different perspective so that we can better recognize the lenses of the people providing the information. "Getting a second opinion" is a principle that doesn't simply apply to medical diagnoses; it is relevant to every area of our lives.

For example, let's consider different accounts of a historical event—the Bat-

Figure 6.10. "The Investigation"

tle of Lexington, which took place during the American Revolution. In high school, you probably read an account similar to the first one, a version written by Samuel Steinberg for a mainstream American History textbook. At that time it was probably the only perspective you were exposed to, and you had little reason to doubt it. But let's analyze the account in the context of a number of other contrasting perspectives. As you read each account, try to answer the following questions:

1. How would you describe the Colonial group? (How many? Professionally trained?)

2. How would you describe the British group?

*Note: This exercise was developed by Kevin O'Reilly, creator of the Critical Thinking in History Project in Boston, Massachusetts.

3. How would you describe what occurred? (Who fired the first shot? How many died?)

4. How did the Colonials behave? (With courage? As cowards?)

5. How did the British behave?

6. How credible is the source of this account? Do you detect any indication of bias?

> In April 1775, General Gage, the military governor of Massachusetts, sent out a body of troops to take possession of military stores at Concord, a short distance from Boston. At Lexington, a handful of "embattled farmers," who had been tipped off by Paul Revere, barred the way. The "rebels" were ordered to disperse. They stood their ground. The English fired a volley of shots that killed eight patriots. It was not long before the swift-riding Paul Revere spread the news of this new atrocity to the neighboring colonies. The patriots of all of New England, although still a handful, were now ready to fight the English. Even in faraway North Carolina, patriots organized to resist them.
>
> from *The United States: Story of a Free People,* by Samuel Steinberg

While this account *sounds* authoritative (as many textbook accounts do), it would be a mistake to accept without question this or any other account. Instead, let's critically analyze the information it provides by examining a contrasting account, written by a former prime minister of England, Winston Churchill.

> At five o'clock in the morning the local militia of Lexington, seventy strong, formed up on the village green. As the sun rose the head of the British column, with three officers riding in front, came into view. The leading officer, brandishing his sword, shouted, "Disperse, you rebels, immediately!"
>
> The militia commander ordered his men to disperse. The colonial committees were very anxious not to fire the first shot, and there were strict orders not to provoke open conflict with the British regulars. But in the confusion someone fired. A volley was returned. The ranks of the militia were thinned and there was a general *melee.* Brushing aside the survivors, the British column marched on to Concord.
>
> from *History of the English Speaking Peoples,* by Winston Churchill

This account sounds just as authoritative as the first account, yet it provides a very different picture of what took place. Can you identify the similarities and differences between the two accounts? What do we do when we are faced with two conflicting authoritative accounts, whether the subject is history or medicine? Which account do we believe? One strategy is to use our critical thinking abilities, first to isolate the areas of agreement and then to analyze the areas of disagreement by evaluating the evidence supporting each perspective.

We also have to take into account the potential bias of the sources. A second strategy is to get an additional perspective in the hope that by analyzing the three perspectives together, a clearer picture will emerge. This next account is an eyewitness version provided by Sylvanus Wood, an American who took part in the conflict.

> The British troops approached us rapidly in platoons, with a General officer on horseback at their head. The officer came up to within about two rods of the centre of the company, where I stood.—The first platoon being about three rods distant. They there halted. The officer then swung his sword, and said, "Lay down your arms, you damn'd rebels, or you are all dead men—fire." Some guns were fired by the British at us from the first platoon, but no person was killed or hurt, being probably charged only with powder. Just at this time, Captain Parker ordered every man to take care of himself. The company immediately dispersed; and while the company was dispersing and leaping over the wall, the second platoon of the British fired, and killed some of our men. There was not a gun fired by any of Captain Parker's company within my knowledge.

> from *Deposition,* by Sylvanus Wood

How does this account compare with the first two accounts? Does the fact that this is an eyewitness account affect your evaluation? Why? How credible do you think the source of this account is? Do you detect any indications of bias? This account was taken in a deposition thirty years after the event so that Mr. Wood could qualify for his military pension. Does this affect your evaluation of the accuracy of the testimony? Why or why not? In order to try to balance the perspectives being presented, the next account is another eyewitness version, this time from a British soldier who took part in the encounter.

> I, John Bateman, belonging to the Fifty-Second Regiment, commanded by Colonel Jones, on Wednesday morning on the nineteenth day of April instant, was in the party marching to Concord, being at Lexington, in the County of Middlesex; being nigh the meeting-house in said Lexington, there was a small party of men gathered together in that place when our Troops marched by, and I testify and declare, that I heard the word of command given to the Troops to fire, and some of said Troops did fire, and I saw one of said small party lay dead on the ground nigh said meeting-house, and I testify that I never heard any of the inhabitants so much as fire one gun on said Troops.

> from *Testimony,* by John Bateman

How does this account compare with the first three accounts? Do you detect any indications of bias? This account was taken in a deposition when Mr. Bateman was a prisoner of war after having been captured by the Colonial forces. Does this affect your evaluation of his testimony? Why or why not?

Having reviewed and analyzed these four different accounts, you might find yourself somewhat confused. However, your responsibility as a critical reader and thinker is to try to determine what you believe happened, even though you might lack some of the information you would like to have. In other words, instead of looking for the one "true" account, you need to analyze all of the available perspectives that you can and then arrive at your own, well-reasoned synthesis, recognizing that your conclusions may change or evolve over time as you learn additional information. In the space below, describe your conclusions and the reasons that led to them.

1. How would you describe the American group? _____

   _____

   Reasons: _____

2. How would you describe the British group? _____

   _____

   Reasons: _____

3. Who fired the first shot?   _____

   _____

   Reasons: _____

4. How many died? _____

   _____

   Reasons: _____

5. How did the Americans behave? _____

   _____

   Reasons: _____

6. How did the British behave? _____

   _____

   Reasons: _____

A critical thinker sees knowledge and truth as goals to achieve, processes we are all actively involved in as we construct our understanding of the world. Developing accurate knowledge about the world is often a challenging process of exploration and analysis in which our understanding evolves over a period of time. All four sources viewed the Battle of Lexington through their own lenses, which shaped and influenced the information they selected, the way they organized it, their interpretations of the individuals involved, and the language they chose to describe it. Despite the differences in these accounts, we *know* that an actual sequence of events occurred at Lexington on that particular day. The challenge is to try to figure out what actually happened by investigating different accounts, evaluating the reliability of the accounts, and putting together a coherent picture of what took place. This is the process of achieving knowledge and truth that occurs in every area of human inquiry—a process of exploration, critical analysis, and understanding.

Thinking Activity 6.8

The need to read critically is not confined to textbooks: it is necessary for virtually everything we read. Let's examine another situation in which a number of different people had somewhat different perceptions about an event they were describing. The following are four different newspaper accounts of the assassination of Malcolm X. After you have read the accounts, critically analyze the different perspectives with the same approach we used for the Battle of Lexington accounts, and construct your own version of what you believe took place on that day. Use these questions to guide your analysis of the varying accounts:

■ Does the account provide a convincing description of what took place?

■ What reasons and evidence support the account?

■ How reliable is the source? What are the author's perceiving lenses that might influence the account?

Malcolm X, the 39-year-old leader of a militant Black Nationalist movement, was shot to death yesterday afternoon at a rally of his followers in a ballroom in Washington Heights. The bearded Negro extremist had said only a few words of greeting when a fusillade rang out. The bullets knocked him over backwards.

A 22-year-old Negro, Thomas Hagan, was charged with the killing. The police rescued him from the ballroom crowd after he had been shot and beaten.

Pandemonium broke out among the 400 Negroes in the Audubon Ballroom at 160th Street and Broadway. As men, women and children ducked under tables and flattened themselves on the floor, more shots were fired. The police said seven bullets struck Malcolm. Three other Negroes were shot. Witnesses reported that as many as 30 shots had been fired. About two hours later the police said the shooting had apparently been a result of a feud between followers of Malcolm and members of the extremist group he broke with last year, the Black Muslims. . . .

The New York Times (February 22, 1965)

His life oozing out through a half dozen or more gunshot wounds in his chest, Malcolm X, once the shrillest voice of black supremacy, lay dying on the stage of a Manhattan auditorium. Moments before, he had stepped up to the lectern and 400 of the faithful had settled down expectantly to hear the sort of speech for which he was famous—flaying the hated white man. Then a scuffle broke out in the hall and Malcolm's bodyguards bolted from his side to break it up—only to discover that they had been faked out. At least two men with pistols rose from the audience and pumped bullets into the speaker, while a third cut loose at close range with both barrels of a sawed-off shotgun. In the confusion the pistol men got away. The shotgunner lunged through the crowd and out the door, but not before the guards came to their wits and shot him in the leg. Outside he was swiftly overtaken by other supporters of Malcolm and very likely would have been stomped to death if the police hadn't saved him. Most shocking of all to the residents of Harlem was the fact that Malcolm had been killed not by "whitey" but by members of his own race.

Life (March 5, 1965)

They came early to the Audubon Ballroom, perhaps drawn by the expectation that Malcolm X would name the men who firebombed his home last Sunday. . . . I sat at the left in the 12th row and, as we waited, the man next to me spoke of Malcolm and his followers: "Malcolm is our only hope. . . . You can depend on him to tell it like it is and to give Whitey hell. . . ."

There was a prolonged ovation as Malcolm walked to the rostrum. . . . Malcolm looked up and said "A salaam aleikum (Peace be unto you)" and the audience replied "We aleikum salaam (And unto you, peace)."

Bespectacled and dapper in a dark suit, sandy hair glinting in the light, Malcolm said: "Brothers and sisters. . . ." He was interrupted by two men in the center of the ballroom . . . who rose and, arguing with each other, moved forward. Then there was a scuffle at the back of the room. . . . I heard Malcolm X say his last words: "Now, brothers, break it up," he said softly. "Be cool, be calm."

Then all hell broke loose. There was a muffled sound of shots and Malcolm, blood on his face and chest, fell limply back over the chairs behind him. The two men who had approached him ran to the exit on my side of the room, shooting wildly behind them as they ran. . . . I heard people screaming, "Don't let them kill him." "Kill those bastards. . . ." At an exit I saw some of Malcolm's men beating with all their strength on two men. . . . I saw a half dozen of Malcolm's followers bending over his inert body on the stage. Their clothes stained with their leader's blood. . . .

Four policemen took the stretcher and carried Malcolm through the crowd and some of the women came out of their shock . . . and one said: " . . . I hope he doesn't die, but I don't think he's going to make it. . . ."

The New York Post (February 22, 1965)

"We interrupt this program to bring you a special newscast. . . ." the announcer said as the Sunday afternoon movie on the TV set was halted temporarily. "Malcolm X was shot four times . . . while addressing a crowd at the Audubon Ballroom on 166th Street." "Oh no!" That was my first reaction to the shocking event that followed one week after the slender, articulate leader of the Afro-American Unity was routed from his East Elmhurst home by a bomb explosion. Minutes later we alighted from a cab at the corner of Broadway and 166th St. just a short 15 blocks from where I live on Broadway. About 200 men and women, neatly dressed, were milling around, some with expressions of awe and disbelief. Others were in small clusters talking loudly and with deep emotion in their voices. Mostly they were screaming for vengeance. One woman, small, dressed in a light gray coat and her eyes flaming with indignation, argued with a cop at the St. Nicholas corner of the block. "This is not the end of it. What they were going to do to the Statue of Liberty will be small in comparison. We black people are tired of being shoved around." Standing across the street near the memorial park one of Malcolm's close associates commented: "It's a shame." Later he added that "if it's war they want, they'll get it." He would not say whether Elijah Muhammed's followers had anything to do with the assassination. About 3:30 P.M. Malcolm X's wife, Betty, was escorted by three men and a woman from the Columbia Presbyterian Hospital. Tears streamed down her face. She was screaming, "They killed him!" Malcolm X had no last words. . . . The bombing and burning of the No. 7 Mosque early Tuesday morning was the first blow by those who are seeking revenge for the cold-blooded murder of a man who at 39 might have grown to the stature of respectable leadership.

The Amsterdam News (February 27, 1965)

Thinking Activity 6.9

Locate three different newspaper or magazine accounts of an important event—a court decision, a crime, and a political demonstration are possible topics. Analyze each of the accounts with the questions listed below, and then construct your own version of what you believe took place.

■ Does the account provide a convincing description of what took place?

■ What reasons and evidence support the account?

■ How reliable is the source? What are the author's perceiving lenses that might influence his account?

■ Is the account consistent with other reliable descriptions of this event?

Thinking Passage

Feeling Down and Getting Back Up

This article gives you the opportunity to apply your critical reading skills to the topic of depression, one of the most emotionally debilitating problems confronting college students. In the words of the authors, Paul A. Grayson and Phillip W. Meilman, "Depression is both a cause and a consequence of personal difficulties . . . a common denominator, sometimes unrecognized, of widely differing concerns." After reading the article, answer the questions that follow.

Feeling Down and Getting Back Up

Paul A. Grayson and Phillip W. Meilman

The concept of depression overlaps with nearly every other problem area. If you feel homesick at college, if you feel academically overstressed, if you have concerns about romance or sex or

→

diet or career, then you can end up depressed. Conversely, if you are depressed, then you may be below par in socializing, studies, romance, sexual performance and so forth. Depression is both a cause and a consequence of personal difficulties. It is a common denominator, sometimes unrecognized, of widely differing concerns.

In this chapter we explain the nature of depression, distinguishing it from sadness. We show how to recognize depression's warning signals, and give strategies for combating it. We also cover the related topics of mood swings, low self-esteem and identity confusion. Finally, we discuss the critical subject of suicidal feelings.

Depression vs. Sadness

Q: I get sad a lot. Is that normal?

A: It depends on what you mean by "sad" and "a lot." If all you have are passing downshifts in mood, episodes of feeling blue, then you're probably no different from anyone else. If, however, you have long bouts of feeling downcast or your down periods are intense and incapacitating— you can't study, eat, sleep, socialize—that's different. You probably are depressed.

Q: But what's the difference between sadness and depression?

A: It's not entirely clear if sadness and depression come from the same root, or if they're essentially unrelated phenomena. Either way, it's important not to confuse the two. Sadness—a temporary state of feeling down—is a limited experience, and for that reason it's not a problem. In fact, it can feel satisfying sometimes to feel sad and have a good cry, to listen to melancholy music or watch a tragic drama. Sadness adds a fitting solemnity to human existence; life would seem shallow without it. Sadness also has lessons to teach. Through recognizing sadness you may discover that a relationship is empty, a need is unfulfilled, a potential has been wasted. You can discover when you're sad who and what matters to you.

Depression is on a different scale. Depression isn't satisfying; it doesn't uplift or teach. A debilitating condition, depression casts a pall over every aspect of life. In its stronger forms, depression can make you unable to continue in college, and can cause you to think about suicide.

You can't eliminate sadness from your life. You can, and should, take steps to fight off depression.

Q: I've known lots of people who say they're being treated for depression, but they don't all seem the same to me. Are there different kinds of depression?

A: Yes, there are. Here's a thumbnail description of some of the most important types:

A *depressive reaction* is, as its name implies, a reaction to some negative event, such as failure at school, a romantic breakup or the death of a parent. A depressive reaction is "normal" in the sense that anyone facing the same circumstances would naturally feel bad. However, depressive reactions certainly don't feel normal. Like any other kind of depression, they can be intense and profound, can last many weeks or even longer and in severe cases are disabling. But they are related to a specific cause, and ordinarily the depression will abate with time.

Other forms of depression aren't due to negative circumstances alone. The person who ex-

→

periences them also has an underlying biological and/or psychological vulnerability to depression; the cause lies at least partly within. Of these forms, *dysthymia* refers to a long-lasting but comparatively mild form of depression. Dysthymic persons manage to get by from day to day, they can bring themselves to study and socialize, but they view whatever they turn to through gray-colored glasses. One psychologist compares dysthymia to "a low-grade infection. Dysthymics never really feel good."

By contrast, a *major depression* has a relatively sudden onset and lasts several weeks to many months. It is paralyzing. College students who suffer a major depression find themselves unable to function and often must withdraw from school. This is the most severe form of "unipolar" depression, meaning that the extreme moods only go in one direction; depression does not alternate with elevated, or high, moods.

With *manic-depressive disorder*—also called bipolar disorder—episodes of being uncontrollably high ("mania") alternate with episodes of depression. Both the up and down extremes are grave problems, although in the manic phase the person has no insight into the dangers. During manic episodes judgment is impaired and inhibitions melt away, and the person may act recklessly by perhaps gambling away money or running away from responsibilities. During depressive episodes he or she despairs and may be suicidal.

A less extreme up-and-down mood pattern is called *cyclothymia.* If even less pronounced, we simply refer to mood swings—which isn't a disorder at all. Neither cyclothymia nor mood swings should be confused with a full-fledged manic-depressive disorder.

Warning Signs

Q: Sometimes I wonder if I'm depressed and don't know it. Is that possible?

A: Very much so. You may not recognize depression if it creeps up on you, or if you're chronically depressed (dysthymic) and so have no normal emotional baseline as a comparison. And if you're severely depressed, your thinking may be so clouded that you don't recognize your condition.

Here are some classic signs and symptoms to identify depression:

- Prolonged sad or depressed mood; crying spells; irritability; or an inability to feel anything at all. (Note: You can be depressed without feeling sad.)
- Loss of interest and pleasure in activities and other people.
- Significant weight loss or weight gain, or marked increase or decrease in appetite.
- Low self-esteem; feelings of worthlessness, guilt and self-blame.
- Poor concentration; you can't read, write or study for a test.
- Difficulty making decisions.
- Feelings of hopelessness; a belief that the future won't be any better than the present.
- Fatigue and loss of energy, or agitation and restlessness.
- Problems with sleep: inability to fall or stay asleep, waking up early and being unable to get back to sleep, or sleeping too much.

⟶

- Worries about health, and physical symptoms such as digestive disorders and nonspecific aches and pains.
- Recurrent thoughts of death or suicide.

Family Influence

Q: Both my parents sometimes get depressed. Will the same thing happen to me?

A: It could. Research shows that being the child of a depressed parent may double or triple the risk of depression in later life. Sometimes this happens because of genetic transmission. Studies suggest that a vulnerability to major depression and particularly to manic-depressive disorder can be inherited. Parents also can transmit depression if they serve as role models demonstrating how to be miserable, or if they don't provide the love, attention and structure that children need.

However, there is nothing certain about any of this. Children take after each parent in some respects, not in others. It's good to be aware of the risk of depression so you'll seek treatment if the need ever arises. But don't assume because of your parents' history that your own fate has been sealed.

Some students are so afraid of following in their depressed parents' footsteps that they won't let themselves feel sad or upset. One student we know wore a constant smile, as if a cheerful face could ward off evil moods. She was determined not to be like her mother, who'd once been hospitalized for depression. Then this student's boyfriend broke up with her, and she could no longer muster the smile. This terrified her. Did her sorrow indicate severe depression? Was she turning into her mother after all? Thanks to several counseling sessions, she finally saw that suffering after a breakup is normal, not a sign of emotional illness.

Seasonal Depression

Q: I often seem to feel bad in the winter months and then start improving when the days grow longer. Is that possible?

A: It sure is. In recent years researchers have found that in colder climates perhaps 5% of the population have a rather serious form of depression during the winter, while an additional 20% suffer mild depressive symptoms. Those who are seriously affected have what is called seasonal affective disorder, or SAD. Common symptoms of SAD are chronically depressed mood, social withdrawal, excessive sleep and a voracious appetite that leads to weight gain.

Researchers' best guess is that winter blues are caused by the relative lack of sunlight. In other words, your outlook could be dark and gray because it's dark and gray outside your window. If you are severely impaired, you should consult a professional, who may refer you to a specialist in treating SAD (the new, recommended treatment involves light therapy). If instead you have a mild case of cold-weather blahs, the treatment is not usually necessary.

Helping Yourself

Q: What should I do if I'm feeling down?

A: If it's just a question of sadness—a low mood—then no major remedies are necessary. Time is your ally. No matter how bad you feel, chances are it will all be better in a day or two.

→

In the meantime, you might let out what's troubling you to someone you trust. A bit of support and blowing off steam can work wonders for a down emotional state. You may also want to take a break from the usual routine by going to a movie or leaving campus for the weekend.

Choose wisely, however, when you select a break. Don't soothe bad feelings by getting drunk, taking other drugs, bingeing on food, missing classes, having careless sexual experiences or buying clothes you can't afford. Such excesses may distract you for the moment, but you're only substituting a new, larger problem for the one that got you down in the first place.

We should emphasize that alcohol is particularly troublesome when you're down. As a depressant drug, alcohol has chemical properties that may make you feel even worse than before. Since it lowers inhibitions, alcohol also increases the likelihood of risky or self-destructive acts, such as unprotected sex or suicide attempts.

Q: How about more serious, lasting depression? Is there anything I can do on my own?

A: Yes. One method, popular among counselors and therapists, is to identify and challenge self-defeating thoughts and beliefs. According to this "cognitive" approach, depression is caused by talking yourself into disturbed feelings and self-defeating behaviors. You have distorted, negative views about yourself, the world and the future, you repeat these views to yourself, and that's why you're depressed. What's more, these internal communications are so familiar, so automatic, that you may not be aware of them; you're giving yourself subliminal messages to be unhappy. To battle depression, then, you need to replace the messages.

The first step with the cognitive approach is to discover your depression-inducing thoughts. So pay close attention next time you feel down or discouraged. What thoughts are crossing through your mind? What were your thoughts when your down mood began? Keep a written record of these thoughts. The goal is to expose hidden thinking to the bright light of conscious awareness.

Next, evaluate the thoughts. How realistic do they look on paper? Chances are you'll notice that your thinking isn't really objective or reasonable. Specifically, you may find yourself falling into some of the following problem thinking patterns:

- *Dwelling on the negative:* You zero in on the negative aspects of a situation while downplaying or explaining away positive details:
  "Sure I got three B's, but that D is going to ruin my average."
  "I only got an A because the test was easy."
  "He's only being nice because he feels sorry for me."
  "She only goes out with me because she doesn't really know me very well."

- *Thinking in all-or-nothing terms:* You interpret things as all-good or all-bad. Either you perform perfectly (which is unlikely) or you perform horribly; events are either completely wonderful (also unlikely) or they're terrible:
  "I said something stupid in that seminar. The whole class must think I'm an idiot."
  "I've gained five pounds. Now, I'm so fat!"
  "Jan and I had a fight. That's the end of our friendship."

→

- *Overgeneralizing:* You draw general conclusions based on minimal information. Absolute-sounding words like "always," "never," "only," "just," "everyone," "everything" and "completely" are clues to this type of thought:

  "I knew I wouldn't make the tennis team. I always screw up at tryouts."

  "This C proves it. I never do anything well at college."

  "Of course Vicki wouldn't go out with me. Everyone thinks I'm a loser."

- *Catastrophizing:* You expect the worst outcomes imaginable and dwell on disastrous future possibilities:

  "I'll never make any good friends here."

  "What if I fail this test?"

  "My parents will blow up when they see my grades."

  "What if I never make it to medical school?"

- *Overassuming:* In the absence of real proof, you assume you know what people are thinking and feeling. In particular, you assume their actions have personal, negative meaning for you. (Taken to an extreme, overassuming becomes paranoia.):

  "Mike didn't call me tonight. He must think I'm boring."

  "Serena is always talking to that other guy. I bet she wants to go out with him."

  "Alice didn't return my sweater yet. She probably plans to keep it."

- *Having unrealistic expectations:* You refuse to accept other people, yourself or conditions as they really are. Instead you are so angry and distraught that reality isn't what you want it to be. You use words like "should" and "shouldn't" and phrases like "it's awful," "I can't believe" and "it's not fair" to express your indignation:

  "Larry should treat me better than he does."

  "It's awful that I'm so short."

  "I can't believe this graduate school rejected me."

  "It's not fair that I got sick right before that party."

Once you recognize your negative thinking patterns, the next step is to challenge and replace flawed thoughts whenever they occur. Counter each one by asking yourself, "Is this an accurate view of the situation?" and "Am I being fair and reasonable?" Then replace the original thought with a realistic alternative. In other words, use your reasoning abilities to restore perspective and ward off depression.

Q: How can I use this cognitive approach?

A: Here's an example:

When Monica didn't smile as they crossed paths on campus, Jerry kept thinking about her expression (dwelling on the negative) and concluded that she didn't like him anymore (overassuming). He overlooked their recent friendly talk, and never considered the possibility that she hadn't noticed him or might be preoccupied with something else. Dwelling on the incident, he decided that most people didn't like him (overgeneralizing) and that something was wrong with him (more overgeneralizing).

To apply the cognitive approach, Jerry would recognize these thoughts, identify the errors

⟶

they contain and replace them with constructive, realistic alternatives. His reasoning might go like this: "Wait! Am I being realistic here? Do I really know what Monica was thinking when she passed me? Usually when I see her she's friendly, so there's no reason to assume that she doesn't like me anymore. And there's certainly no reason to dwell on this little thing or conclude that I'm unpopular. Maybe she was preoccupied. Next time I see her I'm going to go up and talk to her."

Q: What else can I do to fight depression?

A: Reducing an overcrowded schedule may work; so may adding meaningful activities to an unchallenging schedule. Regular exercise, healthy eating and plenty of sleep are also recommended.

Depression is also often associated with social isolation. Although some solitude is good for you, too much time spent alone is demoralizing and can spawn irrational thinking. (Solitary confinement is used as the ultimate in prison punishment.) If, then, you can make one friend, or schedule even a single social activity, you may give yourself a vital boost.

None of these measures is sure-fire. Besides, you may not feel up to them; you may be too depressed to act. If you can try them, though, you may experience relief from depression.

Q: What can I do to prevent mood swings?

A: Again, it depends on the severity. Some emotional variability comes with being human. You think diverse thoughts, you have ever-changing experiences and so naturally you have shifting moods. So for minor ups and downs, nothing special needs to be done.

For more frequent or pronounced emotional swings (perhaps an objective friend can help you recognize them), we recommend trying the cognitive approach explained above. All-or-nothing thinking, over-generalizations, unrealistic expectations and other flawed thoughts can send you on an emotional roller coaster. Substituting realistic thoughts can restore your emotional equilibrium.

On the subject of realistic expectations, it's particularly important to prepare yourself for changing fortunes. Life, after all, is a deliverer of mixed messages. In any given week, count on it that some people will be friendly and others cool, on some matters you'll shine and on others you'll screw up. Inevitably, good, bad and indifferent are all coming your way. If you learn to expect these fluctuations, you won't do emotional flip-flops when they happen.

As an additional suggestion, we encourage building routines or habits into your schedule. Practice consistency in your sleeping schedule, eating habits, exercise program and times of study and leisure. Don't hit the books for 10 hours and then blow off the next three days (while perhaps drinking too much). Don't binge today and starve yourself tomorrow. Consistent practices will cause you to view yourself evenly, and that in turn may stabilize your moods.

Self-Esteem

Q: But I just don't like myself very much. Why is that?

A: How you feel about yourself takes into account your entire lifetime of experiences. Certainly your parents and siblings have done their share to mold your self-image. If they've harshly

→

criticized you, then you may internalize their messages, converting their disapproval into self-disapproval. Teachers, peers and others have also left their mark on you. In addition, you've been your own judge through the years, evaluating yourself at reading, riding a bicycle, swimming or running, driving a car, more recently at fitting in at college, doing your coursework and finding new friends. All those countless times when you've thought "I did great" or "I'm lousy" are evidence you've used to decide what sort of person you are.

It's important to recognize, however, that self-esteem is not a uniform judgment. You may not generally feel competent at doing things but still feel that you're well liked and lovable, or maybe it's the other way around. And even if you don't feel particularly competent or popular, still surely there are many things about yourself that you give a passing grade. Perhaps you don't like your body but do think your smile is attractive; perhaps you don't think of yourself as a funny person but you have a good way with animals and small children. Everyone can find some points about themselves to like and to dislike.

Q: What can I do to improve self-esteem?

A: We do have some suggestions, but you'll need to be patient waiting for results. After all, your feelings about yourself have had two decades to take root. Here, then, are things you can try:

- Employ the cognitive approach described above to identify and replace self-belittling thoughts. For example, do you dwell on your faults and discount your strengths? Do you overgeneralize from a single setback and conclude that you're worthless? Do you disparage yourself for failing to be perfect? Such negative thinking erodes self-esteem. Watch out for these thoughts; you may find they come up often. Challenge them each time they appear, and in their place substitute fairer, more realistic self-appraisals.

- In order to acknowledge your strengths, take an inventory of your positive points. What do you like about yourself? What would others say they like about you? For example, let's say you're a responsible person. When you say you'll do something, it gets done, conscientiously and on time. You may be straightforward and honest as well—you don't play games. These are valuable qualities that can be the cornerstone of self-esteem, but most likely you haven't valued them enough. So write down on a piece of paper all your assets, large and small: "Responsible. Friendly. Sympathetic. Honest. . . . " Study this list. From it you may start to appreciate some of the things that make you worthwhile.

- It may sound odd, but it also helps to catalog your negative points. So consider your short-comings. In what ways are you deficient? How would others say you should improve? Be as honest as you can, neither exaggerating nor glossing over the truth, and write down what you find. Carrying out this exercise helps build esteem because it shows you can look at yourself honestly and unflinchingly. It feels good to know there's nothing so horrible about you that you can't admit it, nothing so dreadful that you can't still look yourself in the eye.

- Consider again the list of negatives and separate out the ones you can't change. For example, are you unhappy with your height? Your basic body type? Your sexual orientation? Your family's circumstances? A learning disability? These are the givens in your life, the cards you've been dealt. Though it's easier said than done, work on accepting these conditions. Reconcile yourself to your limitations. If you can live with them, not blaming yourself, cursing the fates or wishing you were somehow different, you'll have taken a big step toward self-acceptance.

■ Now, take action on the things you want to change. To like who you are, rational thinking is not enough; you also have to behave in constructive ways. This doesn't mean you have to become an A+ student or captain of the football team (those people may not necessarily like themselves either). It does mean, however, that you have to be proud of your efforts. You have to develop skills, take care of basic responsibilities and not run away from important challenges. All in all, you have to respect what you do. It all sounds so simple—"Behave constructively"—yet surprisingly many students fail to grasp the principle. If you like what you do, you will like yourself; if you don't like your actions, you won't.

So examine where you've been slacking off. Are you badly out of shape? Start jogging again. Is your room a mess? Try organizing the chaos. Have you neglected to write to your high school friends at another school? Drop them a note. Every time you behave constructively, even in small matters, you earn a dividend in self-esteem.

Q: But if I start building up self-esteem, won't I become conceited?

A: We doubt it. In fact, often it's the people who don't like themselves who are the conceited ones. They have an exaggerated sense of their own importance or abilities, or at least they try to convince you they're something special, because they're compensating for inner feelings of inadequacy. In contrast, people who have self-esteem are comfortable with their real selves, warts and all. Because they basically like who they are, they don't have to inflate their importance. So it's safe to work on building your self-esteem; you won't turn into an egotistical monster.

Q: I keep hearing this voice saying, "You're stupid, you can't do this, you're a jerk." Why do I do this to myself?

A: Our bet is that you learned it from someone in your past. If you listen carefully to the voice, you may recognize the words or intonation of a critical parent or sibling, or hear again the teasing you got at school. You're now saying to yourself what used to be said to you.

Oddly enough, you also may *want* to criticize yourself. Your harsh words may be intended to goad you to action. ("Try harder, stupid!") They may be a backhanded way of declaring that you're really wonderful. (Thinking "I'm so dumb" when you get a B+ implies that you really consider yourself an A student.) Self-criticism can also be meant to inoculate you from outside criticism. Since you've already said the worst to yourself, you feel no one else's negative words can hurt you.

Despite such subtle motives, you still probably don't enjoy this critic inside your head. To rid yourself of it, we recommend the same cognitive strategy we outlined for eliminating other negative thinking patterns: Make yourself aware of the self-criticisms. Challenge unfair statements—talk back! Substitute fair self-assessments in their place.

It also may help to imagine being a parent someday. Do you want to criticize, find fault, always harp on the negative with your child? Or do you hope to be a supportive parent, patient

→

and encouraging when your son or daughter takes on a challenge? We assume you agree the second way is better. The question now becomes why you'd be any less humane toward yourself than toward your child. Why do you mistreat the child inside of you—we all have one—when you know that method is wrong?

If you can, try to be a good parent to yourself. Like a child, you too will perform better and feel happier if you are told "Come on, you can do it" rather than "You can't do this, stupid."

Suicide

Q: I sometimes think about suicide. Does that mean I'm likely to go through with it someday?

A: Probably not. Practically every one of us has wondered about suicide. College students wonder more than most, since late adolescence and early adulthood are times of asking large questions about the meaning of life and one's own identity. But we need to draw a sharp distinction between thoughts and behaviors, between casual reflections and serious intentions. So long as you're not at all tempted to act on your thoughts, you are not in danger. This doesn't mean your suicidal thoughts are unimportant. They may be a sign of depression, as we mentioned earlier, and therefore, to be on the safe side, you may want to consult a counselor. However, so long as you know you wouldn't carry out a suicidal thought, then it's most unlikely that you'll do it.

The time to start worrying—and get help—is when your suicidal thoughts cross over into serious, hard-to-control urges, or when you find yourself thinking of ways to carry it out. Likewise if thoughts about suicide are persistent and won't go away, it's time to seek professional help.

Q: Two years ago I took an overdose, and I've been having strong suicidal urges again. I know I should seek counseling, but I don't see how that will help me get over the wish to kill myself.

A: Fortunately, almost nobody has a 100% wish to end his or her life. It's usually 60 : 40, or even 51 : 49. The fact that you've resisted recent suicidal impulses says loud and clear that a strong part of you clings to hope and wants to live. It's that life-affirming side of you that counseling can support and reinforce.

Counseling can help you see your situation in perspective. You can be assisted to widen your field of vision beyond your immediate problems. Counseling can give you empathic support during a lonely time, and encourage you to get support from others. Additionally, your counselor can teach you coping methods to resist suicidal impulses. For example, you may learn when you feel suicidal to call a friend, arrange for an immediate visit to your family or get someone to take you to the hospital.

Since inevitably you will continue to encounter both good and bad in life, the key to overcoming suicidal impulses is not to solve all your problems. Rather, the answer lies in a fundamental change inside of you. You must learn to make an inner pact, a binding decision, that in spite of problems you won't use suicide as a way out. You need to hold onto this decision

→

even when the going gets tough. The decision won't come about all at once. It will take hard work in counseling before you're ready to give up the option of suicide once and for all.

For Further Reading:

A. Alvarez, *The Savage God: A Study of Suicide*. New York: Random House, 1970.
Jeffrey Berlant, Irl Extein, and Larry Kirstein, *Guide to the New Medicines of the Mind*. Summit, NJ: PIA Press, 1988.
David Burns, *Feeling Good: The New Mood Therapy*. New York: Morrow, 1980.

Questions for Analysis

1. According to the authors, it is important to distinguish "sadness" from "depression." Describe a time in your life when you were depressed. What factors or experiences do you think caused your depression? What strategies do the authors suggest for combating depression?

2. Almost everyone suffers from low self-esteem at one time or another. According to the authors, what are some approaches you can use for improving your self-esteem?

3. Have you ever known someone who was so depressed that he or she considered suicide? Describe the situation and your response to it.

7
Writing Effectively

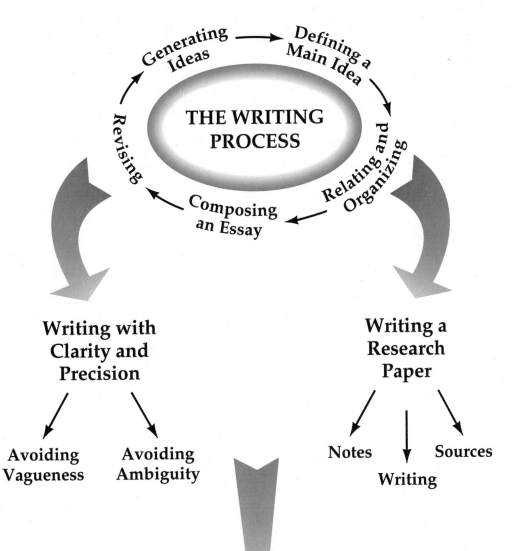

THE WRITING PROCESS

Generating Ideas → Defining a Main Idea → Relating and Organizing → Composing an Essay → Revising

Writing with Clarity and Precision
- Avoiding Vagueness
- Avoiding Ambiguity

Writing a Research Paper
- Notes
- Writing
- Sources

Writing Effectively

One of the greatest challenges of becoming a successful college student is learning to be an effective writer. In your previous education, "good writing" probably meant mastering the mechanics: grammar, spelling, and general organization. These are essential dimensions of language to master, but as a college writer you are expected to do more: to write with depth, insight, and analytical understanding. In order to achieve this level of sophistication, you need to develop comparably advanced thinking abilities. There are intimate, interactive relationships between thinking and language, and these close relationships are particularly evident in the writing process, in which our expression results from this complex interplay.

For example, in the space below, compose a brief message to someone you care about. As you create your message, pay particular attention to the interaction between ideas and words (and emotions!) in your mind as you produce your message.

_____

_____

_____

_____

Becoming an expert writer enables you to represent the rich fabric of your experience with clarity and precision. But as you may have seen when you composed your message, the process of using language also serves to generate ideas and then organize them into coherent form. In a statement that itself demonstrates the dynamic union of thinking and language, the great Russian novelist Leo Tolstoy said this: "The relations of word to thought, and the creation of new concepts is a complex, delicate, and enigmatic process unfolding in our soul." Writing is a vehicle for learning, a tool for developing critical thinking, an approach for creating and communicating ideas, and a catalyst for stimulating personal and intellectual development.

The papers assigned in college range from short essays to very elaborate research papers. Yet despite these different writing contexts, the basic stages in the writing process remain relatively constant:

- Generating ideas
- Defining a main idea
- Organizing ideas
- Composing a paper
- Revising

Generating Ideas

Ideas are not created in isolation but are almost always related to a particular subject. We develop ideas by exploring that subject. Some of the papers assigned to you will have very specific requirements, and others may be more open-ended. In most cases, however, you will be expected to come up with your own ideas. Even when the paper topic is fairly straightforward, you will be expected to bring your own perspective to the subject being explored. There are several strategies to help you generate ideas:

Familiarize Yourself with the Subject

There is no simple formula for developing original ideas for your writing assignments. However, the way to begin is by immersing yourself in the subject and then letting your subconscious work make connections and generate creative ideas. In a way, developing creative ideas is like gardening: you have to prepare the soil, plant the seeds, ensure that there is sufficient food, water, and sunlight— and then wait. Once the ideas begin to emerge, you have to seize them. The creative process is a natural process that works according to its own schedule and rhythm. Familiarize yourself with the subject, allow time for "incubation," and then be prepared to recognize and act on the ideas once they occur to you.

Generating Ideas: A number of strategies like brainstorming and mind-maps can be used to generate ideas for writing assignments.

Brainstorm

Brainstorming is an activity in which, working alone or with a group of people, you generate and record as many ideas as possible on a given theme. The goal is to do this in a fixed period of time. While you are engaged in this idea-generating process, it is important to relax, let your mind run free, build on the ideas of others, and refrain from censoring or evaluating any ideas produced, no matter how marginal they may seem. Brainstorming stimulates your creative juices, and you will be surprised at how many ideas you are able to come up with. And if you work with other people, you will be exposed to fresh perspectives and the *synergy* of people working together as a team.

Create Mind Maps

Mind maps are visual presentations of the various ways ideas can be related to one another. For example, each chapter of this book opens with a "mind map" that visually summarizes the chapter's basic concepts as well as the way these concepts are related to one another. We examined in Chapter 6 how mind maps are effective tools for taking notes on reading assignments. Mind maps are also a powerful approach for writing, helping you generate ideas and begin organizing them into various relationships. They are well suited for the writing process for a number of reasons. First, the organization grows naturally, reflecting the way that your mind naturally makes associations and organizes information. Second, the organization can be easily revised on the basis of new information and your developing understanding of how this information should be organized. Third, you can express a range of relationships among the various ideas. And instead of being identified once and then forgotten, each idea remains an active part of the overall pattern, suggesting new possible relationships. Fourth, you do not have to decide initially on a beginning, subpoints, sub-subpoints, and so on; you can do this after your pattern is complete, saving time and frustration.

The best way to explore the process of generating ideas is to actually engage in it. Listed in Appendix A on page 427 are the annual salaries of various individuals and professions in the United States during 1994. Carefully examine the list, and then explore the information presented by using concepts to classify it in different ways. You might want to use such concepts as

- amount of salary
- type of occupation
- level of education

After classifying the salary information in a variety of ways, examine your categories to see what conclusions you can draw. Questions such as the following might lead to some useful ideas:

1. How do the salaries from the various occupations compare with one another?

Conclusion: _____

_____

2. In what ways do the salaries reflect the level of education? The amount of experience?
   Conclusion: _____

   _____

3. What factors determine the amount of salary?
   Conclusion: _____

   _____

4. *Question:* _____?
   Conclusion: _____

5. *Question:* _____?
   Conclusion: _____

   Now, *brainstorm* ideas with others or by yourself for a period of approximately five minutes. Try to come up with as many ideas as possible, and don't worry if some seem a little wacky—sometimes wacky ideas are the beginning of genuinely creative initiatives. Next, develop a *mind map*, using the following guidelines:

1. Begin with what you consider to be the most important idea as the "center" of the map and then branch out to related ideas.

2. Your ideas should be written on lines that are connected to other lines, in order to express clearly the relationships between the various ideas.

3. Print legibly so that your ideas can be easily read and referred to.

In constructing your map, you might want to begin with the questions and conclusions that you just described. For example, the beginning of a map might look something like the one in Figure 7.1.

After working on your map for a while, you may find that you have exhausted your ideas. When this happens, use the following questions to help stimulate additional ideas and connections.

■ *Can you give examples of the subject?* (What are the salaries of people that you know?)

■ *How do you respond to the subject or feel about it?* (What is your reaction to a counter attendant earning $11,500? An obstetrician earning $110,000?)

■ *Why is the subject valuable or important?* (Why do people focus so much attention on salaries? What do salaries symbolize in our society?)

■ *What are the causes or reasons for this attention?* (What factors determine the amount of salaries?)

■ *What results from the subject?* (What results occur based on the salaries people earn?)

Figure 7.1.
Preliminary mind
map

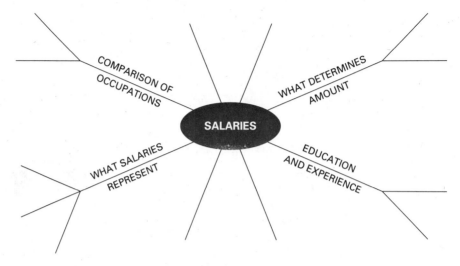

- *How does the subject compare to other things?* (How do different professions compare in terms of salary?)
- *What is my interpretation?* (Am I for or against the way salaries are established? Why?)
- *Have there been changes in the subject?* (What changes have occurred in salary levels over time?)
- *What ought to be done?* (What factors should determine what salary someone earns?)

As you think through these questions, return to your map to generate new ideas and form different relationships. For example, further development of the map may look like the one in Figure 7.2.

Defining a Main Idea

The next step is to define a working main idea suggested by the information and ideas you have been considering. Once selected, your main idea—known as a *thesis*—will act to focus your thinking on a central theme. It will also guide your future explorations and suggest new ideas and other relationships. Of course, a variety of main ideas can develop out of any situation, and your initial working idea will probably need redefining as you further explore your material. Here are some potential main ideas based on the map in Figure 7.2.

1. The amount of money a person earns is an important factor in determining a person's social status.
2. Both high-paying and low-paying jobs have psychological hazards. However, the types of hazards are different.

Using your map as a reference, identify some of the main ideas you could use to focus your thinking on the topic of salaries:

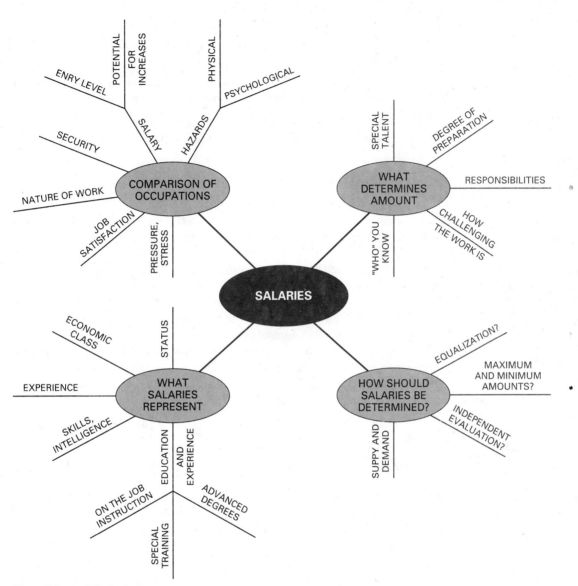

Figure 7.2. Modified mind map

Think carefully about the main ideas you have identified, and select the one that you would like to pursue further:

Main idea: _____

_____

After you decide on a main idea, the next step is to return to the map you created on page 254 and identify all the ideas and relationships connected to the central theme. In our example, the map in Figure 7.2 was used to identify the following ideas and relationships:

1. The amount of salary is related to the amount of responsibility.

2. Occupations differ in terms of the type and amount of stress.

3. The amount of salary is related to the level of decision making.

Exploring a topic is a process of moving back and forth between the various composing activities. This type of interactive exploration stimulates the most comprehensive thinking about the subject. To this end, create a map that uses the main idea you identified above as the starting point and the related ideas you just identified as the initial branches. This map should enable you to further develop and refine your thinking about your particular thesis. If, for example, you had pursued the main idea "Both high-paying and low-paying jobs have psychological hazards; however, the types of hazards are different," the diagram in Figure 7.3 would illustrate an extended treatment of your thesis.

The map you have just created represents your preliminary thinking about a central idea about the subject of salaries. Now you need to turn your attention to how you can shape and organize the results of your explorations. This shaping and organizing will enable you to refine your thinking further and aid you in presenting your ideas to others in written form.

Relating and Organizing Ideas

Each one of us is a "creator." Each of us is actively composing and shaping the world we live in by organizing that world into meaningful patterns, helping us figure out what is going on and what we ought to do. Ideas, things, and events in the world can be related and organized in a variety of ways. Different individuals might take the same furniture and decorations in the same space and arrange them in many different ways, reflecting each person's needs and aesthetic preferences. Or, to take another example, a class of students may develop ideas and write essays about the same subject with widely differing results. In this chapter, we will discuss three basic ways of relating and organizing:

1. *Comparative relationships:* relating things in the same general category in terms of their similarities and dissimilarities

2. *Analogical relationships:* comparing items found in different categories to increase our understanding

3. *Causal relationships:* relating events in terms of the way some event(s) are responsible for bringing about other event(s)

Figure 7.3. ***Mind map of specific thesis.***

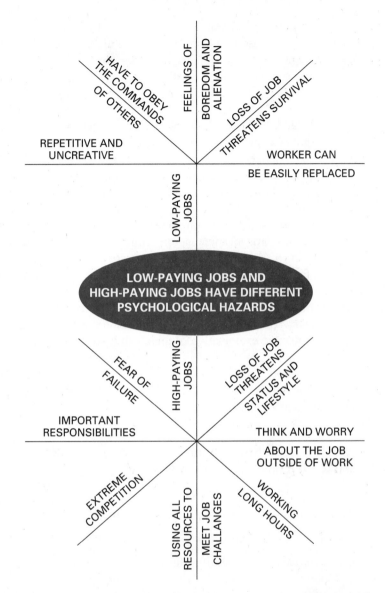

The specific combination of patterns you use to organize your ideas in thinking depends on the subject you are exploring, the goals you are aiming for in your communication, and the audience who will be reading your work.

Comparative Relationships

You compare things all the time, usually without even realizing it. Whenever you select an item on a menu or in a store, or a seat in a theater or on a bus, you are automatically looking for similarities and differences among the various items from which you are selecting, and these similarities and differences help guide your decision. Of course, you do not always engage in a systematic process of comparison. In many cases, the selections and decisions you make seem to be unconscious. Possibly, you have already performed the organized comparison some time in the past and already know what you want and why you want it ("I always choose an aisle seat so I don't have to climb over people").

Sometimes, however, many people make decisions impulsively, without any thought or comparative examination. Maybe someone told them to, maybe they were influenced by a commercial they saw, or maybe they simply said, "What the heck, let's take a chance." Sometimes these impulsive decisions work out, but often they do not because they are simply a result of rolling the dice. On the other hand, when you engage in a critical and comparative examination, you gain information that can help you make intelligent decisions.

In any comparison, some factors, similarities, and differences outweigh others. How do you determine which factors are more important than others and which information is most relevant? Unfortunately, there is no simple formula for answering these questions. But it does help to become *aware* of the factors that are influencing your perceptions and decisions. These *areas of comparison* represent the standards you use to come to conclusions, and a critical and reflective examination of them can help you sharpen, clarify, and improve your standards.

For example, consider each of the subjects listed below and describe the areas of comparison that you think are most important for making an informed and intelligent choice:

1. Selecting a competent surgeon to perform an operation on you
2. Selecting the best philosophy teacher to study under
3. Selecting the most reliable friend to ask an important favor of
4. Selecting a major course of study at college
5. Deciding in what geographical area to live

When making comparisons, there are two major pitfalls to avoid:

■ *Incomplete comparisons.* This difficulty arises when you focus on too few points of comparison. For example, in looking for a competent surgeon, you might decide to focus only on the fee each doctor charges. Even though this may be an important area for comparative analysis, you would be foolish to overlook other areas of comparison, such as medical training, experience, recommendations, and success rates.

■ *Selective comparisons.* This problem occurs when you take a one-sided view of a comparative situation—when you concentrate on the points favoring one side of the things being compared but overlook the points favoring the other side. For example, in selecting a dependable friend to perform a favor for you, you may focus on Bob because he is your best friend and you have known him the longest but overlook the fact that he let you down the last few times you asked him to do something for you.

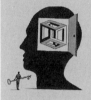

Thinking Activity 7.1

Review the following passages, which use comparative patterns of thinking to organize the ideas being presented. For each passage,

1. Identify the key ideas being compared.
2. Analyze the points of similarity and dissimilarity between the ideas being presented by using a mind map like the diagram in Figure 7.4.
3. Describe the conclusions the passage leads you to.

The difference between an American cookbook and a French one is that the former is very accurate and the second exceedingly vague. American recipes look like doctors' prescriptions. Perfect cooking seems to depend on perfect dosage. You are told to take a teaspoon of this and a tablespoon of that, then to stir them together until thoroughly blended. A French recipe seldom tells you how many ounces of butter to use to make *crepes suzette*, or how many spoonfuls of oil should go into a salad dressing. French cookbooks are full of unusual measurements such as a *pinch* of pepper, a *suspicion* of garlic, or a *generous sprinkling* of brandy. There are constant references to seasoning *to taste,* as if the recipe were merely intended to give a general direction, relying on the experience and art of the cook to make the dish turn out right.

Raoul de Roussy de Sales, "American and French Cookbooks"

Physically and psychically women are by far the superior of men. The old chestnut about women being more emotional than men has been forever destroyed by the facts of two great wars. Women under blockade, heavy bombardment, concentration camp confinement, and similar rigors withstand them vastly more successfully than men. The psychiatric casualties of civilian populations under such conditions are mostly masculine, and there are far more men in our mental hospitals than there are women. The steady hand at the helm is the hand that has had the practice at rocking the cradle. Because of their greater size and weight, men are physically more powerful than women—which is not the same thing as saying that they are stronger. A man of the same size and weight as a woman of comparable background and occupational status would probably not be any more powerful than a woman. As far as constitutional strength is concerned, women are stronger than men. Many diseases from which men suffer can be shown to be largely influenced by their relation to the male Y-chromosome. More males die than females. Deaths from almost all causes are more frequent in males of all ages. Though women are more frequently ill than men, they recover from illnesses more easily and more frequently than men.

Ashley Montagu, *The Natural Superiority of Women*

Return to the ideas about salaries that you generated and mapped on page 256. Select two key ideas that you think might be compared and contrasted in order to further your understanding of the topic. After identifying those key

Figure 7.4. Compar-
ative relationships

COMPARATIVE RELATIONSHIPS

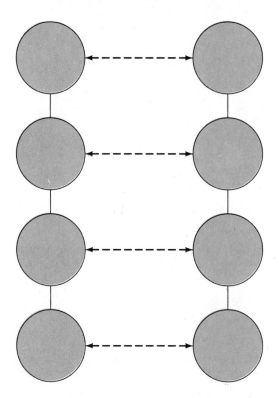

ideas, analyze the relationships between them by setting up and completing a
comparative list. (The following sample comparative list was developed in this
way from the sample map in Figure 7.3.)

Low-paying Occupations	*High-paying Occupations*
1. Work is often repetitive.	1. Work is rarely repetitive—usually demands a high level of analysis and problem solving.
2. Major hazard is feeling bored.	2. Major hazards are stress and pressure.
3. Workers have specific duties and have to obey the directives of others.	3. Workers have more responsibilities, authority, autonomy.
4. The work does not usually involve competition with others.	4. Work usually involves intense competition with others.
5. Fear of losing job is a major concern.	5. Fear of failure is a major concern.

6. Workers usually have fixed hours.	6. Workers often work long hours and take work home.
7. Loss of job threatens survival.	7. Loss of job threatens status and lifestyle.

Analogical Relationships

We noted earlier that comparative relationships involve examining the similarities and differences of two items in the same general category, such as items on a menu or methods of birth control. However, there is a kind of comparison that does *not* focus on things in the same category. Such comparisons are known as *analogies,* and they are used to clarify or illuminate a concept from one category by showing the concept's similarities to one from a different category.

The purpose of an analogy is not the same as the purpose of a comparison. The goal of comparing similar things is usually to make a choice, and the process of comparing can provide information on which we can base an intelligent decision. However, the main use of analogies is not to help us choose or decide; it is to illuminate understanding. Identifying similarities between very different things can often stimulate you to see these things in a new light. Consider the following example:

> Life's but a walking shadow, a poor player
> That struts and frets his hour upon the stage
> And then is heard no more.

> William Shakespeare, *Macbeth*

In this famous quotation, Shakespeare is comparing two things that at first glance don't seem to have anything in common at all: life and an actor. Yet as we look closer at the comparison, we begin to see that even though these two things are unlike in many ways, there are also some very important similarities between them. What are some of these similarities?

1. _____
2. _____
3. _____

Analogy

A comparison between things that are basically dissimilar made for the purpose of illuminating our understanding of the things being compared.

We often create and use analogies to get a point across. Used appropriately, analogies can help illustrate and explain what we are trying to communicate, a particularly important step when we have difficulty in finding the right words to represent our experiences. Powerful or complex emotions can render us speechless or lead us to say such things as "words cannot describe what I feel." Imagine that you are trying to describe your feelings of love and caring for another person. To illustrate and clarify the feelings you are trying to communicate, you might compare your feelings of love to "the first rose of spring," noting the following similarities:

- Like the rose, this is the first great love of your life.
- Like the fragile yet supple petals of the rose, your feelings are tender and sensitive.
- Like the beauty of the rose, the beauty of your love grows with each passing day.

What are some other comparisons of love to a rose?

Like the color of the rose, _____.

Like the fragrance of the rose, _____.

Like the thorns of the rose, _____.

Another frequent use for analogies is to communicate the meaning or purpose of life, which the simple use of the word *life* does not communicate. We have just seen Shakespeare's comparison of life to an actor. Here are some other popular analogies involving life. What are some points of similarity in each comparison?

1. Life is just a bowl of cherries.

   _____

2. Life is a football game.

   _____

3. "Life is a tale told by an idiot, full of sound and fury, signifying nothing."

   _____

Create an analogy for life representing some of your feelings, and explain the points of similarity.

4. Life is   _____

   _____.

In addition to communicating experiences that resist simple characterization, analogies are useful when we are trying to explain a complicated concept. For instance, we might compare the eye to a camera lens or the immunological system of the body to the National Guard (when undesirable elements threaten the well-being of the organism, corpuscles are called to active duty and rush to the scene of danger).

Analogies possess the power to bring things to life by evoking images that illuminate the points of comparison. Consider the following analogies, and explain the points of comparison that the author is trying to make.

1. "Laws are like cobwebs, which may catch small flies, but let wasps and hornets break through."—Jonathan Swift

   _____

2. "I am as pure as the driven slush."—Tallulah Bankhead

   _____

3. "He has all the qualities of a dog, except its devotion."—Gore Vidal

   _____

From the examples discussed so far, we can see that analogies have two parts: an *original subject* and a *compared subject* (what the original is being likened to). In comparing your love to the first rose of spring, the *original subject* is your feelings of love and caring for someone, and the *compared subject* is what you are comparing those feelings to in order to illuminate and express them—namely, the first rose of spring.

In analogies, the connection between the original subject and the compared subject can be either obvious (explicit) or implied (implicit). For example, consider the comment of the great pool hustler "Minnesota Fats": "A pool player in a tuxedo is like a hotdog with whipped cream on it." This is an obvious analogy (known as a *simile*) because we have explicitly noted the connection between the original subject (man in tuxedo) and the compared subject (hotdog with whipped cream) by using the comparative term *like*. (Sometimes the structure of the sentence calls for *as*.)

Simile

An explicit comparison between basically dissimilar things made for the purpose of illuminating our understanding of the things being compared.

We could also use other forms of obvious comparison, such as "is similar to," "reminds me of," or "makes me think of." On the other hand, we could say the following: "A pool player in a tuxedo *is* a hotdog with whipped cream on it." In this case, we are making an implied analogy (known as a *metaphor*), because we have not included any words that point out that we are making a comparison. Instead, we are stating that the original subject *is* the compared subject. Naturally, we are assuming that most people will understand that we are making a comparison between two different things and not describing a biological transformation.

Metaphor

An implied comparison between basically dissimilar things made for the purpose of illuminating our understanding of the things being compared.

Create a *simile* (obvious analogy) for a subject of your own choosing, noting at least two points of comparison.

Subject: _____

1. _____

2. _____

Create a *metaphor* (implied analogy) for a subject of your own choosing, noting at least two points of comparison.

Subject: _____

1. _____

2. _____

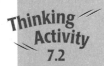

Thinking Activity 7.2

Read the following passage, which uses an analogical pattern of thinking. Identify the major ideas being compared, and describe the points of similarity between them. Explain how the analogy helps illuminate the subject being discussed.

The mountain guide, like the true teacher, has a quiet authority. He or she engenders trust and confidence so that one is willing to join the endeavor. The guide accepts his leadership role, yet recognizes that success (measured by the heights that are scaled) depends upon the close cooperation and active participation of each member of the group. He has crossed the terrain before and is familiar with the landmarks, but each trip is new and generates its own anxiety and excitement. Essential skills must be mastered; if they are lacking, disaster looms. The situation demands keen focus and rapt attention; slackness, misjudgment, or laziness can abort the venture. . . . The teacher is not a pleader, not a performer, not a huckster, but a confident, exuberant guide on expeditions of shared responsibility into the most exciting and least-understood terrain on earth—the mind itself.

Nancy K. Hill, "Scaling the Heights, The Teacher as Mountaineer"

Return to the ideas about salaries, which you generated and mapped on page 256. Create an analogy that might help illuminate your ideas and organize your thinking. Then analyze your analogy by identifying the points of similarity and dissimilarity between your original subject and your compared subject. Here is a sample analogy related to these topics:

> Various occupations can have psychological hazards associated with them in the same way that other occupations can have physical hazards. Coal miners are susceptible to Black Lung disease; dentists are vulnerable to lower back pain; dancers are prone to foot and ankle problems; singers often have throat and voice difficulties. In the same way, people in certain professions are susceptible to various psychological hazards. For instance, assembly-line workers may become bored and depressed because their work has little meaning for them; police officers have an unusually high divorce rate and a suicide rate that is exceeded only by doctors, who also have a high drug addiction and alcoholism rate; people in high-pressure business positions often develop migraine headaches, ulcers, high blood pressure, and heart disease.

<u>Original Subject</u>: the relation between occupations and psychological hazards.
<u>Compared Subject</u>: the relation between occupations and physical hazards.
<u>Similarities</u>:

1. Certain professions seem to be associated with certain hazards, both physical and psychological.

2. The particular hazard—whether physical or psychological—seems to be the result of certain qualities of the occupation.

<u>Dissimilarities</u>:

1. Physical ailments are usually more easily observed and verified than psychological ailments.

2. The relationship between certain occupations and corresponding physical hazards is more easily verified than that between occupations and psychological hazards.

Causal Relationships

Causal patterns of thinking involve relating events in terms of the influence or effect they have on one another. For example, if you were right now to pinch yourself hard enough to feel it, you would be demonstrating a cause-and-effect relationship. Stated very simply, a *cause* is anything that is responsible for bringing about something else—usually termed the *effect*. When we make a causal statement, we are merely stating that a causal relationship exists between two or more things: "The pinch *caused* the pain in my arm." Of course, when we make (or think) causal statements, we do not always use the word *cause*. For example, the following statements are all causal statements. In each case, underline the cause and circle the effect.

1. Since I was the last person to leave, I turned off the lights.

2. Taking lots of vitamin C really cured me of that terrible cold I had.

3. I accidentally toasted my hand along with the marshmallows by getting too close to the fire.

Create three statements that express a causal relationship without actually using the word *cause*.

1. _____

2. _____

3. _____

We are always thinking in terms of causal relationships. In fact, the goal of much of our thinking is to figure out *why* something happened or *how* something came about. If we can figure out how and why things occur, we can then try to *predict* what will happen in the future. These predictions of anticipated results form the basis of many of our decisions. For example, the experience of toasting our hand along with the marshmallows might lead us to choose a longer stick—simply because we are able to figure out the causal relationships involved and then make predictions based on our understanding.

Consider the following activities, which you probably perform daily. Each activity assumes that certain causal relationships exist which influence your decision to perform them. Explain one such causal relationship for each activity.

1. Setting the alarm clock

2. Brushing your teeth

3. Wearing shoes

4. Putting on perfume or cologne

5. Locking the door

Causal Chains.   Although we tend to think of causes and effects in isolation—*A* caused *B*—in reality, causes and effects rarely appear by themselves. Causes and effects generally appear as parts of more complex patterns, including three that we will examine here:

■ *Causal chains*

■ *Contributory causes*

■ *Interactive causes*

Consider the following scenario. Your paper on the topic "Is there life after death?" is due on Monday morning. You have reserved the whole weekend to work on it and are just getting started when the phone rings—your best friend from your childhood is in town and wants to stay with you for the weekend. You say yes. By Sunday night, you've had a great weekend, but have made little progress on your paper. You begin writing, when suddenly you feel stomach cramps—it must have been those raw oysters that you had for lunch! Three hours later, you are ready to continue work. You brew a pot of coffee and get

Causal Chains:
Causes and effects generally appear as parts of more complex patterns such as causal chains, contributory causes, and interactive causes.

started. At 3:00 (A.M.) you are too exhausted to continue. You decide to get a few hours of sleep and set the alarm clock for 6:00 (A.M.), giving you plenty of time to finish up. When you wake up, you find that it's nine o'clock—the alarm failed to go off! Your class starts in forty minutes, and you have no chance of getting the paper done on time. As you ride to school, you go over the causes for this disaster in your mind. You are no longer worried about life after death—you are now worried about life after this class!

1. What causes in this situation are responsible for your paper not being completed on time?

a. _____

b. _____

c. _____

d. _____

2. What do you think is the single most important cause?

_____

3. What do you think your teacher will identify as the most important cause? Why?_____

_____

A causal chain, as we can see from these examples, is a situation in which one thing leads to another, which then leads to another, and so on. There is not just one cause for the resulting effect; there is a whole string of causes. Which cause in the string is the "real" cause? Our answer often depends on our perspective on the situation. In the example of the unfinished paper on the topic "Is there life after death?" we might see the cause as a faulty alarm clock. On the other hand, the teacher might see the cause of the problem as an overall lack of planning. Figure 7.5 illustrates this causal structure.

Thinking Activity 7.3

1. Create a scenario that details a chain of causes resulting in being late for class, standing someone up for a date, failing an exam, or an effect of your own choosing.

2. Review the scenario you have just created. Explain how the "real" cause of the final effect could vary, depending on your perspective on the situation.

Contributory Causes. In addition to operating in causal chains, causes can also act simultaneously to produce an effect. When this happens (as it often does), we have a situation in which a number of different causes are instrumental in bringing something about. Instead of working in isolation, each cause *contributes* to bringing about the final effect. When this situation occurs, each cause serves to support and reinforce the action of the other causes, a structure illustrated in Figure 7.6.

Consider the following situation. It is the end of the term, and you have

Figure 7.5. Causal chain

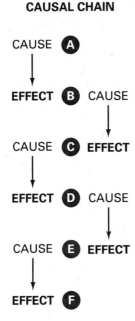

CAUSAL CHAIN

been working incredibly hard at school—writing papers, preparing for exams, finishing up course projects. You haven't been getting enough sleep, and you haven't been eating regular or well-balanced meals. To make matters worse, you have been under intense pressure in your personal life, having had serious arguments with your boyfriend or girlfriend. You find that this problem is constantly on your mind. Also, it is the middle of the flu season, and many of the people you know have been sick with various bugs. Walking home from school one evening, you get soaked by an unexpected shower. By the time you get home, you are shivering. You soon find yourself in bed with a thermometer in your mouth—you are sick!

What was the "cause" of your getting sick? In this situation, you can see it probably was not just *one* thing that brought about your illness; it was a *combination* of different factors that led to your physical breakdown: low resistance, getting wet and chilled, being exposed to various germs and viruses, physical

Figure 7.6. Contributory causes

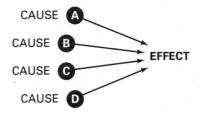

CONTRIBUTORY CAUSES

exhaustion, lack of proper eating, and so on. Taken by itself, no one factor might have been enough to cause your illness. Working together, they all contributed to the outcome.

Think back on situations from your own life in which a number of contributory causes led you to ask someone for a date, choose a major, lose or win a game you played in, or make some other choice. Select one such example, and see if you can identify the various contributory causes involved in bringing about the result.

Interactive Causes.   Our examination of causal relationships has revealed that causes rarely operate in isolation but instead often influence (and are influenced by) other factors. Imagine that you are scheduled to give a speech to a large group of people. As the time for your moment in the spotlight approaches, you become anxious, which results in a dry mouth and throat, making your voice sound more like a croak. The prospect of sounding like a bullfrog increases your anxiety, which in turn dries your mouth and constricts your throat further, reducing your croak to something much worse—silence.

This not uncommon scenario reveals the way that different factors can relate to one another through reciprocal influences that flow back and forth from one to the other. This type of causal relationship, which involves an *interactive* thinking pattern, is an extremely important way to organize and make sense of our experience. For example, to understand social relationships, such as families, teams, groups of friends, and so on, we have to understand the complex ways each individual influences—and is influenced by—all the other members of the group.

Understanding biological systems and other systems is similar to understanding social systems. To understand and explain how an organ such as your heart, liver, or brain functions, you have to describe its complex, interactive relationships with all the other parts of your biological system. The diagram in Figure 7.7 illustrates these dynamic causal relationships.

Thinking Activity 7.4

Read the following passages, which illustrate causal patterns of thinking. For each passage,

1. create mind maps that illustrate cause-and-effect relationships

2. identify the *kind* of causal relationship (direct, chain, contributory, or interactive)

Nothing posed a more serious threat to the bald eagle's survival than a modern chemical compound called DDT. Around 1940, a retired Canadian banker named Charles L. Broley began keeping track of eagles nesting in Florida. Each breeding season, he climbed into more than 50 nests, counted the eaglets and put metal bands on their legs. In the late 1940's, a

→

Figure 7.7.
Interactive causes

INTERACTIVE CAUSES

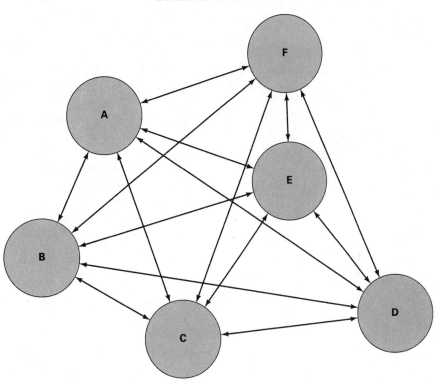

sudden drop-off in the number of young produced led him to conclude that 80 percent of his birds were sterile. Broley blamed DDT. Scientists later discovered that DDE, a breakdown product of DDT, causes not sterility, but a fatal thinning of eggshell among birds of prey. Applied on cropland all over the United States, the pesticide was running off into waterways where it concentrated in fish. The bald eagles ate the fish and the DDT impaired their ability to reproduce. They were not alone, of course. Ospreys and pelicans suffered similar setbacks.

　Jim Doherty, "The Bald Eagle and DDT"

It is popularly accepted that Hitler was the major cause of World War II, but the ultimate causes go much deeper than one personality. First, there were longstanding German grievances against reparations levied on the nation following its defeat in World War I. Second, there were severe economic strains that caused resentment among the German people. Third, there was French and English reluctance to work out a sound disarmament policy and American noninvolvement in the matter. Finally, there was the European fear that communism was a much greater danger than National Socialism. These factors contributed to the outbreak of World War II.

　Gilbert Muller, *The American College Handbook*

We crunch and chew our way through vast quantities of snacks and confectioneries and relieve our thirst with multicolored, flavored soft drinks, with and without calories, for two basic reasons. The first is simple; the food tastes good, and we enjoy the sensation of eating it. Second, we associate these foods, often without being aware of it, with the highly pleasurable experiences depicted in the advertisements used to promote their sale. Current television advertisements demonstrate this point: people turn from grumpiness to euphoria after crunching a corn chip. Others water ski into the sunset with their loved ones while drinking a popular soft drink. People entertain on the patio with friends, cook over campfires without mosquitoes, or go to carnivals with granddad munching away at the latest candy or snack food. The people portrayed in these scenarios are all healthy, vigorous, and good looking; one wonders how popular the food they convince us to eat would be if they would crunch or drink away while complaining about low back pain or clogged sinuses.

Judith Wurtman, *Eating Your Way Through Life*

Return to the ideas about salaries that you generated and mapped in Figure 7.3 on page 256. Describe some of the cause-and-effect relationships that you believe might exist between the key ideas you have identified. (The following description of cause-and-effect relationships was developed based on the ideas mapped in Figure 7.3.)

The psychological hazards of low-paying occupations are often different from the psychological hazards of high-paying occupations because of different causes. For example, think of occupations such as assembly-line workers, typists, and manual laborers. In these types of occupations the tasks are specifically delineated and the workers' responsibilities are limited. However, workers must cope with the tedium of doing the same thing over and over again. In addition, since they are performing only one small part of the overall process in which they are engaged, workers have little sense of connection with what they are producing. In most of these occupations, workers are not challenged to use their creative or critical thinking abilities and so do not have the opportunity to develop a sense of fulfillment in what they are doing. Also, in many low-paying jobs workers are at the mercy of their supervisors, having either to follow their commands without question or risk getting dismissed. It's clear that this sort of situation can result in boredom, depression, feelings of alienation, and eroded sense of self-worth.

In contrast, high-paying occupations often embody different factors that result in other psychological hazards. For example, occupations such as highly placed business executives, successful athletes, airline pilots, and movie stars have a number of qualities in common. In most cases these jobs involve tremendous responsibility. There are high expectations of performance, actions are carefully scrutinized, and people are expected to deliver. In trying to meet this challenge, workers are forced to use as many of their creative and critical thinking abilities as possible in order to maintain or improve their high level of performance, and they must work long hours so that they can stay on top of things. These occupations are often extremely competitive, forcing workers to think about their jobs even when they go home. And since the stakes are so high, the fear of failing is proportionally large. It's obvious that these types of stresses and pressures can result in tension, anxiety, headaches, ulcers, high blood pressure, and other psychological ailments.

Thus far in this chapter, we have explored a sequential process of composing:

■ Generating ideas

■ Defining a main idea

■ Organizing ideas

These steps rarely take place in such a neat, orderly sequence. Instead, there is continual back-and-forth (interactive) movement among these activities as you gradually develop and sharpen your ideas.

Composing a Paper

One purpose of the composing process is to present our ideas to others in a clear fashion. We want readers to understand our thinking, to consider the ideas we are exploring, and to ask intelligent questions. In order to attain this goal, it is useful for us to organize our ideas in a way that will aid others in making sense of our thinking. The form normally used to organize ideas in an essay reflects the basic questions that we raise when discussing ideas with others:

What is your point? (stating the main idea)

I don't quite get your meaning. (explaining the main idea)

Prove it to me. (providing examples, evidence, and arguments to support the main idea)

So what? (drawing a conclusion)*

By using the work you have been doing on the topic of salaries, you can organize your thinking into a basic essay format.

*Source: From Mina Shaghnessy, *Errors and Expectations: A Guide for the Teacher of Basic Writing* (New York: Oxford University Press, 1977), p. 273.

Stating the Main Idea

The first part of your essay should introduce the specific topic you will be exploring. Review your work on page 254, and then write a paragraph introducing your main idea.

Explaining the Main Idea

The next part of your essay should elaborate on your main idea, describing it more fully and with more detail. Review your work on page 256, and then write a paragraph explaining your main idea in more detail.

Providing Examples, Evidence, and Arguments to Support the Main Idea

Once you have stated and explained your main point, your next task is to offer reasons and evidence as support. This support can take a number of different forms:

1. You can *compare and contrast* various ideas.

2. You can suggest *analogies* to illustrate your points.

3. You can suggest *cause-and-effect* relationships.

4. You can give *examples* to illustrate your general ideas, a process we explored in Chapter 6.

5. You can identify *reasons* that support your point of view, a strategy we explored in Chapter 2.

6. You can present *arguments* that attempt to persuade readers that your thinking is accurate and complete, an approach we will be exploring in Chapter 9.

Write two to three paragraphs that provide examples, evidence, and arguments supporting your main point. You might want to work collaboratively with other students in this process, since they will be able to provide you with fresh ideas and an objective analysis of your work.

Drawing a Conclusion

The purpose of a conclusion is to summarize the main idea you have been considering along with the central reasons, evidence, and arguments that support your thinking. You might want to suggest further questions that need to be answered or new directions for pursuing the ideas you have been exploring.

Review the paragraphs you have already written, and then compose a paragraph that summarizes the points you have been addressing. The following essay evolved from the ideas mapped in Figure 7.3:

Psychological Hazards on the Job

Most occupations have psychological hazards for the people performing the work. In general, the psychological hazards in high-paying jobs are different from those in low-paying jobs. This is because different jobs have qualities that create their own unique kinds of stress and pressure.

Psychological hazards are as much a part of an occupation as physical hazards. For example, we know that coal miners are susceptible to Black Lung disease; dentists are vulnerable to lower back pain; dancers are prone to foot and ankle problems; singers often have voice and throat difficulties. In the same way, people in different professions are susceptible to various psychological hazards. For instance, assembly-line workers may become bored and depressed because their work has little meaning for them; police officers have an unusually high divorce rate and a suicide rate that is exceeded only by doctors; doctors also have a high drug addiction and alcoholism rate; people in executive-level business positions often develop migraine headaches, ulcers, high blood pressure, and heart disease. When we consider the various psychological hazards of individual professions, we can see that the pressures and stress of high-paying occupations are generally different from the pressures and stress of low-paying occupations.

For example, consider some of the low-paying occupations in our society, such as assembly-line worker, manual laborer, typist, and short-order cook. In all of these positions the tasks are very specific and the responsibilities are limited. People in these occupations must cope with the tedium of doing the same thing over and over again. Because people are following detailed instructions, they have little opportunity to use their creative and critical thinking abilities. Since people in these jobs are performing only one small part of the overall project they are involved in, they do not really feel connected to what they are doing. Also, in many low-paying jobs, people are at the complete mercy of their supervisors, having to follow commands without questions or risk getting fired. Taken as a whole, it's easy to see how these factors can create significant psychological hazards such as boredom, depression, a feeling of alienation, and an eroded sense of self-worth.

In contrast, high-paying occupations often embody different qualities that result in different psychological hazards. For example, consider some of the high-paying occupations in our society, such as senior business executive, successful athlete, airline pilot, surgeon, the President, and movie star. These occupations have a number of qualities in common. In most cases these jobs involve significant responsibilities—failure usually results in very serious consequences. There are high expectations of people in these positions. Their actions are carefully scrutinized, and they are expected to deliver. In trying to meet these challenges, people are usually forced to use as many of their creative and critical thinking abilities as they can, to work long hours, and to push themselves in order to maintain or improve their high level of performance. These occupations are typically extremely competitive, and people involved in them usually continue to think and worry about them after they go home. And since the stakes are so high, the fear of failing is proportionally greater. Looked at together, it is clear how these factors can create significant psychological hazards such as extreme tension, anxiety, and stress that can lead to migraine headaches, high blood pressure, ulcers, heart conditions, and a variety of other psychological ailments.

In summary, it seems apparent that most occupations have certain psychological hazards associated with them, and the hazards for low-paying jobs tend to be different than for high-paying jobs. Of course, no occupation by itself causes stress, pressure, alienation, or depression. These and other ailments are a result of the way individuals in these occupations react to the demands of their particular job. Some people are able to deal much more effectively with job demands than are others. In the years ahead, it would be a significant advancement if our society would identify the psychological hazards for various occupations—just as physical hazards have been identified—and then help employers and employees devise strategies for minimizing and coping with these hazards.

Revising

In the last few chapters, we have been emphasizing the notion that thinking is an interactive process that involves constantly forming and applying concepts, defining and exemplifying key terms, generating and developing ideas. This same interactive process is a part of the writing process. Most writers find it natural to move back and forth between the various aspects of the writing process as they follow the line of their thinking. In fact, you will probably discover that the process of writing does not merely express your thinking; it also *stimulates* your thoughts, bringing to the surface new ideas and ways to explore them. Because thinking and writing are interactive, in a sense you are continually revising your thinking and writing. The first draft of your writing is usually just that—a first draft. It is then important to go back and "re-see" (the origin of the word *revise*) your writing from a fresh perspective. In addition, it is helpful to have others read what you have written and give their reactions. Effective writing is the result of ongoing evaluation and re-evaluation of your ideas, and integrating the informed perspectives of others is an essential part of this process.

Improving sentence structure and correcting spelling and punctuation are necessary parts of the revising process. However, you also want to take a fresh look at the *thinking* that is being expressed. One useful strategy is to create an outline or a map of the first draft, because this will enable you to identify the main ideas and express their relationships. In turn, you may find ways in which you can clarify your thinking by rearranging different parts, developing certain points further, or deleting what is repetitious or not central to your main idea.

In one sense or another, you have probably been revising all along as you explored, mapped, and drafted your essay on salaries and work. After completing a draft of your essay, you should "re-see" how you have developed and organized your ideas and information by following these steps:

Revision Steps

1. Create a map that expresses the main points and their various relationships as expressed in your paper.

2. Examine your map carefully, looking for ways to clarify and improve your ideas. Determine whether you should
   - rearrange the sequence of your ideas
   - develop certain ideas further
   - delete points that are repetitious or not central to the subject

3. Revise your map (or create a new one to reflect these changes).

4. Compose a revised draft of your paper, using your revision map as a guide.

Writing with Clarity and Precision

Thinking is the organized and purposeful mental *process* that we use to make sense of the world, and language, with its power to represent our thoughts and experiences symbolically, is the most important tool our thinking process has. Although research shows that thinking and language begin as distinct processes, these two processes are so closely related that they are often difficult to separate or distinguish.

Language is a social phenomenon. As children, we internalize language from our social surroundings and develop it through our relations with other people. As we develop our language abilities through these social interactions, our thinking capacities expand as well. Other people help advance our thinking, and as we become literate our interactions with these people help shape our thinking. Social relationships also act as important vehicles for fostering precise thinking and language use: we talk to others and are responded to; we write and then discover how others understand (or misunderstand) our ideas.

Because language and thinking are so closely related, how well we perform one process is directly related to how well we perform the other. In most cases, when we are thinking clearly, we are able to express our ideas clearly in language. For instance, develop a clear and precise thought about the subject of *learning* and then express this thought in language, using the space provided.

_____

_____

_____

If you are *not* able to develop a clear and precise idea of what you are thinking about, then you will have great difficulty in expressing your thinking in language. When this happens, you may say something like this: "I know what I want to say, but I just can't find the right words." Of course, when this happens, you usually *don't* know exactly what you want to say—if you did, you would say it! When you have unclear thoughts, it is usually because you lack a clear understanding of the situation or you do not know the right language to give form to these thoughts.

Not only does unclear thinking contribute to unclear language; unclear language also contributes to unclear thinking. For example, read the following passage from William Shakespeare's *As You Like It,* Act V, Scene i. Here, language is being used in a confusing way for the purpose of confusing our thinking. Examine the passage carefully and then describe, as clearly as you can, the thinking that the author is trying to express:

> Therefore, you clown, abandon—which is in the vulgar, leave—the society—which in the boorish is company—of this female—which in the common is woman; which together is, abandon the society of this female, or, clown, thou perishest; or, to thy better understanding, diest; or, to wit, I kill thee, make thee away, translate thy life into death.

Write your interpretation:

_____

_____

_____

The interactive relationship between thinking and language is particularly well illustrated in the following passage from George Orwell's essay "Politics and the English Language":

> A man may take to drink because he feels himself to be a failure, and then fail all the more completely because he drinks. It is rather the same thing that is happening to the English language. It becomes ugly and inaccurate because our thoughts are foolish, but the slovenliness of our language makes it easier for us to have foolish thoughts. The point is that the process is reversible. Modern English, especially written English, is full of bad habits which spread by imitation and which can be avoided if one is willing to take the necessary trouble. If one gets rid of these habits one can think more clearly.

Just as the drunkard falls into a vicious circle that keeps getting worse, the same is true of the relation between language and thinking. When our use of language is sloppy—that is, vague, general, indistinct, imprecise, foolish, inaccurate, and so on—it leads to thinking of the same sort. Of course, the reverse is also true. Clear and precise language leads to clear and precise thinking.

Vague Language

Although our ability to name and identify gives us the power to describe the world precisely, we often do not use precise words. Instead, we form many of our descriptions of the world by using words that are very imprecise and general—*vague* words. Consider the following sentences:

- I had a *nice* time yesterday.
- That is an *interesting* book.
- She is an *old* person.

In each of these cases, the italicized word is vague because it does not give a precise description of the thought, feeling, or experience that the writer is

Clear vs. Vague Language:
Strong writers have the ability to communicate effectively by using language clearly and precisely.

trying to communicate. A word (or group of words) is vague if its meaning is not clear and distinct. That is, vagueness occurs when a word is used to represent an area of experience in such a way that the area is not clearly defined.

Vague Word
A word that lacks a clear and distinct meaning.

Most words of general measurement—*short, tall, big, small, heavy, light,* and so on—are vague. The exact meanings of these words depend on the specific situation in which they are used and on the particular perspective of the person using them. For example, give specific definitions for the following words in italics by filling in the blanks. Then compare your responses with those of other members of the class. Can you account for the differences in meaning?

1. A *middle-aged* person is one who is _____ years old.
2. A *tall* person is one who is over _____ feet _____ inches tall.
3. It's *cold* outside when the temperature is _____ degrees.
4. A person is *wealthy* when _____.

Although the vagueness of general measurement terms can lead to confusion, other forms of vagueness are more widespread and often more problematic. For example, terms such as *nice* and *interesting*, are imprecise and unclear. Vagueness of this sort permeates every level of human discourse, undermines clear thinking, and is extremely difficult to combat (though there are some situations in which we may choose to be *purposefully* vague). To use language clearly and precisely, we must develop an understanding of the way language functions and commit ourselves to breaking the entrenched habits of vague expression.

Avoiding Vague Words. Let us continue our examination of vagueness—and how to avoid it—by examining the following response to a movie. As you read through the passage, circle all the vague, general words that do not express a clear meaning.

> *Pulp Fiction* is a really funny movie about some really unusual characters in California. The movie consists of several different stories that connect up at different points. Some of the stories are nerve-racking and others are hilarious, but all of them are very well done. The plots are very interesting, and the main characters are excellent. I liked this movie a lot.

Because of the vague language in this passage, it expresses only general approval—it does not explain in exact or precise terms what the experience was like. The writer of the passage has not been successful in communicating his or her experience.

Strong writers have the gift of relating their experiences so clearly that we can actually relive those experiences with them. We can identify with them, sharing the same thoughts, feelings, and perceptions that they had when they underwent (or imagined) the experience.

Clarifying Vague Language. One useful strategy for clarifying vague language often used by journalists is to ask and try to answer the following questions: *Who? What? Where? When? How? Why?* Let us see how this strategy applies to a movie description.

- *Who* were the people involved in the movie? (actors, director, producer, characters, etc.)
- *What* took place in the movie? (setting, events, plot development, etc.)
- *Where* does the movie take place? (physical location, cultural setting, etc.)
- *When* do the events in the movie take place? (historical situation)
- *How* does the film portray its events? (How do the actors create their characters? How does the director use film techniques to accomplish his or her goals?)
- *Why* do I have this opinion of the film? (What are my reasons?)

Even if we don't give an elaborate version of our thinking, we can still communicate effectively by using language clearly and precisely. For example, examine this review of *Pulp Fiction* by the professional film critic David Denby. Compare and contrast it with the earlier review.

> An ecstatically entertaining piece of suave mockery by Quentin Tarantino that revels in every manner of pulp flagrancy—murder and betrayal, drugs, sex, and episodes of sardonically distanced sadomasochism—all told in three overlapping tales. It's a very funky, American sort of pop masterpiece: improbable, uproarious, with bright colors and danger and blood right on the surface.

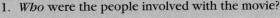

Thinking Activity 7.5

Write a review of a movie that you saw recently, concentrating on expressing your ideas clearly and precisely. Use the following questions to guide your analysis:

1. *Who* were the people involved with the movie?
2. *What* took place in the movie?
3. *Where* does the movie take place?
4. *When* do the events in the movie take place?
5. *How* does the film portray its events?
6. *Why* did you have this opinion about the film?

Virtually all of us use vague language extensively in our day-to-day conversations. In many cases, it is natural that our immediate reaction to an experience would be fairly general ("That's nice," "She's interesting," etc.). If we are truly concerned with sharp thinking and meaningful communication, however, we should follow up these initial general reactions with a more precise clarification of what we really mean:

- I think that she is a nice person *because* . . .
- I think that he is a good teacher *because* . . .
- I think that this is an interesting class *because* . . .

Vagueness is always a matter of degree. In fact, we can think of our descriptive/informative use of language as falling somewhere on a scale between extreme generality and extreme specificity. For example, the following statements move from the general to the specific.

General

She is really smart.
She does well in school.
She gets straight A's.
She got an A in physics.

Specific

Although different situations require various degrees of specificity, we should work at becoming increasingly precise in our use of language. For example, examine the following response to the assignment "Describe what you think about the school you are attending." Circle the vague words.

I really like it a lot. It's a very good school. The people are nice, and the teachers are interesting. There are a lot of different things to do, and students have a good time doing them. Some of the courses are pretty hard, but if you study enough, you should do all right.

Notice how general the passage is. For example, the writer states that "the people are nice" but gives no concrete and specific descriptions of *why* he or she thinks the people are nice. The writer would have been more specific if he or she had used statements such as the following:

- Everyone says hello.
- The students introduced themselves to me in class.
- I always feel welcome in the student lounge.
- The teachers take a special interest in each student.

Although these statements are more precise than saying "The people are nice," they can also be made more specific. To illustrate this, create more specific descriptions for each of these statements:

Everyone says hello.

_____

The students introduced themselves to me in class.

_____

I always feel welcome in the student lounge.

_____

The teachers take a special interest in each student.

_____

Writing a Research Paper

Research papers are more elaborate versions of the standard papers that are typically assigned. In writing a research paper, you will be using the same approach to the composing process that we just explored. The difference is that research papers involve gathering relevant information from appropriate sources, integrating this information into your paper, and then documenting your sources with footnotes and a bibliography. Most research paper assignments will expect you to bring your perspective to the subject; it's just that you are also expected to support your point of view with factual information and evidence drawn from authoritative sources.

Sometimes students writing research papers make the mistake of simply reporting the information from research sources and leave out their own perspective. Other times students make the opposite mistake, using their own ideas with little support from research sources. A properly balanced research paper integrates both.

Research Sources

Imagine that you are assigned the following topic for a research paper:

> Excessive drinking is a significant problem on many college campuses. Write a 5-page research paper that analyzes this problem. Why does it occur, and what can be done to deal with it? Your paper should include relevant research findings as well as your own perspective on this problem.

After taking a deep breath, your initial reaction to this question might reasonably be *Help!* However, there is no need to panic. As a critical thinker, you should have the confidence that this paper is merely a problem to be solved through thoughtful analysis and energy.

Again, your approach should follow the stages in the writing process that we explored: generating and mapping ideas, defining ideas, organizing ideas, and revising. You can start by generating and mapping ideas based on what you know about the subject, before actually beginning your research. This is an effective way to begin organizing your ideas and will in turn help guide your search for the most appropriate research materials. For example, your thinking might lead you to organize your research paper in the following way:

> Part one: one perspective on this problem, supported by appropriate research
>
> Part two: a *contrasting* perspective on this problem, supported by relevant research
>
> Part three: your own well-reasoned perspective, including what approaches might be effective in addressing the problem

Once you have generated and mapped your initial ideas, the next stop is the library. You can spend anywhere from a few hours to a few days in the library, depending on how familiar you are with the research process. The sources that you are looking for will be contained in books, newspaper articles, and scholarly journal articles. There are indexes for these types of sources that will help you track down the information needed. The following are some good places to start:

■ *Encyclopedias:* Depending on your topic, encyclopedias can be a useful place to begin your investigation, serving as a launch pad for more extensive research. In libraries, bound encyclopedias are being replaced by computerized CD-ROM versions, including *Encarta* and *Grolier Encyclope-*

New technologies like CD-ROM encyclopedias, computerized catalogs, and periodical indexes, and multimedia laser disks have made library research faster and more effective.

dia. These computerized versions make searching for information simple— they have many illustrations and even animated sequences, and you can print out useful information, saving you from taking notes or standing in line at the photocopy machine.

■ *Card Catalogs:* These are the basic index system of the library, referencing the collection of books by author, subject, and title. Increasingly, the traditional index cards are being replaced by computerized versions.

■ *Periodical Indexes:* The term *periodicals* refers to magazines and journals that are published at regular intervals. In addition to common magazines such as *Time* and *Newsweek,* there are many "scholarly" journals that contain articles and research findings in all the major fields of inquiry. Periodical indexes are both bound—as is the *Reader's Guide to Periodical Literature*—and computerized. You will also find that in addition to general indexes, there are indexes relating to specific fields, such as the *Social Science Index.* These indexes are usually organized by subject, although you may have to use a number of variations on your topic to ensure that you are locating all of the appropriate references. For example, in looking for information about college drinking, you will likely have to explore a number of different subjects, such as "college life" and "alcohol drinking." The computerized indexes enable you to conduct your exploration with great ease by using the Key Word search and the Boolean search. These software approaches combine key words, such as *college* and *drinking,* to focus your request.

■ *Newspaper Indexes:* A number of the larger newspapers have their own indexes.

Research Notes

Once you collect a group of potential references that you think look promising, the next step is to check them out. Although you will find bound copies of major periodicals, many of your sources will be available only in microfilm or microfiche, so you will have to become familiar with using this technology. The newer machines also give you the ability to make copies of the articles while you are viewing them. If you're not making a copy, you should use a 4″ x 6″ index card to list the title, author, page numbers, publishing information, and your notes detailing the important information contained in the source. Using index cards will give you flexibility when you are organizing and writing your paper. A sample note card is pictured in Figure 7.8.

Research Writing

After you have gathered what seems to be enough information (you may need to go back for additional research once you begin writing the paper), you should organize your ideas and start writing. When the ideas, research, or information that you are expressing is based on one of your sources, you need to give credit to that source. Your teacher will likely provide guidelines on how to do this step. If you are expressing the information in the exact words of the author, then

"Bad Times at Hangover U"
Debra Rosenberg <u>Newsweek</u> 11/19/90 Pg 81
At Boston College, the number of students hospitalized for alcohol related problems has doubled.
At U Mass, 80% of weekend visits to health services are alcohol related.
Study of 1,600 freshman by Harvard School of Public Health found that among those who drink at least once a week, 92% men and 82% women consume at least 5 drinks in a row. 50% said they wanted to get drunk.

Figure 7.8. **Sample note card for research paper**

you need to use quotation marks. Students sometimes commit *plagiarism* by not providing sufficient credit to sources. This sort of "idea stealing" is a primary sin in academic writing, whether the theft is intentional or not, and you should avoid anything close to it. Be sure to ask your teachers to explain their specific definitions of plagiarism. A good rule of thumb is "If in doubt, give credit."

The following is a sample draft of a research paper on student drinking:

Critical Thinking About Uncritical Drinking

There is widespread agreement that excessive student drinking is a serious problem on many college campuses. However, there are different views on the causes of this problem and the best solutions for dealing with it. In this paper I will present two contrasting perspectives on the problem of student drinking and conclude with my own analysis of how best to deal with this serious threat to student health and success.

Perspective One

Why do college students drink to excess? According to many experts, it is mainly due to the influence of the people around them. When most students enter college, they do not have a drinking problem. However, although few realize it, these unwary people are entering a culture in which alcohol is often the drug of choice. It is a drug that can easily destroy their lives. According to some estimates, between 80% and 90% of the students on many campuses drink alcohol.[1] Many of these students are heavy drinkers.[2] One study found that nearly 30% of university students are heavy drinkers, consuming more than 15 alcoholic drinks a week.[3] Another study found that among those who drink at least once a week, 92% of the men and 82% of the women consume at least five drinks in a row, and half said they wanted to get drunk.[4] The results of all this drinking are predictably deadly. Virtually all college administrators agree that alcohol is the most widely used drug among college students and that its abuse is directly related to emotional problems and violent behavior, ranging from date rape to death.[5,6] For example, at one university, a 20-year-old woman became drunk at a fraternity party and fell to her death from the third floor.[7] At another university, two students were killed in a drunk-driving accident after drinking alcohol at an off-campus fraternity house. The families of both students have filed lawsuits against the fraternity.[8] When students enter a college or university, they soon become socialized into the alcohol-sodden culture of "higher education," typically at formal and informal parties. The influence of peer pressure is enormous. When your friends and fellow students are encouraging you to drink, it is extremely difficult to resist giving in to these pressures.

Perspective Two

Other experts believe that while peer pressure is certainly a factor in excessive college drinking, it is only one of a number of factors. They point out that the misuse of alcohol is a problem for all youth in our society, not just college students. For example, a recent study by the Surgeon General's office shows that one in three teenagers consumes alcohol every week. This is an abuse that leads to traffic deaths, academic difficulties, and acts of violence.[9] Another study based on a large, nationally representative sample indicates that although college students are more likely to use alcohol, they tend to drink less quantity per drinking day than nonstudents of the same age.[10] In other words, college students are more social drinkers than problem drinkers. Another sample of undergraduate students found that college drinking is not as widespread as many people think.[11] The clear conclusion is that while drinking certainly takes place on college campuses, it is no greater a problem than in the population at large. What causes the misuse of alcohol? Well, certainly the influence of friends, whether in college or out, plays a role. But influence is not the only factor. To begin with, there is evidence that family history is related to alcohol abuse. For example, one survey of college students found greater problem drinking among students whose parents or grandparents had been diagnosed (or treated) for alcoholism.[12] Another study found that college students who come from families with high degrees of conflict display a greater potential for alcoholism.[13] Another important factor in the misuse of alcohol by young people is advertising. A recent article titled "It isn't Miller time yet, and this Bud's not for you" underscores the influence advertisers exert on the behavior of our youth.[14] By portraying beer drinkers as healthy, fun-loving, attractive young people, advertisers create role models that many youths imitate. In the same way that cigarette advertisers used to encourage smoking among our youth—without regard to the health hazards—so alcohol advertisers try to sell as much booze as they can to whoever will buy it, no matter what the consequences. A final factor in the abuse of alcohol is the people themselves. Although young people are subject to a huge number of influences, in the final analysis, they are free to choose what they want to do. They don't have to drink, no matter what the social pressures. In fact, many students resist these pressures and choose not to drink excessively or at all. In short, some students choose to think critically, and others choose to drink uncritically.

Part Three: My Perspective
Both of these perspectives on excessive drinking on college campuses have merit. I believe that there are a complex variety of factors that are responsible for this problem, and the specific explanation varies from context to context and from individual to individual. With this in mind, I believe that there are a number of strategies that would be effective in solving this problem.

(1) Colleges should create orientation and education programs aimed at preventing alcohol abuse, and colleges should give campaigns against underage drinking top priority.

(2) Advertising and promotion of alcoholic beverages on college campuses and in college publications should be banned. Restrictions should be imposed on liquor distributors that sponsor campus events. In addition, alcoholic beverage companies should be petitioned not to target young people in their ads.

(3) Students at residential colleges should be able to live in "substance-free" housing, offering them a haven from drugs, alcohol, and peer pressure.

(4) Colleges should ban or tightly restrict alcohol use on campus and include stiffer penalties for students who violate the rules.

(5) Colleges should create alcohol-free clubs to combat alcohol abuse and find other entertainment alternatives for students who are under 21.

(6) The drinking age should be reduced to 18 so that students won't be forced to move parties off campus. At off-campus parties there is no college control, and as a result students tend to drink greater quantities and more dangerous concoctions, such as spiked alcohol.

(7) Colleges should ban the use of beer kegs, the symbol of cheap and easy availability of alcohol.

(8) Fraternities should eliminate pledging in order to stop alcohol abuse and hazing.

In conclusion, I believe that alcohol abuse on college campuses is an extremely important problem that is threatening the health and college careers of many students. As challenging as this problem is, I believe that it is one that can be solved if students, teachers, and college officials work together in harmony and with determination.

Notes

1. *Chronicle of Higher Education,* January 17, 1990, pp. A33–A35.
2. *Journal of Studies on Alcohol,* November 1990, p. 41.
3. *Chronicle of Higher Education,* April 12, 1989, p. A43.
4. *Newsweek,* November 19, 1990, p. 81.
5. *Chronicle of Higher Education,* January 17, 1990, pp. A33–A35.
6. *Chronicle of Higher Education,* January 31, 1990, pp. A33–A35.
7. *Chronicle of Higher Education,* January 31, 1990, p. 3.
8. *Chronicle of Higher Education,* June 12, 1991, pp. A29–A30.
9. *Time,* December 16, 1991, p. 64.
10. *Journal of Studies on Alcohol,* 52 (1), January 1991.
11. *Journal of Studies on Alcohol,* 51 (6), November 1990.
12. *Journal of Counseling and Development,* 69, January 1991, pp. 237–240.
13. *Adolescence,* 26 (102), Summer 1991, pp. 341–347.
14. *Business Week,* June 24, 1991, p. 52.

Note the raised numbers used in this essay. Each raised number (known as a *callout*) directs the reader to a note that credits the source of either the information used or the language quoted. If the writer is using a *footnote* style, each note would appear at the bottom of the page on which it is called out. In

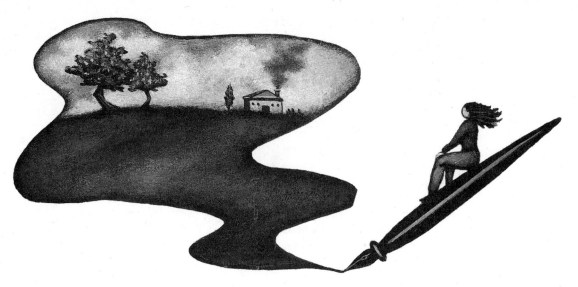

Effective Writing:
Effective writing paints a picture in the mind of the reader.

endnote style, the notes are listed together, in order, after the conclusion of the essay. However, some documentation methods use *parenthetical* style, in which each source is credited, in parentheses, directly after it is used. Whatever style of documentation is used, the last element of the essay will be the bibliography, or reference list. Here, all sources are listed alphabetically. The difference between a note and a reference citation is that the note contains specific information (such as the exact page that was used for a quotation) and the reference citation includes complete information about the source: page range, place of publication, etc.

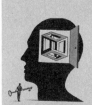

"Young Hate"

A college community is often a microcosm of the larger society: diverse people living and working together. Unfortunately, the intolerance and bigotry that infect society are also often reflected on college campuses, as the following article, "Young Hate" by David Shenk, makes clear. It is tragically ironic that a community of people devoted to education and enlightenment can display incidents of such destructive cruelty. As this article reveals, writing is a powerful vehicle for stimulating us to think critically about complex problems like these, and devising effective

→

A college community is a microcosm of the larger society, diverse people living and working together. Unfortunately, the intolerance and bigotry that infect society as a whole are also often reflected on college campuses.

solutions. After reading this article, respond to the questions that follow.

Young Hate

In the struggle against intolerance, must colleges make a choice between liberty and equality?

David Shenk

Death to gays. Here is the relevant sequence of events: On Monday night Jerry Mattioli leads a candlelight vigil for lesbian and gay rights. *Gay are trash.* On Tuesday his name is in the school paper and he can hear whispers and feel more, colder stares than usual. On Wednesday morning a walking bridge in the middle of the Michigan State campus is found to be covered with violent epithets warning campus homosexuals to *be afraid, very afraid,* promising to *abolish faggots from existence,* and including messages specifically directed at Mattioli. Beginning Friday morning fifteen of the perpetrators, all known to Mattioli by name and face, are rounded up and quietly disciplined by the university. *Go home faggots.* On Friday afternoon Mattioli is asked by university officials to leave campus for the weekend, for his own safety. He does, and a few hours later receives a phone call from a friend who tells him that his dormitory room has been torched. MSU's second annual "Cross Cultural Week" is over.

"Everything was ruined," Mattioli says. "What wasn't burned was ruined by smoke and heat and by the water. On Saturday I sat with the fire investigator all day, and we went through

→

the room, literally ash by ash. . . . The answering machine had melted. The receiver of the telephone on the wall had stretched to about three feet long. That's how intense the heat was."

"Good News!" says Peter Jennings. A recent *Washington Post*/ABC News poll shows that integration is up and racial tension is down in America, as compared with eight years ago. Of course, in any trend there are fluctuations, exceptions. At the University of Massachusetts at Amherst, an estimated two thousand whites chase twenty blacks in a clash after a 1986 World Series game, race riots break out in Miami in 1988 and in Virginia Beach in 1989; and on college campuses across the country, our nation's young elite experience an entire decade's aberration from the poll's findings: incidents of ethnic, religious, and gender-related harassment surge throughout the eighties.

Greatest hits include Randy Bowman, a black student at the University of Texas, having to respectfully decline a request by two young men wearing Ronald Reagan masks and wielding a pistol to exit his eighth-floor dorm room through the window; homemade T-shirts, *Thank God for AIDS* and *Aryan by the Grace of God,* among others, worn proudly on campus; Jewish student centers shot at, stoned, and defaced at Memphis State, University of Kansas, Rutgers (*Six million, why not*), and elsewhere; the black chairperson of United Minorities Council at U Penn getting a dose of hi-tech hate via answering machine: *We're going to lynch you, nigger shit. We are going to lynch you.*

The big picture is less graphic, but just as dreadful: reports of campus harassment have increased as much as 400 percent since 1985. Dropout rates for black students in predominantly white colleges are as much as five times higher than white dropout rates at the same schools and black dropout rates at black schools. The Anti-Defamation League reports a sixfold increase in anti-Semitic episodes on campuses between 1985 and 1988. Meanwhile, Howard J. Ehrlich of the National Institute Against Prejudice and Violence reminds us that "up to 80 percent of harassed students don't report the harassment." Clearly, the barrage of news reports reveals only the tip of a thoroughly sour iceberg.

Colleges have responded to incidents of intolerance—and the subsequent demands of minority rights groups—with the mandatory ethnic culture classes and restrictions on verbal harassment. But what price tranquility? Libertarian and conservative student groups, faculty, and political advisors lash out over limitations on free speech and the improper embrace of liberal political agendas. "Progressive academic administrations," writes University of Pennsylvania professor Alan Charles Kors in the *Wall Street Journal,* "are determined to enlighten their morally benighted students and protect the community from political sin."

Kors and kind bristle at the language of compromise being attached to official university policy. The preamble to the University of Michigan's new policy on discriminatory behavior read, in part, "Because there is tension between freedom of speech, the right of individuals to be free from injury caused by discrimination, and the University's duty to protect the educational process . . . it may be necessary to have varying standards depending on the locus of regulated conduct." The policy tried to "strike a balance" by applying different sets of restrictions to academic centers, open areas, and living quarters, but in so doing, hit a wall. Before the policy could go into effect, it was struck down in a Michigan court as being too vague. At least a dozen schools in the process of formulating their own policies scurried in retreat as buoyant free-speech advocates went on the offensive. Tufts University president Jean Mayer voluntarily dismissed his school's "Freedom of Speech versus Freedom from Harassment" policy after a particularly inventive demonstration by late-night protestors, who used chalk, tape, and poster board to divide the campus into designated free speech, limited speech, and non-free speech zones. "We're not working for a right to offensive speech," says admitted chalker Andrew Zappia, co-editor of the conservative campus paper, *The Primary Source.* "This is about protecting free speech, in general, and allowing the community to set its own standards about what is appropriate. . . .

"The purpose of the Tufts policy was to prosecute people for what the university described as 'gray area'—meaning unintentional—harassment." Zappia gives a hypothetical example: "I'm a Catholic living in a dorm, and I put up a poster in my room [consistent with my faith] saying that homosexuality is bad. If I have a gay roommate or one who doesn't agree with me, he could have me prosecuted, not because I hung it there to offend him, but because it's gray area harassment. . . . The policy was well intended, but it was dangerously vague. They used words like *stigmatizing, offensive, harassing*—words that are very difficult to define."

Detroit lawyer Walter B. Connolly, Jr. disagrees. He insists that it's quite proper for schools to act to protect the victims of discrimination as long as the restrictions stay out of the classroom. "Defamation, child pornography, fighting words, inappropriate comments on the radio—there are all sorts of areas where the First Amendment isn't the preeminent burning omnipotence in the sky. . . . Whenever you have competing interests of a federal statute [and] the Constitution, you end up balancing."

If you want to see a liberal who follows this issue flinch, whisper into his or her ear the name Shelby Steele. Liberals don't like Steele, an English professor at California's San Jose State; they try to dismiss him as having no professional experience in the study of racial discrimination. But he's heavily into the subject, and his analyses are both lucid and disturbing. Steele doesn't favor restrictions on speech, largely because they don't deal with what he sees as the problem. "You don't gain very much by trying to legislate the problem away, curtailing everyone's rights in the process," he says. In a forum in which almost everyone roars against a shadowy, usually nameless contingent of racist thugs, Steele deviates, choosing instead to accuse the accusers. He blames not the racists, but the weak-kneed liberal administrators and power-hungry victims' advocates for the mess on campuses today.

"Racial tension on campus is the result more of racial equality than inequality," says Steele. "On campuses today, as throughout society, blacks enjoy equality under the law—a profound social advancement. . . . What has emerged in recent years . . . in a sense as a result of progress . . . is a *politics of difference,* a troubling, volatile politics in which each group justifies itself, its sense of worth and its pursuit of power, through difference alone." On nearly every campus, says Steele, groups representing blacks, Hispanics, Asians, gays, women, Jews, and any combinations therein solicit special resources. Asked for—often demanded, in intense demonstrations—are funds for African-American (Hispanic . . .) cultural centers, separate (face it, segregated) housing, ethnic studies programs, and even individual academic

⟶

incentives—at Penn State, minority students are given $275 per semester if they earn a C average, twice that if they do better than 2.75.

These entitlements, however, do not just appear *deus ex machina.* Part two of Steele's thesis addresses what he calls the "capitulation" of campus presidents. To avoid feelings of guilt stemming from past discrimination against minority groups, Steele says, "[campus administrators have] tended to go along with whatever blacks put on the table, rather than work with them to assess their real needs. . . . Administrators would never give white students a theme house where they could be 'more comfortable with people of their own kind,' yet more and more universities are doing this for black students." Steele sees white frustration as the inevitable result.

"White students are not invited to the negotiating table from which they see blacks and others walk away with concessions," he says. "The presumption is that they do not deserve to be there, because they are white. So they can only be defensive, and the less mature among them will be aggressive."

Course, some folks see it another way. The students fighting for minority rights aren't wicked political corruptors, but champions of a cause far too long suppressed by the white male hegemony. Responsive administrators are engaged not in capitulation, but in progress. And one shouldn't look for the cause of this mess on any campus, because he doesn't live on one. His address used to be the White House, but then he moved to 666 St. Cloud Road. Ronald Reagan, come on down.

Dr. Manning Marable, University of Colorado: "The shattering assault against the economic, social, and political status of the black American community as a whole [is symbolized by] the Reagan Administration in the 1980s. The Civil Rights Commission was gutted; affirmative action became a 'dead letter'; social welfare, health care, employment training, and educational loans were all severely reduced. This had a disproportionately more negative impact upon black youth."

The "perception is already widespread that the society at large is more permissive toward discriminatory attitudes and behaviors, and less committed to equal opportunity and affirmative action," concluded a 1988 conference at Northern Illinois University. Jon Wiener, writing in *The Nation,* attacks long-standing institutions of bigotry, asserting, for example, that "racism is endemic to the fraternity subculture," and praises the efforts of some schools to double the number of minority faculty and increase minority fellowships. On behalf of progressives across the land, Wiener writes off Shelby Steele as someone who is content to "blame the victim."

So the machine has melted, the phone has stretched to where it is useless. This is how intense the heat is. Liberals, who largely control the administration, faculty, and students' rights groups of leading academic institutions, have, with virtually no intensive intellectual debate, inculcated schools with their answers to the problem of bigotry. Conservatives, with a long history of insensitivity to minority concerns, have been all but shut out of the debate, and now want back in. Their intensive pursuit of the true nature of bigotry and the proper response to it—working to assess the "real needs" of campuses rather than simply bowing to pressure—deserves to be embraced by all concerned parties, and probably would have been by now but

⟶

for two small items: a) Reagan, their fearless leader, clearly *was* insensitive to ethnic/feminist concerns (even Steele agrees with this); and b) some of the more coherent conservative pundits *still* show a blatant apathy to the problems of bigotry in this country. This has been sufficient ammunition for liberals who are continually looking for an excuse to keep conservatives out of the dialogue. So now we have clashes rather than debates: on how much one can say, on how much one should have to hear. Two negatives: one side wants to crack down on expression, the other on awareness. The machine has melted, and it's going to take some consensus to build a new one. Intellectual provincialism will have to end before young hate ever will.

A Month in the Life of Campus Bigotry

April 1. Vandals spray-paint "Jewhaters will pay" and other slogans on the office walls of *The Michigan Daily* (University of Michigan) in response to editorials condemning Israel for policies regarding the Palestinians. Pro-Israeli and pro-Palestinian shanties defaced; one is burned.

U of M: Fliers circulated over the weekend announce "White Pride Month."

Southern Connecticut State University reportedly suspends five fraternity officers after racial brawl.

April 2. Several gay men of the University of Connecticut are taunted by two students, who yell "faggot" at them.

April 3. The University of Michigan faculty meet to discuss a proposal to require students to take a course on ethnicity and racism.

April 4. Students at the University of California at Santa Barbara suspend hunger strike after university agrees to negotiate on demands for minority faculty hiring and the changed status of certain required courses.

April 5. The NCAA releases results of survey on black student athletes, reporting that 51 percent of black football and basketball players at predominantly white schools express feelings of being different; 51 percent report feelings of racial isolation; 33 percent report having experienced at least six incidents of individual racial discrimination.

The *New York Times* prints three op-ed pieces by students on the subject of racial tension on campus.

Charges filed against a former student of Penn State for racial harassment of a black woman.

April 6. University of Michigan: Hundreds of law students wear arm bands, boycott classes to protest lack of women and minority professors.

Michigan State University announces broad plan for increasing the number of minority students, faculty, and staff; the appointment of a senior advisor for minority affairs; and the expansion of multicultural conferences. "It's not our responsibility just to mirror society or respond to mandates," President John DiBioggio tells reporters, "but to set the tone."

→

April 7. Wayne State University (Detroit, Michigan) student newspaper runs retraction of cartoon considered offensive following protest earlier in the week.

Controversy develops at the State University of New York at Stony Brook, where a white woman charges a popular black basketball player with rape. Player denies charges. Charges are dismissed. Protests of racism and sexual assault commence.

April 12. Twelve-day sit-in begins at Wayne State University (Michigan) over conditions for black students on campus.

April 14. Racial brawl at Arizona State.

April 20. Demonstrations at several universities across the country (Harvard, Duke, Wayne State, Wooster College, Penn State, etc.) for improvements in black student life.

Separate escort service for blacks started at Penn State out of distrust of the regular service.

April 21. 200-student sit-in ends at Arizona State University when administrators agree to all thirteen demands.

April 24. Proposed tuition increase at City Universities of New York turns into racial controversy.

April 25. After eighteen months in office, Robert Collin, Florida Atlantic University's first black dean, reveals he has filed a federal discrimination complaint against the school.

Two leaders of Columbia University's Gay and Lesbian Alliance receive death threat. "Dear Jeff, I will kill you butt fucking faggots. Death to CGLA!"

April 26. A black Smith College (Massachusettes) student finds note slipped under door, ". . . African monkey do you want some bananas? Go back to the jungle . . .".

"I don't think we should have to constantly relive our ancestors' mistakes," a white student at the University of North Carolina at Greensboro tells a reporter. "I didn't oppress anybody. Blacks are now equal. You don't see any racial problems anymore."

White Student Union is reported to have been formed at Temple University in Philadelphia, "City of Brotherly Love."

April 28. Note found in Brown University (Rhode Island) dorm. "Once upon a time, Brown was a place where a white man could go to class without having to look at little black faces, or little yellow faces or little brown faces, except when he went to take his meals. Things have been going downhill since the kitchen help moved into the classroom. Keep white supremecy [sic] alive!!! Join the Brown chapter of the KKK today." Note is part of series that began in the middle of the month with "Die Homos." University officials beef up security, hold forum.

April 29. Controversy reported over proposed ban on verbal harassment at Arizona State.

April 30. Anti-apartheid shanty at University of Maryland, Baltimore County, is defaced. Signs read "Apartheid now" and "Trump Plaza."

→

University of California at Berkeley: Resolution is passed requiring an ethnic studies course for all students.

University of Connecticut: Code is revised to provide specific penalties for acts of racial intolerance.

Questions for Analysis

1. Think about the diversity on your own campus. Have you witnessed or heard about incidents of bigotry directed at people because of their race, sexual preference, or some other distinguishing quality? If so, describe one such incident and analyze why you think it occurred. If not, explain why your campus doesn't seem to suffer from problems related to diversity.

2. Have you ever been the victim of prejudice or discrimination? If so, describe one such experience, and explain how the incident made you feel about yourself and the people victimizing you.

3. In Chapter Three you learned an approach for solving complex problems such as those described in "Young Hate." Using the method developed in that chapter, analyze the problem of bigotry—on your campus, if you think it exists there—and develop some practical solutions for dealing with this troubling issue.

8

Discussing and Debating

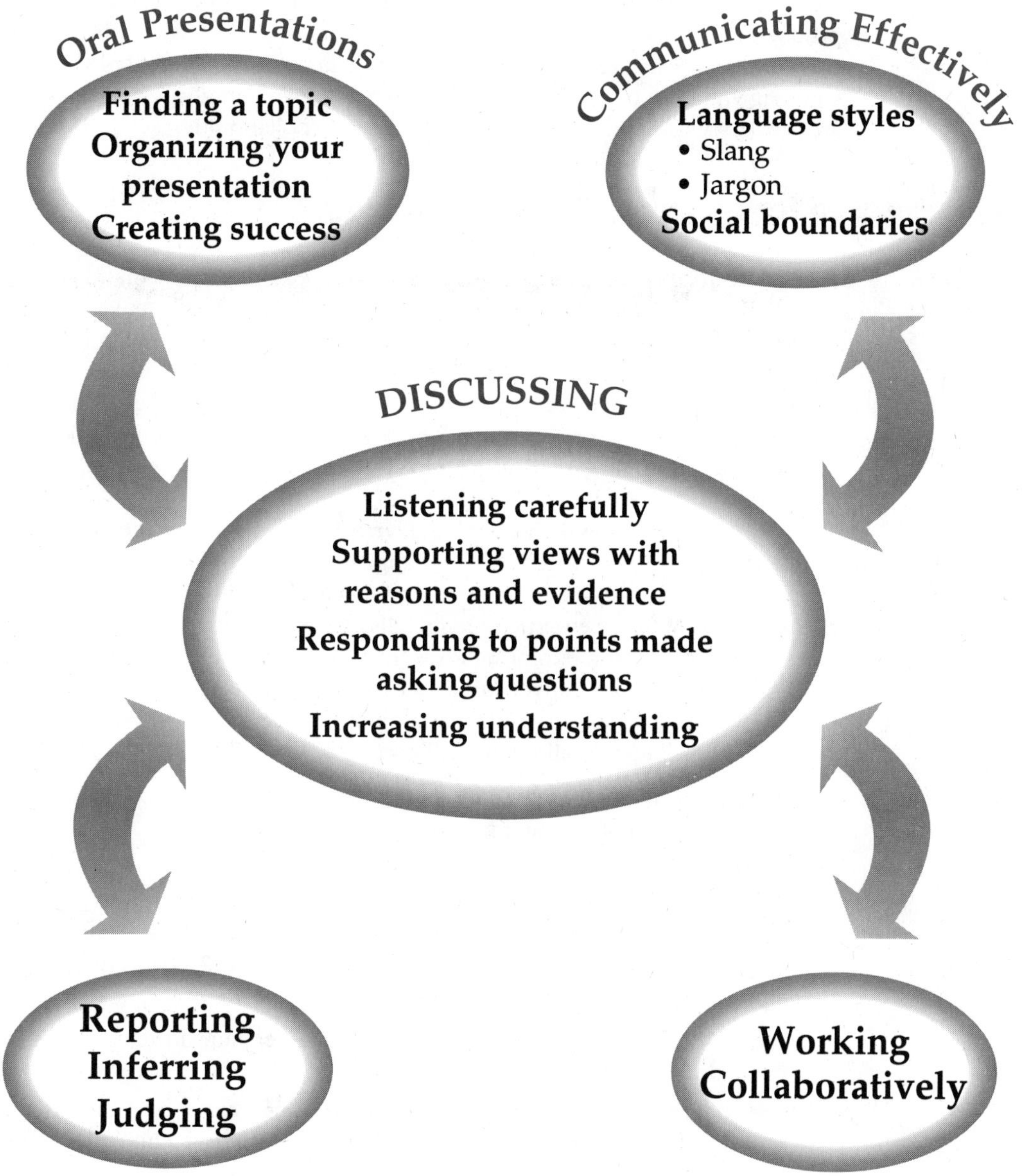

Oral Presentations

Finding a topic
Organizing your presentation
Creating success

Communicating Effectively

Language styles
• Slang
• Jargon
Social boundaries

DISCUSSING

Listening carefully
Supporting views with reasons and evidence
Responding to points made asking questions
Increasing understanding

Reporting
Inferring
Judging

Working
Collaboratively

Success in college and most careers involves becoming a critical reader and an effective writer, but it also means learning how to engage in other forms of thoughtful communication. In your classes, you need to listen carefully, respond to your instructors' questions, ask intelligent questions of your own, and engage in class discussions. Outside of class, you will find that your learning is enhanced if you work collaboratively with others and share ideas. In virtually all careers, successful individuals are able to express their ideas clearly, listen and respond appropriately to the ideas of others, and work productively as members of a group to analyze issues and solve problems. In this chapter we will explore all of these crucial communication abilities, showing you how to extend your critical thinking and language abilities into the areas of discussion, oral presentation, and group collaboration.

Discussing Ideas in an Organized Way

Thinking critically often takes place in a social context, not in isolation. Although it is natural for every person to have his or her perspective on the world, no single viewpoint is adequate for making sense of complex issues, situations, or even people. As we saw in Chapter Six, we each have our own "lenses" through which we view the world—lenses that shape, influence, and often distort the way we see things. The best way to expand your thinking and compensate for the bias that we all have is to discuss your experiences with other people.

This is the way in which thinking develops: being open to the viewpoints of others and willing to listen and exchange ideas with them. This process of give and take, of advancing our views and considering those of others, is known as *discussion*. When we participate in a discussion, we are not simply talking; we are exchanging and exploring ideas in an organized way.

Unfortunately, our conversations with other people about important topics are too often not productive, degenerating into name calling, shouting matches, or worse. Consider the following dialogue:

Person A: I have a friend who just found out she's pregnant and is trying to decide whether she should get an abortion or have the baby. What do you think?

Person B: Well, I think that abortion is murder. Your friend doesn't want to be a murderer, does she?

Person A: How can you call her a murderer? An abortion is a medical operation.

Person B: Abortion *is* murder. It's killing another human being, and your friend doesn't have the right to do that.

Person A: Well, you don't have the right to tell her what to do—it's her body and her decision. Nobody should be forced to have a child that is not wanted.

Communicating Clearly:
Success in college and careers involves expressing ideas clearly and listening carefully to the ideas of others.

Person B: Nobody has the right to commit murder—that's the law.

Person A: But abortion isn't murder.

Person B: Yes, it is.

Person A: No, it isn't.

Person B: Good-bye! I can't talk to anyone who defends murderers.

Person A: And I can't talk to anyone who tries to tell other people how to run their lives.

If we examine the dynamics of this dialogue, we can see that the two people here are not really

- Listening to each other
- Supporting their views with reasons and evidence
- Responding to the points being made
- Asking—and trying to answer—important questions

■ Trying to increase their understanding rather than simply trying to win the argument

In short, the people in this exchange are not *discussing* their views; they are simply *expressing* them and trying to get the other person to agree. Contrast this first dialogue with the following one. Although it begins the same way, it quickly takes a much different direction.

Person A: I have a friend who just found out that she's pregnant and is trying to decide whether she should get an abortion or have the baby. What do you think?

Person B: Well, I think that abortion is murder. Your friend doesn't want to be a murderer, does she?

Person A: Of course she doesn't want to be a murderer! But why do you believe that having an abortion is the same thing as murder?

Person B: Because murder is when we kill another human being, and when you have an abortion, you are killing another human being.

Person A: But is a fetus a human being yet? It certainly is when it is born. But what about before it's born, while it's still in the mother's womb? Is it a person then?

Person B: I think it is. Simply because the fetus hasn't been born doesn't mean that it isn't a person. Remember, sometimes babies are born prematurely, in their eighth or even seventh month of development. And they go on to have happy and useful lives.

Person A: I can see why you think that a fetus in the *last stages* of development—the seventh, eighth, or ninth month—is a person. After all, it can survive outside the womb with special help at the hospital. But what about at the *beginning* of development? Human life begins when an egg is fertilized by a sperm. Do you believe that the fertilized egg is a person?

Person B: Let me think about that for a minute. No, I don't think that a fertilized egg is a person, although many people do. I think that a fertilized egg has the *potential* to become a person—but it isn't a person yet.

Person A: Then at what point in its development do you think a fetus *does* become a person?

Person B: That's a good question, one that I haven't really thought about. I guess you could say that a fetus becomes a person when it begins to look like a person, with a head, hands, feet, and so on. Or you might say that a fetus becomes a person when all of its organs are formed—liver, kidneys, lungs, and so on. Or you might say that it becomes a person when its heart begins to start beating or when its brain is fully developed. Or you might say that its life begins when it can survive outside the mother. I guess determining when the fetus becomes a person all depends on the *standard* that you use.

Person A: I see what you're saying! Since the development of human life is a continuous process that begins with a fertilized egg and ends with a baby, deciding when the fetus becomes a person depends on at what point in the process of development you decide to draw the line. But *how* do you decide where to draw the line?

Person B: That's a good place to begin another discussion. But right now I have to leave for class. See you later.

How would you contrast the level of communication taking place in this dialogue with that of the first dialogue? What are the reasons for your conclusion?

_____

_____

_____

_____

Naturally, discussions are not always quite this organized and direct. Nevertheless, the second dialogue does provide a good model for what can take place in our everyday lives when we carefully explore an issue or a situation with someone else. Let us take a closer look at this discussion process.

Listening Carefully

Review the second dialogue and notice how each person in the discussion *listens carefully* to what the other person is saying and then tries to comment directly on what has just been said. When you are working hard at listening to others, you are trying to understand the point they are making and their reasons for it. This approach enables you to imagine yourself in their position and see things as they do. Listening in this way often brings new ideas and different ways of viewing the situation to your attention that might otherwise never have occurred to you. An effective dialogue in this sense is like a game of tennis— you hit the ball to me, I return the ball back to you, you return my return, and so on. The "ball" the discussants keep hitting back and forth is the subject they are gradually analyzing and exploring. One valuable strategy is paraphrasing the other person's ideas to clarify the point being stated and to determine if your understanding is accurate. For example, such responses as "Are you saying that . . . ?" or "Let me see if I understand your point about . . ." can produce useful results.

Supporting Views with Reasons and Evidence

Critical thinkers strive to support their points of view with evidence and reasons, and they also make sure to develop an in-depth understanding of the evidence and reasons that support other people's opinions. Review the second dialogue and identify some of the reasons used by the participants to support their points of view. For example, Person B expresses the view that "abortion is murder" and supports it with the reasoning that "murder is killing another human being"; if a fetus is a human being, removing it from the womb prematurely is the same thing as murder.

1. *Viewpoint:* _____

   _____

   Supporting Reason: _____

   _____

2. *Viewpoint:* _____

   _____

   Supporting Reason: _____

   _____

Responding to the Points Being Made

When people engage in effective dialogue, they listen carefully to the people speaking and then respond directly to the points being made instead of simply trying to make their own points. In the second dialogue, Person A responds to Person B's view that "abortion is murder" with the question "But is a fetus a human being yet?" When you respond directly to other people's views, and they to yours, you extend and deepen the consideration of the issues being discussed. Although people involved in the discussion may not ultimately agree, they can develop more insightful understanding of the important issues and a greater appreciation of other viewpoints. In the second dialogue, notice how each person keeps responding to what the other is saying, creating an ongoing interactive development.

Asking Questions

Asking questions is one of the driving forces in effective discussion. You can explore a subject by raising important questions and then trying to answer them together, as part of the discussion. This questioning process gradually reveals the various reasons and evidence that support each of the different viewpoints involved. For example, although the two dialogues begin the same way, the second dialogue moves in a completely different direction from the first when Person A poses an important question: "But *why* do you believe that having an abortion is the same thing as murder?" Asking this question directs the discussion toward a mutual exploration of the issues and away from angry confrontation. Identify some of the other key questions that are posed in the dialogue:

1. _____
2. _____
3. _____
4. _____

A guide to the various types of questions that can be posed in exploring issues and situations begins on page 54 of Chapter 2.

Increasing Understanding

When we discuss subjects with others, we often begin by disagreeing. In fact, this is one of the chief reasons that we have discussions. In an effective discussion, however, our main purpose should be to develop our understanding—not to prove ourselves right at any cost. If we are determined to prove that we are right, then we are not likely to be open to the ideas of others and to viewpoints that differ from our own.

Imagine that, instead of ending, the second dialogue had continued for a while. In the space provided, write responses that expand the ideas being examined in the dialogue. Be sure to keep the following discussion guidelines in mind as you continue.

- When we discuss, we have to listen to each other.
- When we discuss, we keep asking—and trying to answer—important questions.
- When we discuss, our main purpose is to develop a further understanding of the subject we are discussing, not to prove that we are right and the other person is wrong.

Person A: I see what you're saying! Since the development of human life is a continuous process that begins with a fertilized egg and ends with a baby, deciding when the fetus becomes a person depends on at what point in the process of development you decide to draw the line. But *how* do you decide where to draw the line?

Person B: _____

_____

Person A: _____

_____

Person B: _____

_____

Read the following dialogue on the issue of capital punishment and then continue the discussion, creating an additional three or four responses for each person.

Person A: I heard on the news yesterday that a group of prisoners in Virginia took some hostages in one floor of the prison to protest the death sentence of one of the inmates who was going to be executed last night. Nine persons were injured in the revolt.

Person B: Why was the man sentenced to die in the electric chair?

Person A: Because he had killed a pregnant woman and her five-year-old daughter a few years ago.

Person B: Do you believe in the death penalty?

Person A: Well, crime has been on the rise year after year. There has to be a way to regulate the increase, and capital punishment is one way.

Person B: It is true that crime has been on the rise, but to take such an option as capital punishment would make us less civilized. There is evidence to suggest that in some states, capital punishment has not deterred heinous crimes.

Person A: It may seem desperate to bring back capital punishment, but what do you suggest instead?

Person B: I think there should be longer prison terms and less plea bargaining. Also, social programs should be available to help prisoners who finish their terms adapt to civilian life.

Person A: That sounds great, but you are talking about a great increase in the budget for correction and social programs. Why not just kill murderers and save the money?

Person B: Killing them is the easy way out. And if we kill them, that would make us just as bad as the criminals. What gives us the right to take a life?

Person A: Suppose someone kills, serves his prison sentence, and then kills again. What then? If he had been executed the first time, this murder of another innocent person would not have occurred.

Now continue the dialogue.

Person A: _____

_____

Person B: _____

_____

Person A: _____

_____

Person B: _____

_____

Select an important social issue and write a dialogue that analyzes the issue from two different perspectives. As you write your dialogue, keep in mind the qualities of effective discussion: listening carefully to each other and trying to comment directly on what has been said, asking and trying to answer important questions about the subject, and trying to develop a fuller understanding of the subject, not simply trying to prove ourselves right.

After completing your dialogue, read it to the class (with a classmate as a partner). Analyze the class's dialogues by using the criteria for effective discussions.

Making Effective Oral Presentations

When I attended college, I felt no particular need to develop my abilities at public speaking, never expecting that I would be making presentations to groups of people. As a result, I was not exactly prepared when, some years later, I walked in to teach my first college class. It was an Introduction to Philosophy class scheduled for three hours on a Saturday morning, and the students waited expectantly to have their minds stimulated. I sat behind a desk, took out my notes, and proceeded to read, in a virtual monotone, a three-hour lecture that covered most of the important events, people, and concepts in the field of philosophy for the past 2,000 years. Although I believed at the time that I had made a brilliant entrance into the teaching profession, I'm certain that my students had a much different opinion. The point is that there will probably be many occasions in your life when you will be expected to speak in front of a group of people, in both professional and personal situations, so it makes sense for you to be more prepared than I was.

Sometimes people fall into the trap of thinking that being an effective public speaker is a genetically inherited trait, a belief expressed in such comments as "She's just a natural speaker in front of others" or "I hate public speaking—it's just the way I am." The truth is that public speaking is a set of skills that every person can develop and refine. Research shows that the quality of an oral presentation is directly tied to the amount of preparation time, the amount of research, the number of rehearsals, and the effort spent on preparing speaking notes and visual aids. No matter how uncomfortable you are speaking publicly, with the right preparation you can become an effective presenter. Who knows—in time, you might actually learn to enjoy speaking publicly!

Getting Started: Finding a Topic

Finding a topic for an oral presentation involves the same approach and strategies that we explored in the last chapter. You need to immerse yourself in the subject; use the techniques of brainstorming, mapping, and freewriting; and then narrow your topic down to a specific, focused theme. In developing your theme, you need to think about what you want to accomplish with your presentation. Do you want to *inform* people about important information or ideas? Do you want to *persuade* them to accept a belief, change a point of view, or take an action? Or do you hope to accomplish some combination of these two basic speaking purposes? In other words, it is useful to begin at the *conclusion* of your presentation by identifying the goals you hope to accomplish and then work backward to construct your presentation so that it meets these goals. As Alice of *Alice in Wonderland* was told, "If you have no idea where you are going, how will you know when you get there?"

We have seen in previous chapters how the versatile thinking tool of mapping can be used to take notes of lectures and reading assignments, generate ideas for writing, and organize writing assignments. Mapping is also an effective aid in generating ideas and preparing for oral presentations. By organizing the information we want to present in this way, we have all the key ideas and their relationships in a single whole. Probably the greatest fear of people making oral presentations is that they will "get stuck" or lose their train of thought. If you have a clear map of the main ideas and their relationships, the chances of this sort of "freeze-up" are considerably reduced.

One of the advantages of using a map is that once you have constructed it, you can place the ideas in whatever new order you may need by simply renumbering them or circling them in different colors. As a result, a map not only represents your key ideas and their relationships simultaneously; it can also be used to construct more traditional outlines or speaking notes.

Organizing Your Presentation

Oral presentations are typically divided into three general sections: the introduction, the main body, and the conclusion.

The Introduction.   The introduction communicates the main ideas that you are trying to express, but it should also engage the interest of your audience. Many speakers like to begin with a personal experience that relates to their theme. This step helps you make a personal connection to the audience, engaging their attention on a friendly level. Other introductory approaches include using a vivid illustration, telling a humorous story, asking the audience to respond to a provocative question, or repeating a memorable quotation: "The philosopher Bertrand Russell once said: 'Most people would rather die than think—in fact they do!'" In creating your introduction, think about what openings engage your attention when *you* are a member of an audience. For example, telling a personal story can illustrate your points in a very concrete and memorable way, form a bond with the audience by letting them know something about you, and generally engage their interest.

The Main Body.   The main body of an oral presentation consists of the development of your key ideas. In addition to clearly articulating your central points, you also need to *support* the points you are making with illustrations, examples, reasons, evidence, and external testimony. The exact organization of the main body depends on the subject of your presentation and the goals you want to accomplish. In Chapter 7 we examined a number of thinking patterns that we can use to organize both written papers and oral presentations:

- Comparison and contrast
- Analogy
- Causal relationships
- Problem/Solution

In this chapter, we will explore three additional thinking patterns:

- Reporting information
- Inferring conclusions based on what is currently known
- Evaluating the worth of something by using specified criteria

And in the next chapter, we will explore one more thinking pattern:

- Constructing arguments

In your oral presentations, as in your writing assignments, you may find that it is appropriate to use several different thinking patterns to organize your presentation. For example, when I conduct workshops with teachers on critical thinking, I do the following:

Compare and *contrast* the qualities of critical and uncritical thinkers

Create *analogies* between effective teaching and good coaching

Analyze the *causes* for the prevalence of uncritical thinking in our culture

Define the *problem* of how to teach people to think critically and discuss possible *solutions*

Report research that explains how traditional teaching approaches often reinforce *uncritical* thinking

Make *inferences* about what will happen if we don't teach students to think critically

Evaluate the effectiveness of strategies for fostering critical and creative thinking

Discuss *arguments* for committing education to the task of helping students become sophisticated thinkers and users of language

It's important to be knowledgeable about all of these thinking patterns so that you can integrate them into your thinking, writing, and speaking in the most appropriate and efficient ways.

The Conclusion. The conclusion of an oral presentation brings everything together, summarizing the main points and ending with a bang, known as "the clincher." Like your introduction, your clincher can be a personal experience, a humorous story, a vivid example, or a memorable quotation. For example, one story that I sometimes use to illustrate the transforming power of education concerns a former student of mine named Gus. He was a very engaging, likable, and enthusiastic young man. The problem was that Gus wasn't completing any of the course assignments, despite my ongoing requests. One morning I asked the class for volunteers to share their homework assignment, a description and analysis of an experience that shaped the way they thought about the world. To my surprise, Gus raised his hand. I naturally called on him, and when he finished reading his paper, everyone in the class was thunderstruck.

A Shaping Experience

I always dreamed of leaving home, but not like this. I walked to the bus and got on. They called it the Gray Goose. There were about forty others on the bus with me. It was a portable jail. Even the driver was fenced off from us. Anger ran through me as I sat down. There was an unnaturalness about the way I felt. I was actually going to prison. Fear started forming in my mind as I looked at the other guys and realized I knew none of them. They were the ugliest faces I had ever seen. Soon we passed through town and men and women at street corners stared at us as we passed, disgust spread over their righteous faces. I turned away from their condemning stares; then I wondered why I felt that way. All they were seeing was some guys on the way to prison. They didn't know me. They would never see me again. I fell asleep, and when I awoke, we were on the bridge leading to Rikers Island. Suddenly there it was, miles of barbed wire fences. Behind them a bunch of buildings of which one was my new home and it didn't seem right at all, but even here, I was cool! This place would never break me! Now I was in the classification center. I knew it was going to be a trip. Not as bad as some of the guys on the bus had said, not as good as some of the virgins thought it might be. You have never been searched until you've been searched coming into Rikers. They've got it down to a science. You name it; they do it. It was as if I had stepped into another world where everything existed, yet nothing existed. A world where reality was an object out there beyond those fences. All that was happening was real, but unbelievable to me. Finally, after a long endless day of processing I was assigned a cell, the gate slammed behind me; what a painful sound. There I was dressed like a janitor. The uniform felt itchy, and the whole place had an odor, the odor of prison. It was an odor made up of frustration and fear, bodies close together, with no sun, twenty men shut in a cell, psychos, murderers, perverts, all in one stinking hole made for ten men. Weak guys made an odor too, an odor of urine and tears and self pity. Sometimes there was an odor of blood and semen, and as if all this weren't enough, the next day was just the beginning!

After reading Gus's essay, I always point out to my audience that education is a means for exploration, it is a means for discovery, and at its very best it is a means for self-transformation. By teaching students to be thoughtful, reflective thinkers, we are equipping them with tools they can use to build a stairway to their dreams.

Creating Success

Having a thoughtfully researched and clearly organized presentation is essential to achieving success in your public speaking, but there are other important factors as well.

Effective presenters speak dynamically and confidently, use supplementary aids, and involve the audience.

Prepare Clear Notes and Speak Dynamically. Although you may have written out your presentation in its entirety, *don't read it.* When you read from a prepared script, your presentation runs the danger of sounding unspontaneous and mechanical, and you will be making insufficient eye contact with your audience. People enjoy being spoken *to,* which means that you should look directly at them and speak dynamically, showing that you are actually *thinking* as you speak instead of simply reading previously prepared thoughts.

You need to rehearse your presentation until you are thoroughly familiar with it and then develop clear notes that remind you of your main ideas. Don't worry during your presentation if you can't find the exact words or perfect phrases contained in the written version of your text: the direct and personal contact you are making with your audience more than compensates for this.

Your notes can be recorded on standard sheets in outline or mapping format, or written on note cards. The choice is a personal preference and depends in part on whether you will have a lectern where you can place your notes or if you will be standing "naked," in which case note cards are less conspicuous.

Use Supplementary Aids. Research shows that people can process and remember only a relatively small portion of what they hear. As a result, visual enhancements such as charts, diagrams, illustrations, photographs, and excerpts from videos are very effective ways of supporting and reinforcing the ideas you are speaking about. They provide your audience with other points of reference that help them integrate your ideas into their own framework of understanding. Many people use overhead projectors to present material, although I personally prefer using handouts that the audience can make notes on and keep for future reference.

Speak Confidently and Energetically.   Although on the inside you may be screaming with panic and insecurity, it is essential that you have a confident appearance. Acting confidently will actually make you *feel* more confident, and it will inspire the audience members to have confidence in you. Stand up straight and look directly at your audience; speak boldly, clearly, and not too fast; and act like you're enjoying yourself. If you act like you believe in yourself and your message, your audience is inclined to believe in you as well, which in turn bolsters your confidence. On the other hand, if you act like you *don't* believe in yourself, appearing apologetic, your audience is drawn into this negative thinking, thus undermining your confidence even more.

Be physically dynamic. A great deal is communicated without language—nonverbally—through facial expressions, gestures, tone of voice, and body movements. Try to loosen up and move your body as you speak, investing energy and feeling into the words you are speaking, the ideas you are communicating. Practice in front of your friends or family members (as well as the mirror!), and ask for their feedback. Remember the advice of the famous orchestra conductor Toscanini: "You don't do anything in a performance that you haven't done a thousand times in practice."

Research has also found that positive visualization can contribute significantly to a successful performance. Imagine yourself speaking dynamically and effectively, to the thunderous applause of the audience. Think only of how things are going to go well, and don't let yourself fall into the trap of focusing on potential disasters that might occur. The more positive your expectations and focus, the more successful the outcome. Regrettably, the reverse is equally true.

You can find additional strategies for relaxation and dealing constructively with anxiety on page 183. These strategies will help you overcome the paralyzing anxiety that almost everyone is vulnerable to, including actors, entertainers, and other public figures.

Involve the Audience.   Successful speakers pay attention to the members of their audience and engage them in active participation as much as possible. Your audience sends out many signals to let you know what they're feeling and thinking. If they start to look bored or distracted, then it's time to shake things up. As you undoubtedly know from personal experience, it's easy to slip into a passive, unthinking frame of mind when listening to someone else speak. That's why if your presentation lasts for more than just a few minutes, you should find ways to engage the minds of your audience:

■ ask them to think about a question and then invite them to respond

■ give them a brief writing assignment

■ invite questions from them

■ assign a brief project in which they speak to their neighbors

■ engage them in an activity to get them out of their seats and moving around

■ alternate your speaking with other presentation modes, such as handouts or video

In other words, do whatever it takes to keep your audience actively engaged in the presentation. It will make the experience more entertaining for you as well.

Reporting, Inferring, Judging

Reporting, inferring, and judging are thinking patterns that produce different kinds of beliefs that we express in our speaking and writing. Our beliefs are the main tools we use to make sense of the world and guide our actions, and the total collection of our beliefs represents our view of the world, our philosophy of life.

All beliefs are not equal. In fact, beliefs differ from one another in many kinds of ways. For example, beliefs differ in accuracy. The belief "the earth is surrounded by stars and planets" is considerably more certain than the belief "the positions of the stars and planets determine our personalities and our destinies." Beliefs differ in other respects besides accuracy. Review the following beliefs, and then analyze some of the differences between them:

1. My bus was late today.

   Type of belief: reporting

2. My bus will probably be late tomorrow.

   Type of belief: inferring

3. The bus system is unreliable.

   Type of belief: judging

As we examine these various statements, we can see that they provide us with different types of information about the world. For example, the first statement *reports* an aspect of the world that we can verify—that is, check for accuracy.

Reporting Factual Information
Describing the world in ways that can be verified through investigation.

Looking at the second statement, we can see immediately that it provides a different sort of information. This *inference* cannot be verified because there is no way to investigate and determine with certainty whether the bus will indeed be late tomorrow. Although this conclusion may be based on factual information, it goes beyond factual information to make a statement about what is not currently known.

Inferring

Describing the world in ways that are based on factual information yet going beyond this information to make statements about what is not currently known.

Finally, the third statement describes the world in ways that express the speaker's evaluation or *judgment* of the bus service. This evaluation is based on certain standards (criteria) that the speaker has used to judge the bus service as unreliable.

Judging

Describing the world in ways that express our evaluation.

We continually use these various ways of describing and organizing our world—reporting, inferring, judging—to make sense of our experience. In most cases, we are not aware that we are actually performing these activities, nor are we usually aware of the differences among them. Yet these three activities work together to help us see the world as a complete picture.

Using these definitions, identify whether the following statements are expressing reports, inferences, or judgments:

1. I have hair on my body. *Type of belief:* _____

2. The sun will rise tomorrow. *Type of belief:* _____

3. I believe that there is some form of life after death. *Type of belief:*
   _____

4. I think that dancing is more fun than jogging. *Type of belief:* _____

5. I believe that we should always act toward others in ways that we would like to have them act toward us. *Type of belief:* _____

6. Each modern atomic warhead has over one hundred times the explosive power of the bomb dropped on Hiroshima. *Type of belief:* _____

7. With all of the billions of planets in the universe, the odds are that there are other forms of life than what is found on earth. *Type of belief:*
   _____

8. In the long run, the energy needs of the world will best be met by solar energy technology rather than by nuclear energy or fossil fuels. *Type of belief:* _____

Thinking Activity 8.2

1. Compose six sentences: two reports, two inferences, and two evaluations.

2. Locate a short article from a newspaper or magazine, and identify the reports, inferences, and judgments it contains.

3. Carefully examine the photograph on page 66. Write five statements based on your observations. Then identify each of your statements as reporting, inferring, or judging, and explain why you classify them as such.

Reporting Factual Information

Statements that result from reporting express the most accurate beliefs we have about the world. Factual beliefs have earned this distinction because they are verifiable, usually by one or more of our senses. For example, consider the following factual statement: "That young woman is wearing a brown hat in the rain." This statement about an event in the world is considered to be factual because it can be verified by our immediate sense experience—what we can (in principle or in theory) see, hear, touch, feel, or smell. It is important to say *in principle* or *in theory,* because we often do not use all our relevant senses to check out what we are experiencing. Look again at our example of a factual statement: "That young woman is wearing a brown hat in the rain." We would normally be satisfied to *see* this event, without insisting on touching or smelling the hat or giving the person a physical examination. If necessary, however, we could perform these additional actions—in principle or in theory.

We use the same reasoning when we believe factual statements that we are not in a position to check out immediately. For instance,

■ The Great Wall of China is more than fifteen hundred miles long.

■ There are large mountains and craters on the moon.

■ Our skin is covered with germs.

We consider these to be factual statements because, even though we cannot verify them with our senses at the moment, we could in theory verify them with our senses

if we were flown to China,

if we were rocketed to the moon, or

if we were to examine our skin with a powerful microscope.

The process of verifying factual statements involves *identifying* the sources of information on which they are based and *evaluating* the reliability of these sources.

We communicate factual information to each other by means of reports. A *report* is a description of something that has been experienced, communicated in as accurate and complete a way as possible. Through reports we can share our experiences with other people, and this mutual sharing enables us to learn much more about the world than if we were confined to knowing only what *we* experience. The recording of factual reports also makes possible the accumulation of knowledge learned by previous generations.

Because factual reports play such an important role in the exchange and accumulation of information about the world, it is important that they be as accurate and complete as possible. This brings us to a problem. We have already seen in Chapter Six that perceptions and observations are often *not* accurate or complete because they are influenced by the "lenses" through which we view the world. Often when we think we are making true factual reports, our reports are actually inaccurate or incomplete. For instance, consider our earlier "factual statement": "That young woman is wearing a brown hat in the rain." Here are some questions we could ask concerning how accurate our statement really is:

- Is the woman really young, or does she merely look young?
- Is the woman really a woman, or a man disguised as a woman?
- Is that really a hat the woman/man is wearing, or something else (for example, a paper bag) being used to keep her/his head dry?

Of course, we could clear up these questions with more detailed observations.

Besides difficulties with observations, the "facts" that we see in the world actually depend on more general *beliefs* that we have about how the world operates. Consider this question: "Why did the man's body fall from the top of the building to the sidewalk?" If we have taken some general science courses, we might say something like "The body was simply obeying the law of gravity," and we would consider this to be a "factual statement." But how did people account for this sort of event before Newton formulated the law of gravity? Some popular responses might have included the following:

- Things always fall down, not up.
- The spirit in the body wanted to join with the spirit of the earth.

When people made statements like these and others, such as "Humans can't fly," they thought that they were making "factual statements." Increased knowledge and understanding have since shown these "factual beliefs" to be inaccurate, so they have been replaced by expanded beliefs. These expanded beliefs are able to explain the world in a way that is more accurate and predictable. Will many of the beliefs we now consider to be factually accurate also be replaced in the future by beliefs that are *more* accurate? If history is any indication, this phenomenon will most certainly happen. For example,

Newton's formulations have been replaced by Einstein's, based on the latter's theory of relativity. And Einstein's have been refined and modified by the theory of quantum mechanics.

Thinking Activity 8.3

1. Locate and carefully read an article that deals with an important social issue.
2. Summarize the main theme and the key points of the article.
3. Describe the factual statements that are used to support the major theme.
4. Evaluate the accuracy of the factual information.
5. Evaluate the reliability of the sources of the factual information.

Inferring

Imagine yourself in the following situations:

1. It is 2:00 (A.M.), and your roommate comes crashing through the door into the room. He staggers unsteadily to his bed and falls across it, dropping (and breaking) a nearly empty whiskey bottle. You rush over and ask, "What happened?" With alcoholic fumes blasting from his mouth, your roommate mumbles, "I juss wanna hadda widdel drink!" What do you conclude?

2. Your friend has just learned that she passed a math exam for which she had done absolutely no studying. Humming the song "My Way," she comes bouncing over to you with a huge grin on her face and says, "Let me buy you dinner to celebrate!" What do you conclude about how she is feeling?

3. It is midnight, and the library is about to close. As you head for the door, you spy a classmate shuffling along in an awkward waddle. His coat is bulged out in front like he's pregnant. When you ask "What's going on?" he gives you a glare and hisses, "Shhh!" Just before he reaches the door, a pile of books slides from under his coat and crashes to the floor. What do you conclude?

In these examples, it would be reasonable to make the following conclusions:

1. Your roommate is drunk.
2. Your roommate is happy.
3. Your roommate is stealing library books.

Although these conclusions are reasonable, they are *not* factual reports; they are *inferences*—conclusions that "go beyond" what is known to what is unknown. You have not directly experienced the other students' "drunkenness," "happiness," or "stealing." Instead, you have *inferred* it based on their behavior and the circumstances. What are the clues in these situations that might lead to these conclusions?

One way of understanding the inferential nature of these views is to ask yourself the following questions:

1. Have you ever pretended to be drunk when you weren't? Could other people tell?

2. Have you ever pretended to be happy when you weren't? Could other people tell?

3. Have you ever been accused of stealing something when you were perfectly innocent? How did this happen?

From these examples we can see that whereas factual beliefs can in theory be verified by direct observation, *inferential beliefs* go beyond what can be directly observed. For instance, in the examples given, your observation of certain actions of your roommate led you to infer things that you were *not* observing directly: "He's drunk," "She's happy," "He's stealing books." Making such simple inferences is something we do all the time and so automatically that we usually are not even aware that we are going beyond our immediate observations. Making such inferences enables us to see the world as a complete picture, to fill in the blanks and round out what is actually being presented to our senses. In a way, we become artists, painting a picture of the world that is consistent, coherent, and predictable.

Our picture also includes *predictions* of what will take place in the near future. These predictions and expectations are also inferences because we attempt to determine what is currently unknown from what is already known.

Of course, our inferences may be mistaken, and in fact they frequently are. You may infer that the woman sitting next to you is wearing two earrings and then discover that she has only one. Or you may expect the class to end at noon and find that the teacher lets you go early—or late. In the last section we concluded that not even factual beliefs are absolutely certain. Comparatively speaking, inferential beliefs are a great deal more uncertain than factual beliefs, and it is important to distinguish between the two. For example, do you ever cross streets with cars heading toward you, expecting them to stop for a red light or because you have the right of way? Is this a factual belief or an inference? Considered objectively, are you running a serious risk when you do this? In evaluating the risk, think of all the motorists who may be in a hurry, not paying attention, drunk, ill, and so on.

Consider these situations, analyzing each situation by asking these questions: Is the action based on a factual belief or an inference? In what ways might the inference be mistaken? What is the degree of risk involved?

- Placing your hand in a closing elevator door to reopen it.
- Taking an unknown drug at a party.
- Jumping out of an airplane with a parachute on.
- Riding on the back of a motorcycle.
- Taking a drug prescribed by your doctor.

Having an accurate picture of the world depends on our being able to evaluate how *certain* our beliefs are. Therefore, it is crucial that we *distinguish* inferences from factual beliefs and then *evaluate* how certain or uncertain our inferences are. This process is known as "calculating the risks," and it is very important to successfully solving problems and deciding what steps to take.

The distinction between what is observed and what is inferred is paid particular attention in courtroom settings, where defense lawyers usually want witnesses to describe *only what they observed*—not what they *inferred*. When a witness includes an inference such as "I saw him steal it," the lawyer may object that the statement represents a "conclusion of the witness" and move to have the observation stricken from the record. For example, imagine that you are a defense attorney listening to the following testimony. At what points would you make the objection "This is a conclusion of the witness"?

> I saw Harvey running down the street, right after he knocked the old lady down. He had her purse in his hand and was trying to escape as fast as he could. He was really scared. I wasn't surprised because Harvey has always taken advantage of others. It's not the first time that he's stolen either, I can tell you that. Just last summer he robbed the poor box at St. Anthony's. He was bragging about it for weeks.

Finally, we should be aware that even though facts and inferences can be distinguished *in theory, in practice* it is almost impossible to communicate with others by using factual observations only. A reasonable approach is to state our inference *along with* the observable evidence upon which the inference is based (for example, John *seemed* happy because . . .). Our language has an entire collection of terms (*seems, appears, is likely,* etc.) that signal we are making an inference and not expressing an observable fact.

Examine the following list of statements, noting which statements are factual beliefs (based on observations) and which are inferential beliefs (conclusions that go beyond observations). For each factual statement, describe how you might go about verifying the information. For each inferential statement, describe a factual observation on which the inference could be based. (Some statements may contain factual beliefs *and* inferential beliefs.)

1. When my leg starts to ache, that means snow is on the way.
2. The grass is wet—it must have rained last night.
3. I think that it's pretty clear from the length of the skid marks that the accident was caused by that person driving too fast.
4. Fifty men lost their lives in the construction of the Queensboro Bridge.
5. Nancy said she wasn't feeling well yesterday—I'll bet she's out sick today.

Now consider the following situations. What inferences might you be inclined to make based on what you are observing? How could you investigate the accuracy of your inference?

1. A student in your class is consistently late for class.
2. You see a friend of yours driving a new car.
3. A teacher asks the same student to stay after class several times.
4. You don't receive any cards on your birthday.
5. Driving on the highway, you observe an area of the road that contains broken glass and skid marks.

We have been exploring relatively simple inferences. However, many of the inferences people make are much more complicated. In fact, much of our knowledge about the world rests on our ability to make complicated inferences in a systematic and logical way. However, just because an inference is more complicated does not mean that it is more accurate; in fact, the opposite is often the case. One of the masters of complex inferences is the legendary Sherlock Holmes. In the following passage, Holmes makes an astonishing number of inferences about Dr. Watson. Study the conclusions he comes to. Are they reasonable? Can you explain how he reaches these conclusions?

> "You appeared to be surprised when I told you, on our first meeting, that you had come from Afghanistan."
>
> "You were told, no doubt."
>
> "Nothing of the sort. I *knew* you came from Afghanistan. From long habit the train of thoughts ran so swiftly through my mind that I arrived at the conclusion without being conscious of intermediate steps. There were such steps, however. The train of reasoning ran, 'Here is a gentleman of a medical type, but with the air of a military man. Clearly an army doctor, then. He is just come from the tropics, for his face is dark, and that is not the natural tint of his skin, for his wrists are fair. He has undergone hardship and sickness, as his haggard face says clearly. His left arm has been injured. He holds it in a stiff and unnatural manner. Where in the tropics could an English army doctor have seen much hardship and got his arm wounded? Clearly in Afghanistan.' The whole train of thought did not occupy a second. I then remarked that you came from Afghanistan, and you were astonished."
>
> Sir Arthur Conan Doyle, *A Study in Scarlet*

Thinking Activity 8.4

Describe an experience in which you made an *incorrect* inference that resulted in serious consequences. For example, it might have been a situation in which you mistakenly accused someone, an accident based on a miscalculation, a poor decision based on an inaccurate prediction, or some other event. Analyze that experience by answering the following questions:

1. What was your mistaken inference?
2. What was the factual evidence on which you based your inference?
3. Looking back, what could you have done to avoid the erroneous inference?

Judging

In the space provided, identify and describe a friend you have, a course you have taken, and the school you attend. Be sure your descriptions are specific and include *what you think* about the friend, the course, and the school.

1. _____ is a friend that I have.

   He/she is _____

   _____.

2. _____ is a course I have taken.

   It was _____

   _____.

3. _____ is the school I attend.

   It is _____

   _____.

Now review your responses. Do they include *factual* descriptions? For each response, note any factual information that can be verified. In addition to factual reports, your descriptions may contain *inferences* based on factual information. Can you identify any inferences? In addition to inferences, your descriptions may also include *judgments* about the person, course, and school—descriptions that express your evaluation based on certain criteria. Facts and inferences are designed to help us figure out what is actually happening (or will happen), but the purpose of judgments is to express our evaluation about what is happening (or will happen). For example,

■ My new car has broken down three times in the first six months. *(Factual report)*

■ My new car will probably continue to have difficulties. *(Inference)*

■ My new car is a lemon. *(Judgment)*

When we pronounce a new car a "lemon," we are making a judgment based on certain criteria or standards. For instance, a "lemon" is usually a newly purchased item with which we have repeated problems—generally an automobile. To take another example of judging, consider the following statements:

■ Carla always does her work thoroughly and completes it on time. *(Factual report)*

■ Carla will probably continue to do her work in this fashion. *(Inference)*

■ Carla is a very responsible person. *(Judgment)*

By judging Carla to be responsible, we are evaluating her on the basis of the criteria or standards that we believe indicate a responsible person. One such criterion is completing assigned work on time. Can you identify additional criteria for judging someone to be responsible? Review your descriptions of a friend, a course, and your school. Can you identify any judgments in your descriptions? If so, list them here.

1. Judgments about your friend: _____

   _____

2. Judgments about your course: _____

   _____

3. Judgments about your school: _____

   _____

For each judgment you have listed, identify the criteria on which the judgment is based.

1. Criteria for judgment about your friend:

   a. _____

   b. _____

2. Criteria for judgment about your course:

   a. _____

   b. _____

3. Criteria for judgment about your school:

   a. _____

   b. _____

When we judge, we are often expressing our feelings of approval or disapproval. Sometimes, however, we make judgments that conflict with what we personally approve of. For example,

Judging:
People judge events differently because they view events through their own evaluation "lenses." Critical thinkers approach differences in judgments by making the judgment criteria *explicit* and identifying the reasons *that justify these criteria.*

▪ I think a woman should be able to have an abortion if she chooses to, although I don't believe it's right.

▪ I can see why you think that person is very attractive, even though he or she is not the type that appeals to me.

In fact, at times it is essential to disregard our personal feelings of approval or disapproval when we judge. For instance, a judge in a courtroom should render evaluations based on the law, not on his or her personal preferences.

Many of our disagreements with other people focus on differences in judgments. As critical thinkers, we need to approach such differences in judgments intelligently. We can do so by following these guidelines:

1. *Make explicit* the criteria used as a basis for the judgment.

2. Try to *establish the reasons* that justify these criteria.

For instance, if I make the judgment "Professor Andrews is an excellent teacher," I am basing my judgment on certain criteria of teaching excellence. Once these standards are made explicit, we can discuss whether they make sense and what the justification is for them. Identify below some of your standards for teaching excellence:

1. _____

2. _____

3. _____

Of course, your idea of what makes an excellent teacher may be different from someone else's, a conclusion you can test by comparing your criteria with those of other class members. When these disagreements occur, our only hope for resolution is to use the two steps previously identified:

1. Make explicit the standards we are using.

2. Give reasons that justify these standards.

For example, "Professor Andrews really gets my mind working, forcing me to think through issues on my own and then defend my conclusions. I earn what I learn, and that makes it really 'mine.'"

In short, not all judgments are equally good or equally poor. The credibility of a judgment depends on the criteria used to make the judgment and the evidence or reasons that support these criteria. For example, there may be legitimate disagreements about judgments on the following points:

▪ Who was the greatest United States President?

▪ Which movie deserves the Oscar this year?

▪ Which is the best baseball team this year?

▪ Which music is best for dancing?

However, in these and countless other cases the quality of judgments depends on identifying the criteria used for the competing judgments and then demonstrating that our candidate best meets those criteria by providing supporting evidence and reasons. With this approach, we can often engage in intelligent discussion and establish which judgments are best supported by the evidence. For example, would you judge a pizza to be "junk food"? Analyze the criteria used by the author of the following passage in reaching his judgment:

> One widely held misconception concerning pizza should be laid to rest. Although it may be characterized as fast food, pizza is *not* junk food. Especially when it is made with fresh ingredients, pizza fulfills our basic nutritional requirements. The crust provides carbohydrates; from the cheese and meat or fish comes protein; and the tomatoes, herbs, onions, and garlic supply vitamins and minerals.
>
> Louis Philip Salamone, "Pizza: Fast Food, Not Junk Food"

Understanding how judgments function encourages us to continue thinking critically about a situation. For instance, the judgment "This course is worthless!" does not encourage further exploration and critical analysis. In fact, it may prevent such an analysis by *discouraging* further exploration. Judgments seem to summarize the situation in a final sort of way. And because judgments are sometimes made *before* we have a clear and complete understanding of the situation, they can serve to *prevent* us from seeing the situation as clearly and completely as we might. Of course, if we understand that all judgments are based on criteria that may or may not be adequately justified, we can explore these judgments further by making the criteria explicit and examining the reasons that justify them.

Communicating Effectively

Its link with thinking makes language so powerful a tool that we not only rely on it as a vehicle for expressing our thoughts and feelings and for influencing others; we also use language to provide a structure for learning. Like a choreographer who creates a dance, language shapes and forms our thoughts. It organizes them. It relates one idea to the other so that their combinations, many and varied, can be reported with strength and vitality, creating meaning that no one idea could convey alone. Used expertly, language *expresses* our thinking in a way that clearly evokes the images, feelings, and ideas that we as speakers and writers want to present. It also *communicates* our thinking in such a way that others can comprehend our meaning and, in turn, make appropriate inferences and judgments and thereby expand their own thinking.

Language Styles

Language is always used in a context. That is, we always speak or write with a person or group of people—an audience—in mind. The group may include friends, coworkers, or strangers. We also always use language in a particular situation. We may converse with our friends, meet with our boss, or carry out a business transaction at a bank or supermarket. Learning to use the appropriate language style, depending on the social context in which we are operating, requires both critical judgment and flexible expertise with various language forms. In each of these cases, we use the *language style* that is appropriate to the social situation. For example, describe how you usually greet the following people when you see them:

- a good friend
- a teacher
- a parent
- an employer
- a restaurant server

When greeting a friend, we are likely to say something like "Hey, Richard, how ya been!" or "Hi, Sue, good to see ya." When greeting our employer, however, or even a coworker, something more like "Good morning, Mrs. Jones" or "Hello, Dan, how are you this morning?" is in order. The reason for this variation is that the two social contexts, personal friendship and the workplace, are very different and call for different language responses. In a working environment, no matter how frequently we interact with coworkers or employers, our language style tends to be more formal and less abbreviated than it is in personal friendships. Conversely, the more familiar we are with someone, the more abbreviated our *style* of language will be in that context. The language we use with someone is more abbreviated when we share a variety of ideas,

Learning to use the appropriate language style, depending on the social context, requires both critical judgment and flexible expertise with various language forms.

opinions, and experiences with that person. The language style identifies this shared thinking and consequently *restricts* the group of people who can communicate within this context.

We all belong to social groups in which we use styles that separate "insiders" from "outsiders." When we use an abbreviated style of language with a friend, we are identifying that person as a friend and sending a social message that says "I know you pretty well, and I can assume many common perspectives between us." On the other hand, when we are speaking in a more elaborate language style to someone at the office, we are sending a different social message, namely, "I know you within a particular context, and I can assume only certain common perspectives between us."

In this way we use language to identify the social context in which we are using it and to define our relationship with the other person. Language styles vary from *informal,* in which we abbreviate not only sentence structure but also the sounds that form words—as in "ya" in the examples—to increasingly *formal,* in which we use more complex sentence structure as well as complete words in terms of sound patterns.

Thinking Activity 8.5

1. Write a conversation you would be likely to carry on with a classmate about a problem you might have had in class.

2. Now rewrite the conversation as if you were explaining the problem to your professor.

3. Finally, rewrite the conversation as if you were explaining the problem to a family member.

4. Compare the similarities and differences between these conversations in terms of their language styles: formality, word choice, sentence construction, and sound patterns.

Slang

Read the following dialogue:

Woman 1: "Hey, did you see that new guy? He's gnarly. I mean, like really radical."

Woman 2: "All the guys in my class are barfo. Geeks or skids or wastoids. Let's blow this clambake. I have to powerdrill."

Now rewrite the dialogue in your own style.

_____

_____

_____

_____

How would you describe the style of the original dialogue? How would you describe the style of your version of the dialogue? The linguist Shoshana Hoose points out the following:

> As any teen will tell you, keeping up with the latest slang takes a lot of work. New phrases sweep into town faster than greased lightning, and they are gone just as quickly. Last year's "hoser" is this year's "dweeb" (both meaning somewhat of a "nerd"). Some slang consists of everyday words that have taken on a new, hip meaning. "Mega," for instance, was used mainly by astronomers and mathematicians until teens adopted it as a way of describing anything great, cool, and unbelievable. Others are words such as *gag* that seem to have naturally evolved from one meaning (to throw up) to another (a person or thing that is gross to the point of making one want to throw up). And then there are words that come from movies, popular music, and the media. "Rambo," the macho movie character who singlehandedly defeats whole armies, has come to mean a muscular, tough, adventurous boy who wears combat boots and fatigues.

> As linguists have long known, the people of any culture create the most words for the things that preoccupy them the most. For example, it has been reported that the Inuits of Alaska and Canada have more than seventy-six words for *ice* and *snow* and that Hawaiians can choose from scores of variations on the word *water.* Most teenage slang falls into one or two categories: words meaning "cool" and words meaning "out of it." A person who is really out of it could be described as a *nerd,* a *goober,* a *geek,* a *tade,* or a *pinhead,* to name just a few possibilities.

Thinking Activity 8.6

Review the slang terms and definitions in the following glossary. How do your terms match up? For each term, list a word that you use (or have heard of) that means the same thing. If your meanings do not match those in the glossary or if you did not recognize some of the words in the glossary, what do you think was the main reason?

Word:	*Your Word:*	*Meaning:*
babe	_____	a good-looking guy/girl
barfo	_____	gross, disgusting
burnout	_____	someone who hangs out, drinks, takes drugs
gnarly	_____	really cool, weird, strange, totally awesome
mongo	_____	really big, cool
posers	_____	showoffs

→

wastoids	_____	druggies, losers
beat	_____	stupid, out-of-date, a drag
nada	_____	no good
powerdrill	_____	study intensely

Slang is a restrictive style of language that limits its speakers to a particular group. Although slang is an important form of communication within your group, problems can occur if you overuse slang in formal settings—such as the workplace—and the effect may interfere with your social acceptability and success.

In addition to slang, where age is usually the determining factor, another form of restricted communication is *jargon,* which is determined by profession or interest group. Let's look at this other type of language style.

Jargon

Jargon is made up of words, expressions, and technical terms that are intelligible to professional circles or interest groups but not to the general public. Consider the following interchanges:

1. *A:* Breaker 1-9. Com'on, Little Frog.

   B: Roger and back to you, Charley.

   A: We got to back down, we got a Smokey ahead.

   B: I can't afford to feed the bears this week. Better stay at 5-5 now.

   A: That's a big 10-4.

   B: I'm gonna cut the co-ax now.

2. OK, Al, number six takes two eggs, wreck 'em, with a whiskey down and an Adam and Eve on a raft. Don't forget the Jack Tommy, express to California.

3. Please take further notice, that pursuant to and in accordance with Article II, Paragraph Second and Fifteen of the aforesaid Proprietary Lease Agreement, you are obligated to reimburse Lessor for any expense Lessor incurs including legal fees in instituting any action or proceeding due to a default of your obligations as contained in the Proprietary Lease Agreement.

Word meaning in these interchanges is shared by (1) CB radio operators; (2) restaurant/diner cooks and servers; and (3) attorneys. Most of the rest of us would be confused when listening to these types of jargon—even if we speak English fluently!

The Social Boundaries of Language

Language is a system of communication, by sounds and markings, among given groups of people. Within each language community, members' thinking patterns are defined in many respects by the specific patterns of meaning that language imposes. Smaller groups within language communities display more distinctive language patterns. When there are some differences from the norm, mainly in vocabulary and length of sentences, we say the speakers are using a specific language style. When the form of the language spoken by these smaller groups shows many differences from the "usual" or "regular" form in words and sentence structure, we call this language form a *dialect.* Both language styles and dialects place boundaries on communication. The most obvious are social; they identify people as belonging to a particular group.

However, we cannot overlook the tie between language and thinking. That is, we cannot ignore the way in which our thoughts about a social situation determine the variety of language we use. The connection between language and thought turns language into a powerful social force that separates us as well as binds us together. The language that we use and the way we use it serve as important clues to our social identity. For example, dialect identifies our geographical area or group, slang marks our age group and subculture, jargon often identifies our occupation, and accent typically suggests the place we grew up and our socioeconomic class. These dimensions of language are important influences in shaping our response to others. Sometimes they can trigger stereo-types we hold about someone's interests, social class, intelligence, personal attributes, and so on. The ability to think critically gives us the insight and the intellectual ability to distinguish people's language use from their individual qualities, to correct inaccurate beliefs about people, and to avoid stereotypical responses in the future.

Thinking Activity 8.7

1. Describe examples, drawn from your personal experience, of each of the following: accent, jargon, slang.

2. Describe your immediate responses to the examples you just provided. For example, what is your immediate response to someone with a British accent? To someone speaking "computerese"? To someone speaking a slang that you don't understand?

3. Analyze the responses you just described. How did they get formed? Do they represent an accurate understanding of the person or a stereotyped belief?

4. Identify strategies for using critical thinking abilities to overcome inaccu-rate and inappropriate responses to others, based on their language use.

Working Collaboratively with Others

Your success in college—and especially in your career—will depend on how well you are able to work constructively with other people. In this chapter we have been exploring many of the language abilities you need to communicate

Working Collaboratively:
The ability to work productively as a member of a group to analyze issues and solve problems is important in both college and careers.

with others. But there are important social skills that you also need. The term *col-laboration* refers to social relationships that typically occur in group situations. Groups can be "small" (3–12 people) or "large" (more than 12 people), and they are usually defined as a collection of people who work together face to face in order to achieve a common goal. The members of a group interact and communicate, assume various roles within the group, and establish a group identity.

Working collaboratively has numerous advantages over working individually. To begin with, the members bring diverse backgrounds and interests that can generate a multiplicity of perspectives. And working with others actually creates ideas that none of the individuals would have come up with on their own. In addition, group members provide support and encouragement for one another, and each person can contribute his or her specialized skills. Finally, the ideas generated by individuals are typically discussed and evaluated by the group as a whole, so the final conclusions should be sound and thoughtful.

Of course, whenever humans get together, there are complications. For example, sometimes one or more group members want to dominate the group deliberations, trying to control and intimidate the other group members. Also, groups are frequently plagued by a member who doesn't want to do his or her share. This is particularly damaging in small groups, where the contribution of each member is essential. And sometimes there are just incompatibilities, when you are expected to work with someone who drives you crazy. As a result, there are some key abilities that people need to develop in order to work collaboratively with others:

■ *Treat all group members with respect.* This is a basic ground rule for collaborative success. Even if the people in your group are not your favorites, you need to treat them and their ideas with professional respect. The quickest way to destroy group dynamics is to be insulting, arrogant, contemptuous, or condescending toward members of the group, even in subtle ways.

■ *Don't hesitate to contribute your ideas.* Every member has an important perspective to contribute, and it is your responsibility to make your contributions. Don't be worried about the reactions of others or let yourself be intimidated by loud, insistent voices.

■ *Encourage diverse ideas from others, and don't judge their ideas prematurely.* In addition to contributing your ideas, you should encourage other group members to contribute theirs. When people offer ideas, respond positively and constructively. You never know where ideas are going to lead, and a supportive attitude encourages a free and open exchange.

■ *Evaluate ideas objectively, not personally.* When the group evaluates ideas from its members, the ideas should be evaluated on the basis of critical thinking: What is the issue or problem? How does this idea address this issue or problem? What reasons or evidence support the idea? What are its risks or disadvantages? It is important for each member to realize that the ideas are being evaluated, not the person who suggested the idea.

- *Keep the group focused and "on task."* Many groups end up wasting time because they cannot stay focused on the task at hand, or they are unable to close their deliberations. It's helpful to establish a time frame that commits you to making a decision, and it's also useful to establish a decision-making process in case there are deep disagreements.

- *Assign the group responsibilities equitably.* It is important that all group members undertake substantive responsibilities, avoiding the divisions between the "workhorses" and the "freeloaders." Everyone has important talents and energy to contribute, and shared responsibility promotes positive group morale.

- *Deal directly with problem members.* Don't let problem members disrupt the group's functioning. If someone tries to dominate the discussion or impose his or her ideas, let the person know directly that this behavior is inappropriate. If a member is excessively negative and critical, encourage that person to participate in a more constructive way. For example, a number of years ago I was the president of the board of trustees for a land conservancy organization. Most of the other trustees were hard-working and positive individuals, but there was one who was unrelentingly negative, critical of everything that I and the other trustees proposed. After several failed efforts to deal with the problem, I finally resorted to critical thinking. To every negative comment from this person, I would respond "You might be right in your criticism—what do *you* suggest as a better idea?" And every time the trustee asked why the organization wasn't doing one thing or another, I would respond "That's an excellent suggestion—I'm putting *you* in charge of implementing this idea." It wasn't long before the silence emanating from this trustee was deafening!

Thinking Passage

"Sex, Lies and Conversation"

Recently, gender differences in language use have reached the forefront of social research, even though variation in language use between the sexes has been observed for centuries. Proverbs such as "A woman's tongue wags like a lamb's tail" historically attest to supposed differences—usually inferiorities—in women's speech and, by implication, their thinking, as opposed to men's. Vocabulary, swearing and taboo language, pronunciation, and verbosity have all been pointed to as contexts that illustrate gender differences in language. Only within the last two decades have scholars of the social use of language paid serious attention to variation between men's and women's language and the social factors that contribute to these differences. The following article by Deborah Tannen reflects the current interest in sociolinguistic variations between women and men.

→

Sex, Lies and Conversation: Why Is It So Hard for Men and Women to Talk to Each Other?

Deborah Tannen

I was addressing a small gathering in a suburban Virginia living room—a women's group that had invited men to join them. Throughout the evening, one man had been particularly talkative, frequently offering ideas and anecdotes, while his wife sat silently beside him on the couch. Toward the end of the evening, I commented that women frequently complain that their husbands don't talk to them. This man quickly concurred. He gestured toward his wife and said, "She's the talker in our family." The room burst into laughter; the man looked puzzled and hurt. "It's true," he explained. "When I come home from work I have nothing to say. If she didn't keep the conversation going, we'd spend the whole evening in silence."

This episode crystallizes the irony that although American men tend to talk more than women in public situations, they often talk less at home. And this pattern is wreaking havoc with marriage.

The pattern was observed by political scientist Andrew Hacker in the late '70s. Sociologist Catherine Kohler Riessman reports in her new book *Divorce Talk* that most of the women she interviewed—but only a few of the men—gave lack of communication as the reason for their divorces. Given the current divorce rate of nearly 50 percent, that amounts to millions of cases in the United States every year—a virtual epidemic of failed conversation.

In my own research, complaints from women about their husbands most often focused not on tangible inequities such as having given up the chance for a career to accompany a husband to his, or doing far more than their share of daily life-support work like cleaning, cooking, social arrangements and errands. Instead, they focused on communication: "He doesn't listen to me," "He doesn't talk to me." I found, as Hacker observed years before, that most wives want their husbands to be, first and foremost, conversational partners, but few husbands share this expectation of their wives.

In short, the image that best represents the current crisis is the stereotypical cartoon scene of a man sitting at the breakfast table with a newspaper held up in front of his face, while a woman glares at the back of it, wanting to talk.

→

Miscommunication: Men and women often have different communication styles that can lead to miscommunication and misunderstanding.

Linguistic Battle of Sexes

How can women and men have such different impressions of communication in marriage? Why the widespread imbalance in their interests and expectations?

In the April issue of *American Psychologist,* Stanford University's Eleanor Maccoby reports the results of her own and others' research showing that children's development is most influenced by the social structure of peer interactions. Boys and girls tend to play with children of their own gender, and their sex-separate groups have different organizational structures and interactive norms.

I believe these systematic differences in childhood socialization make talk between women and men like cross-cultural communication, heir to all the attraction and pitfalls of that enticing but difficult enterprise. My research on men's and women's conversations uncovered patterns similar to those described for children's groups.

For women, as for girls, intimacy is the fabric of relationships, and talk is the thread from which it is woven. Little girls create and maintain friendships by exchanging secrets; similarly, women regard conversation as the cornerstone of friendship. So a woman expects her husband to be a new and improved version of a best friend. What is important is not the individual subjects that are discussed but the sense of closeness, a life shared, that emerges when people tell their thoughts, feelings, and impressions.

Bonds between boys can be as intense as girls', but they are based less on talking, more on doing things together. Since they don't assume talk is the cement that binds a relationship, men don't know what kind of talk women want, and they don't miss it when it isn't there.

Boys' groups are larger, more inclusive, and more hierarchical, so boys must struggle to avoid the subordinate position in the group. This may play a role in women's complaints that men don't listen to them. Some men really don't like to listen, because being the listener makes them feel one-down, like a child listening to adults or an employee to a boss.

But often when women tell men, "You aren't listening," and the men protest, "I am," the men are right. The impression of not listening results from misalignments in the mechanics of conversation. The misalignment begins as soon as a man and a woman take physical positions. This became clear when I studied videotapes made by psychologist Bruce Dorval of children and adults talking to their same-sex best friends. I found that at every age, the girls and women faced each other directly, their eyes anchored on each other's faces. At every age, the boys and men sat at angles to each other and looked elsewhere in the room, periodically glancing at each other. They were obviously attuned to each other, often mirroring each other's movements. But the tendency of men to face away can give women the impression they aren't listening even when they are. A young woman in college was frustrated: Whenever she told her boyfriend she wanted to talk to him, he would lie down on the floor, close his eyes, and put his arm over his face. This signaled to her, "He's taking a nap." But he insisted he was listening extra hard. Normally, he looks around the room, so he is easily distracted. Lying down and covering his eyes helped him concentrate on what she was saying.

Analogous to the physical alignment that women and men take in conversation is their topical alignment. The girls in my study tended to talk at length about one topic, but the boys

→

tended to jump from topic to topic. Girls exchanged stories about people they knew. The second-grade boys teased, told jokes, noticed things in the room and talked about finding games to play. The sixth-grade girls talked about problems with a mutual friend. The sixth-grade boys talked about 55 different topics, none of which extended over more than a few turns.

Listening to Body Language

Switching topics is another habit that gives women the impression men aren't listening, especially if they switch to a topic about themselves. But the evidence of the 10th-grade boys in my study indicates otherwise. The 10th-grade boys sprawled across their chairs with bodies parallel and eyes straight ahead, rarely looking at each other. They looked as if they were riding in a car, staring out the windshield. But they were talking about their feelings. One boy was upset because a girl had told him he had a drinking problem, and the other was feeling alienated from all his friends.

Now, when a girl told a friend about a problem, the friend responded by asking probing questions and expressing agreement and understanding. But the boys dismissed each other's problems. Todd assured Richard that his drinking was "no big problem" because "sometimes you're funny when you're off your butt." And when Todd said he felt left out, Richard responded, "Why should you? You know more people than me."

Women perceive such responses as belittling and unsupportive. But the boys seemed satisfied with them. Whereas women reassure each other by implying, "You shouldn't feel bad because I've had similar experiences," men do so by implying, "You shouldn't feel bad because your problems aren't so bad."

There are even simpler reasons for women's impression that men don't listen. Linguist Lynette Hirschman found that women make more listener-noise, such as "mhm," "uhuh," and "yeah," to show "I'm with you." Men, she found, more often give silent attention. Women who expect a stream of listener-noise interpret silent attention as no attention at all.

Women's conversational habits are as frustrating to men as men's are to women. Men who expect silent attention interpret a stream of listener-noise as overreaction or impatience. Also, when women talk to each other in a close, comfortable setting, they often overlap, finish each other's sentences and anticipate what the other is about to say. This practice, which I call "participatory listenership," is often perceived by men as interruption, intrusion and lack of attention.

A parallel difference caused a man to complain about his wife, "She just wants to talk about her own point of view. If I show her another view, she gets mad at me." When most women talk to each other, they assume a conversationalist's job is to express agreement and support. But many men see their conversational duty as pointing out the other side of an argument. This is heard as disloyalty by women, and refusal to offer the requisite support. It is not that women don't want to see other points of view, but that they prefer them phrased as suggestions and inquiries rather than as direct challenges.

In his book *Fighting for Life,* Walter Ong points out that men use "agonistic" or warlike, oppositional formats to do almost anything; thus discussion becomes debate, and conversation a competitive sport. In contrast, women see conversation as a ritual means of establishing rapport. If Jane tells a problem and June says she has a similar one, they walk away feeling closer to each other. But this attempt at establishing rapport can backfire when used with men. Men take too literally women's ritual "troubles talk," just as women mistake men's ritual challenges for real attack.

The Sounds of Silence

These differences begin to clarify why women and men have such different expectations about communication in marriage. For women, talk creates intimacy. Marriage is an orgy of closeness: you can tell your feelings and thoughts, and still be loved. Their greatest fear is being pushed away. But men live in a hierarchical world, where talk maintains independence and status. They are on guard to protect themselves from being put down and pushed around.

This explains the paradox of the talkative man who said of his silent wife, "She's the talker." In the public setting of a guest lecture, he felt challenged to show his intelligence and display his understanding of the lecture. But at home, where he has nothing to prove and no one to defend against, he is free to remain silent. For his wife, being home means she is free from the worry that something she says might offend someone, or spark disagreement, or appear to be showing off; at home she is free to talk.

The communication problems that endanger marriage can't be fixed by mechanical engineering. They require a new conceptual framework about the role of talk in human relationships. Many of the psychological explanations that have become second nature may not be helpful, because they tend to blame either women (for not being assertive enough) or men (for not being in touch with their feelings). A sociolinguistic approach by which male–female conversation is seen as cross-cultural communication allows us to understand the problem and forge solutions without blaming either party.

Once the problem is understood, improvement comes naturally, as it did to the young woman and her boyfriend who seemed to go to sleep when she wanted to talk. Previously, she had accused him of not listening, and he had refused to change his behavior, since that would be admitting fault. But then she learned about and explained to him the differences in women's and men's habitual ways of aligning themselves in conversation. The next time she told him she wanted to talk, he began, as usual, by lying down and covering his eyes. When the familiar negative reaction bubbled up, she reassured herself that he really was listening. But then he sat up and looked at her. Thrilled, she asked why. He said, "You like me to look at you when we talk, so I'll try to do it." Once he saw their differences as cross-cultural rather than right and wrong, he independently altered his behavior.

Women who feel abandoned and deprived when their husbands won't listen to or report daily news may be happy to discover their husbands trying to adapt once they understand the place of small talk in women's relationships. But if their husbands don't adapt, the women may still be comforted that for men, this is not a failure of intimacy. Accepting the difference, the wives may look to their friends or family for that kind of talk. And husbands who can't provide it shouldn't feel their wives have made unreasonable demands. Some couples will still decide to divorce, but at least their decisions will be based on realistic expectations.

→

In these times of resurgent ethnic conflicts, the world desperately needs cross-cultural understanding. Like charity, successful cross-cultural communication should begin at home.

Questions for Analysis

1. Identify the distinctive differences between the communication styles of men and women, according to Deborah Tannen, and explain how these differences can lead to miscommunication and misunderstanding.

2. Based on your experience, explain whether you believe Dr. Tannen's analysis of these different communication styles is accurate. Provide specific examples to support your viewpoint.

9
Reasoning Logically

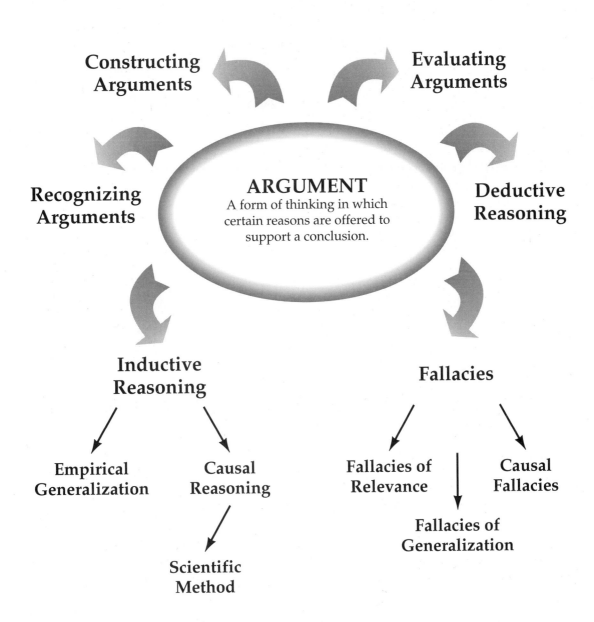

Constructing Arguments

Evaluating Arguments

Recognizing Arguments

ARGUMENT
A form of thinking in which certain reasons are offered to support a conclusion.

Deductive Reasoning

Inductive Reasoning

Fallacies

Empirical Generalization

Causal Reasoning

Fallacies of Relevance

Causal Fallacies

Scientific Method

Fallacies of Generalization

What exactly is "reasoning"? It is a type of thinking in which you offer reasons in support of conclusions, and it is the hallmark of an educated thinker. You have been engaged in the reasoning process throughout this book, as well as in much of your life, as you have tried to explain, justify, and predict things by offering reasons in support of conclusions. The technical term for this reasoning process is *argument*.

> **Argument**
>
> A form of thinking in which certain statements (reasons) are offered in support of another statement (a conclusion).

This definition of *argument* is somewhat different from the meaning of the concept in our ordinary language. In common speech, *argument* usually refers to a dispute or quarrel between people, often involving intense feelings. (For example: "I got into a terrible argument with the idiot who hit the back of my car.") Very often these quarrels involve people presenting arguments in the sense that we have defined the concept, although the arguments are usually not carefully reasoned or clearly stated because the people are so angry. Instead of this common usage, in this chapter we will use the term's more technical meaning. Using this definition, we can define the main ideas that make up an argument:

> **Reasons**
>
> Statements that support another statement (known as a conclusion), justify it, or make it more probable.

> **Conclusion**
>
> A statement that explains, asserts, or predicts on the basis of statements (known as reasons) that are offered as evidence for it.

Recognizing Arguments

We use arguments in our everyday thinking in order to

- Decide
- Explain
- Predict
- Persuade

An example of each of these different types of arguments is given in the following sections. After each example, construct an argument of the same type.

Deciding

Reason: Throughout my life, I've always been interested in electricity.

Reason: There are many attractive job opportunities in the field of electrical engineering.

Conclusion: I will work toward becoming an electrical engineer.

Reason: _____

Reason: _____

Conclusion: _____

Explaining

Reason: I was delayed leaving my house because my dog needed an emergency walk.

Reason: There was an unexpected traffic jam caused by motorists slowing down to view an overturned chicken truck.

Conclusion: Therefore, I was late for our appointment.

Reason: _____

Reason: _____

Conclusion: _____

Predicting

Reason: Some people will always drive faster than the speed limit allows, no matter whether the limit is 55 or 65 mph.

Reason: Car accidents are more likely at higher speeds.

Conclusion: It follows that the reinstated 65 mph limit will result in more accidents.

Reason: _____

Reason: _____

Conclusion: _____

Persuading

Reason: Chewing tobacco can lead to cancer of the mouth and throat.

Reason: Boys sometimes are led to begin chewing tobacco by ads for the product that feature sports heroes.

Conclusion: Therefore, ads for chewing tobacco should be banned.

Reason: _____

Reason: _____

Conclusion: _____

Arguments:

We use arguments (a form of thinking in which reasons are offered in support of a conclusion) in our everyday lives to persuade, decide, explain, and predict.

Of course, your reasoning—and the reasoning of others—is not always correct. For example, the reasons someone offers may not really support the conclusion that is intended. Or the conclusion may not really follow from the reasons stated. Nevertheless, whenever you accept a conclusion as likely or true based on certain reasons or whenever you offer reasons to support a conclusion, you are using arguments to engage in reasoning—even if your reasoning is weak or faulty, and needs to be improved. In this chapter you will be carefully exploring both the way to construct effective arguments and the way to evaluate arguments in order to develop and sharpen your reasoning abilities. Let's begin by analyzing a dialogue in which the participants use a variety of arguments to try to prove their point about the issue of legalizing marijuana:

Dennis: Did you hear about the person who was sentenced to fifteen years in prison for possessing marijuana? I think this is one of the most outrageously unjust punishments I've ever heard of! In most states, people who are convicted of armed robbery, rape, or even murder don't receive fifteen-year sentences. And unlike the possession of marijuana, these crimes violate the rights of other people.

Caroline: I agree that this is one case in which the punishment doesn't seem to fit the crime. But you have to realize that drugs pose a serious threat to the young people of our country. Look at all the people who are addicted to drugs, who have had their lives ruined, and who often die at an early age of overdoses. And think of all the crimes committed by people to support their drug habits. As a result, sometimes society has to make an example of someone—like the person you mentioned—to convince others of the seriousness of the situation.

Dennis: That's ridiculous. In the first place, it's not right to punish someone unfairly just to provide an example. At least not in a society that believes in justice. And in the second place, smoking marijuana is nothing like using drugs such as heroin or even cocaine. It follows that smoking marijuana should not be against the law.

Caroline: I don't agree. Although marijuana might not be as dangerous as some other drugs, smoking it surely isn't good for you. And I don't think that anything that is a threat to your health should be legal.

Dennis: What about cigarettes and alcohol? We *know* that they are dangerous. Medical research has linked smoking cigarettes to lung cancer, emphysema, and heart disease, and alcohol damages the liver. No one has proved that marijuana is a threat to our health. And even if it does turn out to be somewhat unhealthy, it's certainly not as dangerous as cigarettes and alcohol.

Caroline: That's a good point. But to tell you the truth, I'm not so sure that cigarettes and alcohol should be legal. And in any case, they are already legal. Just because cigarettes and alcohol are bad for your health is no reason to legalize another drug that can cause health problems.

Dennis: Look—life is full of risks. We take chances every time we cross the street or climb into our car. In fact, with all of these loonies on the road, driving is a lot more hazardous to our health than any of the drugs around. And many of the foods we eat can kill. For example, red meat contributes to heart disease, and artificial sweeteners can cause cancer. The point is, if people want to take chances with their health, that's up to them. And many people in our society like to mellow out with marijuana. I read somewhere that over

70% of the people in the United States think that marijuana should be legalized.

Caroline: There's a big difference between letting people drive cars and letting them use dangerous drugs. Society has a responsibility to protect people from themselves. People often do things that are foolish if they are encouraged or given the opportunity to. Legalizing something like marijuana encourages people to use it, especially young people. It follows that many more people would use marijuana if it were legalized. It's like society saying "This is all right—go ahead and do it."

Dennis: I still maintain that marijuana isn't dangerous. It's not addictive—like heroin is—and there is no evidence that it harms you. Consequently, anything that is harmless should be legal.

Caroline: Marijuana may not be physically addictive like heroin, but I think that it can be psychologically addictive, because people tend to use more and more of it. I know a number of people who spend a lot of their time getting high. What about Carl? All he does is lie around and get high. This shows that smoking it over a period of time definitely affects your mind. Think about the people you know who smoke a lot. Don't they seem to be floating in a dream world? How are they ever going to make anything of their lives? As far as I'm concerned, a pothead is like a zombie—living but dead.

Dennis: Since you have had so little experience with marijuana, I don't think that you can offer an informed opinion on the subject. And, anyway, if you do too much of anything it can hurt you. Even something as healthy as exercise can cause problems if you do too much of it. But I sure don't see anything wrong with toking up with some friends at a party or even getting into a relaxed state by yourself. In fact, I find that I can even concentrate better on my schoolwork after taking a little smoke.

Caroline: I think you're just trying to rationalize your drug habit. Smoking marijuana doesn't help you concentrate—it takes you away from reality. And I don't think that people can control it. Either you smoke and surrender control of your life, or you don't smoke because you want to retain control. There's nothing in between.

This discussion is an illustration of two people engaging in *dialogue,* which we defined in Chapter Eight as the systematic exchange of ideas. Participating in this sort of dialogue is one of the keys to thinking critically because it stimulates you to develop your mind by carefully examining the way you make sense of the world. Discussing issues with others encourages you to be mentally active, to ask questions, to view issues from different perspectives, and to develop reasons to support conclusions.

Let's examine the discussion about marijuana. After Dennis presents the argument with the conclusion that the fifteen-year prison sentence is an unjust punishment (argument 1), Caroline considers that argument. Although she acknowledges that in this case "the punishment doesn't seem to fit the crime," she goes on to offer another argument (argument 2), giving reasons that lead to a conclusion that conflicts with the one Dennis made:

> *Reason:* Drugs pose a very serious threat to the young people of our country.
>
> *Reason:* Many crimes are committed to support drug habits.
>
> *Conclusion:* As a result, sometimes society has to make an example of someone to convince people of the seriousness of the situation.
>
> Can you identify an additional reason that supports this conclusion?
>
> Reason: _____

Cue Words for Arguments

Language provides signposts that help identify reasons and conclusions. Certain key words, known as *cue words,* signal that a reason is being offered in support of a conclusion or that a conclusion is being announced on the basis of certain reasons. For example, in response to Caroline's conclusion that society sometimes has to make an example of someone to convince people of the seriousness of the situation, Dennis gives the following argument (argument 3):

> *Reason:* In the first place, it's not right to punish someone unfairly just to provide an example.
>
> *Reason:* In the second place, smoking marijuana is nothing like using drugs such as heroin or even cocaine.
>
> *Conclusion:* It follows that smoking marijuana should not be against the law.

In this argument, the phrases *in the first place* and *in the second place* signal that reasons are being offered in support of a conclusion. Similarly, the phrase *it follows that* signals that a conclusion is being announced on the basis of certain reasons. Here is a list of the most commonly used cue words for reasons and conclusions:

Cue Words Signaling Reasons

since	in view of
for	first, second
because	in the first (second) place
as shown by	may be inferred from
as indicated by	may be deduced from
given that	may be derived from
assuming that	for the reason that

Cue Words Signaling Conclusions

therefore	then
thus	it follows that
hence	thereby showing
so	demonstrates that
consequently	allows us to infer that
(which) proves/shows that	suggests very strongly that
implies that	you see that
points to	leads me to believe that
as a result	allows us to deduce that

Of course, identifying reasons, conclusions, and arguments involves more than looking for cue words. The words and phrases listed here do not always signal reasons and conclusions, and in many cases arguments are made without the use of cue words. However, cue words do help signal that an argument is being made.

Thinking Activity 9.1

1. Review the discussion on marijuana, and underline any cue words signaling that reasons are being offered or that conclusions are being announced.

2. With the aid of cue words, identify the various arguments contained in the discussion on marijuana. For each argument, describe

   a. the *reasons* offered in support of a conclusion

   b. the *conclusion* announced on the basis of the reasons

Before you start, review the three arguments we have examined so far in this chapter.

Evaluating Arguments

To know how to construct an effective argument, it's critical to understand how to evaluate an argument's effectiveness, or soundness. This entails investigating two aspects of each argument independently to determine the soundness of the argument as a whole:

1. How *true* are the reasons being offered to support the conclusion?
2. To what extent do the reasons *support* the conclusion, or to what extent does the conclusion follow from the reasons offered?

Truth: How True Are the Supporting Reasons?

Does each reason make sense? What evidence is being offered as part of each reason? Do I know each reason to be true, based on my experience? Is each reason based on a source that can be trusted? You can use these questions and others like them to analyze the reasons offered and to determine how true they are. Evaluating the sort of beliefs usually found in arguments as reasons is a complex and ongoing challenge. Let's evaluate the truth of the reasons presented in the discussion on pages 343–344.

Argument 1

Reason: Possessing marijuana is not a serious offense.

Evaluation: As it stands, this reason needs further evidence to support it. The major issue of the discussion is whether possessing (and using) marijuana is in fact a serious offense or no offense at all. This reason would be strengthened by adding to it: "Possessing marijuana is not as serious an offense as armed robbery, rape, and murder, according to the overwhelming majority of legal statutes and judicial decisions."

Reason: There are many other more serious offenses—such as armed robbery, rape, and murder—that don't receive such stiff sentences.

Evaluation: The accuracy of this reason is highly doubtful. It is true there is wide variation in the sentences handed down for the same offense. The sentences vary from state to state and also vary within states and even within the same court. Nevertheless, on the whole, serious offenses like armed robbery, rape, and murder do receive long prison sentences. The real point here is a fifteen-year sentence for possessing marijuana is extremely unusual when compared with other sentences for marijuana possession.

Argument 2

Reason: Drugs pose a very serious threat to the young people of our country.

Evaluation: As the later discussion points out, this statement is much too vague. "Drugs" cannot be treated as being all the same. Some drugs (such as aspirin) are beneficial, while other drugs (such as heroin) are highly dangerous. To strengthen this reason, we would have to be more specific: "Drugs such as heroin, amphetamines, and cocaine pose a very serious threat to the young people of our country." We could increase the accuracy of the reason even more by adding the qualification "*some* of the young people of our country," because many young people are not involved with dangerous drugs.

Reason: Many crimes are committed to support drug habits.

Evaluation: _____

_____

_____

Argument 3

Reason: It's not right to punish someone unfairly just to provide an example.

Evaluation: This reason raises an interesting and complex ethical question that has been debated for centuries. The political theorist Machiavelli stated that "the ends justify the means," which implies that if we bring about desirable results it does not matter how we go about doing it. He would probably disagree with this reason, since using someone as an example might bring about desirable results, even though it might be unfair to the person being used as an example. In our society, however, which is based on the idea of fairness under the law, most people would probably agree with this reason.

Reason: Smoking marijuana is nothing like using drugs such as heroin or cocaine.

Evaluation: _____

_____

_____

Review the other arguments from the discussion on marijuana that you identified in Thinking Activity 9.1. Evaluate the truth of each of the reasons contained in the arguments.

Validity: Do the Reasons Support the Conclusion?

In addition to determining whether the reasons are true, evaluating arguments involves investigating the *relationship* between the reasons and the conclusion. When the reasons support the conclusion, so that the conclusion follows from the reasons being offered, the argument is *valid*. (In formal logic, the term *validity* is reserved for deductively valid arguments in which the conclusions follow necessarily from the premises. See the discussion of deductive arguments later in this chapter.) If, however, the reasons do *not* support the conclusion so that the conclusion does *not* follow from the reasons being offered, the argument is *invalid*.

> **Valid Argument**
>
> Argument in which the reasons support the conclusion so that the conclusion follows from the reasons offered.
>
> **Invalid Argument**
>
> Argument in which the reasons do not support the conclusion so that the conclusion does *not* follow from the reasons offered.

One way to focus on the concept of validity is to *assume* that all the reasons in the argument are true and then try to determine how probable they make the conclusion. The following is an example of one type of valid argument:

Reason: Anything that is a threat to our health should not be legal.

Reason: Marijuana is a threat to our health.

Conclusion: Therefore, marijuana should not be legal.

This is a valid argument because, if you assume that the reasons are true, then the conclusion necessarily follows. Of course, you may not agree that either or both of the reasons are true and so not agree with the conclusion. Nevertheless, the *structure* of the argument is valid. This particular form of thinking is known as *deduction*, and we will examine deductive reasoning more closely in the pages ahead.

The Soundness of Arguments

"Truth" and "validity" are not the same concepts. An argument can have true reasons and an invalid structure or false reasons and a valid structure. In both cases the argument is *unsound*. To be sound, an argument must have *both* true reasons and a valid structure. For example, consider the following argument:

Reason: For a democracy to function most effectively, citizens should be able to think critically about important social and political issues.

Reason: Education plays a key role in developing critical thinking abilities.

Conclusion: Therefore, education plays a key role in ensuring that a democracy is functioning most effectively.

A good case could be made for the soundness of this argument because the reasons are persuasive and the argument structure is valid. Of course, someone might contend that one or both of the reasons are not completely true, which illustrates an important point about the arguments we construct and evaluate. Many of the arguments you encounter in life fall somewhere between complete soundness and complete unsoundness because you may not be sure if the supporting reasons are completely true. Throughout this book you have found that developing accurate beliefs is an ongoing process and that your beliefs are subject to clarification and revision. As a result, the conclusion of any argument can be only as certain as the reasons supporting this conclusion.

To sum up, evaluating arguments involves both the truth of the reasons and the validity of the argument structure. The degree of soundness an argument has depends on how accurate its reasons turn out to be and how valid the argument's structure is.

Deductive Arguments

You use a number of basic argument forms to organize, relate, and make sense of the world. Two of the major types of argument forms are *deductive arguments* and *inductive arguments.* The deductive argument is the one most commonly associated with the study of logic. Although it has a variety of valid forms, they all share one characteristic: if you accept the supporting reasons (also called *premises*) as true, then you must necessarily accept the conclusion as true.

> **Deductive Argument**
>
> A form of argument in which one reasons from premises that are known or assumed to be true to a conclusion that follows logically from these premises.

Consider the following famous deductive argument:

Reason/Premise: All men are mortal.

Reason/Premise: Socrates is a man.

Conclusion: Therefore, Socrates is mortal.

In this example of deductive thinking, accepting the premises of the argument as true means that the conclusion necessarily follows; it cannot be false. Many deductive arguments, like the one just given, are structured as *syllogisms*, an argument form that consists of two supporting premises and a conclusion. However, there are also a large number of *invalid* deductive forms, one of which is illustrated below:

> *Reason/Premise:* All men are mortal.
>
> *Reason/Premise:* Socrates is a man.
>
> *Conclusion:* Therefore, all men are Socrates.

In the next several pages, we will briefly examine some common valid deductive forms.

Applying a General Rule

Whenever you reason with the form illustrated by the valid syllogism illustrated above, you are using the following argument structure:

> *Premise:* All A (men) are B (mortal).
>
> *Premise:* S is an A (Socrates is a man).
>
> *Conclusion:* Therefore, S is B (Socrates is mortal).

This basic argument form is valid no matter what terms are included. For example,

> *Premise:* All politicians are untrustworthy.
>
> *Premise:* Bill White is a politician.
>
> *Conclusion:* Therefore, Bill White is untrustworthy.

Notice again that, with any valid deductive form, *if* you assume that the premises are true, then you must accept the conclusion. Of course, in this case there is considerable doubt that the first premise is actually true. When we diagram this argument form Figure 9.1, it becomes clear why it is a valid way of thinking:

*Figure 9.1. **Basic syllogism in graphic format***

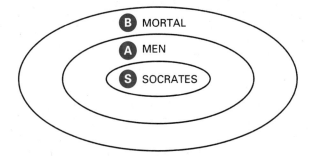

The *first premise* states that classification *A* (men) falls within classification *B* (mortal).

The *second premise* states that *S* (Socrates) is a member of classification *A* (men).

The *conclusion* simply states what has now become obvious—namely, that *S* (Socrates) must fall within classification *B* (mortal).

Although you may not always be aware of it, you use this basic type of reasoning whenever you apply a general rule in the form *All A is B.* For instance,

Premise: All children eight years old should be in bed by 9:30 P.M.

Premise: You are an eight-year-old child.

Conclusion: Therefore, you should be in bed by 9:30 P.M.

Review the dialogue at the beginning of this chapter to see if you can identify a deductive argument that uses this form.

Premise: _____

Premise: _____

Conclusion: _____

Modus Ponens

Another valid deductive form that you commonly use in your thinking is called *modus ponens*—that is, "affirming the antecedent"—and is illustrated by the following example:

Premise: If I have prepared thoroughly for the final exam, then I will do well on the exam.

Premise: I prepared thoroughly for the exam.

Conclusion: Therefore, I will do well on the exam.

When you reason like this, you are using the following argument structure:

Premise: If *A* (I have prepared thoroughly), then *B* (I will do well).

Premise: *A* (I have prepared thoroughly).

Conclusion: Therefore, *B* (I will do well).

Like all valid deductive forms, this form is valid no matter what specific terms are included. For example,

Premise: If the Democrats are able to register 20 million new voters, then they will win the presidential election.

Premise: The Democrats were able to register more than 20 million new voters.

Conclusion: Therefore, the Democrats will win the presidential election.

As with other valid argument forms, the conclusion will be true *if* the reasons are true. Although the second premise in this argument expresses information that can be verified, the first premise would be more difficult to establish.

Review the dialogue at the beginning of this chapter to see if you can identify a deductive argument that uses this form.

Premise: _____

Premise: _____

Conclusion: _____

Modus Tollens

A third commonly used valid deductive form has the name *modus tollens*—that is, "denying the consequence"—and is illustrated by the following example:

Premise: If Michael were a good friend, he would lend me his car for the weekend.

Premise: Michael refuses to lend me his car for the weekend.

Conclusion: Therefore, Michael is not really a good friend.

When you reason in this fashion, you are using the following argument structure:

Premise: If *A* (Michael is a good friend), then *B* (He will lend me his car).

Premise: Not *B* (He won't lend me his car).

Conclusion: Therefore, not *A* (He's not really a good friend).

Again, like other valid reasoning forms, this form is valid no matter what subject is being considered. For instance,

Premise: If alcoholic beverage manufacturers were really concerned about the health of young people, they would not target them in their advertising and promotions.

Premise: Alcoholic beverage manufacturers do target young people in much of their advertising and promotions.

Conclusion: Therefore, alcoholic beverage manufacturers are not really concerned about the health of young people.

This conclusion—and any other conclusion produced by this form of reasoning—can be considered accurate *if* the reasons are true. In this case, the second premise would probably be easier to verify than the first.

Review the dialogue at the beginning of this chapter to see if you can identify a deductive argument that uses this reasoning form.

Premise: _____

Premise: _____

Conclusion: _____

Disjunctive Syllogism

A fourth common type of valid deductive argument is known as a *disjunctive syllogism,* an argument form in which we reason from several "either/or" alternatives presented. This form is illustrated in the following example:

Premise: Either I left my wallet on my dresser or I have lost it.

Premise: The wallet is not on my dresser.

Conclusion: Therefore, I must have lost it.

When you reason in this way, you are using the following argument structure:

Premise: Either *A* (I left my wallet on my dresser) or *B* (I have lost it).

Premise: Not *A* (I didn't leave it on my dresser).

Conclusion: Therefore, *B* (I have lost it).

This valid reasoning form can be applied to any number of situations and still yield valid results. For example,

Premise: Either your stomach trouble is caused by what you are eating or it is caused by nervous tension.

Premise: You tell me that you have been taking special care with your diet.

Conclusion: Therefore, your stomach trouble is caused by nervous tension.

To determine the accuracy of the conclusion, you must determine the accuracy of the premises. If they are true, then the conclusion must be true.

Review the dialogue at the beginning of this chapter to see if you can identify a deductive argument that uses this reasoning form.

Premise: _____

Premise: _____

Conclusion: _____

All these basic argument forms—applying a general rule, *modus ponens, modus tollens,* and disjunctive syllogism—are found not only in informal, every-day conversations but also at more sophisticated levels of thinking. They appear in academic disciplines, in scientific inquiry, in debates on social issues, and so on. Many other argument forms—both deductive and inductive—also are a part of human reasoning. By sharpening your understanding of these ways of thinking, you will be better able to make sense of the world by constructing and evaluating effective arguments.

Analyze the arguments below by completing the following operations.

1. Summarize the reasons and conclusions given.

2. Identify which, if any, of the deductive argument forms are used:
   - Applying a general rule
   - *Modus ponens* (affirming the antecedent)
   - *Modus tollens* (denying the consequence)
   - Disjunctive syllogism (reasoning from several "either/or" alternatives)

3. Evaluate the truth of the reasons that support the conclusion.

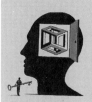

For if the brain is a machine of ten billion nerve cells and the mind can somehow be explained as the summed activity of a finite number of chemical and electrical reactions, [then] boundaries limit the human prospect—we are biological and our souls cannot fly free.

Edward O. Wilson, *On Human Nature*

The state is by nature clearly prior to the family and to the individual, since the whole is of necessity prior to the part.

Aristotle, *Politics*

There now is sophisticated research that strongly suggests a deterrent effect [of capital punishment]. Furthermore, the principal argument against the deterrent effect is weak. The argument is that in most jurisdictions where capital punishment has been abolished there has been no immediate, sharp increase in what had been capital crimes. But in those jurisdictions, the actual act of abolition was an insignificant event because for years the death penalty had been imposed rarely, if at all. Common sense—which deserves deference until it is refuted—suggests that the fear of death can deter some premeditated crimes, including some murders.

George F. Will, *Cleveland Plain-Dealer*, March 13, 1981

To fully believe in something, to truly understand something, one must be intimately acquainted with its opposite. One should not adopt a creed by default, because no alternative is known. Education should prepare students for the "real world" not by segregating them from evil but by urging full confrontation to test and modify the validity of the good.

Robert Baron, "In Defense of 'Teaching' Racism, Sexism, and Fascism"

The inescapable conclusion is that society secretly *wants* crime, *needs* crime, and gains definite satisfactions from the present mishandling of it! We condemn crime; we punish offenders for it; but we need it. The crime and punishment ritual is a part of our lives. We need crimes to wonder at, to enjoy vicariously, to discuss and speculate about, and to publicly deplore. We need criminals to identify ourselves with, to envy secretly, and to punish stoutly. They do for us the forbidden, illegal things we *wish* to do and, like scapegoats of old, they bear the burdens of our displaced guilt and punishment—"the iniquities of us all."

Karl Menninger, "The Crime of Punishment"

The extreme vulnerability of a complex industrial society to intelligent, targeted terrorism by a very small number of people may prove the fatal challenge to which Western states have no adequate response. Counterforce alone will never suffice. The real challenge of the true terrorist is to the basic values of a society. If there is no commitment to shared values in Western society—and if none are imparted in our amoral institutions of higher learning—no increase in police and burglar alarms will suffice to preserve our society from the specter that haunts us—not a bomb from above but a gun from within.

James Billington, "The Gun Within"

Thinking Activity 9.4

Select a current issue of interest to you. (Possible choices are animal rights, helmet laws for motorcyclists, mandatory AIDS testing, and drug testing for athletes.) Following these guidelines, construct an argumentative essay that explores the issue.

1. Locate two articles about the issue you have selected, and use them as resources. (It would be helpful to find articles with opposing points of view.)

2. List arguments on both sides of the issue, organizing them into premises and conclusions.

3. Make notes evaluating the strengths and weaknesses of each argument.

4. Identify the most important arguments, and make an outline including the arguments you plan to use in the essay.

5. Using the outline and notes as a guide, write your essay. The essay should begin with a paragraph that introduces the issue and should end with a paragraph that sums it up.

Inductive Arguments

Although *deductive* forms of reasoning are crucial to understanding the world and making informed decisions, much of our reasoning is nondeductive. The various nondeductive argument forms are typically included under the general category of *inductive* reasoning. In contrast to deductive arguments, inductive arguments rarely provide conclusions that are totally certain. The premises merely offer some evidence in support of the conclusion.

> **Inductive Argument**
>
> Argument form in which one reasons from premises that are known or assumed to be true to a conclusion that is supported by the premises but does not follow logically from them.

When you reason inductively, your premises provide evidence that makes it more or less probable (but not certain) that the conclusion is true. The following statements are examples of conclusions reached through inductive reasoning:

1. A recent Gallup poll reported that 74% of the American public believes that abortion should remain legalized.

2. On the average, a person with a college degree will earn over $830,000 more in his or her lifetime than a person with just a high school diploma.

3. In a recent survey, twice as many doctors interviewed stated that if they were stranded on a desert island, they would prefer Bayer Aspirin to Extra Strength Tylenol.

4. The outbreak of food poisoning at the end-of-year school party was probably caused by the squid salad.

5. The devastating disease AIDS is caused by a particularly complex virus that may not be curable.

6. The solar system is probably the result of an enormous explosion—a "big bang"—that occurred billions of years ago.

The first three statements are forms of inductive reasoning known as *empirical generalization,* a general statement about an entire group made on the basis of observing some members of the group. The final three statements are examples of *causal reasoning,* a form of inductive reasoning in which it is claimed an event (or events) is the result of another event (or events). We will be exploring the ways each of these forms of inductive reasoning function in our lives and in various fields of study.

In addition to examining various ways of reasoning logically and effectively, we will also explore certain forms of reasoning that are not logical and, as a result, usually not effective. These ways of pseudoreasoning (false reasoning) are often termed *fallacies:* arguments that are not sound because of various errors in reasoning. Fallacious reasoning is typically used to influence others. It seeks to persuade not on the basis of sound arguments and critical thinking but rather on the basis of illogical factors.

> ### Fallacies
> Unsound arguments that are often persuasive because they appear to be logical, they usually appeal to our emotions and prejudices, and they often support conclusions that we want to believe are accurate.

Empirical Generalization

Have you ever wondered how the major television and radio networks can accurately predict election results hours before the polls close? These predictions are made possible by the power of *empirical generalization,*

Empirical Generalization:
Empirical generalizations are general statements made about an entire group based on observing some members of the group. Although an important form of reasoning, care must be taken to avoid the fallacy of hasty generalization.

which is defined as reasoning from a limited sample to a general conclusion based on this sample.

> **Empirical Generalization**
>
> A form of inductive reasoning in which a general statement is made about an entire group (the "target population") based on observing some members of the group (the "sample population").

Network election predictions, as well as public opinion polls that occur throughout a political campaign, are based on interviews with a select number of people. Ideally, pollsters would interview everyone in the *target population* (in this case, voters), but doing so would hardly be practical. Instead, the pollsters select a relatively small group of individuals from the target population, known as a *sample,* who they have determined will adequately represent the group as a whole. Pollsters believe that they can then generalize the opinions of this smaller group to the target population. And with a few notable exceptions (such as in the 1948 presidential election, when New York Governor Thomas Dewey went to bed believing he had been elected President and woke up a loser to Harry Truman), these results are highly accurate. (Polling techniques are much more sophisticated today than they were in 1948.)

There are three key criteria for evaluating inductive arguments:

■ Is the sample known?

■ Is the sample sufficient?

■ Is the sample representative?

Is the Sample Known?

An inductive argument is only as strong as the sample on which it is based. For example, sample populations described in vague and unclear terms—"highly placed sources" or "many young people interviewed," for example—provide a treacherously weak foundation for generalizing to larger populations. In order for an inductive argument to be persuasive, the sample population should be explicitly *known* and clearly identified. Natural and social scientists take great care in selecting the members in the sample groups, and this selection is an important part of the data and is made available to outside investigators who may want to evaluate and verify the results.

Is the Sample Sufficient?

The second criterion for evaluating inductive reasoning is to consider the *size* of the sample. It should be large enough to give an accurate sense of the group as a whole. In the polling example discussed earlier, you would be concerned if only a few registered voters were interviewed and the results of these interviews were generalized to a much larger population. Overall, the larger the sample, the more reliable the inductive conclusions. Natural and social scientists have developed precise guidelines for determining the size of the sample needed to achieve reliable results. For example, poll results are often accompanied by a qualification such as "These results are subject to an error factor of ± 3 percentage points." If the sample reveals that 47% of those interviewed prefer candidate X, then we can reliably state that 44% to 50% of the target population prefer candidate X. Because a sample is usually a small portion of the target population, we can rarely say that the two match each other exactly—there must always be some room for variation. The exceptions are situations in which the target population is completely homogeneous. For example, tasting one sip from a container of milk is usually enough to tell you whether or not the entire container is fresh or sour.

Is the Sample Representative?

The third crucial element in effective inductive reasoning is the *representativeness* of the sample. If you are to generalize with confidence from the sample to the target population, then you have to be sure the sample is similar in all relevant aspects to the larger group from which it is drawn. For instance, in the polling example the sample population should reflect the same percentage of men and women, of Democrats and Republicans, of young and old, and so on, as the target population. It is obvious that many characteristics, such as hair color, favorite food, and shoe size, are not relevant to the comparison. However, the better the sample reflects the target population in terms of *relevant* qualities, then the better the accuracy of the generalizations. On the other hand, when the sample is *not* representative of the target population—for example, if the election pollsters interviewed only women between the ages of thirty and thirty-five—then the sample is termed *biased,* and any generalizations made about the target population will be highly suspect.

How do you ensure that the sample is representative of the target population? One important device is *random selection*, a selection strategy in which every member of the target population has an equal chance of being included in the sample. For example, the various techniques used to select winning lottery tickets are supposed to be random—each ticket is supposed to have an equal chance of winning. In complex cases of inductive reasoning—such as polling—random selection is often combined with the confirmation that all the important categories in the population are adequately represented. For example, an election pollster would want to be certain that all significant geographical areas are included, and the pollster would then randomly select individuals from within those areas to compose the sample.

Understanding the principles of inductive reasoning is crucial to effective thinking because you are continually challenged to construct and evaluate inductive arguments in your life.

Thinking Activity 9.5

Read the following passages, which are examples of inductive arguments. For each argument, evaluate the quality of the thinking by answering these questions:

1. Is the sample known?
2. Is the sample sufficient?
3. Is the sample representative?
4. Do you believe that the conclusions are likely to be accurate? Why or why not?

1. In a study of a possible relationship between pornography and antisocial behavior, questionnaires went out to 7,500 psychiatrists and psychoanalysts, whose listing in the directory of the American Psychological Association indicated clinical experience. Over 3,400 of these professionals responded. The result: 7.4 percent of the psychiatrists and psychologists had cases in which they were convinced that pornography was a causal factor in antisocial behavior; an additional 9.4 percent were suspicious; 3.2 percent did not commit themselves; and 80 percent said they had no cases in which a causal connection was suspected.

2. A survey by the Sleep Disorder Clinic of the VA hospital in La Jolla, California (involving more than one million people), revealed that people who sleep more than ten hours a night have a death rate 80 percent higher than those who sleep only seven or eight hours. Men who sleep less than four hours a night have a death rate 180 percent higher, and women with less [than four hours of] sleep have a rate 40 percent higher. This might be taken as indicating that too much and too little sleep cause death.

3. "U.S. Wastes Food Worth Millions." Americans in the economic middle waste more food than their rich and poor counterparts, according to a study published Saturday. Carried out in Tucson, Arizona, by University of Arizona students under the direction of Dr. William L. Rathje, the study analyzed 600 bags of garbage each week for three years from lower-, middle-, and upper-income neighborhoods. They found that city residents throw out around 10 percent of the food they brought home—about 9,500 tons of food each year. The figure amounts to $9 to $11 million worth of food. Most of the waste occurred in middle-class neighborhoods. Both the poor and the wealthy were significantly more frugal.

4. "Young People's Moral Compasses." A recent survey of 5,012 students from 4th grade through high school yields important insights about how young people make moral decisions. Asked how they would decide what to do if "unsure of what was right or wrong in a particular situation," these were the responses and how they were described by the researchers:

■ 23% said they would "do what was best for everyone involved," an orientation the researchers labeled "civic humanist."

■ 20% would "follow the advice of an authority, such as a parent, teacher or youth leader"—"conventionalist."

■ 18% of respondents said they would do what would make them "happy" —"expressivist."

■ 16% would "do what God or Scriptures" say "is right"—"theistic."

■ 10% would "do what would improve their own situations"—"utilitarian."

■ 9% did not know.

■ 3% wrote that they would follow "conscience."

When young people were asked their beliefs about anything from lying, stealing and using drugs to abortion or reasons for choosing a job, these rudimentary ethical systems or "moral compasses" turned out to be more important than the background factors that social scientists habitually favor in their search for explanations, like economic status, sex, race and even religious practice.

New York Times, March 17, 1990

Fallacies of False Generalization

When you construct empirical generalizations, you try to reach a general conclusion based on a limited number of examples and then apply this conclusion to other examples. Although this process is extremely useful in helping you make sense of the world, it can also give rise to fallacious ways of thinking, including the following:

■ Hasty generalization

■ Sweeping generalization

■ False dilemma

Hasty Generalization

Consider the following examples of reasoning. Do you think that the arguments are sound? Why or why not?

My boyfriends have never shown any real concern for my feelings. My conclusion is that men are insensitive, selfish, and emotionally superficial.

My mother always gets upset over insignificant things. This leads me to believe that women are very emotional.

In both of these cases, a general conclusion has been reached that is based on a very small sample. As a result, the reasons provide very weak support for the conclusions being developed. It just does not make good sense to generalize from a few individuals to all men or all women. The conclusion is *hasty* because the sample is not large enough and/or not representative enough to provide adequate justification for the generalization. Of course, a similar generalization could be more warranted than the two given here because the conclusion is based on a sample that is larger and more representative of the group as a whole:

> I have done a lot of research in a variety of automotive publications on the relationship between the size of cars and the gas mileage they get. In general, I think it makes sense to conclude that large cars tend to get fewer miles per gallon than smaller cars.

In this case, the conclusion is generalized from a larger and more representative sample than those in the preceding two arguments. As a result, the reason for the last argument provides much stronger support for the conclusion.

Unfortunately, many of the general conclusions we reach about groups of people are not legitimate because they are based on samples that are too small or are not representative. In these cases, the generalization is a distortion because it creates a false impression of the group that is being represented. These illegitimate generalizations are sometimes called *stereotypes*. Stereotypes affect our perception of the world because they encourage us to form an inaccurate idea of an entire group based on insufficient evidence ("Men are insensitive and selfish"). Even if we have experiences that conflict with our stereotype ("This man is not insensitive and selfish"), we tend to overlook the conflicting information in favor of the stereotype ("All men are insensitive and selfish—except for this one").

Thinking Activity 9.6

There are many stereotypes in our culture—in advertising, in the movies, on television, in literature, and so on.

1. Describe one such stereotype and identify some specific examples of places where this stereotype is found.
2. Explain the reasons why you think this stereotype developed.
3. Have you ever been the victim of a stereotyped generalization? Describe the experience and explain why you believe that you were subjected to this kind of generalization.

Sweeping Generalization

Whereas the fallacy of hasty generalization deals with errors in the process of generalizing, the fallacy of *sweeping generalization* focuses on difficulties in the process of interpreting. Consider the following examples of reasoning. Do you think that the arguments are sound? Why or why not?

Vigorous exercise contributes to overall good health. Therefore, vigorous exercise should be practiced by recent heart-attack victims, people who are out of shape, and women who are about to give birth.

People should be allowed to make their own decisions, providing that their actions do not harm other people. Therefore, people who are trying to commit suicide should be left alone to do what they want.

In both of these cases, generalizations that are true in most cases have been deliberately applied to instances that are clearly intended to be exceptions to the generalizations because of special features. Of course, the use of sweeping generalizations should stimulate you to clarify the generalization, rephrasing it to exclude instances that have special features. For example, the first generalization could be reformulated as "Vigorous exercise contributes to overall good health, *except for* recent heart-attack victims, people out of shape, and women who are about to give birth." Sweeping generalizations become dangerous only when they are accepted without critical analysis and reformulation.

Read the following examples of sweeping generalizations, and in each case reformulate the statement so that it becomes a legitimate generalization:

1. A college education stimulates you to develop as a person and prepares you for many professions. Therefore, all persons should attend college, no matter what career they are interested in.

   _____

   _____

2. Drugs such as heroin and morphine are addictive and therefore qualify as dangerous drugs. This means that they should never be used, even as painkillers in medical situations.

   _____

   _____

3. Once criminals have served time for the crimes they have committed, they have paid their debt to society and should be permitted to work at any job they choose.

   _____

   _____

False Dilemma

The fallacy of the *false dilemma*—also known as the either/or fallacy or the black-or-white fallacy—occurs when you are asked to choose between two extreme alternatives without being able to consider additional options. For example, someone may say, "Either you're for me or against me," meaning that a choice has to be made between these alternatives. Sometimes giving people only two choices on an issue makes sense ("If you decide to swim the English Channel, you'll either make it or you won't"). At other times, however, viewing situations in such extreme terms may be a serious error—it would mean viewing a complicated situation in terms that are much too simple.

The following statements are examples of false dilemmas. After analyzing the fallacy in each case, suggest different alternatives than those presented.

> *Example:* "Everyone in Germany is a National Socialist—the few outside the party are either lunatics or idiots." (Adolf Hitler, quoted by the *New York Times,* April 5, 1938)
>
> *Analysis:* This is a gross mischaracterization. Hitler is saying that if you are not a Nazi, then you are a lunatic or an idiot. By limiting the population to these groups, Hitler is simply ignoring all the people who do not qualify as Nazis, lunatics, or idiots.

1. "America—love it or leave it!"

   _____

   _____

2. "She loves me; she loves me not."

   _____

   _____

3. "If you're not part of the solution, then you're part of the problem." (Eldridge Cleaver)

   _____

   _____

Causal Reasoning

A second major type of induction is *causal reasoning*.

> **Causal Reasoning**
>
> A form of inductive reasoning in which an event (or events) is claimed to be the result of another event (or events).

As you use your thinking abilities to try to understand the world we live in, you often ask the question "Why did that happen?" For example, if the engine of your car is running roughly, your natural question is "What's wrong?" If you wake up one morning with an upset stomach, you usually want to figure out "What's the cause?" Or maybe your softball team has been losing recently. You may wonder "What's going on?" In each of these cases you assume that there is some factor (or factors) responsible for what is occurring, some *cause* (or causes) that results in the *effect* (or effects) you are observing (the rough engine, the upset stomach).

As we saw in Chapter Seven, causality is one of the basic patterns of thinking you use to organize and make sense of your experience. For instance, imagine how bewildered you would feel if a mechanic looked at your car engine and told you there was no explanation for your poorly running engine. Or suppose you take your upset stomach to the doctor, who examines you and then concludes that there is no possible causal explanation for the malady. In each case you would be understandably skeptical of the diagnosis and would probably seek another opinion.

The Scientific Method

Causal reasoning is also the backbone of the natural and social sciences; it is responsible for the remarkable understanding of our world that has been achieved. The *scientific method* works on the assumption that the world is constructed in a complex web of causal relationships that can be discovered through systematic investigation. Scientists have devised an organized approach for discovering causal relationships and testing the accuracy of conclusions. The sequence of steps is as follows:

Steps in the Scientific Method

1. Identify an event or relationship between events to be investigated.
2. Gather information about the event (or events).
3. Develop a theory or hypothesis to explain what is happening.
4. Test the theory or hypothesis through experimentation.
5. Evaluate the theory or hypothesis.

Scientific Hypothesis: Scientists propose possible explanations called hypotheses to account for a set of facts and to use as a basis for further investigation.

How does this sequence work when applied to the situation of the rough-running engine we mentioned earlier?

1. *Identify an event to be investigated.* In this case, the event is obvious—your car engine is running poorly, and you want to discover the cause of the problem so you can fix it.

2. *Gather information about the event.* This step involves locating any relevant information about the situation that will help you solve the problem. You initiate this step by asking and trying to answer a variety of questions: When did the engine begin running poorly? Was it abrupt or gradual? When did I last get a tune-up? Are there other mechanical difficulties that might be related?

3. *Develop a theory or hypothesis to explain what is happening.* After reviewing the relevant information, you want to identify the most likely explanation of what has happened. This possible explanation is known as a *hypothesis.* (A *theory* is normally a more complex model that involves a number of interconnected hypotheses, such as the theory of quantum mechanics in physics.)

Hypothesis

A possible explanation that is introduced to account for a set of facts and that can be used as a basis for further investigation.

Although a hypothesis may be suggested by the information you have, the hypothesis goes beyond the information and so must be tested before you commit yourself to it. In this case the hypothesis you might settle on is "water in the gas." This hypothesis was suggested by your recollection that the engine troubles began right after you bought gas in the pouring rain. This hypothesis may be correct, or it may be incorrect—you have to test it to find out. When you devise a plausible hypothesis to be tested, you should keep three general guidelines in mind:

■ *Explanatory power:* The hypothesis should effectively explain the event you are investigating. A hypothesis that damaged windshield wipers are causing the engine problems doesn't seem to provide an adequate explanation of the difficulties.

■ *Economy:* The hypothesis should not be unnecessarily complex. An explanation that the engine difficulty is the result of sabotage by an unfriendly neighbor is possible but unlikely. There are simpler and more direct explanations we should test first.

■ *Predictive power:* The hypothesis should allow you to make various predictions to test its accuracy. If the "water in the gas" hypothesis is accurate, you can predict that removing the water from the gas tank and gas line should clear up the difficulty.

4. *Test the theory or hypothesis through experimentation.* Once you identify a hypothesis that meets these three guidelines, the next task is to devise an experiment to test its accuracy. In the case of your troubled car, you could test your hypothesis by pouring several containers of "dry-gas" into the tank, blowing out the gas line, and cleaning the carburetor or fuel injectors. By removing the moisture in the gas system, you should be able to determine whether the hypothesis is correct.

5. *Evaluate the theory or hypothesis.* After reviewing the results, you usually can assess the accuracy of your hypothesis. If the engine runs smoothly after you remove moisture from the gas line, then this strong evidence supports your hypothesis. On the other hand, if the engine does *not* run smoothly after your efforts, then this persuasive evidence suggests your hypothesis was not correct. However, there is a third possibility. Removing the moisture from the gas system might improve the engine's performance somewhat but not entirely. In that case, you might want to construct a *revised* hypothesis along the lines of "Water in the gas system is partially responsible for the rough-running engine, but another cause (or causes) might be involved as well."

If the evidence does not support your hypothesis or supports a revised version of it, you then begin the entire process again by identifying and testing a new hypothesis. The natural and social sciences engage in an ongoing process of developing theories and hypotheses and testing them through experimental

The Scientific Method:
The scientific method works on the assumption that the world is constructed in a complex web of causal relationships that can be discovered through systematic investigation.

Figure 9.2.

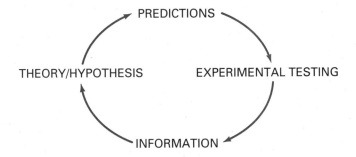

PREDICTIONS

THEORY/HYPOTHESIS   EXPERIMENTAL TESTING

INFORMATION

design. Many theories and hypotheses are much more complex than our "water in the gas" and take years of generating, revising, and testing. For example, determining the subatomic structure of the universe and finding cures for various kinds of cancers have been the subjects of countless theories, hypotheses, and experiments. We might diagram this operation of the scientific process as follows:

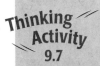

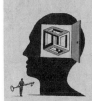

Thinking Activity 9.7

Select one of the following situations or describe a situation of your own choosing. Then analyze the situation by working through the steps of the scientific method listed directly after.

- Situation 1: You have been experiencing unexplained tension and headaches.
- Situation 2: Your grades have been declining all semester.
- Situation 3: (You choose.)

1. *Identify an event or a relationship between events to be investigated.* Describe the situation you have selected.

2. *Gather information about the event.* Elaborate the situation by providing additional details. Be sure to include a variety of possible causes for the event.

3. *Develop a theory or hypothesis to explain what is happening.* Based on the information you have described, identify a plausible hypothesis that (a) explains what occurred, (b) is clear and direct, and (c) leads to predictions that can be tested.

4. *Test the theory or hypothesis through experimentation.* Design a way of testing your hypothesis that results in evidence proving or disproving it.

5. *Evaluate the theory or hypothesis.* Describe the results of your experiment and explain whether the results lead you to accept, reject, or revise your hypothesis.

Controlled Experiments

Although your analysis of causal reasoning has focused on relationships between specific events, much of scientific research addresses causal factors influencing populations composed of many individuals. In these cases, the causal relationships tend to be much more complex than the simple formulation *A* causes *B*. For example, on every package of cigarettes sold in the United States appears a message such as this: "Surgeon General's Warning: Smoking Causes Lung Cancer, Heart Disease, Emphysema, And May Complicate Pregnancy." This does not mean that every cigarette smoked has a direct impact on one's health, nor does it mean that everyone who smokes moderately, or even heavily, will die prematurely of cancer, heart disease, or emphysema. Instead, the statement means that if you habitually smoke, your chances of developing one of the diseases normally associated with smoking are significantly higher than are those of someone who does not smoke or who smokes only occasionally. How were scientists able to arrive at this conclusion?

The reasoning strategy scientists use to reach conclusions like this one is the *controlled experiment*, and it is one of the most powerful reasoning strategies ever developed. For example, imagine you have developed a new cream you believe will help cure baldness, and you want to evaluate its effectiveness. What do you do? To begin with, you have to identify a group of people that accurately represents all the balding men and women in the world, because testing it on all balding people simply isn't feasible. Your approach involves following the guidelines for inductive reasoning we explored in the last section. The group you select to test must be *representative* of all balding people (known as the *target population*), because you hope your product will grow hair on all types of heads. For example, if you selected only men between the ages of twenty and thirty to test, the experiment would establish only whether the product works for men of these ages. Additional experiments would have to be conducted for women and other age groups. This representative group is known as a *sample*. Scientists have developed strategies for selecting sample groups to ensure that they mirror the larger group from which they are drawn.

Once you have selected your sample of balding men and women—say, 200 people—the next step is to divide the sample into two groups of 100 people who are alike in all relevant respects. The best way to ensure that the groups are essentially alike is through the technique of *random selection*, which means that each individual selected has the same chance of being chosen as everyone else. You then designate one group as the *experimental group* and the other group as the *control group*. You next give the individuals in the experimental group treatments of your hair-growing cream, and you give either no treatments or a harmless, non-hair-growing cream to the control group. At the conclusion of the testing period, you compare the experimental group with the control group to evaluate hair gain and hair loss.

Suppose that a number of individuals in the experimental group do indeed show evidence of more new hair growth than the control group. How can we be sure this is because of the cream and not simply a chance occurrence? Scientists have developed a statistical formula based on the size of the sample and the frequency of the observed effects. For example, imagine that thirteen persons in your experimental group show evidence of new hair growth, whereas no one in the control group shows any such evidence. Statisticians have determined that we can say with 95% certainty that the new hair growth was caused by your new cream—in other words, the results were not merely the result of chance. This type of experimental result is usually expressed by saying that the experimental results were significant at the 0.05 level, a standard criterion in experimental research.

Thinking Activity 9.8

Read the following experimental situations. For each situation,

1. Describe the proposed causal relationship (the theory or hypothesis).

2. Evaluate:

   a. the representativeness of the sample

   b. the randomness of the division into experimental and control groups

3. Explain how well the experimental results support the proposed theory or hypothesis.

1. "Birthdays: A Matter of Life and Death." A new study, based on 2,745,149 deaths from natural causes, has found that men tend to die just before their birthdays, while women tend to die just after their birthdays. Thus an approaching birthday seems to prolong the life of women and precipitate death in men. The study, published in the journal *Psychosomatic Medicine*, found 3 percent more deaths than expected among women in the week after a birthday and a slight decline the week before. For men, deaths peaked just before birthdays and showed no rise above normal afterward.

    New York Times, September 22, 1993

2. "Cheating on Sleep." Experts in sleep behavior and sleep disorders have found that a majority of people are sleeping at least an hour to 90 minutes less each night than they should, based on a series of studies of several hundred college and graduate students between the ages of 18 and 30. In one representative experiment with young adults who were generally healthy and got an average of seven to eight hours sleep a night, sleep researchers discovered that 20 percent of these apparently normal students could fall asleep almost instantaneously throughout the day if allowed to lie down in a darkened room, evidence that they were sleep deprived. Researchers further discovered that even the students who seemed alert and did not quickly fall asleep under test conditions could benefit from more sleep. If they spent one week getting to bed a hour to 90 minutes earlier than usual, the students improved their performance markedly on psychological and cognitive tests. Such results

⟶

seem to suggest that most people who think they are sleeping enough would be better off with an extra portion of rest.

New York Times, May 15, 1990

3. "Nicotine Patches: Cure or Con?" The ads seem too good to be true: Slap a patch on the arm, change it every day, and two or three months later, you've kicked the habit. However, the truth is more elusive. Studies submitted to the F.D.A. indicated that smokers who used nicotine patches for 8 to 12 weeks were about twice as likely to have quit at the end of that period as were those who used dummy patches without nicotine. But as any smoker will testify, quitting is easy; the problem is that starting up again is even easier. So smokers wonder whether the patches will conquer their craving for nicotine and help them quit permanently or whether they will have to continue to purchase the patches at a cost of $300 for the 12 week supply. So far, research suggests that those who quit with the help of patches relapse at about the same rate as anyone else. In one series of follow-up studies, the share of individuals still smoke-free six months after they stopped using patches ranged from zero to 48 percent, as compared with a six-month success rate of zero to 40 percent for those who did not use them. Other studies indicate that success rates then continue to drop for at least a year, with patch users retaining some of their initial edge. Taken together, the figures suggest that the patches can help a small fraction of smokers. Each year 17 million Americans try to quit smoking, but only 1.3 million manage to do so.

New York Times, April 8, 1992

4. "Left-Handedness May Be Hazardous to Your Health." A survey of 5000 people by Stanley Coren found that while 15 percent of the population at age 10 was left-handed, there was a pronounced drop-off as people grew older, leaving 5 percent among 50-year-olds and less than 1 percent for those aged 80 and above. Where have all the lefties gone? They seem to have died. Lefties have a shorter life expectancy than righties, by an average of 9 years in the general population, apparently due to the ills and accidents they are more likely to suffer by having to live in a "righthanded world."

New York Times, January 23, 1992

Causal Fallacies

Because causality plays such a dominant role in the way we make sense of the world, it is not surprising that people make many mistakes and errors in judgment in trying to determine causal relationships. The following are some of the most common fallacies associated with causality:

■ Questionable cause

■ Misidentification of the cause

■ False cause

■ Slippery slope

Questionable Cause

The fallacy of *questionable cause* occurs when someone presents a causal relationship for which no real evidence exists. Superstitious beliefs, such as "If you break a mirror you will have seven years of bad luck," usually fall into this category. Some people feel that astrology, a system of beliefs tying one's personality and fortunes to the position of the planets at the moment of the person's birth, also falls into this category.

Consider the following passage from St. Augustine's *Confessions.* Does it seem to support or deny the causal assertions of astrology? Why or why not?

> Firminus had heard from his father that when his mother had been pregnant with him, a slave belonging to a friend of his father's was also about to bear. . . . It happened that since the two women had their babies at the same instant, the men were forced to cast exactly the same horoscope for each newborn child down to the last detail, one for his son, the other for the little slave. . . . Yet Firminus, born to wealth in his parents' house, had one of the more illustrious careers in life . . . whereas the slave had no alleviation of his life's burden.

Other examples of this fallacy include explanations such as those given by fourteenth-century sufferers of the bubonic plague who claimed that "the Jews are poisoning the Christians' wells." This was particularly nonsensical since an equal percentage of Jews were dying of the plague as well. The evidence did not support the explanation.

Misidentification of the Cause

In causal situations you may not always be certain about what is causing what—in other words, what the cause is and what the effect is. *Misidentifying the cause* is easy to do. For example, which are the causes and which are the effects in the following pairs of items? Why?

- Poverty and alcoholism
- Headaches and tension
- Failure in school and personal problems
- Shyness and lack of confidence
- Drug dependency and emotional difficulties

Of course, sometimes a third factor is responsible for both of the effects you are examining. For example, your headaches and tension may both be the result of a third element—such as some new medication you are taking. If you overlook this possibility, you are said to commit the fallacy of *ignoring a common cause.* On the other hand, there also exists the fallacy of *assuming a common cause*—for example, assuming that both a sore toe and an earache stem from the same cause.

False Cause

The Latin name of the fallacy of *false cause* is *post hoc ergo propter hoc* ("After it, therefore because of it"). False cause refers to those situations in which, because two things occur close together in time, we assume one caused the other. For example, if your team wins the game each time you wear your favorite shirt, you might be tempted to conclude that the one event (wearing your favorite shirt) has some influence on the other event (winning the game). As a result, you might continue to wear this shirt "for good luck." It is easy to see how this sort of mistaken thinking can lead to all sorts of superstitious beliefs.

Consider the following causal conclusion arrived at by Mark Twain's fictional character Huckleberry Finn. How would you analyze the conclusion that he comes to?

> I've always reckoned that looking at the new moon over your left shoulder is one of the carelessest and foolishest things a body can do. Old Hank Bunker done it once, and bragged about it; and in less than two years he got drunk and fell off a shot tower and spread himself out so that he was just a kind of layer. . . . But anyway, it all come of looking at the moon that way, like a fool.

Can you identify any of your own superstitious beliefs or practices that might have been the result of *post hoc* thinking?

Slippery Slope

The causal fallacy of *slippery slope* is illustrated in the following advice:

> Don't smoke that first marijuana cigarette. If you do, it won't be long before you are smoking hashish. Then you will soon be popping pills and snorting cocaine. Before you know it, you will be hooked on heroin and you will end your life with a drug overdose in some rat-infested hotel room.

Slippery slope thinking asserts that one undesirable action will lead to a worse action, which will lead to a worse one still, all the way down the "slippery slope" to some terrible disaster at the bottom. Although this progression may indeed happen, there is certainly no causal guarantee that it will. Think about slippery slope scenarios for one of the following warnings:

1. If you get behind on one credit card payment . . .
2. If you fail that first test . . .
3. If the United States lets too many illegal immigrants enter the country . . .

———————————

Identify and explain the causal pitfalls illustrated in the following examples:

1. The person who won the lottery says that she dreamed the winning number. I'm going to start writing down the numbers in my dreams. _____

2. Yesterday I forgot to take my vitamins, and I immediately got sick. That mistake won't happen again! _____

_____

3. I'm warning you—if you start missing classes, it won't be long before you flunk out of school and ruin your future. _____

_____

4. I always take the first seat in the bus. Today I took another seat, and the bus broke down. And you accuse me of being superstitious! _____

_____

5. I think the reason I'm not doing well in school is because I'm just not interested. Also, I simply don't have enough time to study. _____

_____

Fallacies of Relevance

Many fallacious arguments appeal for support to factors that have little or nothing to do with the argument being offered. In these cases, false appeals substitute for sound reasoning and a critical examination of the issues. Such appeals, known as *fallacies of relevance,* include the following kinds of fallacious thinking:

- Appeal to authority
- Appeal to pity
- Appeal to fear
- Appeal to ignorance
- Appeal to personal attack

Appeal to Authority

When you rely on the advice of authorities, they should have legitimate expertise in the area in which they are advising—such as an experienced mechanic diagnosing a problem with a car. However, people often appeal to authorities who are not qualified to give an expert opinion. Consider the reasoning in the following advertisements. Do you think the arguments are sound? Why or why not?

- Hi. You've probably seen me out on the football field. After a hard day's work crushing halfbacks and sacking quarterbacks, I like to settle down with a cold, smooth Maltz beer.
- SONY. Ask anyone.
- Over 11 million women will read this ad. Only 16 will own the coat.

Fallacies:

Fallacies are unsound arguments that are often persuasive because they appeal to our emotions and prejudices in order to support illogical conclusions. Choosing fallacious reasoning leads to oversimplified and inaccurate conclusions, while choosing logical reasoning results in sound, intelligent conclusions.

Each of these arguments is intended to persuade you of the value of a product through the appeal to various authorities. In the first case, the authority is a well-known sports figure; in the second, the authority is large numbers of people; and in the third, the authority is a select few, appealing to our desire to be exclusive ("snob appeal"). Unfortunately, none of these authorities offers legitimate expertise about the product. Football players are not beer experts, large numbers of people are often misled, and exclusive groups of people are frequently mistaken in their beliefs. To evaluate authorities properly, you have to ask these questions:

■ What are the professional credentials on which the authorities' expertise is based?

■ Is their expertise in the area they are commenting on?

■ What potential bias or self-interest might influence the information presented?

Appeal to Pity

Consider the reasoning in the following arguments. Do you think the arguments are sound? Why or why not?

I know that I haven't completed my term paper, but I really think that I should be excused. This has been a very difficult semester for me. I caught every kind of flu that came around. In addition, my brother has a drinking problem, and this has been very upsetting to me. Also, my dog died.

I admit that my client embezzled money from the company, your honor. However, I would like to bring several facts to your attention. He is a family man, with a wonderful wife and two terrific children. He is an important member of the community. He is active in the church, coaches a Little League baseball team, and has worked very hard to be a good person who cares about people. I think that you should take these things into consideration in handing down your sentence.

In each of these arguments, the reasons offered to support the conclusions may indeed be true. However, they are not relevant to the conclusion. Instead of providing evidence that supports the conclusion, the reasons are designed to make you feel sorry for the person involved and agree with the conclusion out of sympathy. Although these appeals are often effective, the arguments are not sound. The probability of a conclusion can only be established by reasons that support and are relevant to the conclusion.

Appeal to Fear

Consider the arguments presented below, and evaluate them in terms of their soundness:

I'm afraid I don't think you deserve a raise. After all, there are many people who would be happy to have your job at the salary you are currently receiving. I would be happy to interview some of these people if you really think that you are underpaid.

If you continue to disagree with my interpretation of *The Catcher in the Rye,* I'm afraid you won't get a very good grade on your term paper.

In both of these arguments, the conclusions being suggested are supported by an appeal to fear, not by reasons that provide evidence for the conclusions. In the first case, the threat is if you do not let up on your salary demands, your job may be in jeopardy. In the second case, the threat is if you do not agree with the teacher's interpretation, then you will do badly on the assignment. In neither instance are the real issues—is a salary increase deserved? is the student's interpretation legitimate?—being discussed. People who appeal to fear to support their conclusions are interested only in prevailing, regardless of which position might be more justified.

Appeal to Ignorance

Evaluate the reasoning in the following arguments, and determine whether you think the reasoning is sound or not:

You say that you don't believe in God. But can you prove that He doesn't exist? If not, then you have to accept the conclusion that He does in fact exist.

Greco Tires are the best. No others have been proved better.

With me, abortion is not a problem of religion. It's a problem of the Constitution. I believe that until and unless someone can establish that the unborn child is not a living human being, then that child is already protected by the Constitution, which guarantees life, liberty, and the pursuit of happiness to all of us.

Ronald Reagan, October 8, 1984

When this argument form is used, the person offering the conclusion is asking his or her opponent to *disprove* the conclusion. If the opponent is unable to do so, then the conclusion is asserted to be true. This argument form is not valid because it is the job of the person proposing the argument to prove the conclusion. Simply because an opponent cannot *disprove* the conclusion offers no evidence that the conclusion is justified.

Appeal to Personal Attack

Consider the reasoning in the following arguments. Do you think the arguments are sound? Why or why not?

Your opinion on this issue is false. It's impossible to believe anything you say.

How can you have an intelligent opinion about abortion? You're not a woman, so this is a decision that you'll never have to make.

Well, I guess I'm reminded a little bit of what Will Rogers once said about Hoover. He said it's not what he doesn't know that bothers me, it's what he knows for sure just ain't so.

Walter Mondale characterizing Ronald Reagan, October 8, 1984

This argument form has been one of the most frequently used fallacies through the ages. Its effectiveness results from ignoring the issues of the argument and focusing instead on the personal qualities of the person making the argument. By trying to discredit the other person, the effort is being made to discredit the argument—no matter what reasons are offered. This fallacy is also referred to as the *ad hominem* argument, which means "to the man" rather than to the issue, and *poisoning the well,* because we are trying to ensure that any water drawn from our opponent's well will be treated as undrinkable.

The effort to discredit can take two forms, as illustrated in the examples above. The fallacy can be *abusive* in the sense you are directly attacking the credibility of your opponent (as in the third example). In addition, the fallacy can also be *circumstantial* in the sense that you are claiming that the person's circumstances, not character, render his or her opinion so biased or uninformed that it cannot be treated seriously (as in the second example). Other examples of the circumstantial form of the fallacy would include disregarding the views on nuclear plant safety given by an owner of a plant or ignoring the views of a company comparing a product it manufactures with competing products.

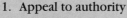

Locate (or develop) an example of each of the following kinds of false appeals. For each example, explain why you think that the appeal is not warranted.

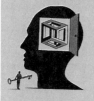

1. Appeal to authority
2. Appeal to pity
3. Appeal to fear
4. Appeal to ignorance
5. Appeal to personal attack

Reasoning Critically and Creatively

If we think of concepts as the vocabulary of thought, then the forms of reasoning constitute the rules of syntax that we use to organize concepts into intelligible patterns. The forms of reasoning we have been exploring in this and other chapters structure our thinking in informal, everyday contexts and also in more formal settings as well: academic disciplines, scientific inquiry, debates on social issues.

As with all forms of effective thinking, reasoning logically involves both the ability to think critically and to think creatively. For example, we think creatively when we construct effective arguments, design research models, or develop hypotheses as part of scientific inquiry. Similarly, we think critically when we evaluate the soundness of arguments, analyze the results of inductive research, or test hypotheses through controlled experiments. The final chapter of this text explores the way we use our reasoning process to develop and revise our beliefs about the world, beliefs that ultimately become incorporated into our philosophy of life.

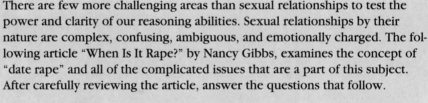

Exploring Sexual Relationships

There are few more challenging areas than sexual relationships to test the power and clarity of our reasoning abilities. Sexual relationships by their nature are complex, confusing, ambiguous, and emotionally charged. The following article "When Is It Rape?" by Nancy Gibbs, examines the concept of "date rape" and all of the complicated issues that are a part of this subject. After carefully reviewing the article, answer the questions that follow.

When Is It Rape?

Nancy Gibbs

Be careful of strangers and hurry home, says a mother to her daughter, knowing that the world is a frightful place but not wishing to swaddle a child in fear. Girls grow up scarred by caution and enter adulthood eager to shake free of their parents' worst nightmares. They still know to be wary of strangers. What they don't know is whether they have more to fear from their friends.

Most women who get raped are raped by people they already know—like the boy in biology class, or the guy in the office down the hall, or their friend's brother. The familiarity is enough to make them let down their guard, sometimes even enough to make them wonder afterward whether they were "really raped." What people think of as "real rape"—the assault by a monstrous stranger lurking in the shadows—accounts for only one out of five attacks.

So the phrase "acquaintance rape" was coined to describe the rest, all the cases of forced sex between people who already knew each other, however casually. But that was too clinical for headline writers, and so the popular term is the narrower "date rape," which suggests an ugly ending to a raucous night on the town.

These are not idle distinctions. Behind the search for labels is the central mythology about rape; that rapists are always strangers, and victims are women who ask for it. The mythology is hard to dispel because the crime is so rarely exposed. The experts guess—that's all they can do under the circumstances—that while one in four women will be raped in her lifetime, less than 10 percent will report the assault, and less than 5 percent of the rapists will go to jail.

Women charge that date rape is the hidden crime; men complain it is hard to prevent a crime they can't define. Women say it isn't taken seriously; men say it is a concept invented by women who like to tease but not take the consequences. Women say the date-rape debate is the first time the nation has talked frankly about sex; men say it is women's unconscious reaction to the excesses of the sexual revolution. Meanwhile, men and women argue among themselves about the "gray area" that surrounds the whole murky arena of sexual relations, and there is no consensus in sight.

In court, on campus, in conversation, the issue turns on the elasticity of the word *rape,* one of the few words in the language with the power to summon a shared image of a horrible crime.

At one extreme are those who argue that for the word to retain its impact, it must be strictly defined as forced sexual intercourse: a gang of thugs jumping a jogger in Central Park, a psychopath preying on old women in a housing complex, a man with an ice pick in a side street. To stretch the definition of the word risks stripping away its power. In this view, if it happened on a date, it wasn't rape. A romantic encounter is a context in which sex *could* occur, and so what omniscient judge will decide whether there was genuine mutual consent?

Others are willing to concede that date rape sometimes occurs, that sometimes a man goes too far on a date without a woman's consent. But this infraction, they say, is not as ghastly a crime as street rape, and it should not be taken as seriously. The New York *Post,* alarmed by the Willy Smith case, wrote in a recent editorial, "If the sexual encounter, *forced or not,* has been preceded by a series of consensual activities—drinking, a trip to the man's home, a walk on a deserted beach at three in the morning—the charge that's leveled against the alleged offender should, it seems to us, be different than the one filed against, say, the youths who raped and beat the jogger."

This attitude sparks rage among women who carry scars received at the hands of men they knew. It makes no difference if the victim shared a drink or a moonlit walk or even a passionate kiss, they protest, if the encounter ended with her being thrown to the ground and forcibly violated. Date rape is not about a misunderstanding, they say. It is not a communications problem. It is not about a woman's having regrets in the morning for a decision she made the night before. It is not about a "decision" at all. Rape is rape, and any form of forced sex—even between neighbors, co-workers, classmates and casual friends—is a crime.

A more extreme form of that view comes from activists who see rape as a metaphor, its definition swelling to cover any kind of oppression of women. Rape, seen in this light, can occur not only on a date but also in a marriage, not only by violent assault but also by psychological pressure. A Swarthmore College training pamphlet once explained that acquaintance rape

→

"spans a spectrum of incidents and behaviors, ranging from crimes legally defined as rape to verbal harassment and inappropriate innuendo." No wonder, then, that the battles become so heated. When innuendo qualifies as rape, the definitions have become so slippery that the entire subject sinks into a political swamp. The only way to capture the hard reality is to tell the story.

A 32-year-old woman was on business in Tampa last year for the Florida supreme court. Stranded at the courthouse, she accepted a lift from a lawyer involved in her project. As they chatted on the ride home, she recalls, "he was saying all the right things, so I started to trust him." She agreed to have dinner, and afterward, at her hotel door, he convinced her to let him come in to talk. "I went through the whole thing about being old-fashioned," she says. "I was a virgin until I was twenty-one. So I told him talk was all we were going to do."

But as they sat on the couch, she found herself falling asleep. "By now, I'm comfortable with him, and I put my head on his shoulder. He's not tried anything all evening, after all." Which is when the rape came. "I woke up to find him on top of me, forcing himself on me. I didn't scream or run. All I could think about was my business contacts and what if they saw me run out of my room screaming rape."

"I thought it was my fault. I felt so filthy, I washed myself over and over in hot water. Did he rape me?, I kept asking myself. I didn't consent. But who's gonna believe me? I had a man in my hotel room after midnight." More than a year later, she still can't tell the story without a visible struggle to maintain her composure. Police referred the case to the state attorney's office in Tampa, but without more evidence it decided not to prosecute. Although her attacker has admitted that he heard her say no, maintains the woman, "he says he didn't know that I meant no. He didn't feel he'd raped me, and he even wanted to see me again."

Her story is typical in many ways. The victim herself may not be sure right away that she has been raped, that she had said no and been physically forced into having sex anyway. And the rapist commonly hears but does not heed the protest. "A date rapist will follow through no matter what the woman wants because his agenda is to get laid," says Claire Walsh, a Florida-based consultant on sexual assaults. "First comes the dinner, then a dance, then a drink, then the coercion begins." Gentle persuasion gives way to physical intimidation with alcohol as the ubiquitous lubricant. "When that fails, force is used," she says. "Real men don't take no for an answer."

The Palm Beach case serves to remind women that if they go ahead and press charges, they can expect to go on trial along with their attacker, if not in a courtroom then in the court of public opinion. The New York *Times* caused an uproar on its own staff not only for publishing the victim's name but also for laying out in detail her background, her high-school grades, her driving record, along with an unattributed quote from a school official about her "little wild streak." A freshman at Carleton College in Minnesota, who says she was repeatedly raped for four hours by a fellow student, claims that she was asked at an administrative hearing if she performed oral sex on dates. In 1989 a man charged with raping at knife point a woman he knew was acquitted in Florida because his victim had been wearing lace shorts and no underwear.

From a purely legal point of view, if she wants to put her attacker in jail, the survivor had better be beaten as well as raped, since bruises become a badge of credibility. She had better have reported the crime right away, before taking the hours-long shower that she craves, before burning her clothes, before curling up with the blinds down. And she would do well to be a woman of shining character. Otherwise the strict constructionist definitions of rape will prevail in court. "Juries don't have a great deal of sympathy for the victim if she's a willing participant up to the nonconsensual sexual intercourse," says Norman Kinne, a prosecutor in Dallas. "They feel that many times the victim has placed herself in the situation." Absent eyewitnesses or broken bones, a case comes down to her word against his, and the mythology of rape rarely lends her the benefit of the doubt.

She should also hope for an all-male jury, preferably composed of fathers with daughters. Prosecutors have found that women tend to be harsh judges of one another—perhaps because to find a defendant guilty is to entertain two grim realities: that anyone might be a rapist, and that every woman could find herself a victim. It may be easier to believe, the experts muse, that at some level the victim asked for it. "But just because a woman makes a bad judgment, does that give the guy a moral right to rape her?" asks Dean Kilpatrick, director of the Crime Victim Research and Treatment Center at the Medical University of South Carolina. "The bottom line is, Why does a woman's having a drink give a man the right to rape her?"

Last week the Supreme Court waded into the debate with a 7-to-2 ruling that protects victims from being harassed on the witness stand with questions about their sexual history. The Justices, in their first decision on "rape shield laws," said an accused rapist could not present evidence about a previous sexual relationship with the victim unless he notified the court ahead of time. In her decision, Justice Sandra Day O'Connor wrote that "rape victims deserve heightened protection against surprise, harassment, and unnecessary invasions of privacy."

That was welcome news to prosecutors who understand the reluctance of victims to come forward. But there are other impediments to justice as well. An internal investigation of the Oakland police department found that officers ignored a quarter of all reports of sexual assaults or attempts, though 90 percent actually warranted investigation. Departments are getting better at educating officers in handling rape cases, but the courts remain behind. A New York City task force on women in the courts charged that judges and lawyers were routinely less inclined to believe a woman's testimony than a man's.

The present debate over degrees of rape is nothing new; all through history, rapes have been divided between those that mattered and those that did not. For the first few thousand years, the only rape that was punished was the defiling of a virgin, and that was viewed as a property crime. A girl's virtue was a marketable asset, and so a rapist was often ordered to pay the victim's father the equivalent of her price on the marriage market. In early Babylonian and Hebrew societies, a married woman who was raped suffered the same fate as an adulteress—death by stoning or drowning. Under William the Conqueror, the penalty for raping a virgin was castration and loss of both eyes—unless the violated woman agreed to marry her attacker, as she was often pressured to do. "Stealing an heiress" became a perfectly conventional means of taking—literally—a wife.

It may be easier to prove a rape case now, but not much. Until the 1960s it was virtually impossible without an eyewitness; judges were often required to instruct jurors that "rape is a charge easily made and hard to defend against; so examine the testimony of this witness with

→

caution." But sometimes a rape was taken very seriously, particularly if it involved a black man attacking a white woman—a crime for which black men were often executed or lynched.

Susan Estrich, author of *Real Rape,* considers herself a lucky victim. This is not just because she survived an attack 17 years ago by a stranger with an ice pick, one day before her graduation from Wellesley. It's because police, and her friends, believed her. "The first thing the Boston police asked was whether it was a black guy," recalls Estrich, now a University of Southern California law professor. When she said yes and gave the details of the attack, their re-action was, "So, you were really raped." It was an instructive lesson, she says, in understanding how racism and sexism are factored into perceptions of the crime.

A new twist in society's perception came in 1975, when Susan Brownmiller published her book *Against Our Will: Men, Women and Rape.* In it she attacked the concept that rape was a sex crime, arguing instead that it was a crime of violence and power over women. Throughout history, she wrote, rape has played a critical function. "It is nothing more or less than a conscious process of intimidation, by which *all men* keep *all women* in a state of fear."

Out of this contention was born a set of arguments that have become politically correct wisdom on campus and in academic circles. This view holds that rape is a symbol of women's vulnerability to male institutions and attitudes. "It's sociopolitical," insists Gina Rayfield, a New Jersey psychologist. "In our culture men hold the power, politically, economically. They're socialized not to see women as equals."

This line of reasoning has led some women, especially radicalized victims, to justify flinging around the term rape as a political weapon, referring to everything from violent sexual assaults to inappropriate innuendos. Ginny, a college senior who was really raped when she was sixteen, suggests that false accusations of rape can serve a useful purpose. "Penetration is not the only form of violation," she explains. In her view, rape is a subjective term, one that women must use to draw attention to other, nonviolent, even nonsexual forms of oppression. "If a woman did falsely accuse a man of rape, she may have had reasons to," Ginny says. "Maybe she wasn't raped, but he clearly violated her in some way."

Catherine Comins, assistant dean of student life at Vassar, also sees some value in this loose use of "rape." She says angry victims of various forms of sexual intimidation cry rape to regain their sense of power. "To use the word carefully would be to be careful for the sake of the violator, and the survivors don't care a hoot about him." Comins argues that men who are unjustly accused can sometimes gain from the experience. "They have a lot of pain, but it is not a pain that I would necessarily have spared them. I think it ideally initiates a process of self-exploration. 'How do I see women?' 'If I didn't violate her, could I have?' 'Do I have the potential to do to her what they say I did?' Those are good questions."

Taken to extremes, there is an ugly element of vengeance at work here. Rape is an abuse of power. But so are false accusations of rape, and to suggest that men whose reputations are destroyed might benefit because it will make them more sensitive is an attitude that is sure to backfire on women who are seeking justice for all victims. On campuses where the issue is most inflamed, male students are outraged that their names can be scrawled on a bathroom-wall list of rapists and they have no chance to tell their side of the story.

"Rape is what you read about in the New York *Post* about seventeen little boys raping a jogger in Central Park," says a male freshman at a liberal-arts college, who learned that he had been branded a rapist after a one-night stand with a friend. He acknowledges that they were both very drunk when she started kissing him at a party and ended up back in his room. Even through his haze, he had some qualms about sleeping with her: "I'm fighting against my hormonal instincts, and my moral instincts are saying, 'This is my friend and if I were sober, I wouldn't be doing this.'" But he went ahead anyway. "When you're drunk, and there are all sorts of ambiguity, and the woman says 'Please, please' and then she says no sometime later, even in the middle of the act, there still may very well be some kind of violation, but it's not the same thing. It's not rape. If you don't hear her say no, if she doesn't say it, if she's playing around with you—oh, I could get squashed for saying it—there is an element of say no, mean yes."

The morning after their encounter, he recalls, both students woke up hung over and eager to put the memory behind them. Only months later did he learn that she had told a friend that he had torn her clothing and raped her. At this point in the story, the accused man starts using the language of rape. "I felt violated," he says, "I felt like she was taking advantage of me when she was very drunk. I never heard her say 'No!,' 'Stop!,' anything." He is angry and hurt at the charges, worried that they will get around, shatter his reputation and force him to leave the small campus.

So here, of course, is the heart of the debate. If rape is sex without consent, how exactly should consent be defined and communicated, when and by whom? Those who view rape through a political lens tend to place all responsibility on men to make sure that their partners are consenting at every point of a sexual encounter. At the extreme, sexual relations come to resemble major surgery, requiring a signed consent form. Clinical psychologist Mary P. Koss of the University of Arizona in Tucson, who is a leading scholar on the issue, puts it rather bluntly: "It's the man's penis that is doing the raping, and ultimately he's reponsible for where he puts it."

Historically, of course, this has never been the case, and there are some who argue that it shouldn't be—that women too must take responsibility for their behavior, and that the whole realm of intimate encounters defies regulation from on high. Anthropologist Lionel Tiger has little patience for trendy sexual politics that make no reference to biology. Since the dawn of time, he argues, men and women have always gone to bed with different goals. In the effort to keep one's genes in the gene pool, "it is to the male advantage to fertilize as many females as possible, as quickly as possible and as efficiently as possible." For the female, however, who looks at the large investment she will have to make in the offspring, the opposite is true. Her concern is to "select" who "will provide the best set-up for their offspring." So, in general, "the pressure is on the male to be aggressive and on the female to be coy."

No one defends the use of physical force, but when the coercion involved is purely psychological, it becomes hard to assign blame after the fact. Journalist Stephanie Gutmann is an ardent foe of what she calls the date-rape dogmatists. "How can you make sex completely politically correct and completely safe?" she asks. "What a horribly bland, unerotic thing that would be! Sex is, by nature, a risky endeavor, emotionally. And desire is a violent emotion. These people in the date-rape movement have erected so many rules and regulations that I don't know how people can have erotic or desire-driven sex."

Nonsense, retorts Cornell professor Andrea Parrot, co-author of *Acquaintance Rape: The Hidden Crime*. Seduction should not be about lies, manipulation, game playing or coercion of any kind, she says. "Too bad that people think that the only way you can have passion and excitement and sex is if there are miscommunications, and one person is forced to do something he or she doesn't want to do." The very pleasures of sexual encounters should lie in the fact of mutual comfort and consent: "You can hang from the ceiling, you can use fruit, you can go crazy and have really wonderful sensual erotic sex, if both parties are consenting."

It would be easy to accuse feminists of being too quick to classify sex as rape, but feminists are to be found on all sides of the debate, and many protest the idea that all the onus is on the man. It demeans women to suggest that they are so vulnerable to coercion or emotional manipulation that they must always be escorted by the strong arm of the law. "You can't solve society's ills by making everything a crime," says Albuquerque attorney Nancy Hollander. "That comes out of the sense of overprotection of women, and in the long run that is going to be harmful to us."

What is lost in the ideological debate over date rape is the fact that men and women, especially when they are young, and drunk, and aroused, are not very good at communicating. "In many cases," says Estrich, "the man thought it was sex, and the woman thought it was rape, and they are both telling the truth." The man may envision a celluloid seduction, in which he is being commanding, she is being coy. A woman may experience the same event as a degrading violation of her will. That some men do not believe a woman's protests is scarcely surprising in a society so drenched with messages that women have rape fantasies and a desire to be overpowered.

By the time they reach college, men and women are loaded with cultural baggage, drawn from movies, television, music videos and "bodice ripper" romance novels. Over the years they have watched Rhett sweep Scarlett up the stairs in *Gone With the Wind;* or Errol Flynn, who was charged twice with statutory rape, overpower a protesting heroine who then melts in his arms; or Stanley rape his sister-in-law Blanche du Bois while his wife is in the hospital giving birth to a child in *A Streetcar Named Desire*. Higher up the cultural food chain, young people can read of date rape in Homer or Jane Austen, watch it in *Don Giovanni* or *Rigoletto*.

The messages come early and often, and nothing in the feminist revolution has been able to counter them. A recent survey of sixth- to ninth-graders in Rhode Island found that a fourth of the boys and a sixth of the girls said it was acceptable for a man to force a woman to kiss him or have sex if he has spent money on her. A third of the children said it would not be wrong for a man to rape a woman who had had previous sexual experiences.

Certainly cases like Palm Beach, movies like *The Accused* and novels like Avery Corman's *Prized Possessions* may force young people to reexamine assumptions they have inherited. The use of new terms, like acquaintance rape and date rape, while controversial, has given men and women the vocabulary they need to express their experiences with both force and precision. This dialogue would be useful if it helps strip away some of the dogmas, old and new, surrounding the issue. Those who hope to raise society's sensitivity to the problem of date rape would do well to concede that it is not precisely the same sort of crime as street rape, that there may be very murky issues of intent and degree involved.

→

On the other hand, those who downplay the problem should come to realize that date rape is a crime of uniquely intimate cruelty. While the body is violated, the spirit is maimed. How long will it take, once the wounds have healed, before it is possible to share a walk on a beach, a drive home from work or an evening's conversation without always listening for a quiet alarm to start ringing deep in the back of the memory of a terrible crime?

Questions for Analysis

1. If rape is "sex without consent," as the author of this article suggests, how would you define "date rape"? Provide an example to illustrate your definition.

2. Do you know of someone who has been involved in a date rape situation? If so, describe this person's experience (without divulging his or her identity).

3. Some people explain date rape as a breakdown of communication; others see it as the result of the sex roles in our culture. Explain why you believe date rape occurs.

4. Some feminists contend that even false accusations of rape serve a useful purpose. How can society protect the rights of both the accused and the accuser in the effort to ensure that justice is served?

5. Imagine that you were the Dean of Students at your college. Describe what actions you would take to address this problem, and explain why you chose these actions.

10

Creating a Life Philosophy

Living Creatively

CREATIVITY
The process of developing innovative ideas or productive solutions

Understand and Trust the Creative Process

Eliminate the "Voice of Judgment"

Make Creativity a Priority

Establish a Creative Environment

Creating a Life Philosophy

Developing Beliefs

BELIEFS
Interpretations, evaluations, conclusions, and predictions about the world that we endorse as true

Developing Knowledge by Thinking Critically About Beliefs

Forming and Revising Beliefs

Developing Beliefs About Complex Issues

ou are an artist, creating your life portrait, and your paints and brush strokes are the choices that you make each day of your life. We introduced this metaphor in the opening chapter of this book to provide you with a way to think about your personal development, underscoring your responsibility for making the most intelligent decisions possible. Sometimes students become discouraged about their lives, concluding that their destinies are shaped by forces beyond their control.

Although difficult circumstances *do* hamper our striving for success, this fatalistic sentiment can also reflect a passivity that is the opposite of thinking critically. As a critical thinker, you should be confident that you can shape the person that you want to become through insightful understanding and intelligent choices.

In this book you have been developing the abilities and attitudes needed to become an educated thinker and a successful student. In this final chapter, we will integrate these goals into a larger context, exploring how to live a life that is creative, professionally successful, and personally fulfilling. By using both your creative and critical thinking abilities, you can develop informed beliefs and an enlightened life philosophy. In the final analysis, the person who looks back at you in the mirror is the person you have created.

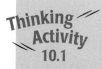

Thinking Activity 10.1

1. Describe a portrait of yourself as a person. What sort of person are you? What are your strengths and weaknesses? In what areas do you feel you are creative?

2. Describe some of the ways you would like to change yourself.

Living Creatively

Every day you encounter a series of choices, forks in your life path that have the cumulative effect of defining you as a person: What will be my schedule for the day? Who will I seek out, and what will I say? Will I participate in class? What will be my social agenda for the day? How will I approach my studying? What activities will I do after school: exercise? sleep? watch television? write in my journal? compose a poem?

In thinking about these questions, you may discover that there are habitual patterns in your life that rarely change. If you find that your life is composed of

Living Creatively:
You are an artist, creating your life portrait, and your paints and brush strokes are the choices that you make each day of your life.

a collection of similar activities and routines, don't despair—this is typical, not unusual. However, it may be an indication that you are not living your life in the most creative fashion possible, that your choices have become automatic, and that your experiences are fixed in certain "ruts." If this is the case, it may be time to reflect on your life, re-evaluate the choices you are making, and consider living your life in a more creative fashion.

Over two thousand years ago the Greek philosopher Socrates said this: "The unexamined life is not worth living." He was suggesting that if you live your life unreflectively, simply reacting to life's situations and not trying to explore its deeper meanings, then your life has diminished value. An unreflective person is not making use of the distinctive human capacity to think deeply about important issues and develop thoughtful conclusions about herself and her world.

Conversely, humans have a nearly limitless capacity to be creative, for our imaginations give us the power to conceive of new possibilities and put these innovative ideas into action. Using creative resources in this way enriches our lives and brings a special meaning to our activities. While we might not go to the extreme of saying that "the *uncreative* life is not worth living," it is surely preferable to live a life enriched by the qualities of creativity.

Can I Be Creative?

The first day of my Creative Thinking: Theory and Practice course, I always ask the students if they think they are creative. Typically, less than half of the class members raise their hands. One reason for this is that people often confuse being "creative" with being "artistic"—skilled at art, music, poetry, creative writing, drama, dance. Although artistic people are certainly creative, there are an infinite number of ways to be creative that are *not* artistic. This is a mental trap that I fell into when growing up. In school, I always dreaded art class because I was so inept. My pathetic drawings and art projects were always good for a laugh, and I felt no overwhelming urges to write poetry, paint, or compose music. I was certain that I had simply been born "uncreative," and I accepted this "fact" as my destiny. It wasn't until I graduated from college that I began to change this view of myself. I was working as a custom woodworker to support myself, designing and creating specialized furniture for people when it suddenly struck me: I was being creative! I then began to see other areas of my life in which I was creative: playing sports, decorating my apartment, even writing research papers. I finally understood that being creative was a state of mind and a way of life. As the writer Eric Gill expresses it, "The artist is not a different kind of person, but each one of us is a different kind of artist."

Are you creative? Yes! Think of all of the activities that you enjoy doing: cooking, creating a wardrobe, raising children, playing sports, cutting or braiding hair, dancing, playing music. Whenever you are investing your own personal ideas, putting on your own personal stamp, you are being creative. For example, imagine that you are cooking your favorite dish. To the extent that

Creative Inspiration:
"If you do not expect the unexpected you will not find it, for it is not to be reached by search or trail."
Heraclitus

you are expressing your unique ideas developed through inspiration and experimentation, you are being creative. (Of course, if you are simply following someone else's recipe without significant modification, your dish may be tasty—but it is not creative.) Similarly, if your moves on the dance floor or the basketball court express your distinctive personality, you are being creative, as you are when you stimulate the original thinking of children or make your friends laugh with your brand of humor.

Creativity

The process of developing innovative ideas or productive solutions.

Living your life creatively means bringing your unique perspective and creative talents to all the dimensions of your life. Described below are passages written by students about creative areas in their lives. After reading the passages, complete Thinking Activity 10.2, which gives you the opportunity to describe a creative area of your own life.

1. One of the most creative aspects of my life is my diet. I have been a vegetarian for the past five years, while the rest of my family has continued to eat meat. I had to overcome many obstacles to make this lifestyle work for me, including family dissension. The solution was simple: I had to learn how to cook creatively. I have come to realize that my diet is an ongoing learning process. The more I learn about and experiment with different foods, the healthier and happier I become. I feel like an explorer setting out on my own to discover new things about food and nutrition. I slowly evolved from a person who could cook food only if it came from a can, into someone who could make bread from scratch and grow yogurt cultures. I find learning new things about nutrition and cooking healthful foods very relaxing and rewarding. I like being alone in my house baking bread; there is something very comforting about the aroma. Most of all I like to experiment with different ways to prepare foods, because the ideas are my own. Even when an effort is less than successful, I find pleasure in the knowledge that I gained from the experience. I discovered recently, for example, that eggplant is terrible in soup! Making mistakes seems to be a natural way to increase creativity, and I now firmly believe that people who say that they do not like vegetables simply have not been properly introduced to them!

2. As a tropical fish hobbyist, I create an ecosystem most suited to the variety of fish I keep. My most recent choice of fish has been Pacus, a close cousin of the Piranha native to South America and Africa. I then added two Barracuda of the same approximate size. These two genera are nervous, aggressive fish not ordinarily found together in nature. As "dither fish," which are used as a distraction between two or more gen-

era, I chose two Jack Dempseys, which are large territorial cichlids. Since these fish require different habitats, it was necessary to create a blend of environments. The Pacus need an area to be well planted, providing cover, which I placed in the corners of the aquarium. The Dempseys require rocks, caves, and tree branches to do their cavorting and establish their domain. The Barracuda, being the most dominant and aggressive of the lot, got the center area of the tank to swim about freely. When raising fish, you become familiar with their distinct personalities, and you have to be both knowledgeable and creative to develop appropriate habitats for them.

3. As any parent knows, children have an abundance of energy to spend, and toys or television do not always meet their needs. In response, I create activities to stimulate their creativity and preserve my sanity. For example, I involve them in the process of cooking, giving them the skin from peeled vegetables and a pot so they can make their own "soup." Using catalogs, we cut out pictures of furniture, rugs, and curtains, and they paste them onto cartons to create their own interior decors: vibrant living rooms, plush bedrooms, colorful family rooms. I make beautiful boats from aluminum paper, and my children spend hours in the bathtub playing with them. We "go bowling" with empty soda cans and a ball, and they star in "track meets" by running an obstacle course we set up. When it comes to raising children, creativity is a way of survival!

4. After quitting the government agency I was working at because of too much bureaucracy, I was hired as a carpenter at a construction site, although I had little knowledge of this profession. I learned to handle a hammer and other tools by watching other coworkers, and within a matter of weeks I was skilled enough to organize my own group of workers for projects. Most of my fellow workers used the old-fashioned method of construction carpentry, building panels with inefficient and poorly made bracings. I redesigned the panels in order to save construction time and materials. My supervisor and site engineer were thrilled with my creative ideas, and I was assigned progressively more challenging projects, including the construction of an office building that was completed in record time.

5. My area of creativity is hair braiding, an activity that requires skill, talent, and patience that is difficult for most people to accomplish. Braiding hair in styles that are being worn today consists of braiding small to tiny braids, and it may include adding artificial hair to make the hair look fuller. It takes anywhere from ten to sixteen hours depending on the type of style that is desired: the smaller the braids, the longer it takes. In order to braid, I had to learn how to determine the right hair and color for peo-

ple that wanted extensions, pick out the right style that would fit perfectly on my customers' faces, learn to cut hair in an asymmetric fashion, put curls in the braids, and know the sequence of activities. Doing hair is a rewarding experience for me because when I am through with my work, my customers think the result is gorgeous!

Thinking Activity 10.2

1. Describe a creative area of your life in which you are able to express your unique personality and talents. Be specific and give examples.

2. Analyze your creative area by answering the following questions:
   - Why do you feel that this activity is creative? Give examples.
   - How would you describe the experience of being engaged in this activity? Where do your creative ideas come from? How do they develop?
   - What strategies do you use to increase your creativity? What obstacles block your creative efforts? How do you try to overcome these blocks?

Becoming More Creative

Although we each have nearly limitless potential to live creatively, most people use only a small percentage of their creative gifts. In fact, there is research to suggest that people typically achieve their highest creative point as young children, after which there is a long, steady decline into uncreativity. Why? Well, to begin with, young children are immersed in the excitement of exploration and discovery. They are eager to try out new things, act on their impulses, and make unusual connections between widely differing ideas. They are not afraid to take risks in trying out untested solutions, and they are not compelled to identify the socially acceptable "correct answer." Children are willing to play with ideas, creating improbable scenarios and imaginative ways of thinking, without fear of being ridiculed.

All this tends to change as we get older. The weight of "reality" begins to smother our imagination, and we increasingly focus our attention on the nuts and bolts of living, rather than playing with possibilities. The social pressure to conform to group expectations increases dramatically. Whether the group is our friends, schoolmates, or fellow employees, there are clearly defined "rules" for dressing, behaving, speaking, and thinking. When we deviate from these rules, we risk social disapproval, rejection, or ridicule. Most groups have little tolerance for individuals who want to think independently and creatively. As we become older, we also become more reluctant to pursue untested courses of action, because we become increasingly afraid of failure. Pursuing creativity inevitably involves failure, for we are trying to break out of established ruts and go beyond traditional methods. For example, going beyond the safety of a proven recipe to create an innovative dish may involve some disasters, but it's

The Payoff:
Using creative resources enriches our lives and brings a special meaning to our activities.

the only way to create something genuinely unique. The history of creative discoveries is littered with failures, a fact we tend to forget when we are debating whether we should risk an untested idea.

Thinking Activity 10.3

Reflect on your own creative development and describe some of the fears and pressures that inhibit your creativity. For example, have you ever been penalized for trying out a new idea that didn't work out? Have you ever suffered the wrath of the group for daring to be different and violating the group's unspoken rules? Do you feel that your life is so filled with responsibilities and the demands of reality that you don't have time to be creative?

Although the forces that discourage us from being creative are powerful, they can nevertheless be overcome with the right approaches. We are going to explore four productive strategies:

- Understand and trust the creative process
- Eliminate the "Voice of Judgment"
- Establish a creative environment
- Make creativity a priority

Understand and Trust the Creative Process. Discovering your creative talents requires that you understand how the creative process operates and then have confidence in the results it produces. There are no fixed procedures or formulas for generating creative ideas; creative ideas *by definition* go beyond established ways of thinking to the unknown and the innovative. As the ancient Greek philosopher Heraclitus once said, "You must expect the unexpected, because it cannot be found by search or trail."

Although there is no fixed path to creative ideas, there are activities we can pursue to make the birth of creative ideas possible. In this respect, generating creative ideas is similar to gardening. We need to prepare the soil; plant the seeds; ensure proper water, light, and food; and then be patient until the ideas begin to sprout. Here are some steps for cultivating your creative garden:

- *Absorb yourself in the task:* Creative ideas don't occur in a vacuum. They emerge after a great deal of work, study, and practice. For example, if you want to come up with creative ideas in the kitchen, you need to become knowledgeable about the art of cooking. The more knowledgeable you are, the better prepared you are to create valuable and innovative dishes. Similarly, if you are trying to develop a creative perspective for a research paper in college, you need to immerse yourself in the subject, developing an in-depth understanding of the central concepts and issues. Absorbing yourself in the task "prepares the soil" for your creative ideas.

■ *Allow time for ideas to incubate:* After absorbing yourself in the task or problem, the next stage in the creative process is to *stop* working on the task or problem. Although your conscious mind has separated itself from the task, the unconscious part of your mind continues working—processing, organizing, and ultimately generating innovative ideas and solutions. This process is known as *incubation* because it mirrors the process in which baby birds gradually evolve inside the egg until the moment when they break out. In the same way, your creative mind is at work while you are going about your business until the moment of *illumination,* when the incubating idea finally erupts to the surface of your conscious mind. People report that these illuminating moments—when their mental light bulbs go on—often occur when they are engaged in activities completely unrelated to the task. One of the most famous cases was that of the Greek thinker Archimedes, whose moment of illumination came while he was taking a bath, causing him to run naked through the streets of Athens shouting "Eureka" ("I have found it").

■ *Seize on the ideas when they emerge, and follow them through:* Generating creative ideas is of little use unless we recognize them when they appear and then act on them. Too often, people don't pay much attention to these ideas when they occur, or they dismiss them as too impractical. We have to have confidence in the ideas we create, even if they seem wacky or far out. Many of the most valuable inventions in our history started as improbable ideas, ridiculed by the popular wisdom. For example, the idea of Velcro started with burrs covering the pants of the inventor as he walked through a field, and Post-It Notes resulted from the accidental invention of an adhesive that was weaker than normal. In other words, thinking effectively means thinking creatively *and* thinking critically. After we use our *creative thinking* abilities to generate innovative ideas, we must then employ our *critical thinking* abilities to evaluate and refine the ideas, and design a practical plan for implementing them.

Eliminate the Voice of Judgment.

The biggest threat to our creativity lies within ourselves, the negative Voice of Judgment (VOJ), a term coined by Michael Ray and Rochelle Myers. The VOJ can undermine your confidence in every area of your life, including your creative activities, with such statements as these:

"This is a stupid idea, and no one will like it."

"Even if I could pull this idea off, it probably won't amount to much."

"Although I was successful the last time I tried something like this, I was lucky and I won't be able to do it again."

Eliminate Fear:
The biggest threat to our creativity lies within ourselves, the irrational fears and negative judgments that make us doubt ourselves and the quality of our creative thinking.

These statements, and countless others like them, have the ongoing effect of making us doubt ourselves and the quality of our creative thinking. As we lose confidence, we become more timid, reluctant to follow through on ideas and present them to others. After a while our cumulative insecurity discourages us from even generating ideas in the first place, and we end up simply conforming to established ways of thinking and the expectations of others. And in so doing we surrender an important part of ourselves, the vital and dynamic creative core of our personality that defines our unique perspective on the world.

Where do these negative voices come from? Often they originate in the negative judgments we experienced while growing up, destructive criticisms that became internalized as a part of ourselves. In the same way that praising children helps make them feel confident and secure, consistently criticizing them does the opposite. Although parents, teachers, and acquaintances often don't intend these negative consequences, the unfortunate result is still the same: a Voice of Judgment that keeps hammering away at the value of ourselves, our ideas, and our creations. As a teacher, I see the VOJ when students present their creative projects to the class with apologies like "This isn't very good, and it probably doesn't even make sense."

How do we eliminate this unwelcome and destructive voice within ourselves? There are a number of effective strategies you can use, although you should be aware that the fight, though worth the effort, will not be easy.

- *Become aware of the VOJ:* You have probably been listening to the negative messages of the VOJ for so long that you may not even be consciously aware of it. To conquer the VOJ, you need to first recognize when it speaks. In addition, it is helpful to analyze the negative messages, try to figure out how and why they developed, and then create strategies to overcome them. A good strategy is to keep a VOJ journal, described in Thinking Activity 10.4.

- *Restate the judgment in a more accurate or constructive way:* Sometimes there is an element of truth in our self-judgments, but we have blown the reality out of proportion. For example, if you fail a test, your VOJ may translate this as "You're a failure." Or if you ask someone for a date and get turned down, your VOJ may conclude "You're a social misfit with emotional bad breath!" In these instances, you need to translate the reality accurately: "I failed this test—I wonder what went wrong and what I can do to improve my performance in the future." "This person turned me down for a date—I guess I'm not his or her type."

- *Get tough with the VOJ:* You can't be a wimp if you hope to overcome the VOJ. Instead, you have to be strong and determined, telling yourself as soon as the VOJ appears, "I'm throwing you out and not letting you back in!" This attack might feel peculiar at first, but it will soon become an automatic response when those negative judgments appear. Don't give in to the judgments, even a little bit, by saying "Well, maybe I'm just a little bit of a jerk." Get rid of the VOJ entirely, and good riddance to it!

▪ *Create positive voices and visualizations:* The best way to destroy the VOJ for good is to replace it with positive encouragements. As soon as you have stomped on the judgment "I'm a jerk," you should replace it with "I'm an intelligent, valuable person with many positive qualities and talents." Similarly, you should make extensive use of positive visualization, as you "see" yourself performing well on your examinations, being entertaining and insightful with other people, and succeeding gloriously in the sport or dramatic production in which you are involved. If you make the effort to create these positive voices and images, they will eventually become a natural part of your thinking. And since positive thinking leads to positive results, your efforts will become self-fulfilling prophecies.

▪ *Use other people for independent confirmation:* The negative judgments coming from the VOJ are usually irrational, but until they are dragged out into the light of day for examination, they can be very powerful. Sharing your VOJ with others you trust is an effective strategy because they can provide an objective perspective that reveals to you the irrationality and destructiveness of these negative judgments. This sort of "reality testing" strips the judgments of their power, a process enhanced by the positive support of concerned friends you have developed relationships with over a period of time.

Thinking Activity 10.4

1. For one day, take a small notebook or pad and record every negative judgment that you make about yourself. At the end of the day, classify your judgments by category—for example, negative judgments about your physical appearance, your popularity with others, your academic ability.

2. Analyze the judgments in each of the categories, and try to determine where they came from and how they developed.

3. Use the strategies described above, and others of your own creation, to start fighting these judgments when they occur.

Establish a Creative Environment. An important part of eliminating the negative voices in your mind is to establish environments in which your creative resources can flourish. You should find or develop physical environments conducive to creative expression as well as find or develop supportive social environments. Sometimes working with other people is stimulating and energizing to creative juices; other times we require a private place where we can work without distraction. For example, I have a specific location in which I do much of my writing: sitting on a comfortable couch, with a calm, pleasing view, music on the stereo, a cold drink, a supply of Tootsie Roll Pops. I'm ready for creativity to strike me, although I sometimes have to wait awhile.

Different environments work for different people: you have to find the environment(s) best suited to your own creative process and then make a special effort to do your work there.

The people who form our social environment play an even more influential role in encouraging or inhibiting our creative process. When we are surrounded by those who are positive and supportive, our confidence is increased and we are encouraged to take the risk to express our creative vision. These people can stimulate our creativity by providing us with fresh ideas and new perspectives. By engaging in brainstorming, they can work with us to generate ideas and then later help us figure out how to refine and implement the most valuable ones.

However, when the people around us tend to be negative, critical, or belittling, then the opposite happens: we lose confidence and are reluctant to express ourselves creatively. Eventually, we begin to internalize these negative judgments, incorporating them into our VOJ. When this occurs, we have the choice of telling people that we will not tolerate this sort of destructive behavior or, if they can't improve their behavior, moving them out of our lives. Of course, sometimes this is difficult because we work with them or they are related to us. In this case, we have to try to diminish their negative influence and spend more time with those who support us.

Make Creativity a Priority.   Having diminished the power of the VOJ, established a creative environment, and committed yourself to trusting your creative gifts, you are now in a position to live more creatively. How do you actually do this? Start small. Identify some habitual patterns in your life, and break out of them. Choose new experiences whenever possible—for example, unfamiliar items on a menu or getting to know people outside of your circle of friends—and strive to develop fresh perspectives on things in your life. Resist falling back into the ruts you were previously in by remembering that living things are supposed to be continually growing, changing, and evolving, not acting in repetitive patterns like machines. The student essay below summarizes many of the reasons why choosing to live creatively may be one of the most fulfilling decisions that you make.

Creativity

Creativity is an energizing force: powerful, generative, productive. Sadly, for the most part, its potential remains unused, as men and women circle the periphery of its domain. The author Kahlil Gibran writes: "For the self is a sea, boundless and measureless," and for many of us that sea remains largely undiscovered. Creativity is a treasure that if nurtured can become a harvest of possibilities and riches. Why is creativity important? Very simply, creativity brings fulfillment and enrichment to every dimension of our lives. A creative disposition sees difficulties not as problems but as challenges to be met. The intuitive thinker draws upon the combined resources of insight, illumination, imagination and an inner

Find a special place in which your creative resources can flourish.

strength. He puts ideas and strategies into effect, while developing a sense of competency and control over his environment. Creativity fosters limitless opportunities because it draws upon the power of discovery and invention.

Creativity's realm is in the vast uncharted portions of the mind. What we call full consciousness is a very narrow thing, and creativity springs from the unknown and unconscious depths of our being. In the words of Gibran: "Vague and nebulous is the beginning of all things." Creativity always begins with a question, and we must abandon preconceived ideas and expectations. But while the phenomenon of creativity involves innovating, developing, playing and speculating, there must ultimately be a point of synthesis. Ideas in flight are of little use; a convergence and application gives substance to our visions. Fostering our creative gifts is a lifelong project. The Buddhists use the term "mindfulness" to describe the creative state of being. Mindfulness involves developing an openness to ideas, suggestions and even once discarded thoughts. The goal is to increase our sensitivity and awareness to the mystery and beauty of life. We must adopt a playful attitude, a willingness to fool around with ideas, with the understanding that many of these fanciful notions will not be relevant or practical. But some will, and these creative insights can lead to profound and wondrous discoveries. At the same time, cultivating a creative attitude stretches our imaginations and makes our lives vibrant and unique.

Worry and mental striving create anxiety that clogs rather than stimulates the flow of ideas. It is impossible to impose one's will with brute force on the chaos. We must be gentle with ourselves, harmonize rather

Creativity:
The creative process requires patience, not brute force, and "the solution will present itself quietly and say 'Here I am'" (Albert Einstein).

than try to conquer, and in the words of Albert Einstein, "The solution will present itself quietly and say 'Here I am.'" And while we need critical evaluation to provide direction and focus for our creative efforts, a premature and excessive critical judgment suppresses, overpowers and smothers creative spontaneity. This "Voice of Judgment" shrinks our creative reservoir and undermines our courage to take creative risks. The author Napoleon Hill has stated, "Whatever the mind can conceive and believe, it can achieve." Similarly, if we approach our lives with a mindful sense of discovery and invention, we can continually create ourselves in ways that we can only imagine. In such lives, there are no predetermined outcomes, only creativity searching for seeds of progress.

Thinking Activity 10.5

Select an area of your life in which you would like to be more creative: in school, at your job, in an activity you enjoy, or in a personal relationship. Make a special effort to inject a fresh perspective and new ideas into your area, and keep a journal recording your efforts and their result. Be sure to allow yourself sufficient time to break out of your ruts and establish new patterns of thinking, feeling, and behaving. Focus on your creative perceptions as you "expect the unexpected," and pounce on new ideas when they emerge from the depths of your creative resource.

Developing Beliefs to Guide Your Life

It seems to be a natural human impulse to try to understand the world we live in, and beliefs are the main tools we use to make sense of the world and guide our actions. The total collection of your beliefs represents your view of the world, your philosophy of life. For example, consider the following statements and answer "Yes," "No," or "Not sure" to each.

1. Humans need to eat to stay alive.
2. Smoking marijuana is a harmless good time.
3. Every human life is valuable.
4. Developing our minds is as important as taking care of our bodies.
5. People should care about other people, not just themselves.

Your responses to these statements reflect certain beliefs you have, and these beliefs help you explain why the world is the way it is and how you ought to behave.

What exactly are "beliefs"? If we examine the concept closely, we can see that beliefs represent an interpretation, evaluation, conclusion, or prediction about the nature of the world. Note the following examples:

■ The statement "I believe that the whale in the book *Moby-Dick* symbolizes a primal, natural force that men are trying to destroy" represents an *interpretation* of that novel.

■ To say "I believe that watching soap operas is unhealthy because they focus almost exclusively on the seamy, evil side of human life" expresses an *evaluation* of soap operas.

■ The statement "I believe that one of the main reasons two out of three people in the world go to bed hungry each night is that industrially advanced nations like the United States have not done a satisfactory job of sharing their knowledge" expresses a *conclusion* about the problem of world hunger.

■ To say "If drastic environmental measures are not undertaken to slow the global warming trend, then I believe that the polar icecaps will melt and the earth will be flooded" is to make a *prediction* about events that will occur in the future.

Besides expressing an interpretation, evaluation, conclusion, or prediction about the world, beliefs also express an *endorsement* of the accuracy of the beliefs by the speaker or author.

Beliefs

Interpretations, evaluations, conclusions, predictions about the world that we endorse as true.

In the space provided, describe beliefs you have in each of these categories (interpretation, evaluation, conclusion, prediction) and then explain the reason(s) you have for endorsing the beliefs.

1. *Interpretation. Example:* Poetry enables humans to communicate deep, complex emotions and ideas that resist simple expression.

   I believe that _____

   _____.

   Supporting Reason(s): _____

   _____

2. *Evaluation. Example:* Children today spend too much time watching television and too little time reading.

   I believe that _____

   _____.

   Supporting Reason(s): _____

   _____

3. *Conclusion. Example:* An effective college education provides not only mastery of information and skills, but also evolving insight and maturing judgment.

   I believe that _____

   _____.

Supporting Reason(s): _____

_____

4. *Prediction. Example:* With the shrinking and integration of the global community, there will be an increasing need in the future for Americans to become bilingual.

I believe that   _____

_____.

Supporting Reason(s): _____

_____

Knowledge and Truth

Most people in our culture are socialized to believe that knowledge and truth are absolute and unchanging. One major goal of our social institutions, including family, school system, and religion, is to transfer to us the knowledge that has been developed over the ages. Under this model, the role of learners is to absorb this information passively, like sponges. However, achieving knowledge and truth is a much more complicated process than this. Instead of simply relying on the testimony of such authorities as parents, teachers, textbooks, and religious leaders, critical thinkers have a responsibility to engage *actively* in the learning process and participate in developing their own understanding of the world.

The need for this active approach to knowing is underscored by the fact that authorities often disagree about the true nature of a given situation or the best course of action. For example, it is not uncommon for doctors to disagree about a diagnosis, for economists to differ on the state of the economy, for psychiatrists to disagree on whether a convicted felon is a menace to society or a harmless victim of social forces, and for religions to present conflicting approaches to achieving eternal life.

What do we do when experts disagree? As critical thinkers, we must analyze and evaluate all the available information, develop our own well-reasoned beliefs, and recognize when we don't have sufficient information to arrive at well-founded beliefs. We must realize that beliefs may evolve over time as we gain information or improve our insight.

Although there are compelling reasons to view knowledge and truth in this way, many people resist it. Either they take refuge in a belief in the absolute, unchanging nature of knowledge and truth, as presented by the appropriate authorities, or they conclude that there is no such thing as knowledge or truth and that trying to seek either is a futile enterprise. In this latter view of the world, known as *relativism,* all beliefs are considered as "relative" to the person or context in which they arise. For the relativist, all opinions are equal in validity to all others; we are never in a position to say with confidence that one view is right and another view is wrong.

Although a relativistic view is appropriate in some areas of experience—for example, in many matters of taste—in many other areas it is not. Although knowledge is often difficult to achieve, in the form of well-supported beliefs, it does exist. Some beliefs are better than others, not because an authority has proclaimed them so but because they meet the following criteria:

- How effectively do our beliefs *explain what is taking place?*
- To what extent are these beliefs *consistent with other beliefs* we have about the world?
- How effectively do our beliefs help us *predict what will happen* in the future?
- To what extent are our beliefs supported by *sound reasons and compelling evidence* derived from *reliable sources?*

A critical thinker sees knowledge and truth as goals that we are striving to achieve, processes that we are all actively involved in as we construct our understanding of the world. Developing accurate knowledge about the world is often a challenging process of exploration and analysis in which our understanding grows and evolves over a period of time. In Chapter 6 we examined four contrasting media accounts of the assassination of Malcolm X. All four authors, we found, viewed the event through their own perceiving spectacles, which shaped and influenced the information they selected, the way they organized it, their interpretations of the individuals involved, and the language they chose to describe it. Despite the differences in these accounts, we *know* that an actual sequence of events occurred on that February day in 1965. The challenge for us is to try to figure out what actually happened by investigating different accounts, evaluating the reliability of the accounts, and putting together a coherent picture of what took place. This process of achieving knowledge and truth occurs in every area of human inquiry—a matter of exploration, critical analysis, and evolving understanding.

Forming and Revising Your Beliefs

As we attempt to make sense of the world, our thinking abilities give us the means to do the following:

1. Ask questions about our experience.
2. Work toward forming beliefs that will enable us to answer these questions and make useful decisions.

When we ask questions, it means that we are not simply content to take things for granted, as we saw in Chapter 2. Asking questions encourages us to try to form more accurate beliefs to explain what is taking place. By questioning our experience, we are better able to understand the situation we are in and to take control.

Let us explore how asking questions and forming beliefs enable us to make sense of our world. Read carefully the following passage, in which a student whom we will call Maria describes her experiences with the "system."

A few years ago my oldest son went to a party. On his way home (about 11 P.M.) he was accosted by three individuals who tried to take his belongings. Seeing guns, my son's first reaction was to run away, which he did. While running he was shot. His wounds left him paralyzed from his neck down. As he lay in the intensive care unit of the hospital, I started to receive threatening phone calls telling us that "if we identify them to the police, they will finish the work."

At this time I reported the phone calls to both the police and the telephone company. I was irritated by the way the police handled the whole situation. I was told that there was no reason why the city should pay for having a police officer protect my son and was asked what he was doing in the streets at this time. (The time was 11 p.m., and my son was almost eighteen years old.) Finally I was told there was nothing that could be done. In my anger, I called the mayor's office, the senator's office, and the councilman. Also, I immediately wrote a letter to the police commissioner regarding the whole situation and mailed it special delivery, registered, for proof in case the matter became worse. In less than a few hours, there was an officer at my son's bedside making sure that nothing further happened to him.

I learned that although there are many laws to protect citizens, if citizens don't fight for their rights these laws will never be exercised. My opinion of the "system" changed after this experience. I believe that I shouldn't have had to go through so much red tape in order to have my legal rights. I feel that if you don't take a stand, there is no one who will go out of the way to instruct you or to help out. I was never informed at the police headquarters about what to do and how to go about doing it. I was left standing without any hope at all. I feel sorry for those persons who are ignorant about how you can make the system work for you.

Maria's story illustrates the process by which we form and re-form our beliefs, a process that often follows the following sequence:

1. We *form* beliefs to explain what is taking place. (These initial beliefs are often based on our past experiences.)
2. We *test* these beliefs by acting on the basis of them.
3. We *revise* these beliefs if our actions do not result in our desired goals.
4. We *retest* these revised beliefs by acting on the basis of them.

This process of critical exploration enables us to develop a greater understanding of various situations in our experience and also gives us the means to exert more control over these situations.

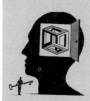

Thinking Passage

"Why I Quit the Klan"

Examine the process of forming and re-forming beliefs by reading the following interview, which Studs Terkel conducted with C. P. Ellis. Ellis, who was fifty-three years old when the interview took place, was once president (Exalted Cyclops) of the Durham, North Carolina, chapter of the Ku Klux Klan. He is currently a business manager of the International Union of Operating Engineers in Durham, North Carolina. Answer the questions that follow the passage.

Why I Quit the Klan

C. P. Ellis

All my life, I had work, never a day without work, worked all the overtime I could get and still could not survive financially. I began to see there's something wrong with this country. I worked my butt off and just never seemed to break even. I had some real great ideas about this nation. They say to abide by the law, go to church, do right and live for the Lord, and everything'll work out. But it didn't work out. It just kept gettin worse and worse. . . .

Tryin to come out of that hole, I just couldn't do it. I really began to get bitter. I didn't know who to blame. I tried to find somebody. Hatin America is hard to do because you can't see it to hate it. You gotta have somethin to look at to hate. The natural person for me to hate would be black people, because my father before me was a member of the Klan. . . .

So I began to admire the Klan. . . . To be part of somethin. . . . The first night I went with the fellas . . . I was led into a large meeting room, and this was the time of my life! It was thrilling. Here's a guy who's worked all his life and struggled all his life to be something, and here's the moment to be something. I will never forget it. Four robed Klansmen led me into the hall. The lights were dim and the only thing you could see was an illuminated cross. . . . After I had taken my oath, there was loud applause goin throughout the buildin, musta been at least four hundred people. For this one little ol person. It was a thrilling moment for C. P. Ellis. . . .

The majority of [the Klansmen] are low-income whites, people who really don't have a part in something. They have been shut out as well as blacks. Some are not very well educated either. Just like myself. We had a lot of support from doctors and lawyers and police officers.

Maybe they've had bitter experiences in this life and they had to hate somebody. So the natural person to hate would be the black person. He's beginnin to come up, he's beginnin to . . . start votin and run for political office. Here are white people who are supposed to be superior to them, and we're shut out. . . . Shut out. Deep down inside, we want to be part of this great society. Nobody listens, so we join these groups. . . .

We would go to the city council meetings, and the blacks would be there and we'd be there. It was a confrontation every time. . . . We began to make some inroads with the city councilmen and county commissioners. They began to call us friend. Call us at night on the

→

telephone: "C. P., glad you came to that meeting last night." They didn't want integration either, but they did it secretively, in order to get elected. They couldn't stand up openly and say it, but they were glad somebody was sayin it. We visited some of the city leaders in their homes and talked to em privately. It wasn't long before councilmen would call me up: "The blacks are comin up tonight and makin outrageous demands. How about some of you people showin up and have a little balance?" . . .

We'd load up our cars and we'd fill up half the council chambers, and the blacks the other half. During these times, I carried weapons to the meetings, outside my belt. We'd go there armed. We would wind up just hollerin and fussin at each other. What happened? As a result of our fightin one another, the city council still had their way. They didn't want to give up control to the blacks nor the Klan. They were usin us.

I began to realize this later down the road. One day I was walkin downtown and a certain city council member saw me comin. I expected him to shake my hand because he was talkin to me at night on the telephone. I had been in his home and visited with him. He crossed the street [to avoid me]. . . . I began to think, somethin's wrong here. Most of em are merchants or maybe an attorney, an insurance agent, people like that. As long as they kept low-income whites and low-income blacks fightin, they're gonna maintain control. I began to get that feelin after I was ignored in public. I thought: . . . you're not gonna use me any more. That's when I began to do some real serious thinkin.

The same thing is happening in this country today. People are being used by those in control, those who have all the wealth. I'm not espousing communism. We got the greatest system of government in the world. But those who have it simply don't want those who don't have it to have any part of it. Black and white. When it comes to money, the green, the other colors make no difference.

I spent a lot of sleepless nights. I still didn't like blacks. I didn't want to associate with them. Blacks, Jews or Catholics. My father said: "Don't have anything to do with em." I didn't until I met a black person and talked with him, eyeball to eyeball, and met a Jewish person and talked to him, eyeball to eyeball. I found they're people just like me. They cried, they cussed, they prayed, they had desires. Just like myself. Thank God, I got to the point where I can look past labels. But at that time, my mind was closed.

I remember one Monday night Klan meeting. I said something was wrong. Our city fathers were using us. And I didn't like to be used. The reactions of the others was not too pleasant: "Let's just keep fightin them niggers."

I'd go home at night and I'd have to wrestle with myself. I'd look at a black person walkin down the street, and the guy'd have ragged shoes or his clothes would be worn. That began to do something to me inside. I went through this for about six months. I felt I just had to get out of the Klan. But I wouldn't get out. . . .

[Ellis was invited, as a Klansman, to join a committee of people from all walks of life to make recommendations on how to solve racial problems in the school system. He very reluctantly accepted. After a few stormy meetings, he was elected co-chair of the committee, along with Ann Atwater, a black woman who for years had been leading local efforts for civil rights.]

A Klansman and a militant black woman, co-chairman of the school committee. It was impossible. How could I work with her? But it was in our hands. We had to make it a success. This give me another sense of belongin, a sense of pride. This helped the inferiority feeling I had. A man who has stood up publicly and said he despised black people, all of a sudden he was willin to work with em. Here's a chance for a low-income white man to be somethin. In spite of all my hatred for blacks and Jews and liberals, I accepted the job. Her and I began to reluctantly work together. She had as many problems workin with me as I had workin with her.

One night, I called her: "Ann, you and I should have a lot of differences and we got em now. But there's something laid out here before us, and if it's gonna be a success, you and I are gonna have to make it one. Can we lay aside some of these feelins?" She said: "I'm willing if you are." I said: "Let's do it."

My old friends would call me at night: "C. P., what the hell is wrong with you? You're sellin out the white race." This begin to make me have guilt feelins. Am I doin right? Am I doin wrong? Here I am all of a sudden makin an about-face and tryin to deal with my feelins, my heart. My mind was beginnin to open up. I was beginnin to see what was right and what was wrong. I don't want the kids to fight forever. . . .

One day, Ann and I went back to the school and we sat down. We began to talk and just re-flect. . . . I begin to see, here we are, two people from the far ends of the fence, havin identical problems, except hers bein black and me bein white. . . . The amazing thing about it, her and I, up to that point, has cussed each other, bawled each other, we hated each other. Up to that point, we didn't know each other. We didn't know we had things in common. . . .

The whole world was openin up, and I was learning new truths that I had never learned before. I was beginning to look at a black person, shake hands with him, and see him as a human bein. I hadn't got rid of all this stuff. I've still got a little bit of it. But somethin was happenin to me. . . .

. . . They say the older you get, the harder it is for you to change. That's not necessarily true. Since I changed, I've set down and listened to tapes of Martin Luther King. I listen to it and tears come to my eyes cause I know what he's sayin now. I know what's happenin.

Questions for Analysis

1. What were C. P. Ellis's most important *initial beliefs?* From where did his stereotypes originate?

2. What were some of the *experiences* that helped form these initial beliefs?

3. What *actions* did he take based on these initial beliefs?

4. What *experiences* raised doubts about his initial beliefs? Why was he able to say: "Thank God, I got to the point where I can look past labels. . . . I was beginning to look at a black person, shake hands with him, and see him as a human being."

5. What *revised beliefs* did he form to make better sense of his experiences?

We can now see that two aspects of the way we make sense of the world, perceiving and believing, continually influence each other. On one hand, the experiences we perceive influence what we come to believe. For example, the fact that C. P. Ellis's friends and family insulted and disparaged blacks, Jews, and Catholics led him to form racist beliefs about these groups. On the other hand, our beliefs influence the way we perceive things; that is, they influence the perceptual lenses we use to view the world. The racist beliefs that C. P. Ellis had formed were reflected in his perceptual stereotypes of blacks, Jews, and Catholics.

Fortunately, beliefs do not stand still in the minds of critical thinkers. We continue to form and re-form our beliefs, based in part on what we are experiencing and how we think about what we are experiencing. For C. P. Ellis, the experience of meeting and working with people from other ethnic groups broke down his perceptual stereotypes of them: "I found they're people just like me. They cried, they cussed, they prayed, they had desires. Just like myself."

Thinking Activity 10.6

1. Interview another person about a belief he or she once held but no longer holds. Ask that person the following questions. (Try asking the questions in the course of a conversation you have with the person rather than confronting him or her with an intimidating series of formal questions. Most people like to be asked about their beliefs and are very cooperative.)

   a. What is the belief?

   b. On what evidence did you hold that belief?

   c. What caused you to change the belief?

   d. What were your feelings when you found that changing the belief was necessary?

   e. How do you feel now about changing the belief?

Next, write a summary of the interview. Begin by describing the person and explaining your relationship with him or her. Then give his or her answers to the questions. Make your summary as detailed as possible.

2. Describe your reaction to the other person's experience. What did you learn about perception and belief from this person?

Thinking Critically and Living Creatively

The purpose of this text has been to introduce the thinking abilities you need to become successful, not just in your studies, but in all areas of your life. Creating yourself as a person is a lifelong process that involves developing your intellectual abilities and your creative potential. And becoming a critical thinker involves using these abilities to develop informed beliefs, make intelligent decisions, and empathize genuinely with viewpoints other than your own. It is a process tied to your personal growth as a mature and socially responsible individual.

The important decisions that you make in life reflect your *values,* the principles that you consider to be most important. When you make decisions regarding "right" and "wrong" behavior in your relationships with others, the values that these decisions express are *moral* values. Each one of us possesses a "moral compass" that we use to guide our decisions in moral situations.

Your moral compass is an important part of your core beliefs, your philosophy of life, and it is important to use your critical thinking abilities to develop the soundest moral beliefs possible. For example, the hallmark of thinking critically is to understand perspectives other than our own, to think empathetically within other viewpoints, and to appreciate others' unique circumstances. This moral perspective is a central belief in many of the world religions and moral theories, and it is embodied in the Golden Rule: "Do unto others as you would have them do unto you." In other words, deciding on the morally right thing to do requires that we mentally and emotionally place ourselves in the positions of other people who might be affected by our action, and then make our decision based on what will be best for their interests *as well as* our interests.

We should not abandon our own views or automatically sacrifice our own interests. It simply means that as we work toward creating a fulfilling life for ourselves that we take other people's interests into consideration. We do not exist in isolation: we are members of communities to which we are related in complex and interdependent ways. According to this point of view, achieving happiness and fulfillment in life does not mean pursuing our own narrow desires; instead, it involves pursuing our dreams in a context of empathy and understanding for other people. To become truly fulfilled as a human being involves living a life that is woven into the fabric of others' lives, contributing to their happiness as they contribute to ours.

You are the artist of your life, and your brush strokes express your philosophy of life, a vision that incorporates your most deeply held values, aspirations, and convictions. The challenge you face is to create a coherent view of the world that expresses who you are and who you want to become. It should be a vision that not only guides your actions but also enables you to understand the value of your experiences, the significance of your relationships, and the meaning of your life.

Creating Yourself

The process of creating yourself through your choices is a lifelong one that involves all the creative and critical thinking abilities that we have been exploring in this book. The processes of creative thinking and critical thinking are related to one another in complex, interactive ways. We use the creative thinking process to develop ideas that are unique, useful, and worthy of further elaboration, and we use the critical thinking process to analyze, evaluate, and refine these ideas. Creative thinking and critical thinking work as partners, enabling us to create meaningful products and lead

$\longrightarrow$

fulfilling lives. The first of the following articles, "Original Spin," by Lesley Dormen and Peter Edidin, provides a useful introduction to creative thinking and suggests strategies for increasing your creative abilities. The second article, "Discovering Your Personal Myth," by Sam Keen, encourages you to discover—and create—the overarching personal "myth" that gives your life meaning and purpose. After reading the articles and reflecting on their ideas, answer the questions that follow.

Original Spin

Lesley Dormen and Peter Edidin

> Creativity is not just for geniuses and artists. But unlocking your creative potential requires rethinking the way you think.

Creativity, somebody once wrote, is the search for the elusive "Aha," that moment of insight when one sees the world, or a problem, or an idea, in a new way. Traditionally, whether the discovery results in a cubist painting or an improved carburetor, we have viewed the creative instant as serendipitous and rare—the product of genius, the property of the elect.

Unfortunately, this attitude has had a number of adverse consequences. It encourages us to accept the myth that the creative energy society requires to address its own problems will never be present in sufficient supply. Beyond that, we have come to believe that "ordinary" people like ourselves can never be truly creative. As John Briggs, author of *Fire in the Crucible: The Alchemy of Creative Genius,* says, "The way we talk about creativity tends to reinforce the notion that it is some kind of arbitrary gift. It's amazing the way 'not having it' becomes wedded to people's self-image. They invariably work up a whole series of rationalizations about why they 'aren't creative,' as if they were damaged goods of some kind." Today, however, researchers are looking at creativity, not as an advantage of the human elite, but as a basic human endowment. As Ruth Richards, a psychiatrist and creativity researcher at McLean Hospital in Belmont, MA, says, "You were being creative when you learned how to walk. And if you are looking for something in the fridge, you're being creative because you have to figure out for yourself where it is." Creativity, in Richards' view, is simply fundamental to getting about the world. It is "our ability to adapt to change. It is the very essence of human survival."

In an age of rampant social and technological change, such an adaptive capability becomes yet more crucial to the individual's effort to maintain balance in a constantly shifting environment. "People need to recognize that what Alvin Toffler called future shock is our daily reality," says Ellen McGrath, a clinical psychologist who teaches creativity courses at New York University. "Instability is an intrinsic part of our lives, and to deal with it every one of us will need to find new, creative solutions to the challenges of everyday life. I think creativity will be the survival skill of the '90s."

But can you really become more creative? If the word *creative* smacks too much of Picasso at his canvas, then rephrase the question in a less intimidating way: Do you believe you could deal with the challenges of life in a more effective, inventive and fulfilling manner? If the answer is yes, then the question becomes, "What's stopping you?"

→

Defining Yourself as a Creative Person

People often hesitate to recognize the breakthroughs in their own lives as creative. But who has not felt the elation and surprise that come with the sudden, seemingly inexplicable discovery of a solution to a stubborn problem? In that instant, in "going beyond the information given," as psychologist Jerome Bruner has said, to a solution that was the product of your own mind, you were expressing your creativity.

This impulse to "go beyond" to a new idea is not the preserve of genius, stresses David Henry Feldman, a developmental psychologist at Tufts University and the author of *Nature's Gambit,* a study of child prodigies. "Not everybody can be Beethoven," he says, "but it is true that all humans, by virtue of being dreamers and fantasizers, have a tendency to take liberties with the world as it exists. Humans are always transforming their inner and outer worlds. It's what I call the 'transformational imperative.'"

The desire to play with reality, however, is highly responsive to social control, and many of us are taught early on to repress the impulse. As Mark Runco, associate professor of psychology at California State University at Fullerton and the founder of the new *Creativity Research Journal,* says, "We put children in groups and make them sit in desks and raise their hands before they talk. We put all the emphasis on conformity and order, then we wonder why they aren't being spontaneous and creative."

Adults too are expected to conform in any number of ways and in a variety of settings. Conformity, after all, creates a sense of order and offers the reassurance of the familiar. But to free one's natural creative impulses, it is necessary, to some extent, to resist the pressure to march in step with the world. Begin small, suggests Richards. "Virtually nothing you do can't be done in a slightly different, slightly better way. This has nothing to do with so-called creative pursuits but simply with breaking with your own mindsets and trying an original way of doing some habitual task. Simply defer judgment on yourself for a little while and try something new. Remember, the essence of life is not getting things right, but taking risks, making mistakes, getting things *wrong.*"

But it also must be recognized that the creative life is to some degree, and on some occasions, a solitary one. Psycholinguist Vera John-Steiner, author of *Notebooks of the Mind: Explorations of Thinking,* is one of many creativity researchers who believe that a prerequisite for creative success is "intensity of preoccupation, being pulled into your activity to such an extent that you forget it's dinnertime." Such concentration, John-Steiner believes, is part of our "natural creative bent," but we learn to ignore it because of a fear that it will isolate us from others. To John-Steiner, however, this fear is misplaced. Creative thought, she has written, is a "search for meaning," a way to connect our inner sense of being with some aspect of the world that preoccupies us. And she believes that only by linking these two aspects of reality—the inner and the outer—can we gain "some sense of being in control of life."

Avoiding the Myths

David Perkins, co-director of Project Zero at the Harvard Graduate School of Education, asks in *The Mind's Best Work,* "When you have it—creativity, that is—what do you have?" The very impalpability of the subject means that often creativity can be known only by its products. Indeed, the most common way the researchers define creativity is by saying it is whatever produces something that is: a. original; b. adaptive (i.e., useful); c. meaningful to others. But because we don't understand its genesis, we're often blocked or intimidated by the myths that surround and distort this mercurial subject.

One of these myths is, in Perkins's words, that creativity is "a kind of 'stuff' that the creative person has and uses to do creative things, never mind other factors." This bit of folk wisdom, that creativity is a sort of intangible psychic organ—happily present in some and absent in others—so annoys Perkins that he would like to abolish the word itself.

Another prevalent myth about creativity is that it is restricted to those who are "geniuses"—that is, people with inordinately high IQs. Ironically, this has been discredited by a study begun by Stanford psychologist Lewis Terman, the man who adapted the original French IQ test for America. In the early 1920s, Terman had California school teachers choose 1,528 "genius" schoolchildren (those with an IQ above 135), whose lives were then tracked year after year. After six decades, researchers found that the putative geniuses, by and large, did well in life. They entered the professions in large numbers and led stable, prosperous lives. But very few made notable creative contributions to society, and none did extraordinary creative work.

According to Dean Simonton, professor of psychology at the University of California at Davis and the author of *Genius, Creativity and Leadership* and *Scientific Genius*, "There just isn't any correlation between creativity and IQ. The average college graduate has an IQ of about 120, and that is high enough to write novels, do scientific research, or any other kind of creative work."

A third myth, voiced eons ago by Socrates, lifts creativity out of our own lives altogether into a mystical realm that makes it all but unapproachable. In this view, the creative individual is a kind of oracle, the passive conduit or channel chosen by God, or the tribal ancestors, or the muse, to communicate sacred knowledge.

Although there *are* extraordinary examples of creativity, for which the only explanation seems to be supernatural intervention (Mozart, the story goes, wrote the overture to *Don Giovanni* in only a few hours, after a virtually sleepless night and without revision), by and large, creativity begins with a long and intensive apprenticeship.

Psychologist Howard Gruber believes that it takes at least 10 years of immersion in a given domain before an eminent creator is likely to be able to make a distinctive mark. Einstein, for example, who is popularly thought to have doodled out the theory of relativity at age 26 in his spare time, was in fact compulsively engaged in thinking about the problem at least from the age of 16.

Finally, many who despair of ever being creative do so because they tried once and failed, as though the truly creative always succeed. In fact, just the opposite is true, says Dean Simonton. He sees genius, in a sense, as inseparable from failure. "Great geniuses make tons of mistakes," he says. "They generate lots of ideas and they accept being wrong. They have a kind of internal fortress that allows them to fail and just keep going. Look at Edison. He held over 1,000 patents, but most of them are not only forgotten, they weren't worth much to begin with."

Mindlessness vs. Mindfulness

"Each of us desires to share with others our vision of the world, only most of us have been taught that it's wrong to do things differently or look at things differently," says John Briggs. "We lose confidence in ourselves and begin to look at reality only in terms of the categories by which society orders it."

→

This is the state of routinized conformity and passive learning that Harvard professor of psychology Ellen Langer calls, appropriately enough, mindlessness. For it is the state of denying the perceptions and promptings of our own minds, our individual selves. Langer and her colleagues' extensive research over the past 15 years has shown that when we act mindlessly, we behave automatically and limit our capacity for creative response. Mired down in a numbing daily routine, we may virtually relinquish our capacity for independent thought and action.

By contrast, Langer refers to a life in which we use our affective, responsive, perceptive faculties as "mindful." When we are mindful, her research has shown, we avoid rigid, reflexive behavior in favor of a more improvisational and intuitive response to life. We notice and feel the world around us and then act in accordance with our feelings. "Many, if not all, of the qualities that make up a mindful attitude are characteristic of creative people," Langer writes in her new book, *Mindfulness*. "Those who can free themselves of mindsets, open themselves to new information and surprise, play with perspective and context, and focus on process rather than outcome are likely to be creative, whether they are scientists, artists, or cooks."

Much of Langer's research has demonstrated the vital relationship between creativity and uncertainty, or conditionality. For instance, in one experiment, Langer and Alison Piper introduced a collection of objects to one group of people by saying, "This is a hair dryer," and "This is a dog's chew toy," and so on. Another group was told "This *could be* a hair dryer," and "This *could be* a dog's chew toy." Later, the experimenters for both groups invented a need for an eraser, but only those people who had been conditionally introduced to the objects thought to use the dog's toy in this new way.

The intuitive understanding that a single thing is, or could be, many things, depending on how you look at it, is at the heart of the attitude Langer calls mindfulness. But can such an amorphous state be cultivated? Langer believes that it can, by consciously discarding the idea that any given moment of your day is fixed in its form. "I teach people to 'componentize' their lives into smaller pieces," she says. "In the morning, instead of mindlessly downing your orange juice, *taste it*. Is it what you want? Try something else if it isn't. When you walk to work, turn left instead of right. You'll notice the street you're on, the buildings and the weather. Mindfulness, like creativity, is nothing more than a return to who you are. By minding your responses to the world, you will come to know yourself again. How you feel. What you want. What you want to do."

Creating the Right Atmosphere

Understanding the genesis of creativity, going beyond the myths to understand your creative potential, and recognizing your ability to break free of old ways of thinking are the three initial steps to a more creative life. The fourth is finding ways to work that encourage personal commitment and expressiveness.

Letting employees learn what they want to do has never been a very high priority in the workplace. There, the dominant regulation has always been, "Do what you are told."

Today, however, economic realities are providing a new impetus for change. The pressure on American businesses to become more productive and innovative has made creative thinking a hot commodity in the business community. But innovation, business is now learning, is likely

→

to be found wherever bright and eager people *think* they can find it. And some people are looking in curious places.

Financier Wayne Silby, for example, founded the Calvert Group of funds, which today manages billions of dollars in assets. Silby, whose business card at one point read Chief Daydreamer, occasionally retreats for inspiration to a sensory deprivation tank, where he floats in warm water sealed off from light and sound. "I went into the tank during a time when the government was changing money-market deposit regulations, and I needed to think how to compete with banks. Floating in the tank I got the idea of joining them instead. We wound up creating an $800-million program. Often we already have answers to our problems, but we don't quiet ourselves enough to see the solution bubbling just below the surface." Those solutions will stay submerged, he says, "unless you create a culture that encourages creative approaches, where it's OK to have bad ideas."

Toward this goal, many companies have turned to creativity consultants, like Synectics, Inc., in Cambridge, MA. Half the battle, according to Synectics facilitator Jeff Mauzy, is to get the clients to relax and accept that they are in a safe place where the cutthroat rules of the workplace don't apply, so they can allow themselves to exercise their creative potential in group idea sessions.

Pamela Webb Moore, director of naming services (she helps companies figure out good names for their products) at Synectics, agrees. One technique she uses to limber up the minds of tightly focused corporate managers is "sleight of head." While working on a particular problem, she'll ask clients to pretend to work on something else. In one real-life example, a Synectics-trained facilitator took a group of product-development and marketing managers from the Etonic shoe corporation on an "excursion," a conscious walk away from the problem—in this case, to come up with a new kind of tennis shoe.

The facilitator asked the Etonic people to imagine they were at their favorite vacation spot. "One guy," Moore says, "was on a tropical island, walking on the beach in his bare feet. He described how wonderful the water and sand felt on his feet, and he said, 'I wish we could play tennis barefoot.' The whole thing would have stopped right there if somebody had complained that while his colleague was wandering around barefoot, they were supposed to come up with a *shoe.* Instead, one of the marketing people there was intrigued, and the whole group decided to go off to play tennis barefoot on a rented court at 10 at night."

While the Etonic people played tennis, the facilitator listed everthing they said about how it felt. The next morning, the group looked at her assembled list of comments, and they realized that what they liked about playing barefoot was the lightness of being without shoes, and the ability to pivot easily on both the ball of the foot and the heel. Nine months later, the company produced an extremely light shoe called the Catalyst, which featured an innovative two-piece sole that made it easier for players to pivot.

The Payoff

In *The Courage to Create,* Rollo May wrote that for much of this century, researchers had avoided the subject of creativity because they perceived it as "unscientific, mysterious, disturbing and too corruptive of the scientific training of graduate students." But today researchers are coming to see that creativity, at once fugitive and ubiquitous, is the mark of human nature itself.

→

Whether in business or the arts, politics or personal relationships, creativity involves "going beyond the information given" to create or reveal something new in the world. And almost invariably, when the mind exercises its creative muscle, it also generates a sense of pleasure. The feeling may be powerfully mystical, as it is for New York artist Rhonda Zwillinger, whose embellished artwork appeared in the film *Slaves of New York*. Zwillinger reports, "There are times when I'm working and it is almost as though I'm a vessel and there is a force operating through me. It is the closest I come to having a religious experience." The creative experience may also be quiet and full of wonder, as it was for Isaac Newton, who compared his lifetime of creative effort to "a boy playing on the seashore and diverting himself and then finding a smoother pebble or prettier shell than ordinary, while the greater ocean of truth lay all undiscovered before me."

But whatever the specific sensation, creativity always carries with it a powerful sense of the mind working at the peak of its ability. Creativity truly is, as David Perkins calls it, the mind's best work, its finest effort. We may never know exactly how the brain does it, but we can feel that it is exactly what the brain was meant to do.

Aha!

Questions for Analysis

1. According to the authors, "Creativity . . . is the search for the elusive 'Aha,' that moment of insight when one sees the world, or a problem, or an idea, in a new way." Describe an "aha" moment that you have had recently. Identify the origin of your innovative idea and how you implemented it.

2. Name some of the influences in your life that have inhibited your creative development, including the "myths" about creativity that are described in the article.

3. Using the ideas contained in this chapter and also in this article, identify some of the strategies that you intend to use in order to become more creative in your life—for example, becoming more "mindful," destroying the "Voice of Judgment," and creating a more conducive atmosphere.

Discovering Your Personal Myth

Sam Keen

It seems that Americans are finally taking seriously what Carl Jung, this Swiss psychologist, said is the most important question we can ask ourselves: "What myth are we living?" . . .

What Is a Myth?

What is a myth? Few words have been subject to as much abuse and been as ill-defined as *myth*. Journalists usually use it to mean a "lie," "fabrication," "illusion," "mistake," or something similar. It is the opposite of what is supposedly a "fact," of what is "objectively" the case, and of

→

what is "reality." In this usage myth is at best a silly story and at worst a cynical untruth. Theologians and propagandists often use myth as a way of characterizing religious beliefs and ideologies other than their own.

Such trivialization of the notion of myth reflects false certainties of dogmatic minds, an ignorance of the mythic assumptions that underlie the commonly accepted view of "reality," and a refusal to consider how much our individual and communal lives are shaped by dramatic scenarios and "historical" narratives that are replete with accounts of the struggle between good and evil empires: our godly heroes versus the demonic enemy.

In a strict sense *myth* refers to "an intricate set of interlocking stories, rituals, rites, and customs that inform and give the pivotal sense of meaning and direction to a person, family, community, or culture." A living myth, like an iceberg, is 10 percent visible and 90 percent beneath the surface of consciousness. While it involves a conscious celebration of certain values, which are always personified in a pantheon of heroes (from the wily Ulysses to the managing Lee Iacocca) and villains (from the betraying Judas to the barbarous Moammar Kadafi), it also includes the unspoken consensus, the habitual way of seeing things, the unquestioned assumptions, the automatic stance. It is differing cultural myths that make cows sacred objects for Hindus and hamburgers meals for Methodists, or turn dogs into pets for Americans and roasted delicacies for the Chinese.

People's Myths Are Primarily Unconscious

At least 51 percent of the people in a society are not self-consciously aware of the myth that informs their existence. Cultural consensus is created by an unconscious conspiracy to consider the myth "the truth," "the way things *really* are." In other words, a majority is made up of literalists, men and women who are not critical or reflective about the guiding "truths"— myths—of their own group. To a tourist in a strange land, an anthropologist studying a tribe, or a psychologist observing a patient, the myth is obvious. But to the person who lives within the mythic horizon, it is nearly invisible.

For instance, most Americans would consider potlatch feasts, in which Northwest Indian tribes systematically destroy their wealth, to be irrational and mythic but would consider the habit of browsing in malls and buying expensive things we do not need (conspicuous consumption) to be a perfectly reasonable way to spend a Saturday afternoon. To most Americans the Moslem notion of *jihad*—holy war—is a dangerous myth. But our struggle against "atheistic communism" is a righteous duty. Ask a born-again Christian about the myth of the atonement, and you will be told it is no myth at all but a revealed truth. Ask a true believer of Marxism about the myth of the withering away of the state, and you will get a long explanation about the "scientific" laws of the dialectic of history.

What Is a Myth?

I use myth to mean the systematic, unconscious way of structuring reality that governs a culture as a whole, or a people, or a tribe. It can govern a corporation, a family, or a person. It's the underlying story.

Sam Keen in *A World of Ideas II*, 1990.

I suggest two analogies that may help to counteract the popular trivialized notion of myth. The dominant myth that informs a person or a culture is like the "information" contained in DNA or the program in the systems disk of a computer. Myth is the software, the cultural DNA, the unconscious information, the metaprogram that governs the way we see "reality" and the way we behave.

Myths Can Be Creative or Destructive

The organizing myth of any culture functions in ways that may be either creative or destructive, healthful or pathological. By providing a world picture and a set of stories that explain why things are as they are, it creates consensus, sanctifies the social order, and gives the individual an authorized map of the path of life. A myth creates the plotline that organizes the diverse experiences of a person or a community into a single story.

But in the same measure that myth gives us security and identity, it also creates selective blindness, narrowness, and rigidity because it is intrinsically conservative. It encourages us to follow the faith of our fathers, to hold to the time-honored truths, to imitate the way of the heroes, to repeat the formulas and rituals in exactly the same way they were done in the good old days. As long as no radical change is necessary for survival, the status quo remains sacred, the myth and ritual are unquestioned, and the patterns of life, like the seasons of the year, repeat themselves. But when crisis comes—a natural catastrophe, a military defeat, the introduction of a new technology—the mythic mind is at a loss to deal with novelty. As Marshall McLuhan said, it tries to "walk into the future looking through a rearview mirror."

Families Have Myths

Every family, like a miniculture, also has an elaborate system of stories and rituals that differentiate it from other families. The Murphys, being Irish, understand full well that Uncle Paddy is a bit of a rogue and drinks a tad too much. The Cohens, being Jewish, are haunted each year at Passover when they remember the family that perished in the Holocaust. The Keens, being Calvinists, are predestined to be slightly more righteous and right than others, even when they are wrong. And within the family each member's place is defined by a series of stories. Obedient to the family script, Jane, "who always was very motherly even as a little girl," married young and had children immediately, while Pat, "who was a wild one and not cut out for marriage," sowed oat after oat before finding fertile ground.

The Task of Tasks

I asked myself, "What is the myth you are living?" and found that I did not know. So . . . I took it upon myself to get to know "my" myth, and I regarded this as the task of tasks . . . I simply had to know what unconscious or preconscious myth was forming me.

C. J. Jung in *The Portable Jung,* 1976.

Family myths, like those of the Kennedy clan, may give us an impulse to strive for excellence and a sense of pride that helps us endure hardship and tragedy. Or they may, like the myths of alcoholic or abusive families, pass a burden of guilt, shame, and failure from

→

generation to generation as abused children, in turn, become abusive parents, ad nauseam. The sins, virtues, and myths of the fathers are passed on to the children of future generations.

Every Individual Has a Personal Myth

Finally, the entire legacy and burden of cultural and family myth comes to rest on the individual. Each person is a repository of stories. To the degree that any one of us reaches toward autonomy, we must begin a process of sorting through the trash and treasures we have been given, keeping some and rejecting others. We gain the full dignity and power of our persons only when we create a narrative account of our lives, dramatize our existence, and forge a coherent personal myth that combines elements of our cultural myth and family myth with unique stories that come from our experience. As my friend David Steere once pointed out to me, the common root of "authority" and "authorship" tells us a great deal about power. Whoever authors your story authorizes your actions. We gain personal authority and power in the measure that we question the myth that is upheld by "the authorities" and discover and create a personal myth that illuminates and informs us.

What Do You Believe?

I began to examine my own experience at a very crucial and disturbed period in my life—when my own tenacious clinging to the Christian worldview and the Christian myth began to crumble, when I couldn't believe it anymore—and I had to ask myself the question, well, what do you believe? How do you find any rock upon which to put your feet? For a long time I was at a loss, and suddenly it occurred to me that instead of looking at the answers that myth gave, I could look at the questions. I began to interrogate my own life using those questions. Who are my heroes? Who are my villains? What is my source? Where did I come from? Who are my people? I discovered that I could find within my own autobiography, as it were, a complete but undeveloped mythology. And as I began to look at those stories and recover those stories for myself, I had a mythology that gave me a story by which I lived.

Sam Keen in *A World of Ideas II,* 1990.

What George Santayana said about cultures is equally true for individuals: "Those who do not remember history are condemned to repeat it." If we do not make the effort to become conscious of our personal myths gradually, we become dominated by what psychologists have variously called repetition compulsion, autonomous complexes, engrams, routines, scripts, games. One fruitful way to think of neurosis is to consider it a tape loop, an oft-told story that we repeat in our inner dialogues with ourselves and with others. "Well, I'm just not the kind of person who can . . ." "I never could . . ." "I wouldn't think of . . .". While personal myths give us a sense of identity, continuity, and security, they become constricting and boring if they are not revised from time to time. To remain vibrant throughout a lifetime we must always be inventing ourselves, weaving new themes into our life-narratives, remembering our past, re-visioning our future, reauthorizing the myth by which we live.

Questions for Analysis

1. The author defines *myth* as "an intricate set of interlocking stories, rituals, rites, and customs that inform and give the pivotal sense of meaning and direction to a person, family, community, or culture." Describe examples of myths from both your culture and your family, and explain how these myths provide meaning and influence the behavior of the people who participate in the myth.

2. Myths, as we saw in the previous article regarding "myths of creativity," can be destructive, repressive, and encourage uncritical thinking. On the other hand, myths can be constructive and liberating, encouraging creative expression and independent thought. Describe a myth in your life that is destructive and one that is constructive. Discuss how you might go about diminishing the destructive myth and empowering the constructive myth.

3. The author concludes by saying "To remain vibrant throughout a lifetime, we must always be inventing ourselves, weaving new themes into our live-narratives. . . ." Describe new themes that you are currently trying to weave into your own personal myth as you project yourself into the future.

Appendix: National Average Starting Salaries

Accountant $26,500
Accountant (Tax) $22,700
Actor $16,500
Advertising manager $37,900
Airplane inspector $24,500
Airplane flight attendant $20,500
Anesthesiologist $118,400
Radio announcer $22,500
Architect $33,500
Assembler (production) $13,200
Astronomer $31,800
Athlete (professional) $37,000–$5 million
Athletic trainer $18,400
Attorney (tax) $33,700
Attendant (service station) $12,000
Bagger $7,100
Baker $17,000
Barber $13,500
Bartender $15,000
Beekeeper $15,000
Bellhop $7,000
Biologist $27,800
Bookkeeper $16,000
Bricklayer $16,000
Botanist $28,000
Box maker $11,200
Boat builder $21,200
Boat loader $36,600
Butcher $16,800
Cabinetmaker $11,400
Carpenter $22,000
Caseworker (child welfare) $20,500
Cashier $12,500
Chef $22,900
Chauffeur $16,000
Chemist $29,600
Child care attendant (school) $10,200

Chiropractor $77,000
Clergy member $22,400
Clerk (accounting) $15,000
Clerk (file) $13,000
Clerk (post office) $23,500
Clerk-typist $15,000
Collector (toll) $17,000
Composer (music) $28,600
Conductor (orchestra) $31,900
Conductor (passenger car) $33,000
Construction worker $16,700
Cook $11,500
Correction officer $19,000
Counselor $23,000
Counter attendant (coffee shop) $11,500
Dancer $18,500
Dental assistant $17,000
Dentist $60,500
Derrick operator $27,100
Designer (clothes) $25,000
Detective $25,900
Die maker (bench) $26,900
Dining room attendant $10,000
Disc jockey $22,500
Dog groomer $12,400
Donut machine operator $12,600
Dragline operator $27,000
Driver (bus) $18,300
Driver (tractor-trailer truck) $21,600
Driver (taxi) $15,300
Driver (concrete mixing truck) $20,100
Economist $25,600
Editor (newspaper) $28,000
Electrician $28,500
Engineer (mechanical) $35,500
Engineer (nuclear) $34,000
Engraver $16,000

Envelope machine operator $10,500
Executive secretary $19,000
Exterminator $15,000
Faculty member (college) $27,500
Farmer (general) $22,000
Farmworker $7,900
Financial analyst $28,500
Fire chief $35,900
Firefighter $20,400
Fire inspector $25,400
Fisherman (net) $14,500
Food service worker $15,900
Forest worker $22,000
Funeral director $20,500
Garbage collector $16,500
Geologist $26,500
Guard (security) $18,500
Home attendant $10,600
Horse trainer $20,300
Host/hostess (restaurant) $13,100
Housecleaner $7,200
Humorist $23,800
Illustrator $21,400
Interpreter $23,000
Janitor $13,800
Jockey $24,400
Judge $64,900
Keypunch operator $14,600
Knitting machine operator $11,300
Laborer (construction) $14,500
Lathe operator $18,000
Lawyer (corporation) $38,500
Librarian $21,000
Library assistant $13,300
Lithographic plate maker $19,000
Loan officer $21,000
Locksmith $23,000
Locomotive engineer $54,500
Logger $16,000
Machinist $19,200
Mail carrier $25,000
Manager (fast foods) $18,500
Manicurist $14,500
Mason (cement) $17,000
Mate (ship) $36,200
Mechanic (aircraft) $26,700
Mehanic (automobile) $19,000
Medical assistant $17,500
Meteorologist $30,000

Meter reader $13,500
Milling machine operator $18,300
Miner $21,500
Model $25–$300 per hour
Narcotics investigator $20,900
Newswriter $20,500
Nurse's aide $12,000
Nurse (licensed practical) $21,000
Nurse (midwife) $27,500
Obstetrician $110,000
Office manager $20,000
Optometrist $50,000
Ordinary seaman $14,000
Painter (construction) $18,500
Paper hanger $16,000
Park ranger $19,000
Parole officer $20,500
Pattern maker (metal) $17,200
Pediatrician $110,000
Pharmacist $37,500
Personnel manager $27,000
Photograph finisher $20,500
Photo journalist $15,600
Physicist $34,500
Piano tuner $15,500
Pilot (airplane, commercial) $77,100
Pilot (test) $43,000
Plasterer (construction) $15,000
Police captain $37,100
Police officer $22,500
Postmaster $25,000–$67,000
Power-shovel operator $20,400
Principal $29,500
Private investigator $25,500
Programmer (information system) $24,000
Proofreader $17,500
Psychologist (clinical) $31,700
Psychologist (industrial, organizational) $28,400
Rancher (livestock) $22,000
Receptionist $13,700
Repairer (appliance) $16,500
Repairer (instrument) $20,500
Retail store manager $15,000
Ring maker (jewelry) $19,500
Rock-Drill operator $29,000
Sales agent (real estate) $20,500
Scientist (animal) $24,000
Scientist (soil) $25,000
Secretary $18,600

Set decorator $20,200
Sheriff (deputy) $22,600
Singer $27,500
Social worker $20,500
Stage director $26,900
Sports instructor $20,500
Stenographer $16,000
Stonemason $16,000
Stunt performer $34,500
Surgeon $179,000
Surgical technician $22,000
Systems analyst $33,000
Tailor $13,900
Taxidermist $15,300

Teacher's aide $10,000
Tool-and-die maker $24,500
Tree surgeon $19,500
Typist $15,000
Umpire $4,200
Urban planner $25,000
Veterinarian $35,500
Weaver (hand loom) $10,400
Welder (arc) $21,100
Word processing operator $16,000
Writer (editorial) $23,800
Writer (screen) $27,800
Writer (technical publications) $24,500
Zoologist $32,000

Index

Text and Art Credits

Chapter 1   Photo of Students on Lawn © Myrleen Ferguson/PhotoEdit; New Possibilities Warren Gebert; Goals Warren Gebert; The Career Ladder Warren Gebert; Where Are You? © United Technologies Corporation 1984. Used by permission. Photo of Doctor with Baby © Gaye Hilsonrath/The Picture Cube; Photo of Teenager Drawing © Elizabeth Crews/The Image Works; The Right Match Warren Gebert.

Chapter 2   Thinking Independently Warren Gebert; Gardner Lindzey, Calvin S. Hall, and Richard F. Thompson From Gardner Lindzey, Calvin S. Hall, and Richard F. Thompson, *Psychology,* Second Edition, Worth Publishers, New York, 1978; Abortion Protest © Hazel Hankin/Stock Boston; Being Open-minded Warren Gebert; Photo of Police Car and Chimp © George Mars Cassidy/The Picture Cube; The Educated Thinker Warren Gebert; Aspiring Student and Teacher © Frank Siteman/The Picture Cube; Donna Farbi Schuster "On Becoming a Better Student." Copyright © 1987 by *The Yoga Journal.* Used with permission; John Lawry Questions based on material from John Lawry, *College 101: A Freshman Reader,* 1992, p. 82.

Chapter 3   Analyzing Problems Warren Gebert; Boys Drinking at Bar © Bruce Ayres/Tony Stone Images; Mother-daughter Talk © Harriet Gans/The Image Works; Generating Alternatives Warren Gebert; Evaluating Possible Solutions Warren Gebert; Debra Rosenberg From *Newsweek,* November 19, 1990, Copyright © 1990, Newsweek, Inc. All rights reserved. Reprinted by permission; Nancy A. Gleason From *Journal of American College Health,* 42(6) (May 1994). Reprinted with permission of the Helen Dwight Reid Educational Foundation. Published by Heldref Publications, 1319 Eighteenth Street, N.W., Washington, DC 20036–1802. Copyright © 1994.

Chapter 4   Girl Studying Skull © Charles Gupton/Tony Stone Images; Teaching Ceramics © Lionell J-M Delevigne/Stock Boston; Approaches to Learning Warren Gebert; Girl Studying in Dorm © Mark Richards/Photoedit; Cramming vs. Learning Over Time Warren Gebert; Girl Studying on Porch © Chip Henderson/Tony Stone Images; Jennifer Crichton "College Friends" by Jennifer Crichton as seen in *Ms.* Magazine. Reprinted by permission of the author.

Chapter 5   Fear of Tests Warren Gebert; Being Well Prepared Warren Gebert; Girl Meditating © Richard Hutchings/PhotoEdit; Michelle Stacey "Diary of an Eating Disorder" by Michelle Stacey, originally in *Allure,* April 1994 reprinted by permission of Ellen Levine Literary Agency. William C. Rader "Dangerous Diets" by William C. Rader, M.D., The Rader Institute, Los Angeles, CA.

Chapter 6   Metacognition Warren Gebert; Engineers with Plans © Kaluzny/Thatcher/Tony Stone Images; Female Helicopter Pilot © Bob Daemmrich/The Image Works; Susan Brownmiller Reprinted by permission of Simon & Schuster, Inc., from *Femininity* by Susan Brownmiller. Copyright © 1983 by Susan Brownmiller. Perceiving Lenses Warren Gebert; Cartoon The Investigation © John Jonik. Reproduced with permission. This cartoon first appeared in *Psychology Today,* February 1984, p. 26. Paul A. Grayson and Phillip W. Meilman From *Beating the College Blues* by Paul A. Grayson and Phillip W. Meilman. Copyright

Chapter 7 GENERATING IDEAS Warren Gebert; CAUSAL CHAINS Warren Gebert; CLEAR VS. VAGUE LANGUAGE Warren Gebert; CARTOON Roget's Brontosaurus. Drawing by M. Stevens © 1975 The New Yorker Magazine, Inc.; LIBRARY COMPUTER © David Young—Wolff/PhotoEdit; EFFECTIVE WRITING Warren Gebert; DAVID SHENK "Young Hate" by David Shenk, first appeared in CV Magazine.

Chapter 8 COMMUNICATING CLEARLY Warren Gebert; MOTIVATIONAL SPEAKER © Paul Meredith/Tony Stone Images; JUDGING Warren Gebert; MEN GREETING ON STREET © Chester Higgins, Jr./Photo Researchers, Inc.; WORKING COLLABORATIVELY Warren Gebert; DEBORAH TANNEN From *You Just Don't Understand: Women and Men in Conversation* by Deborah Tannen. Copyright © 1990 by Deborah Tannen. Reprinted by permission of International Creative Management, Inc.; MISCOMMUNICATION Warren Gebert.

Chapter 9 ARGUMENTS Warren Gebert; EMPIRICAL GENERALIZATION Warren Gebert; SCIENTIFIC HYPOTHESIS Warren Gebert; THE SCIENTIFIC METHOD Warren Gebert; FALLACIES Warren Gebert; NANCY GIBBS "When Is It Rape?" by Nancy Gibbs from *Time,* June 3, 1991. Copyright © 1991 Time Inc. Reprinted by permission.

Chapter 10 LIVING CREATIVELY Warren Gebert; CREATIVE INSPIRATION Warren Gebert; THE PAYOFF Warren Gebert; ELIMINATE FEAR Warren Gebert; GIRL AT WINDOW © Jean-Claude Lejeune/Stock Boston; USING CONCEPTS Warren Gebert; C.P. ELLIS From *American Dreams: Lost and Found* by Studs Terkel. Copyright © 1980 by Studs Terkel. Reprinted by permission of Pantheon Books, a division of Random House, Inc.; LESLEY DOMEN AND PETER EDIDIN Reprinted by permission from *Psychology Today* Magazine, Copyright © 1989 Sussex Publishers, Inc.; SAM KEEN Reprinted by permission of The Putnam Publishing Group/Jeremy P. Tarcher, Inc. from *Your Mythic Journey* by Sam Keen and Anne Valley-Fox. Copyright © 1989 by Sam Keen and Anne Valley-Fox.